Valuation Challenges and Solutions in Contemporary Businesses

Sinem Derindere Köseoğlu
Independent Researcher, Turkey

IGI Global
DISSEMINATOR OF KNOWLEDGE

A volume in the Advances in Business Information Systems and Analytics (ABISA) Book Series

Published in the United States of America by
IGI Global
Business Science Reference (an imprint of IGI Global)
701 E. Chocolate Avenue
Hershey PA, USA 17033
Tel: 717-533-8845
Fax: 717-533-8661
E-mail: cust@igi-global.com
Web site: http://www.igi-global.com

Library of Congress Cataloging-in-Publication Data

Names: Derindere Köseoğlu, Sinem, 1981- editor.
Title: Valuation challenges and solutions in contemporary businesses / Sinem Derindere Köseoğlu, editor.
Description: Hershey, PA : Business Science Reference, [2020] | Includes bibliographical references and index. | Summary: "This book examines challenges, issues, and solutions for firm evaluation"-- Provided by publisher.
Identifiers: LCCN 2019024174 (print) | LCCN 2019024175 (ebook) | ISBN 9781799810865 (hardcover) | ISBN 9781799810872 (paperback) | ISBN 9781799810889 (ebook)
Subjects: LCSH: Business enterprises--Valuation.
Classification: LCC HG4028.V3 V32 2020 (print) | LCC HG4028.V3 (ebook) | DDC 658.15--dc23
LC record available at https://lccn.loc.gov/2019024174
LC ebook record available at https://lccn.loc.gov/2019024175

This book is published in the IGI Global book series Advances in Business Information Systems and Analytics (ABISA) (ISSN: 2327-3275; eISSN: 2327-3283)

British Cataloguing in Publication Data
A Cataloguing in Publication record for this book is available from the British Library.

All work contributed to this book is new, previously-unpublished material. The views expressed in this book are those of the authors, but not necessarily of the publisher.

For electronic access to this publication, please contact: eresources@igi-global.com.

Advances in Business Information Systems and Analytics (ABISA) Book Series

Madjid Tavana
La Salle University, USA

ISSN:2327-3275
EISSN:2327-3283

Mission

The successful development and management of information systems and business analytics is crucial to the success of an organization. New technological developments and methods for data analysis have allowed organizations to not only improve their processes and allow for greater productivity, but have also provided businesses with a venue through which to cut costs, plan for the future, and maintain competitive advantage in the information age.

The **Advances in Business Information Systems and Analytics (ABISA) Book Series** aims to present diverse and timely research in the development, deployment, and management of business information systems and business analytics for continued organizational development and improved business value.

Coverage

- Business Models
- Big Data
- Algorithms
- Data Governance
- Geo-BIS
- Data Management
- Performance Metrics
- Statistics
- Management Information Systems
- Legal information systems

IGI Global is currently accepting manuscripts for publication within this series. To submit a proposal for a volume in this series, please contact our Acquisition Editors at Acquisitions@igi-global.com or visit: http://www.igi-global.com/publish/.

The Advances in Business Information Systems and Analytics (ABISA) Book Series (ISSN 2327-3275) is published by IGI Global, 701 E. Chocolate Avenue, Hershey, PA 17033-1240, USA, www.igi-global.com. This series is composed of titles available for purchase individually; each title is edited to be contextually exclusive from any other title within the series. For pricing and ordering information please visit http://www.igi-global.com/book-series/advances-business-information-systems-analytics/37155. Postmaster: Send all address changes to above address.

Titles in this Series

For a list of additional titles in this series, please visit:
https://www.igi-global.com/book-series/advances-business-information-systems-analytics/37155

Strategic IT Governance and Performance Frameworks in Large Organizations
Yassine Maleh (The National Port Agency, Morocco) Abdelkebir Sahid (Hassan 1st University, Morocco) and Mustapha Belaissaoui (Hassan 1st University, Morocco)
Business Science Reference • © 2019 • 413pp • H/C (ISBN: 9781522578260) • US $195.00 (our price)

Modeling Methods for Business Information Systems Analysis and Design
Selin Erben (Beykent University, Turkey)
Business Science Reference • © 2019 • 267pp • H/C (ISBN: 9781522555223) • US $215.00 (our price)

Big Data Analytics for Entrepreneurial Success
Soraya Sedkaoui (Khemis Miliana University, Algeria & SRY Consulting Montpellier, France)
Business Science Reference • © 2019 • 300pp • H/C (ISBN: 9781522576099) • US $215.00 (our price)

Sentiment Analysis and Knowledge Discovery in Contemporary Business
Dharmendra Singh Rajput (VIT University, India) Ramjeevan Singh Thakur (Maulana Azad National Institute of Technology, India) and S. Muzamil Basha (VIT University, India)
Business Science Reference • © 2019 • 333pp • H/C (ISBN: 9781522549994) • US $215.00 (our price)

Law, Ethics, and Integrity in the Sports Industry
Konstantinos Margaritis (University of Crete, Greece)
Business Science Reference • © 2019 • 307pp • H/C (ISBN: 9781522553878) • US $195.00 (our price)

Institutional and Organizational Transformations in the Robotic Era Emerging Research and Opportunities
Albena Antonova (Sofia University, Bulgaria)
Business Science Reference • © 2019 • 178pp • H/C (ISBN: 9781522562702) • US $155.00 (our price)

Utilizing Big Data Paradigms for Business Intelligence
Jérôme Darmont (Université Lumière Lyon 2, France) and Sabine Loudcher (Université Lumière Lyon 2, France)
Business Science Reference • © 2019 • 313pp • H/C (ISBN: 9781522549635) • US $210.00 (our price)

Handbook of Research on Expanding Business Opportunities With Information Systems and Analytics
George Leal Jamil (Informações em Rede Consultoria e Treinamento Ltda, Brazil)
Business Science Reference • © 2019 • 455pp • H/C (ISBN: 9781522562252) • US $245.00 (our price)

IGI Global
DISSEMINATOR OF KNOWLEDGE

701 East Chocolate Avenue, Hershey, PA 17033, USA
Tel: 717-533-8845 x100 • Fax: 717-533-8661
E-Mail: cust@igi-global.com • www.igi-global.com

Editorial Advisory Board

Table of Contents

Detailed Table of Contents

This chapter is an introduction to the book and provides basic information to help readers in the following chapters. This book analyzes all kinds of problems and develops solutions in firm valuation process. The needs and purposes of firm valuation are briefly explained. Basic Concepts, such as Cost, Price, Value, Valuation, Evaluation, Free Cash Flow, and different types of value, are explained. Face value, issue price, fair value, intrinsic value, market value, book value, going-concern value, liquidation value, replacement value, enterprise value, and equity value are explained within the different types of value. Then, "financial statements" and "elements of financial statements", which will form the basis of all valuation approaches, are explained and emphasized. The value drivers for businesses are discussed. Business valuation approaches' general features are given.

Despite the existence of International Valuation Standards (IVS) and Financial Reporting Standards (IFRS), countries that have transferred to adopting IFRS face the large challenge of the difference in interpretation and application of the standards. Because they include various concepts, bases, and approaches for valuation and measurement, and although there are common objectives for each of the International Valuation Standards Council (IVSC) and International Accounting Standards Board(IASB), each works independently and has their own objectives and different target groups. Thus, more improvements are needed to consistently apply valuation and financial reporting standards. This chapter compares and converges the concepts, bases, and approaches adopted by the IVSC and the IASB to increase consistency in valuation practices for financial reporting purposes and to create bridges between accountants and auditors and professional valuers.

Capital structure decisions of management affect the value of a firm. This fact leads to the creation of an extremely rich capital structure literature over the last 60 years. This chapter explains main theories of capital structure and discusses the concept of target leverage which maximizes the firm value. The roles of tax payments, profitability, firm size, asset tangibility, growth opportunities, income volatility, and non-debt tax shields are examined as determinants of capital structure. The current status of capital structure research and some important empirical issues are discussed. Considerations for future research are presented.

It is generally believed that, in determining the real value of a company, the best results are obtained by using the Dicounted FCF method. The overall value of the firm itself or the value of equity is determined by discounting the "appropriate" cash flows by "appropriate" discount rates. We basically need to determine three major parameters: free cash flows, cost of capital, and the terminal value. All these three parameters have sub-parameters within themselves. Because all these parameters and their sub-parameters are to be future values, many factors like the riskiness of the firm in question, its leverage ratio, whether it is a profitable firm, newly-established or public company will not only influence the calculation of these parameters/sub-parameters but will also make it more difficult for the analyst. This chapter explains what variables are needed for company valuation, how they are determined, and what problems may be faced in calculating these values. Finally, authors propose solutions to all the problems analysts will likely face.

Capital asset pricing model (CAPM) brings deep intuitive understanding of the relationship between expected return and risk. Unfortunately, the empirical record of the CAPM has not been satisfactory since its commencement. The empirical testing of CAPM is void in most cases due to the use of an inefficient index as a proxy for market portfolio. Plausible tests require a well-diversified market portfolio which so far has been unfeasible to obtain. Lack of validity in empirical records has been caused by complexity in exerting valid estimations of the beta coefficient. This chapter judges which of the indices provides investors the best beta forecast and questions which time period should be selected for beta calculation. This chapter reveals that the choice of return intervals causes variations in beta estimation of the security. Applying higher frequency has an advantage in that it increases the number of observations, but a shortfall is that beta tends to have substantial bias with shorter return intervals used.

This chapter presents solutions to some challenges when calculating CAPM Beta. Three methods for calculating traditional beta are presented and illustrated through the case of Facebook. Different choices of market index, data frequency, and sample size result in different values of beta; however, in all cases beta was greater than one. The chapter explores ordinal beta as an alternative measure to treat outliers in both developed and thin markets. Using a sample of 84 US stocks, there was no statistical difference between median traditional and ordinal betas. This was not the case for a sample of 47 Colombian stocks, which questions the usefulness of traditional beta in thin markets. In contrast with median traditional beta, median ordinal beta did not change significantly as a result of irregular data series. The contrary occurred when the observation (sampling) period was reduced; this leaves open the question of subjectivity when defining such period. Finally, the process of valuing a private company was illustrated through the case of Palmoil Ltd., a Colombian company.

This book mostly concentrates on firms with positive earnings, but this chapter focuses on the negative earnings firms or firms with very low earnings. It is easier to value a positive earning firm than a company with negative earnings. Analyzing negative earning firms has always created problems for researchers and analysts. In case of a negative earning firm, growth rates cannot be predicted or used in the valuation of firms. When current income of the firms is negative, growth rate will make it more negative. Tax computation becomes more complicated and the Going Concern Assumption does not apply properly. Authors start with complications in valuing negative earning firms, discuss the causes of negative earnings, and whether the problem is short-term, long-term, or cyclical in nature. Finally, authors provide the appropriate valuation technique for each case.

This chapter analyzes startups and methods for valuing them. Startup means a process for activating a job or action. Startup as a young innovative company has a dominant and key role in modern economies. Startups are newborn or young companies struggling to achieve their potential and growth. One of the most challenging issues in corporate finance is to decide on firm valuation. It is even more difficult to evaluate companies that do not generate income. Deciding the value of a Startup is similar to valuing a specific table. The valuation at this stage is very important. Since startup is a company, it is necessary to look at the methods developed specifically for Startups. Nasser (2016) determines 9 different valuation methods to determine Pre-Money Valuation; Berkus Method, Risk Factor Summation Method, Scorecard Valuation Method, Comparable Transactions Method, Book Value Method, Liquidation Value Method, Discounted Cash Flow Method, First Chicago Method, and Venture Capital Method. Traditional valuation methods are also applicable in valuation.

This chapter investigates the challenges faced by sell-side analysts in engaging with companies with material stranded assets through the lens of Becksian risk society theory. The research unravels the usefulness of sustainability reports in deriving the intrinsic value of energy companies in the UK, and whether they take Environmental Social and Governance (ESG) factors into consideration in doing so. Qualitative data were collected via dual methods comprising longitudinal participant observation at IR meetings and interview of sell-side analysts and institutional shareholder. Findings indicate dissatisfaction with the existing risk reporting system is a key factor in divestment decisions and asset stranding. The growing Responsible Investment (RI) awareness notwithstanding, the inadequate risk reporting system continues to represent a major source of agitation amongst shareholders and analysts, making the overhaul of the current financial reporting system inevitable.

This chapter examines in particular the valuation of banks which can be classified into five parts. It introduces several valuation approaches to find out whether there is a superior method. This chapter starts with a description of bank regulations and their impact on bank valuations and continues with an overview of valuation approaches. The second part applies the banking sector decision Models. The third section shows banking sector valuation models. The fourth part presents the input factors that are needed to value a company. In the last part, financial statements have been used to analyze the main ratios of the Bank of America, and the calculated values were then compared over time (2014-2018) to assess the explanatory power of the bank.

In the business arena, particularly in the field of corporate finance, the scope of valuation is highly significant. There are several value drivers for a firm. However, due to its nature of business, a bank's valuation is affected by several unique drivers including earnings diversification, risk capabilities, assets mix, and a lot of intangible factors. Since banking is a highly regulated sector, this chapter is designed to address the missing links between Basel capital and liquidity regulations, banking system resilience, and bank valuation.

The growth and diversification of investment and management property have development requirements, so achieving first place economically requires transfer of share of ownership from government to private sector. One of the major requirements of these operations is pricing of shares through stock exchange. The accurate and transparent assessment in assignment of stock value has great importance. So, it has been tried to design optimal model and then determine the bank stock value in public offerings. In this regard, the review of conventional models of stock valuation has been analyzed and the effect of functional variables and balance sheet on the value of bank stocks is investigated. In the statistical stage, the relevant tests have been accepted for 16 banks in Tehran Stock Exchange and Iranian OTC market on a three-year timeframe. The results of research lead to design and specify the optimal model for evaluating of Bank stock.

The challenge of the stock price forecast is the most crucial component for companies and equity traders to predict future revenues. A successful and accurate prediction to the future stock prices ultimately results in profit maximisation. This chapter proposes the use of autoregressive integrated moving average (ARIMA) and the artificial neural networks (ANNs) models to predict the future prices of the stock. Using Walmart's stock index, the results show that both ARIMA and the ANNs models provide accurate forecasting performance. However, for short-term forecasting, the performance of ANNs outperformed ARIMA models.

The value of a firm is equal to the value of all projects in its assets. Investment decision is taken based on expected costs, knowledge of techniques, and risk perception; all of which are parameters of firm valuation. The research in this chapter is based on a real company in the household appliance industry. The company has a factory storage in Istanbul, Turkey. Two alterative heating projects (infrared and natural gas) are developed for the storage space according to project characteristics and heating requirements. The initial investments and operating costs are determined by market prices. According to the results, electric infrared heating is most of the time more favorable when the ceiling is high. An investment decision specifically for the factory storage is made. A discussion section on results is also available. Heating and cooling is a strategic industry for European Commission. The research can guide academicians and practitioners in this field.

Preface

Firm valuation is one of the most important and long-discussed issues of finance. Today, valuation has become an integral part of financial management. The question of what the value of your firm is a strategic subject in a firm's ongoing activities. Although many senior managers and the owner of the companies know accurately the value of capital assets, vehicles, machines, cars, or more simply the computer that they uses, when the question is asked about the value of the business, which is the main subject of them, they often give answers rarely accurate and questionable. In real life, the value of the company is an important tool not only for selling, acquisition or merger but also for making medium and long-term plans properly. All these needs keep the company valuation subject up to date for finance and leads to the development of new valuation methods and to seek solutions for the problems facing during the valuation process. The main purpose of finance managers is to maximize the market value of the firm, and thus the maximum amount of money that will remain to shareholders. The managers who exhibit a value-based management approach will determine factors affecting the value of the company, which are called value drivers. And they will give importance to these issues in the company's medium and long-term strategic plans.

Although the business valuation is not a new issue, its importance increases. The business valuation has become a more professional subject in need of legal action, buying the firm, mergers, acquisitions, taxation and many legal cases. It may cause many rights losses as long as the valuation not being done professionally. For example, a shareholder who wishes to withdraw from the partnership will receive a lower amount when the value of the share is not determined correctly. Or, if an accurate value is not determined in the sales of the company, an unfair situation will arise between the buyer and seller. These examples can be reproduced. Therefore, the business valuation has become more professional and valuation techniques has become more advanced in the business and academic world.

There are three traditional approaches for firm valuation: Income-based, Market-based and Asset-based valuation approaches. In income-based valuation models it is begun by forecasting earnings and cash flows and discount these cash flows back at an appropriate discount rate to arrive at the value of a firm or asset. This operation can be easy when valuing firms with positive earnings and a long history of performance firms. If when one or more of these conditions does not hold, how we can value the firm. Second in market-based valuation methods it is begun by finding comparable firms and comparable multiplies for valuation. However, if there are not a large number of comparable firms in the sector, how we can manage this problem. Lastly in asset-based valuation methods, we need to value the assets that the company has, but if the company has got many intellectual properties such as patents, trade secret, know-how and other licenses, how we can value these intangible assets and manage the firm valuation process.

The firm valuation process can be easy when everything is in normal situations, however there are many challenges in real life. For example, valuing firms such as negative earnings, no history, no comparables, cyclical companies, financial services companies such as banks are challenges of valuation. In addition, estimating some variables such as beta, cash flow and growth rate are also challenging issues for valuation process. In this book, we try to answer all these challenging questions and give solutions for these situations for contemporary businesses.

The aim of the book is that it will be a resource that addresses all the challenges aspects of the firm valuation and their solution together. Although there are separate studies on each challenge, there is no collecting study in this way. Thus, the book will be about the firm valuation for all challenging issues and solutions for these problems.

In the first chapter of the book, it is explained the needs and purposes of valuation, parties benefit from valuation, financial statement concepts, other concepts of valuation and the business value drives. And finally, three different firm valuation approaches have been explained. Thus, the aim of this chapter is to give general knowledge about firm valuation as an introduction of this book titled “Valuation Challenges and Solutions in Contemporary Businesses”.

International standards are important in order to speak the same language all over the world. It is also needed standards for valuation process. The International Valuation Standards (IVS) that published by International Valuation Standards Council (IVSC) is recognized as the key global valuation standards which applied by many companies in many countries and often acts as the basis for all valuation activities. Despite the multiplicity and diversity objectives of international standards, including valuation standards and financial reporting standards, these standards played a significant role in achieving harmonization in professional practices, as well as make the reliability of the information extracted based on them. And it can be considered as guidelines for professionals and academics in the field of business world. However, the biggest challenge facing these professionals and academics is the different interpretation and application of the concepts contained in these standards in some cases, and conflict between them in the other cases. Although they deal with similar cases, the main reason is these standards were set by different professional bodies. Accordingly, the concepts and procedures applied in the international standards need more research and analysis to remove the ambiguity surrounding them and reach clear and easy explanations in the application. Chapter 2 in this book addresses these issues and attempts to resolve them by bridging the relationship between international Valuation standards (IVS) and International Financial Reporting Standards (IFRS). The chapter especially focused on the IVS 200, in an attempt to reach a valuation of entire Business.

Because, the aim of the financial managers is maximizing the firm value, they constantly determine factors affecting the value of the company, which are called value drivers. And they will give importance to these issues in the company’s medium and long-term strategic plans. These managers exhibit value-based management approach. The value of the firm is a function of various factors including the capital structure. Hence, finance scholars diligently tried to find a correct answer to the question of what is the optimal capital structure to maximize the value of the firm. Their fruitful efforts lead to the emergence of a notable literature of capital structure. Therefore, main theories of capital structure are explained in detail and the concept of optimal capital structure is discussed in Chapter 3, titled “Optimal Capital Structure for Maximizing the Firm Value”. Besides, some firm level factors such as tax payments, profitability, firm size, asset tangibility, growth opportunities, income volatility and non-debt tax shields are examined as determinants of capital structure. Lastly, the current status of the empirical capital structure research is revealed and some considerations for future research are presented.

Many business valuations models and methods from very simple to highly complex ones are used in finance literature and practice. While these methods and models are based on very different assumptions, some of the methods have some common features and can be categorized together. With the classification of a number of common valuation methods together, a wider concept of valuation approach emerges. The three different approaches used in business valuation; first, market-based approach is also known as relative valuation. In this approach, the value of the business is obtained by the comparison of the business with similar-class businesses and securities sold in the market. In other words, the real market values are examined to figure out what your business value is. The basis of market-based valuation is the assumption that similar assets will be traded at similar prices in efficient market conditions. Multiples (comparables) are used to obtain business value. There are several multiples within the Market Approach. When there are a sufficient number of similar businesses/assets/securities in the market the possibility to work well of this approach increases.

Asset based approach depends on the assets and the liabilities of the company's balance sheet. The value of a company consists of assets and liabilities within the scope of this approach. The equity value is obtained by reducing total value of the company's liabilities from the total value of the company's assets. The proponents of this approach argue that an accounting-based company value estimate gives more accurate results than valuation models based on all predictive assumptions for the future. Indeed, the balance sheet elements give general picture of business value. However, it is not enough to give complete and accurate picture. This approach is based on accounting records. Since it is a static valuation method, it does not take into account the future expectation of the company, the company's situation in the sector, the future cash flows and the factors that are not reflected in the accounting tables such as the agreements made by the company.

Income-based approach is also known as Discounted Cash Flow Valuation, where the value is determined by discounting future cash flows to the present using a required rate of return. The income-based business valuation approach is based on the future income to be generated by a company. According to this approach a company can only create value as long as it generates cash in the future. Therefore, the present value of a company is determined by the present value of the cash flows of that company generated in the future.

In the income-based approach, it is taken into account of the company's future expectations. Therefore, it is argued that this approach gives more accurate picture of a business' true value. However, it is difficult to calculate and is based on many projections. Because the calculations are mostly based on projections and predictions, the probability of biases increase due to the human factors.

There are three common income-based business valuation approaches that are commonly used when valuing a business; Discounted Free Cash Flow Method, Discounted Dividend Method and Capitalization of Earnings/Cash Flow Method. The discounted free cash flow method is one of the most widely used methods by both the experts and investors who are interested in the company valuation especially for intrinsic value. Taking into account the future cash flows, the risk level of these cash flows and the risk level of the company are the main reasons for the common use of this method. However, the fundamental variables of the method; the free cash flows that the company will create in the future, company's cost of capital and its terminal value are highly sensitive to assumptions. This sensitivity can also prevent realistic results in determining the value we aim to determine. Although this method is considered as one of the best methods, it is important to examine this method with many challenges and to offer solutions to these problems. Therefore, Chapter 4 explains the cash flow analysis and discusses the problems facing the analyst while applying this method and tries to give solutions to these problems.

The main principle of applying Discounted FCF method is the need to match free cash flows to discount rates: equity cash flows to the cost of equity (required rate of equity) and firm cash flows to the cost of capital (weighted average cost of capital). While determining present value of FCFF by using WACC (k_o) gives the entire company value, determining present value of FCFE by using cost of equity (k_e) gives equity value of a company. It is needed beta while calculating both (k_o) and (k_e). The cost of equity is an opportunity cost. Therefore, a number of models are used to determine the cost of equity. Like CAPM, APT, Fama-French 3-Factor Model or multi-factor models etc. However, in practice the most commonly used one among the models is CAPM. In the CAPM, in order to determine the cost of equity, a risk premium is added to the risk-free rate of return. Naturally, risk premium will be higher for investments with higher risk and vice versa. In this model, the risk premium of a firm will be equal to the multiplication of the market risk premium with the Beta of the equity of the firm in question, which measures the sensitivity of the shares of that firm to the changes in the market portfolio. Almost all of the risk-return equilibrium models in finance assure that the investors do good diversification, eliminate non-systematic risk and therefore expect to get a return for the systematic risk they take. Beta calculated as such may have some problems need to be solved.

Chapter 5, titled "Challenges in Estimation of Beta: Market Models Used for Risk Estimation", aims to make a judgment as to which of the indices provides the investors the best beta forecast. Furthermore, this chapter aims to question which time period should be selected for beta calculation. This study reveals that the choice of return intervals causes variations in beta estimation of the security. Applying higher frequency has an advantage in that it increases the number of observations; however, it does come with a shortage. That is, beta tends to have substantial bias with shorter return intervals used. Without clear understanding of the challenges that analysts and investors face while estimating beta it is impossible to find the possible solutions and obtain the best beta that would maintain an exact fit between the data and econometric model. This chapter will contribute to the improvement of analytical and investment decisions made both domestically and internationally. By using both theoretical and practical applications this study ventures to cease the gap and will contribute to the existing bulk of academic literature in terms of obtaining the beta for a plausible comparison that will be used to reflect future investment decisions.

Chapter 6 also presents solutions to some challenges when calculating CAPM Beta. Three methods for calculating traditional beta are presented and illustrated through the case of Facebook. Different choices as of market index, data frequency and sample size result in different values of beta; however, in all cases beta was greater than one. The chapter explores ordinal beta as an alternative measure to treat outliers in both developed and thin markets. Using a sample of 84 US stocks, there was no statistical difference between median traditional and ordinal betas. This was not the case for a sample of 47 Colombian stocks, which questions the usefulness of traditional beta in thin markets. In contrast with median traditional beta, median ordinal beta did not change significantly as a result of irregular data series. The contrary occurred when the observation (sampling) period was reduced; this leaves open the question of subjectivity when defining such period. Finally, the process of valuing a private company was illustrated through the case of Palmoil Ltd., a Colombian company.

In addition, in determining the future cash flows of the company to be valued, it is normally taking into consideration the past cash flows of the company as well, but in a company with negative earning we do not have such data available. Similarly, we have the same problem for start-ups as well. Determining the growth rate of the future cash flows of such companies is rather difficult. Thus, this situation creates a serious setback for the valuation of such companies. Therefore, it is conceivable to say that in valuing startup, young firms or companies with negative earnings, the use of cash flows approach will have major pitfalls in determining the FCFs needed for the valuation process.

Chapter 7 titled "Valuation of Negative Earning Firms" addresses the issue of valuation of businesses who incur losses. The chapter addresses a different and one of the important issues regarding valuation of the firms. Many developed and developing countries have been promoting starts up to stabilize and accelerate their economic growth and they often incur losses initially. With the rise of e-business and e-commerce, many firms incur negative cash flows. Valuation of negative earning firms needs different approach and methodology than the firms with positive earnings. This chapter has dealt this issue by classifying the negative earning firms into three parts based on the time span they incur negative earnings. The chapter has provided the practical examples along with theory. This chapter will pave the way for further studies on the topic of valuing negative earning firms.

In general, it has been faced similar difficulties for Startups. Deciding the value of a Startup is similar to valuing a specific table. The valuation at this stage is very important. Startups investors/analysts need to use different methods to deal with the difficulties in the cash flow and valuation by focusing on similar indicators about startups. Nine Pre-Money Valuation methods, which are Berkus Method, Risk Factor Summation Method, Scorecard Valuation Method, Comparable Transactions Method, Book Value Method, Liquidation Value Method, Discounted Cash Flow (DCF) Method, First Chicago Method, The Venture Capital Method are explained theoretically.

In addition, professionals can face with specific challenges while valuation process. Valuation of companies with material stranded assets is a one of the important specific issues. Chapter 9 sets out to investigate the challenges being faced by sell-side analysts in companies with material stranded assets through the lens of Becksian risk society theory. The research seeks to unravel the basis for arriving at the intrinsic value of these companies, and whether they take Environmental Social and Governance (ESG) factors into consideration in doing so. Qualitative data were collected via multiple methods comprising longitudinal historiographic method, participant observation at IR meetings and interview of sell-side analysts. Findings indicate dissatisfaction with the existing risk reporting system is a key factor in divestment decisions and asset stranding. The growing Responsible Investment (RI) awareness notwithstanding, the inadequate risk reporting system continues to represent a major source of agitation amongst shareholders and analysts, making the overhaul of the current financial reporting system inevitable.

Financial services firms, such as banks, financial services, insurance companies and investment banks, are different from other corporates, in terms of general operation and financial tables. Therefore, valuing those companies has always been difficult. According to the both market capitalization and the number figures within the financial services firms, banks has higher importance in country's economies. Therefore, there are three chapters about bank or bank stock valuation in the book.

In Chapter 10, it is examined in particular the valuation of banks which can be classified into five parts. It introduces several valuation approaches to find out whether there is a method that is superior over another. This chapter starts with a description of bank regulations and their impact on bank valuations and continues with an overview of valuation approaches. The second part applies the banking sector decision models. The third section shows banking sector valuation models. The fourth part presents the input factors that are needed to value a company. The last part have been used to analyze the main ratios of the Bank of America, the calculated values were then compared over time (2014-2018) to assess the explanatory power of the bank. The importance of valuating banking sector stems from the value of these institutions and its role in economic development. Assessing the value of a bank is a quite challenging task. Banks differ from other companies in multiple ways, which necessarily leads to different valuation approaches. This chapter highlighted the importance of measuring and valuing the commercial banks by providing a comprehensive picture of the various approaches. There are multiple approaches to assess the value of banks, but in general they share one specific characteristic. Assessing the value of a bank is a quite challenging task. Banks differ from other companies in multiple ways, which necessarily leads to different valuation approaches. Additionally, banks are traditionally highly leveraged. Another important point in what distinguishes a bank from any other business is the way a bank is regulated. However, this chapter introduced the most appropriate approaches for valuation of banks. It discussed some previous studies included theories and decision models, valuation models, input factors and financial analysis of banking sector which will add a significance value on the book.

There are several value drivers for firms. However, due to its nature of business, a bank's valuation is affected by several unique drivers including earnings diversification, risk capabilities, assets mix, and a lot of intangible factors. Since, banking is a highly regulated sector, Chapter 11 is designed to address the missing links between Basel capital and liquidity regulations, banking system resilience, and bank valuation.

There is a chapter about bank stock valuation in the book as well. A stock is a security representing a share in a corporation. The equity value can be calculated by multiplying "a stock price" and "the number of shares outstanding of a business". The equity value of a business is the value of the shareholders' claims in the business. Therefore, designing optimal model for valuation of a stock is an important task and helps finding real equity value of banks.

With a different perspective, investors exchange their cash that they don't need today for a share in a claim in stock exchanges. It means deferring consumption now in order to consume more in the future. Valuation is the mechanism behind this ability to trade cash for claims. So, if it is wanted to invest thoughtfully, investors must learn how to value stocks.

The growth and diversification of investment and management property have development requirements, so achieving first place in economic in both of which have been explained, requires transfer of the share of ownership from government to private sector. One of the major requirements of these operations is pricing of shares through stock exchange. Thus, the accurate and transparent assessment in assignment of stock value has great importance. The government is trying to reduce his involvement in economic fields, especially in banking system. Due to these challenges, it has been tried to design optimal model and then determine the bank stock value in public offerings. In this regard, the review of conventional models of stock valuation has been analyzed and effect of functional variables and balance sheet on the value of bank stocks is investigated. In the statistical stage, the relevant tests have been accepted for 16 banks in Tehran Stock Exchange and Iranian OTC market on a three-year timeframe (One year before and one year after the launch). The results of research lead to design and specify the optimal model for evaluating of Bank stock. By investigating the results P/E, earnings per share (EPS), Total costs, total incomes, capital adequacy ratio, the ratio of loans to deposits and fixed assets, these are associated with both high and low growth in earnings per share.

Stock valuation is an important task not only for banks but also for all of companies in the business environment. Stock markets are the beating hearts in the global economy which trade around-the-clock. While you are reading this chapter, fortunes made and lost as shares on stock trade at global stock exchanges such as New York, Nasdaq, London, Tokyo, Hong Kong and Shanghai. Making a successful investment decision is one of the contemporaneous challenges facing investors recently; therefore, this book is designed to overcome these challenges. The analyses are built on comprehensive quantitative methods to tackle persistent issues that are preventing businesses from maximising profits and market growth. Thus, in this chapter, we have used up-to-date forecasting methods to predict the future prices of the stock markets accurately. If there is one common theme to the vast range of the stock market's forecasting techniques, it is the one applied in this chapter where we used a set of examples to identify the potential opportunities of buying and selling the stock of interest.

According to the NPV method, which is one of the most common project valuation methods, a project with a positive NPV value is accepted. Because, in this way, the related project increases the value of the company and serve the value maximization aim. The increase is up to the NPV value. The value of the firms is actually equal to the sum of the NPV values of all their investment projects. Therefore, the valuation of each investment project of a firm is also closely related to the firm value as well. According to this perspective, this book contains real world project valuation examples.

For example, "The Valuation of a Firm With Alternative Projects" is a chapter that provides theoretical framework and valuation for a realworld company with mutually exclusive projects in heating industry. This is a strategic industry for the European Commission particularly to battle with climate change. The place where the valuation takes place is a factory storage. Two alternative projects are developed which are electrical and natural gas heating. These projects are designed and the value of investment and operating costs are determined by the best offers of suppliers in the market and actual energy prices. The chapter also includes methodological discussion and project discussion sections.

Chapter 15, titled "Valuation of Logistics Hubs: A Case Study From Turkey", also presents a specific valuation for the establishment of a logistics center. Logistics structures are key components of the national asset portfolio and play significant roles in the economic development paths of countries. Such structures are irreversible investments and require long-time commitment, maintenance, and operation. The exact valuation of them could be difficult due to various uncertainties and problems. Within this scope, the chapter illustrates a methodological way to be able to make an investment decision about the creation of a logistics hub project in Of-Iyidere region located in Turkey. Furthermore, the chapter discusses basic project valuation challenges and presents solutions to improve the practice of logistics hub appraisal. In this regard, the chapter provides an essential guidance and policy support tool to highlight the potential of logistics hub infrastructure.

The book aims to guides professionals, academicians, company managers, company owners, corporate professionals, master and doctoral students in dealing with some of the special valuation challenges that they are likely to encounter.

Chapter 1
Introduction to Business Valuation

Sinem Derindere Köseoğlu
Independent Researcher, Turkey

Saad Salman Awad Almeany
University of Baghdad, Iraq

ABSTRACT

This chapter is an introduction to the book and provides basic information to help readers in the following chapters. This book analyzes all kinds of problems and develops solutions in firm valuation process. The needs and purposes of firm valuation are briefly explained. Basic Concepts, such as Cost, Price, Value, Valuation, Evaluation, Free Cash Flow, and different types of value, are explained. Face value, issue price, fair value, intrinsic value, market value, book value, going-concern value, liquidation value, replacement value, enterprise value, and equity value are explained within the different types of value. Then, "financial statements" and "elements of financial statements", which will form the basis of all valuation approaches, are explained and emphasized. The value drivers for businesses are discussed. Business valuation approaches' general features are given.

INTRODUCTION

The question of what the value of your company is a strategic subject in a firm's ongoing activities. Although many senior managers and the owner of the companies know accurately the value of capital assets, vehicles, machines, cars, or more simply the computer that they uses, when the question is asked about the value of the company, which is the main subject of them, they often give answers rarely accurate and questionable. In real life, the value of the company is an important tool not only for selling, acquisition or merger but also for making medium and long-term plans properly. The main purpose of finance managers is to maximize the market value of the firm, and thus the maximum amount of money that will remain to shareholders. The managers who exhibit a value-based management approach will determine factors affecting the value of the company, which are called value drivers. And they will give importance to these issues in the company's medium and long-term strategic plans.

DOI: 10.4018/978-1-7998-1086-5.ch001

Although the business valuation is not a new issue, its importance increases. The business valuation has become a more professional subject in need of legal action, buying the firm, mergers, acquisitions, taxation and many legal cases. It may cause many rights losses as long as the valuation not being done professionally. For example, a shareholder who wishes to withdraw from the partnership will receive a lower amount when the value of the share is not determined correctly. Or, if an accurate value is not determined in the sales of the company, an unfair situation will arise between the buyer and seller. These examples can be reproduced. Therefore, the business valuation has become more professional and valuation techniques has become more advanced in the business and academic world.

In this chapter, it is explained the needs and purposes of valuation, parties benefit from valuation, financial statement concepts, other concepts of valuation and the business value drives. Thus, the aim of this chapter is to give general knowledge about firm valuation as an introduction of this book titled "valuation challenges and solutions in contemporary businesses".

THE NEEDS AND THE PURPOSES OF VALUATION

There are many reasons for businesses to need valuations. For instance; purchasing a new business, acquisition, merger, selling your existing business, initial public offering, privatization, credit rayting, determining the values of Intellectual Property rights such as trademark, patent, copyright, and registered transactions, in the process of bankruptcy and liquidation, tax issues, disputes between shareholders, withdrawal from the partnership, adding new shareholders to partnership, transfering equity in your existing business to a family member or key employee, determination of the share values of existing shareholders, long term financing plannig, and financial reporting are some reasons to need and purposes of firm valuation. AICPA (American Institute of Certified Public Accountants) states that the valuation is accurued for numerous purposes such as *"transactions, financings, taxation planning and compliance, intergenerational wealth transfer, ownership transition, financial accounting, bankruptcy, management information, and planning and litigation support long term financing"*.

However, company owners and senior managers should have an idea about the firm value without these specific reasons as well. The established business and the point where this business comes is an important success for owners. The time, effort and capital of company owners dedicated to the business over the years have often grown into their most significant asset.

Companies that have reached a certain maturity after making a serious labor and capital investment need to make an effective planning to sustain these achievements. There are three vital components to this effective planning: i. Knowing your business value, ii. Protecting your business and key employees – Business succession and protection plans allow you to prepare for the unexpected, as well as the future success of your business, iii. Protecting your lifestyle – Retirement, income protection and legacy and estate planning solutions help you and your family maintain your lifestyle. Because the value of your business is such an integral part of effective planning, that's a great place to start. You probably have a good idea of what your business is worth. Therefore, the business valuation is a great start towards sustaining your business' success.

It is very important to know the value of the company and determine the factors affecting this value in order to make a correct and effective planning and to keep these plans up to date. For this reason, company valuation has become an important issue for effective long-term planning of your company except for a number of specific reasons, which are explained in detail below.

Identifying the purpose/need of the company valuation is a crucial first step in the process as it dictates the "basis of value" or "standard of value" to be applied, which, in turn, impacts the selection of approaches, inputs and assumptions considered in the valuation (Barnes, 2017). The firm valuation is carried out in parallel with various targets and taking into account certain objectives (Hitcher, 2003: 2). The different uses of business valuation and cases where professional firm valuation is required are explained below:

- **Portfolio Management and Valuation:** The importance of firm valuation in portfolio management may vary according to active (short-term) and passive (long-term) investors. The valuation of portfolio management for a passive investor is very small. However, for an active investor, who are active in the market conditions, valuation is of great importance. The equity value obtained by using firm valuation methods is compared with the share value in the market. Shares are included in the portfolio if they are low valued in the market comparing to estimation. A firm value determined under realistic assumptions is an indicator of whether stocks are high or low valued in the market. (Ercan vd., 2006: 9-10; Damodaran, 2002: 8).
- **Financial Management and Valuation:** Considering that the most fundamental objective of financial management is to maximize corporate value, it is important to know the real firm value and increase this value. Financial decisions such as capital structure of the firm, financing mix, dividend policy, new investments and refinancing should be serve maximizing firm value. All decisions taken by the financial manager should increase the value of the firm, and make decisions in this direction. Firm valuation helps managers to manage their business.
- **Mergers, Acquisitions, and Valuation:** Firms can grow in two ways: organically or through mergers and acquisitions (Barbara and Kenneth, 2013: 3). As a result of the synergy effect, the aim of the merger and acquisition is to increase the value of the new firm above the sum of the each firm values separately (Ercan vd., 2006: 1-2). Merger and Acquisition are general terms that express the general consolidation of companies. The merger is the economic and legal merger of two or more firms to emerge as a single company under a new legal entity/firm. The merged firms lose their legallity. Acquisation refers to the fact that a firm maintains its legallty, but other company or companies are included in the legally protected company with all of its assets and liabilities. The real values of the companies subject to transactions in both mergers and acquisitions are the basis and focus of the transaction.
- **Privitization and Valuation:** When we look at the economies of the world in the recent period, it is seen that the share of the States decreased especially in some special sectors. Privatization means reducing the share of the State in the economy, providing the funds of local and foreign investors to the related fields, selling the state institutions to the private sector in order to increase efficiency. Some enterprises under the control of the State can be transferred to the private sector in order to increase efficiency. Here, public assets are being transferred to the private sector in order to operate the market mechanism and increase efficiency. The result of the valuation studies shows which value should be taken in the related privatization process. (Kissin ve Zulli, 1989: 39).
- **Bankruptcy, Liquidation, and Valuation:** Valuation is an obligation for companies that have to end their operations due to different reasons. If the company goes bankrupt, it is necessary to liquidate the entire company assets and find its value. The liquidation value of the assets is the minimum amount that will receive for the quick sale of these assets. At this point, the determina-

tion of the true cash values of the assets of the company, namely the liquidity value, is important for the protection of the rights of all parties during the liquidation phase (Ercan vd., 2006: 12).

- **Leaving from Partnership or Taking New Shareholder and Valuation:** A shareholder who wishes to leave the company will want to know his share value in the company. It is also a requirement for the new shareholder to determine the price per share. The company may want to take new shareholders because to grow. In these cases, valuation will also become a necessity.
- **Legal Disputes and Valuation:** Valuation is needed for disputes of shareholder rights, pressures of dissenting shareholder and minority shareholder, minority shareholder rights, compensation calculations, property disputes, and the value to be paid to the counterparty who are not agree to sale.
- **Public Offering and Valuation:** One of the ways in which companies provide financing through equity is to sell their shares to the public and provide funds from the capital markets. In order to sell their own shares, the public is called for and the company finances are made by selling the shares. Companies can provide the opportunity to finance new investments by providing financing in this way. At this point, the value and price of the publicly traded shares are the focus of the transaction. During the public offering, it is important that the company's shares, which are publicly traded in terms of individual investors, are valued in a way that reflects the reality. The determination of the fair value depends on the determination of the cash flow of the stock as the future capital gain and dividend and discounting these cash flows an accurate discount rate.
- **Business Sale:** While selling a company or buying another, a firm valuation provides a detailed analyse for the company subjected.
- **Credit Rating / Solvency Analysis and Valuation:** Credit Institutions, which provide loans to firms make decisions to lend, taking into account the value of the firm, the ability to pay debt and the future cash generation capacity. In this process, the business valuation can be performed by the lender and the firm. If the mortgage is required for the loan, it is necessary to determine the value of the asset, the asset group or the entire firm (Ercan vd., 2006: 11).
- **Intellectual Property Rights (trademark, patent, copy rights etc.) and Valuation:** Some companies have many intellectual property rights such as trademarks, patent, know-how and copyrights. The share of these intellectual property rights within the entire firm value can be quite large. In cases where the value of intellectual property rights becomes important, the value created by these rights must be determined seperatly. This issue becomes even more important, especially if a significant portion of the value of the firm is confined to the brand value it has created. The contribution of these elements to the value should be analyzed in a good way especially in the fields of company sales, mergers and acquisitions.
- **Other issues that is needed business valuation:**
    - Sales of firm shares (block sales: minority shares or majority shares)
    - Financial Reporting Purposes/Providing Information: As a basis for audit reports.
    - Employee Stock Ownership Plans: It will need to be valued in determining how and to what extent company employees will be owner of the company (Hitcher, 2003: 2).
    - Taxation: in the case of the determination of the inheritance tax, real estate and income tax, the company value needs to be determined.
    - Donations for charitable organizations and foundations: Valuation is a requirement if the company shares or assets are donated to charities and there is a possibility to deduct this amount from taxes.

- In legal cases of divorce and inheritance; the value of the asset or company must be determined in order to share the company and / or assets fairly between the spouses and heirs. (Kissin ve Zulli, 1989: 39).

BASIC CONCEPTS

The Concept of Valuation

Valuation activities refer to the process of determining the value of an asset. Valuation is determining of the current market value of economic assets as money. In other words, it can be defined as the appreciation and estimation of the value of a firm's total assets such as current assets (like inventory), fixed assets/non-current assets (like lands, buildings, properties, machinery, plant, equipments and vehicles) and intangible assets (like goodwill and other intangible assets). Valuation is to investigate to what extent a fixed asset, intangible asset or a service provides the expected benefit from them and to give an opinion about their properties in order to determine their value (Chambers, 2009: 5-7). Since the valuation of the firm is a function of the future of the firm, the "expression of art rather than science" is used for firm valuation process (Ertugrul, 2008: 143).

It is also worth mentioning the concepts of ***"valuation"*** and ***"evaluation"*** here. The ***"valuation"*** and ***"evaluation"*** concepts have different meanings and the determination of the economic value of an asset is called valuation, while the evaluation refers to the analysis of the performance of an asset. Firm value generally refers to the total value of the current market values of firm's liabilities and equity. From the shareholders' point of view, equity value is found with the deduction of the current value of the debts from the total current value of all assets of the company. Due to the fact that value is a relative concept and it is difficult to determine exactly, firm valuation is one of the most complex issues of financial management. (Ercan vd., 2003: 1). As in the determination of the economic meaning of value concept, the meaning of value for firms, value drivers and different measurements are also very complex and remain the focus of intensive discussions. When we look at the economic fundamentals of value, the value of the company is defined and calculated from time to time as a function of the cost or utility (like cash flows, profit or dividend, that the company generated in the future) (Ertugrul, 2008: 147).

Distinguish Between "Cost", "Price", and "Value"

It is very important to distinguish between cost, price and value, because all valuation approaches as we will see later depend on these concepts. We need the amount of costs in determining the profits and estimating the future cash flows when using the income approach in the valuation. And we use the price when using the market approach, whether the value is at the exchange or the value in use, and the valuer must have the ability to clearly distinguish between these three concepts so that the valuation decisions are correct and accurate.

Cost

There is no agreed definition of the term cost and the general definition of costs as they came The Committee of Concepts and Cost Standards As an economic sacrifice measured by the unity of monetary, has occurred or is expected Occurrence, achievement of a specific purpose (Hilton & Platt, 2011:72). *"A **cost** is a resource sacrificed or forgone to achieve a specific objective. A cost (such as the cost of labor or advertising) is usually measured as the monetary amount that must be paid to acquire goods or services. An **actual cost** is the cost incurred (a historical or past cost), as distinguished from a **budgeted cost,** which is a predicted, or forecasted, cost (a future cost)"* (Horngren, et al, 215: 51).

There are four characteristics synonymous with these definitions:

- **Sacrifice**: Cost must be measured as a sacrifice, offering this sacrifice now or in the future to reduce cash or other assets or increase current liabilities.
- **Value Money**: The use of resources is measured under the unit of monetary, these resources are materials, wages, and other services (factory overhead).
- **Objective Stated**: When economic sacrifice occurs, it must be associated to obtain benefit. The cost must therefore be associated with a specific objective .In the absence of benefits, we are shift from the concepts of cost to the concept of loss .
- It must be within the standard range (that is, it does not include natural tolerances)

Price

Price is the amount of cash or equivalent cash paid by the buyer to the seller in exchange for any product or service. the amount charged by the seller for a product is known as its price, which included cost add the profit margin. But not necessarily that the price is over the cost. in the some case the seller sell his/her product less than the cost under certain circumstances and this price is call **Bargain price.** The cost of construction of the building represents the amounts paid for the purchase of raw materials, wages and salaries of workers and employees, the amounts spent on electricity, fuel and other services provided for the completion of the building, while the amount received from the sale of it represent the price, and if the building purchased by the properties investment company, the amount paid represents the cost, and when sold later the amount of the sale represents the price. With related it to the cost and value Kotler and Armstrong, defined *"the price is as the amount of money to pay for a product or service, or the value of the exchange help customers receive a product or service for a certain amount. Thus, the direct cost of the period is the amount of money the buyer has to pay for the product or service that is likely to buy it. The price may also be defined as a monetary expression of value for the consumer agrees to pay."* (Isoraite, 2016:30)

Value

What is said is that it is an economic resource if it has two characteristics: scarcity and utility. Scarcity means that obtaining something requires a cost (not a free one) and that the benefit is the ability of the thing to satisfy human needs .Thus, cost and benefit are the basis for the value of the commodity or service Parker (2015) described value as *"the estimate of an amount assuming- exchange, specific date, buyer willing to buy, seller willing to buy, no buyer-seller relationship, period of marketing has occurred, and parties had each acted knowledgeably, prudently and without compulsion; Worth is seen as the value of a commodity to the owner or a potential owner for individual investment or operational objectives."* (Olajide,et al,2016:54) For valuation purposes, the value can be expressed in several formats according to the objective of the valuation, such as Book value, Fair value, Intrinsic value, Market value, Face Value, Face value, issue price, fair value, intrinsic value, market value, book value, going-concern value, liquidation value, replacement value, enterprise value and equity value etc. These terms will be dealt with in detail below.

The Relationship Between Cost, Price, and Value

After presenting these concepts, it is necessary to clarify the relationship between them, as we found that the cost is actual amounts spent by the company for the purpose of producing the goods or service, and that these amounts can be verified in the records of the company, it is characterized by high reliability and there are not many differences in how to calculate except for the recognition of the expense and the timing of recognition, Costs in planning when adopting a cost-cutting policy to compete with other companies operating in the same sector, as well as using control to avoid waste of economic resources, as well as being a basis for pricing policy.

The price is the cost plus a profit margin determined by the management in case the company is given the price, but in the market of high competition, the market is the one that imposes the price and the company in this case took the price and this price is called the target price, When the target profit margin is subtracted from the target price we get the so-called target cost, and then the company must produce the commodity at a cost equal to or less than the target cost.

Although there may be no direct correlation between value and cost, but the value may depend on cost and utility, as economists see, because utility alone does not interpret value as Marshall sees it. For example, the Diamond has a low utility but is sold at a very high price because its cost is very high. Conversely, water has a very high utility but is sold at a low price because it costs very low.

Value is the price that pays the customer who wants to buy a specific commodity, the value is the perceived benefit of the commodity by the customer (buyer), and the benefit varies from one person to another and from one place to another, the person who is addicted to smoking, for example, the value of cigarettes is high at the opposite of the person who not to smoke, as well as VIP people pay a high price to buy luxury cars regardless of the benefits contained in those cars. While the conditions of supply and demand in the market determine the prices of ordinary cars, it is thus possible to conclude that the relationship between price and value is not a linear relationship. Accordingly, the relations between the three concepts can be expressed as follows:

Figure 1. The relationship between cost, price, and value

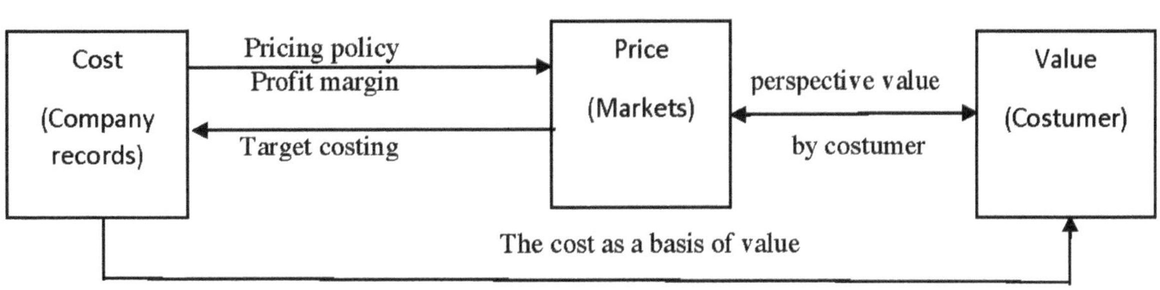

The Differences Between Cost, Price, and Value

Although there is a relationship between the three concepts of cost, price and value as explained earlier, there are many areas of differences, Table 1. focuses on six areas: The first basis for comparison is a meanings which discussed in the previous pages of this chapter, the next is measurement basis that focuses on what the amount was In which the concept is actually expressed or estimated. The third is deal with relation of the concept with the production of the commodity or service in terms of it represents inputs or output, costs represent the inputs of production, either the price expresses the outputs of production are indicators of the process of production, as the efficiency can be expressed by the productivity of maximizing output from a specific input. The other basis of comparison is those who use these concepts, although all concepts are used by multiple parties, However, a particular party (such as management, accountent department) uses a particular concept (such as cost, value) more than others. For example, the management uses the cost for planning, control and decision-making purposes. The fifth comparison relates to the ascertainment, the cost is determined from the perspective of the producer, the price from the perspective of the customer, and the value from the perspective of the user. The last basis for comparison compares the three concepts with the valuation approaches (which the chapters of this book are interested in). The cost is linked to the cost approach and the price is linked to the income approach, while the value is associated with the market approach.

The Concept of "Free Cash Flow" (FCF)

The most important variables that determine the real value of a business or shares is the "**free cash flows that the company will create in the future**". The cash flows generated by a business are referred as "Free Cash Flows". FCF is the cash left over after paying operating expenses and capital expenditures of the company. It is used "free" term due to paying operating expenses, capital expenditures and also tax. Cash flows that are free from all expenses and taxes. Free cash flows to the firm (FCFF) and free cash flows to equity (FCFE) are the cash flows available to, respectively, all of the investors in the company and to common shareholders. The FCFF concept refers to expected cash flows left to shareholders and

Table 1. The Differences Between Cost, Price and Value

Value	Price	Cost	Basis for comparison
Value is the utility of a good or service	Price is the amount paid for acquiring any product or service	Cost is the amount incurred in producing and manufacturing a product.	Meaning
Through opinion/ Estimated	Through policy	Actual	Measurement
Value added	Output	Input	Input /output
Multi-end such as management, markets, government	Multi-end such as management, markets, government	Management	Users
Value is ascertained from the user's perspective	Price is ascertained from the customer's perspective	Cost is ascertained from the producer's perspective	Ascertainment
Market approach	Income approach	Cost approach	Related with valuation approaches

Source: Olajida, et. al., 2016:55 (It is added and deleted some aspects by authors)

long-term lenders, who are main financial source providers of the firm. They shape the capital structure of the company. In other words, Free cash flows to firm (FCFF) expresses cash flow left to all beneficiaries of the company apart from government. The beneficiaries of a firm are stockholders, bond holders and government. Because Free Cash Flow is calculated by deducting tax payments, it refers to the remaining cash to other beneficiaries after government. On the other hand, The FCFE concept refers to expected cash flows in the future left to shareholders only. Because, FCFE is calculated by deducting interest payments and other commitments.

DIFFERENT TYPES OF VALUES

It is possible to view value concepts on a micro and macro perspective. According to this different perspective, the value in the micro base is the value of the stock and the value in the macro basis is the value of the company.

Common stocks (shares) are the securities which give the owner to the right of being a partner of the firm and also can be bought and sold in secondary markets. There is a price level that the buyer and seller deem appropriate for the stock and the stock price increases or decreases according to the change in the estimated value of this stock. There may be different opinions between the values for the stocks, and these different opinions actually shapes the related market. The "real value" determination of each market player's or analyst's for the same stock may be different. As a result, depending on these explanations, the company's equity value will be found after multiplying the number of firm's shares by the value of a stock.

Company valuation cannot be carried out without determining a specific situation of a firm (Is the firm is an ongoing business, private or public business or a business in bankruptcy&liquity procces?); without referring to a specific person (value for who and whom?); without determining a specific purpose (value for what?) and without selecting a specific valuation technique (which valuation approach?). In other words, business value depends to a great extent on for what, for whom, for what purpose and how valuation is performed (Pereiro, 2002: 34).

Concepts Used for "Business Value" and "Share Value" (Types of Value)

- ***Face Value (Par Value, Nominal Value):*** It is the value written/printed on a financial security; spesifically common stocks for our chapter. Face Value is also used as nominal value or par value. The nominal value of a stock is used for accounting processes that required to determine and register the total capital in a firm. This value does not indicate a common stock trading value in the market. The nominal value is not the price. A stock may be purchased and sold at a price below or above the nominal value. There is a difference between the nominal concept used in the economy and the nominal concept used in finance. Nominal concept in the economy means a data that is not corrected by inflation, for a particular year or a period, while nominal concept in finance refers the printed value of a security.
- ***Market Value:*** It is the price that shares are bought and sold in the market depending on supply and demand. The market value of a share is determined by supply and demand fluctuations. Market conditions effects the share value. If the related stocks are traded on the stock exchange, in other words traded in publicly traded stocks, the market value is also called the "stock exchange value".

The equity market value is calculated by multiplying "the stock exchange price" and "the number of shares outstanding of a business". It is called market capitalization. "Market capitilization", or commonly reffered to as "market cap", means the total market value of a business' all outstanding shares. An important point should be underlined here; the "market cap" may often not reflect the real business value it should have. Intrinsic value research should also be done.

- ***Fair Value (or Fair Market Value):*** In investing, it refers to a security sale price agreed upon by a willing purchaser and seller, assuming both are completely knowledgable and enter the transaction freely. It is the value that is considered to be the basis for the exchange between a willing buyer and a willing seller who acts in the light of all known information without any influence in an open and unrestricted market. It is not directly the same as market value. Because this concept assumes and uses hypothetical buyers and sellers who are all rational and perfectly informed.
- ***Intrinsic Value:*** It is the real value of a common stock. Real value is closely related to the future cash inflow generation potential of a business. The most important value for investors is the real value of a business, but it is also difficult to determine. After estimating the real value of a common stock, investors then compare this value with the current market price of the stock. If the real value is above the market value, it is thought the stock is traded cheap and if it is below the market value, it is thought the stock price is expensive.
- ***Issue Price:*** It refers to the "*initial public offering price*". The difference between the issue price and the nominal value is called the "*share premium*". Publicly traded companies may issue shares below the nominal value depending on certain conditions.
- ***Book Value:*** The book value of equity represents the value calculating by deducting book value of the debts from the book value of business. The book value is also known as accounting value. The book value of a share is calculated by dividing the total book value of equity by the total number of shares outstanding. Paid-in capital is the product of the nominal value of a share and the number of shares outstanding. For example, if the nominal value is 1 $, the number of shares is equal to the paid-in capital. Book value generally does not have an important function in determining the real value of the busieness' equity. Book value generally does not have an important function in determining the real/intrinsic value of the firm. Mostly, there are significant differences between the book values and current market values of businesses. However, book value can be used as an important benchmark in valuation. It is used in the valuation method known as MV / BV ratio (market value to book value). Book value of Equity is the sum of the components of Paid-in capital, common stocks, retained earnings, reserves and earning.
- ***Business Value (Enterprise value, Firm Value, Company Value):*** It is the total value of the current market value of the debt and equity of the firm. In other words, the business value of a company specifies the value of the entire company to all its claimholders. There is a significant distinction between "equity value" and "business value".
- ***Equity Value:*** In terms of shareholders, it is the value of the equity obtained by deducting the current market value of debt from the current market value of the assets of the business. In other words, the equity value of a business is the value of the shareholders' claims in the business.
  Enterprise Value = Equity Value + Market Value of Debt
- ***Net Asset Value:*** The asset value of a business is the total market value of its all assets. Net asset value is the net amount obtained by deducting the market value of debts from the total market value of all business assets. In summary, net asset value is the amount that will be left after pay-

ing all debts from the cash obtained by selling all of business assets. It is expected and normal to have differences between the book value and market value of a business' assets. In this case, the accounting values are corrected according to the current market values.

- ***Liquidation Value:*** Liquidation means the closure of a business and termination of its all activities. Liquidation value of the business is the amount remaining after debt paymets from the cash obtained after the rapid sale of all assets of the business. Liquidation value is a concept related to the asset group of the business. This asset group may be unable to perform the expected function of themself. In this situation, the market value of this asset group is less then the situation that performs the expected function of themself.

Although, liquidation value may look similar to the net asset value, the assets of a company that is in liquidation phase will be priced well below normal market conditions due to the necessity and urgency of the sale. Liquidation value is interpreted as the lowest value determined for a company.

- ***Going-concern-value;*** It can be defined as the value that will arise if the business is transferred/ sold as a whole. Going concern value ***represents the value to be obtained if a firm is sold in an all integrated state. In other words, the all asset group is in a working state and performs expectedly. This asset group is interconnected as they should be.*** In this value concept, it is assumed that the business will continue to operate indefinitely (opposite of liquidation value concept). This concept represents the value determined by considering the value of intangible assets such as having a trained workforce, functional facilities, useful licenses/patents, systems and procedures in a business. Goodwill is also added the value. We can formulate the going concern value as follows:

Going-concern-value: Total Market value of all tangible assets of a business + value of the organization (business operation).

This means that a business value is greater than its combined of all tangiable assets. The goodwill of a business increases its value, as qualities such as the firm's customer base, brands, products, location, workforce, and reputation show the firm's proven track record of generating cash.

The value of the organization is consisted of goodwill and intangible assets value.

The organization value here is also expressed in the literature as synergy, including elements such as goodwill, image and brand value.

The value found as a result of firm valuation process represents the real value. The lowest value in the determination of value on a business basis is the liquidation value, while the highest in the determination of value is the going concern value.

In economic terms, the most meaningful business value concept among the other concepts is the value of the going concern value. However, in exceptional and spesific cases and for businesses in spesific sectors, other value concepts may also make sense. For example, the liquidation value is meaningful for the enterprises in liquidation. However, these types of values are generally only supportive indicators when determining the real value of an ongoing business. Going concern value is determined according to analyst's forecasts of future cash flows generated by the business. Therefore, this value calculation is prejudiced and subjective most of the time. In other words, one analyst can make different judgments about the future of a business while another can make different interpretation, and as a result they can reach different values. In fact, this is the basis of transactions in stock exchanges. Investors, who believe that the real value of a share is lower than the market value, sell their shares, while those who believe that the real value of the share is higher than the market value buy these shares. Thus, daily market values of businesses emerge as a result of the supply and demand of analysts with different judgments. Actually, the market value is "price" rather than "value" for the investor who thinks that the market value is different from the real value. Because these investors believe that this is not the real value, but the price that has deviated from the real value for different reasons (Ertugrul, 2008: 153).

- ***Aquisition value:*** It refers to all costs that it is beared when an integrated asset group of a business is acquired in the current market conditions. The integrated asset group of a business performs effectively and have a snergy effect. Acquisition value is not the same with acquisition cost. Acquisition Cost is the cost that a business records on its books for a property. On the other hand, the Acquisition Value contains the measure of terms like "Synergy". This value also considers how much value the company is creating by a particular acquisition for itself.
- ***Replacement Value:*** Replacement value is the value that is the sum of buying costs off all assets, which are identical with company's asset, at the valuation date. That is, in this method, the sum of the costs for the re-purchase of all company's assets will give the replacement value, and also firm value.

FINANCIAL STATEMENTS

Accounting has two main functions: **measurement and communication**. The measurement is based on the set of rules principles and bases accumulated by accountants over number of centuries. It was later called the Generally Accepted Accounting Principles (GAAP). This accumulation of knowledge was referred to conceptual framework as an alternative to accounting theory. There are many bodies issued frameworks for accounting, for example, the conceptual framework issued by the Financial Accounting Standards Board (FASB) in the United States in 1980, and the conceptual framework issued by the International Accounting Standards Board (IASB) and followed by the joint project between the two bodies issued in 2010, which was conducted by multiple amendments to the latest version of the 2018. Accordance with these conceptual frameworks, accounting standards are continually issued to regulate the work of accountants and are considered as guidance in their measurement and disclosure and are based for auditors on them in expressing their neutral professional opinion on the financial statements. On the other hand, accounting standards include a set of presentation and disclosure requirements that should be included in financial reports, including financial statements. These reports represent the second function of accounting (communication). Financial statements represent the main source of disclosure of the financial information of the entity, and reflect the financial position, financial performance and cash flows. The understanding of the contents of these statements is very important for internal and external users to make their decisions for each aspect, especially to assess the performance of the entity and determine real value of firm. However, there are four common statements:

Balance Sheet (Statement of Financial Position)

This statement provides the financial position of entity at specific point in time. In other words, balance sheet represents equity of entity to other parties against equity of other parties to entity. The elements of this statement are as follows:

1. Assets
2. Liabilities
3. Owners' Equity

Income Statement

This statement reflects the financial performance of an entity over certain period. Basic elements found in an income statement are as follows:

1. Revenues
2. Expenses
3. Gains
4. Losses

Statement of Cash Flows

This statement shows the source and uses of cash for the certain period or cash inflow and outflow for specific period. Basic elements of cash flows are three activities:

1. Cash flows from operating activities
2. Cash flows from investment activities
3. Cash flows from financing activities

Statement of Changes in Owners' Equity

This statement represents the increase or decrease of equity during accounts' certain period. Basic elements of this statement are as follow:

- Common stock (Capital)
- Paid in capital
- Reserves
- Returned earnings

ELEMENTS OF FINANCIAL STATEMENTS

The concepts of the elements of the financial statements can be presented in one of the following views: (Belkaoui, 2000: 128)

a. The asset / liability view.
b. The revenue / expenses view.
c. The unrelated view (The no articulated view).

The first approach is named as the balance sheet approach or the capital maintenance approach. This view means that the increase in revenue and expenses is only due to changes in assets and liabilities. For example; expenses are the decrease of assets or a rise in liabilities (Belkaoui, 2000: 126) Revenue is a rise in assets or a decrease in liabilities. The second view is called the income statement approach or the match principle approach. Revenue (or timing of recognition) is recognized through the principle of recognition, according to this view expenses, which represents only those costs that have been expired in produce revenue of one of the following recognition methods: (Belkaoui, 2000: 127)

- Causal relationship (relationship of cause and effect) such as the cost of goods sold.
- Systematic and rational distribution, such as depreciation expenses.

Direct recognition, such as sales and marketing expenses. According to the last (unrelated) view, the asset and liability definitions form the basis of the financial position presentation, and the definitions of revenues and expenses dominate the income measurement. Both statements have an independent and independent means, this view is a critical view because it not currently applicable.

The Elements of Income Statement

Revenues

The Financial Accounting Standards Board (FASB) defines revenue as cash inflows, or increases in assets or decrease in liabilities (or both) arising from the production or producing of services, or other major or continuing activities of the economic unit (FASB, 2000).: 78) Revenue here represents cash inflows (or cash equivalent), actual or expected, that occurred or will occur as a result of the completion of the unit for its central operations (Ibid: 79), although it refers to the production of goods and the provision of services, In cash flows (or cash equivalent) this conclusion leads us to two sub-directions on revenue. The first trend focuses on the inflow within the form of assets as a result of the operational activities of the unit is called the financial flow.

The second trend focuses on the production of goods and services (external flow) by the unit and transfers them to consumers or other producers and is called material flow. Therefore, the FASB has taken the view of the asset / liability and direction of financial flow.

The IASB used the term **income** to denote both expenses and gains once because it adopted a comprehensive income approach to measure the company's performance. Income was defined as: *"increases in assets or decreases in liabilities which result in increases in equity, other than those relating to contributions from holders of equity claims."* (IASB,2018: pragra.4.68)

Expenses

The concept of expenses is similar to the concept of revenues as a process of flow. If the point of asset/ liability view is used, the concept of expenses represents a decreased in assets or increased liabilities and through the use of economic resources and services during a specified period (Belkaoui, 2000: 130) Expenses means the use or consumption of goods and services in the process of obtaining revenue, (expenses are expired to serve the factors directly or indirectly associated with the production and sale of the Company's products (Hendriksen & Meashil, 1992: 333) activity as a result Final consumption, or by converting the product to customers.

The concept of expenses is the same as the revenue concept. If a destination is used, the (FASB) defines expenditure as: *"Cash outflow or other use of assets or increase in liabilities (or both) resulting from the production and delivery of goods, the rendering of services, or other major continuing activities of the economic unit"* (FASB, 2000: 80)

The expenses here represent actual or anticipated cash outflows (or cash equivalents) that have occurred or will occur as a result of the major activities (Ibid: 81). This means that the Committee has focused on the financial flow.

In the same direction of income definition by focusing on changes in assets and liabilities, the IASB recognized expenditure are defined as *"decreases in assets or increases in liabilities which result in decreases in equity, other than those relating to distributions to holders of equity claims."* (IASB, 2018: parag.4.69)

The proposed framework also recognizes other changes in resources and claims, being either contributions from, and distributions to, holders of equity claims, or exchanges which do not result in increases or decreases in equity (for example, acquiring an asset for cash).

As will be seen from the above, the proposed framework continues to define income and expenses in terms of changes in assets and liabilities but also notes that important decisions on matters such as recognition and measurement are driven by considering the nature of the resulting information about both financial performance and financial position.

Gains and Losses

According to the revenue / asset perspective, the gains are defined as the increase in receipts over costs, or other benefits obtained at the time that there is no sacrifice. the losses are defined as impairment in market value or other measurement of value observable At the time of sale or impairment of assets, or at the time of total or partial spoilage to the asset, or any costs that would have been incurred without generating income and therefore losses could not be met with revenue. In this view, they are independent of the definitions of the other elements.

The Elements of Balance Sheet (Financial Position)

Assets

Assets are the property or legal rights owned by an entity to which money value can be attached. In other words, it is an item of economic value that is expected to yield a benefit in the future. Economists emphasize that assets are only economic resources, and that what is said to be an economic resource if you have two main interests is scarcity and utility. The scarcity means that getting a thing requires a cost (not something free) and that the benefit is the ability of the commodity to satisfy human needs, so it is said that cost and benefit are the basis for the value of the product or service.

The accountants differentiate between the asset and its cost. (FASB, 2000: 242) finds that, although assets require acquisition or use, the costs incurred are not the same and that the substance of the asset is its future benefits. Assets are treated as future benefits regardless of whether they are acquired at cost or not. However, cost is necessary to apply the concept of assets and in at least two areas as evidence of acquisition of the asset and a measurement instrument. Realistically, accountants determine the benefits of their ability to generate cash sooner or later. According to the asset / liability view, the asset is an economic asset of the entity that represents future benefits that are expected to result, directly or indirectly, in net cash flows (and will exclude from the definition of assets and economic resources that do not have the exchangeability and severability, Service and economic resources are defined as: (Belkaoui, 2000: 129)

- The productive resources of the enterprise.
- The contractual rights of economic resources.
- Products (inventories).
- Money.
- Commitments to receive money.
- Shares in other entities (investments in other entities)

The FASB did not go beyond that. The assets were defined as *"probable future benefits, owned or controlled by the economic unit, as a result of past operations or events."*

The Board considers that the probable economic benefits are the capacity of an existing entity or through consolidation with another asset to contribute directly and indirectly to the achievement of net cash flow, that the Board also considers that the asset has other characteristics, such as being acquired at cost (as a component of economic resources)), Or are tangible, have the capacity to exchange and have legal status, yet these characteristics are not essential characteristics of the assets (as the Board itself sees it) (FASB, 2000: 188). Mack Neal believes that a commodity that lacks the capacity to exchangeability should not have economic value because selling or buying it is impossible. And thus have no market price (Kam, 2000: 151).

The IASB neglected the ownership aspect and focused on the control side and also focus on the condition of potential benefits as all future benefits of economic resources.

"Asset is defined as a present economic resource controlled by the entity as a result of past events. An economic resource is defined as a right that has the potential to produce economic benefits". (IASB, 2018: parag.4.3). An economic resource is a right that has the potential to produce economic benefits.

This section discusses three aspects of those definitions:

- Right
- Potential to produce economic benefits and
- Control

Assets can be classified as "tangible assets", "intangible assets", "fixed assets" and "current assets"

- **Tangible Assets**: These assets have physical existence. For instance; they can be seen and touched. Machinery, furniture, building are some examples of tangible assets.
- **Intangible Assets**: These assets have physical existence. In another words, they cannot be touched and seen. Goodwill, patents, trademarks are some examples of intangible assets.
- **Fixed Assets:** These assets are put to use for more than one accounting period and its benefit is derived over a longer period. Computer, machinery, land are examples of fixed assets.
- **Current Assets**: These assets which are readily convertible into cash and generally absorbed within one accounting period. Debtors exist to convert them into cash, bills receivable are some example of current assets.

Liabilities

This paragraph includes two elements of the financial statements, namely, liabilities and equity, which are to be accounted for together for two reasons: first, the importance of determining the line between liabilities and equity; and secondly, the definition of equity depends primarily on the definition of assets and liabilities.

The liabilities are the obligation of the entity to transfer economic resources to the other unit in the future (Belkaoui, 2000: 129). The FASB went in the same direction and defined the liabilities as: (a) potential future sacrifices of economic benefits arising from current liabilities (FASB, 2000: 191) that the characteristics of this definition are presented by the Board itself and by the following:

- The substance of liabilities is obligations or requirements to be sacrificed in the future that the emergence of the obligation shows with it receipts, usually cash or equivalent cash (purchase of inventory in the future for example)
- Not all future economic sacrifices are liabilities

A liability is defined as a *"present obligation of the entity to transfer an economic resource as a result of past events"* (IASB, 2018: parag. 4.26).

Liabilities are generally categorized into two broad categories i.e. Current Liabilities and Non-Current Liabilities.

- **Current Liabilities:** It refers to those obligations or payments which are repayable during the current period. Examples of current liabilities are Creditors, accounts payable
- **Non Current Liabilities:** It comprises of those payments which are due for payment over a long period of time and there is no need to payment it current period immediately. For example, bonds, long term loans, etc.

Equity

Equity represents ownership interest in a firm in the form of common stock . Being precise in the accounting terms, it is the difference between fair value of assets and fair vale liabilities of something owned. It is mainly a residual amount adjusted by the assets against liabilities. In the other words, *"equity represents the interests of the owners in the net assets of an entity. It shows the cumulative net results of past transactions and other events affecting the entity since its inception"* (Alibahi, et.al, 2018: 77) . Equity is defined as *"the residual interest in the assets of the entity after deducting all its liabilities."* (IASB,2018: parag.4.63) According to this definition equity is expressed in the following equation:

Equity = Assets – Liabilities

FACTORS EFFECTING OF A BUSINESS VALUE (VALUE DRIVERS)

Since the most important objective of management in a company is to maximize the value of the firm (Rappaport, 1986; Black et al. 2001; Chandra, 2011 and among other), it is important for the senior managers, shareholders and financial managers to know the factors affecting the firm value and to manage these factors in order to serve the main purpose of the firm. Determining all kinds of decisions, such as long-term strategies, performance and future targets in accordance with the value maximization target by management is called the "value-based management" approach. That is, focusing on value maximization by managers and shareholders of a business is value-based management.

In the literature, the factors/variables affecting firm value are called "value drivers". Value drivers can be defined as any variables and factors affecting firm value. It is necessary to define and understand how to use value drivers in order to make financial decisions properly and realize the value maximization target. In fact, all variables used in the firm valuation methods can be listed as value drivers.

Identifying, defining and managing value drivers helps management focus their attention on specific activities which will have the greatest impact on the firm value. Focusing on these points enables the management to direct their effort to specific activities that are likely to create this value.

The first step in value-based management is to identify elements and factors which affect firm value, what is also referred to as value drivers. Value drivers are basically divided into "internal" and "external" factors. Internal value creator factors are related to all kinds of operational and managerial processes, activities, measurements and performance that are directly or indirectly related to the field of activity of the firm. The internal factors creating value should be identified, improved, and monitored of its performance. In addition, the investments of the firm should be examined as value creating factors and the contribution of each investment decisions to the firm value should be determined and followed.

External value drivers are like merger, acquisition or buying processes. The importance of these kind of processes have been increasing recently. The vertical or horizontal merger/aquasition of the firm with another firm should be identified as a value creating process and the results of the process should be monitored in terms of the value creation capacity.

BUSINESS VALUATION APPROACHES, METHODS, AND DIFFICULTIES

Many business valuation models and methods from very simple to highly complex ones are used in finance literature and practice. While these methods and models are based on very different assumptions, some of the methods have some common features and can be categorized together. With the classification of a number of common valuation methods together, a wider concept of valuation approach emerges. In the literature, valuation approaches can be classified in three ways.

Table 2. Internal and External Value Drivers

	QUALITATIVE	QUANTITATIVE
INTERNAL	*Management Quality, *Corporate Governance *Specific features such as; • Quality of products and services • Employee job guarantee • Productivity • Market share • Employee satisfaction • Training of employees • Inventions	*Financial indicators: Sales growth *Operating profit margin *Tax rate *Working capital *capital investments *Cost of capital *Growth period/competitive advantage period
EXTERNAL	*Credit rating, *Consumer behavior, *Customer satisfaction *Mergers, acquisitions	*macro-economic factors

The business valuation approaches are Income Based Approach, Market Based Approach and Asset Based Approach - and within each of these approaches, there are various methods for determining the business value. The different valuation approaches and methods has been given in Figure 2.

The three different approaches used in business valuation are summarized as follows:

Figure 2. Business Valuation Approaches and Methods

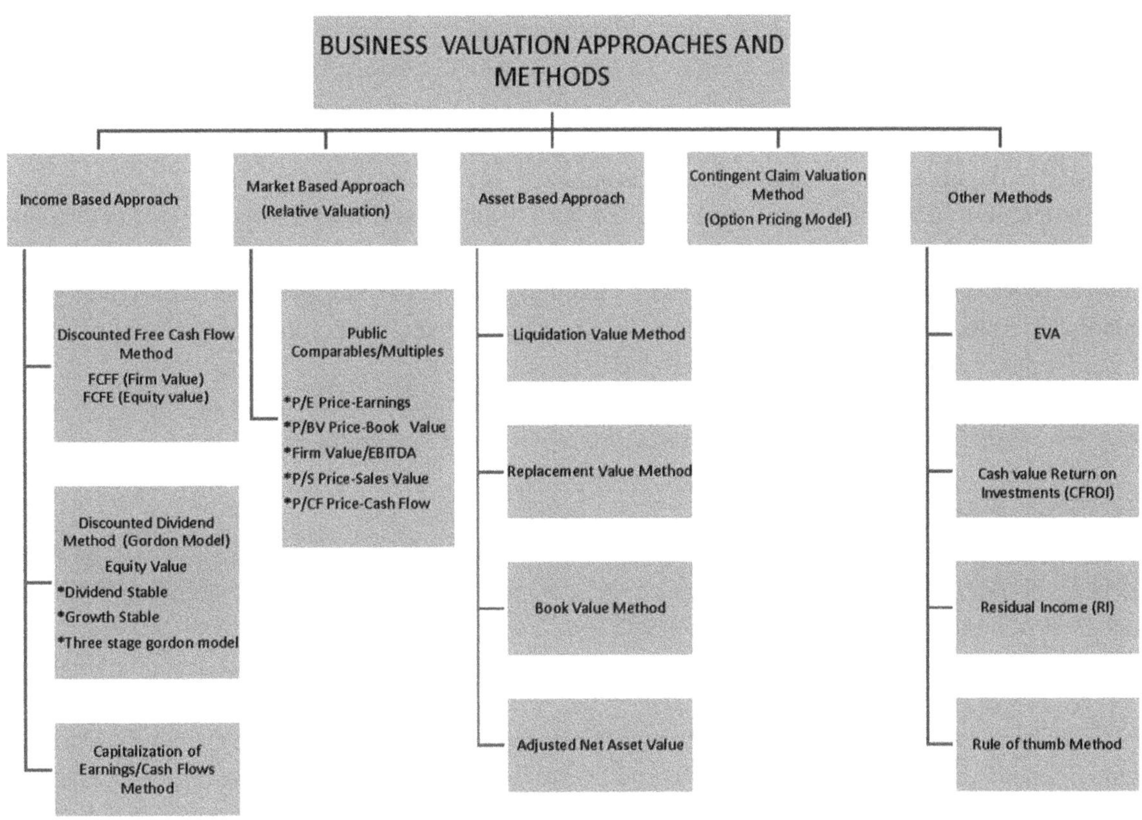

Valuation Approaches

Income Based Approach

This approach is also known as Discounted Cash Flow Valuation, where the value is determined by discounting future cash flows to the present using a required rate of return. The income-based business valuation approach is based on the future income to be generated by a company. According to this approach a company can only create value as long as it generates cash in the future. Therefore, the present value of a company is determined by the present value of the cash flows of that company generated in the future.

The income based business valuation approach is based on the expected future cash flows of the company.

In the income-based approach, it is taken into account of the company's future expectations. Therefore, it is argued that this approach gives more accurate picture of a business' true value. However, it is difficult to calculate and is based on many projections. Because the calculations are mostly based on projections and predictions, the probability of biases increase due to the human factors.

Market Based Approach

This approach is also known as relative valuation. In this approach, the value of the business is obtained by the comparison of the business with similar-class businesses and securities sold in the market. In other words, the real market values are examined to figure out what your business value is. The basis of market-based valuation is the assumption that similar assets will be traded at similar prices in efficient market conditions. Multiples (comparables) are used to obtain business value. There are several multiples within the Market Approach. When there are a sufficient number of similar businesses/assets/securities in the market the possibility to work well of this approach increases.

Although, this approach is simple and uses real market data, it sometimes might be difficult to find similar data. In addition, it is a difficult task to figure out if it is really similar and identified company or not. It is also sometimes very difficult to find enough comparables businesses according to subject business. Therefore, this approach is not flexible. The expectations for the future of the companies and therefore related risks are also not fully included in this approach.

The market based business valuation approach is based on the comparables in the market.

Asset Based Approach

The basis of asset based approach depends on the assets and the liabilities of the company's balance sheet. The value of a company consists of assets and liabilities within the scope of this approach. The equity value is obtained by reducing total value of the company's liabilities from the total value of the company's assets.

The proponents of this approach argue that an accounting-based company value estimate gives more accurate results than valuation models based on all predictive assumptions for the future. Indeed, the balance sheet elements give general picture of business value. However, it is not enough to give complete and accurate picture. This approach is based on accounting records. Since it is a static valuation method, it does not take into account the future expectation of the company, the company's situation in the sector, the future cash flows and the factors that are not reflected in the accounting tables such as the agreements made by the company.

The asset based business valuation approach depends on total up all the value of company assets.

The asset based business valuation approach is based on the principle that total value of all assets of the company.

The advantages and disadvantages of those three business valuation approaches have been given in Table 3.

CONCLUSION

In the modern business environment, the valuation is a great start to achieve sustaining your business success. Interest for valuation has increased after the shift towards a knowledge economy and attention to intellectual capital, because the value of intangible assets represents a large percentage of the total assets of the organization, including human resources, soft infrastructure and intellectual capital such as patent, copyrights and know-how. Determining the value of a company is more difficult in today's business environment. Because the valuation process requires special methods and procedures carried

Table 3. The advantages and disadvantages of three business valuation approaches

	Advantages	Disadvantages
Income Based Approach	*Takes into account mainly company related data, *Takes into account company risk, *Takes into account time value of money, *It is more accurate approach to find real economic value of a business, *It is more flexible than other approaches, *It doesn't require to find similar company and comparables,	*High sensitivity to the cash flows and required rate of return/capitalization rate *Mainly based on projection and many assumptions, *It can be more subjective, *It is more complex than other approaches and requires more time, *Start-ups, early stage businesses have no historical record for tracking to estimate expected future cash flows, *Very good sector expertise must conduct the analyse, it requires in good understanding value drives of the company
Market Based Approach	*Is is easy and quick to implement and therefore time consuming, *It can be a check point for Income Approach, *It can be appropriate method for especially public companies, *The method captures both tangible and intangible value	*It is possible that there are no similar company and comparables in the market, many companies can be unique, * It can be no public market comparables, *the data can be inaccurate and its accuracy should be confirmed
Asset Based Approach	*It is a good starting point for valuation, *It is a proper approach for businesses going liquidation,	*It doesn't take into account expected future income and risk of the business, * For ongoing businesses, the real value of the business is most probably higher than selling its assets, *It is not appropriate methods for businesses which have more intangible assets

out by highly qualified professional valuers who have knowledge of the nature of the markets and the factors affecting the valuation process. A business continuously needs to identify factors influencing valuation for accurate decision-making and effective planning and to make its plans more dynamic. Different value types for different purposes, as well as the different concepts of this process such as cost, price, and value has been explained in this chapter. Before starting the valuation process, a distinction must be made between the concepts of valuation and evaluation. The first is to give value to the assets and liabilities and the second is to analyze the performance of the assets valuated. It should distinguish between cost, price and value, this distinction must be based on the inputs and outputs of users of valuation information. Cost is the input of management (users in general) to make decisions, while the price is outputs of this decisions, and representing the value that the result or outcome derives from its decisions. Moreover, the value itself takes different concepts and these concepts depend on the place and time that derives from them, if the source of the records of the company is called the book value, and if based on the market is called the market value and so forth. Besides understanding these concepts, describing of the components and elements of financial statements is also essential for practitioners because they represent important inputs to valuation approaches. Then all elements of the financial statements it issues become subject to valuation, such as assets (including intangible assets) and liabilities are reflected in the evaluation of the business' performance (income).

Accordingly, there are three main valuation approaches are used. Asset based approach, which deals with the establishment of assets and liabilities recorded in the company's records and represents actual rather than estimates. It does not relate to a particular unit but depends on market prices and deals mutual recurrence. The income approach is based on the expected future cash flows of the company. The present value of a company is determined by the present value of the cash flows of that company generated in the future. Lastly, the value of the business is obtained by the comparison of the business with similar-class businesses and securities sold in the market. From all of the above we can reach a final conclusion that the valuation is an integrated process, which we have all referred to in the previous conclusions parts of it and we cannot neglect any part.

REFERENCES

Aktaş, R.; Başçı S., Değere Dayalı Yönetim ve Firma Değerinin Tespiti, chapter 11, Sakarya Üniversitesi Sürekli Eğitim Uygulama ve Araştırma Merkezi.

Alibhai, S., & … . (2018). *Interpretation and Application of IFRS Standards.* UK: John Wiley.

Belkaoui, A. R. (2000). Accounting theory: Thomson Learning, London, UK, 4th ed.

Black, A. & Wright, P. (2001). *In search of shareholder value: Managing the drivers of performance,* 2nd ed., Financial Times Prentice Hall.

Chambers, N. (2009). *Firma Değerlemesi.* İstanbul, Turkey: Beta Basım Yayın.

Chandra, P. (2011). *Corporate valuation and value creation* (1st ed.). Delhi, India: Tata McGraw-Hill Education.

Cingöz, A. (2014). İndirgenmiş Nakit Akımlari Yöntemine Göre Firma Değerleme ve Enerji Sektöründe Bir Uygulama, Selçuk University, Doctoral Study, Konya, İstanbul.

Damodaran, A. (2002). *Investment valuation: Tools and techniques for determining the value of any asset*. New York, NY: John Wiley & Sons.

Ercan, M., Öztürk, M., Küçükkaplan, İ., Başçı, Demirgüneş, K. (2006). Firma Değerlemesi ve Banka Uygulaması. İstanbul, Literatür Yayıncılık.

Ercan, M. K., Öztürk, M. B., & Demirgüneş, K. (2003). Değere Dayalı Yönetim ve Entelektüel Sermaye, Gazi Kitabevi, 1st ed., Ankara, Turkey.

Ertugrul, M. (2008). Değer-Fiyat Ayrımı ve İşletme Değeri: Kuramsal Bir Bakış. *Eskişehir Orhangazi Üniversitesi İİBF Derigisi, 3*(2), 143–154.

Financial Accounting Standards Board (FASB) (1999-2000). Statement of Financial Accounting Concepts. John Wiley & Sons Inc.

Hendriksen, E., & Michael, B. (1992). *Accounting theory* (1st ed.). Homewood, IL: Richard Irwin.

Hitcher, J. R. (2003). *Financial valuation*. Hoboken, NJ: John Wiley & Sons.

Hong Kong Institute of Certified Public Accountants. (2018). Hong Kong: Conceptual Framework for Financial Reporting.

Horngren, T. C., Datar, S. M., & Rajan, M. (2015). Cost accounting A managerial emphasis, 15th ed. (Global Edition), Pearson Education Limited.

Isoraite, M. (2016). Marketing Mix Theoretical Aspects, *International Journal Research Granthaalayah, 4*(6), 25-37. Retrieved from www.grathaalayah.com

Jimari, R., & Kumar, B. (2015). Drivers of firm's value: panel data evidence from Indian manufacturing industry. *Asian Journal of Finance & Accounting, 7*(2).

Kam, V. (2000). *Accounting theory. Translation by Al-mosul University published hall* (1st ed.). Mosul Iraq.

Kissin, W. & Zulli, R. (1989). Valuation of a closely held business, *Journal of Accountancy, 16*(6). LGA, CPAs and Business Advisors, 4 Questions to Ask Valuations. Retrieved from https://www.lgallp.com/wp-content/uploads/2018/10/LGA-4-Questions-to-Ask-Valuations.pdf

Olajide, S. E., Lizam, M., & Olajide, E. B. (2016). Understanding the conceptual definitions of cost, price worth and value, *Journal of Humanities & Social Science, 20*(9), 53-57, Retrieved from www.iosrjournal.org

Pereiro, L. E. (2002). *Valuation of companies in emerging markets, ABD*. John Wiley & Sons.

Petitt, B. S. & Ferris, K. R. (2013). Valuation for mergers and acquisitions, Pearson Education, 2nd ed.

Rappaport, A. (1998). *Creating shareholder value: a guide for managers and investors*. New York, NY: Simon and Schuster.

Roland, G., & Platt, D. (2011). *Managerial accounting*. USA: Mc Graw-Hill Irwin.

The Institute of Cost and Works Accountants of India. (2010). Business Valuation Management, 12, Sudder Street, Kolkata - 700 016, paper 18.

Chapter 2
International Business Valuation Standards:
Accounting Perspective

Saad Salman Awad Almeant
University of Baghdad, Iraq

ABSTRACT

Despite the existence of International Valuation Standards (IVS) and Financial Reporting Standards (IFRS), countries that have transferred to adopting IFRS face the large challenge of the difference in interpretation and application of the standards. Because they include various concepts, bases, and approaches for valuation and measurement, and although there are common objectives for each of the International Valuation Standards Council (IVSC) and International Accounting Standards Board(IASB), each works independently and has their own objectives and different target groups. Thus, more improvements are needed to consistently apply valuation and financial reporting standards. This chapter compares and converges the concepts, bases, and approaches adopted by the IVSC and the IASB to increase consistency in valuation practices for financial reporting purposes and to create bridges between accountants and auditors and professional valuers.

INTRODUCTION

Valuation standards have a significant role to play in helping to harmonize professional practice at domestic and global levels, and are widely used and reliable in domestic and international financial markets, to be included in the financial statements of listed companies in those markets, or to support secured lending, acquisition and merger transactions(Adair et al, 2014) .The International Valuation Standards Council (IVSC) promotes leading practice approaches for the conduct and competency of professional valuers The International Valuation Standards (IVS) issued by (IVSC) also are standards for undertaking valuation assignments using generally recognized concepts and principles that promote transparency and consistency in valuation practice (IVSC Framework, 2017). Although these standards are not geared to

DOI: 10.4018/978-1-7998-1086-5.ch002

financial reporting only, however, one of IVSC's objectives is to help reduce differences in how companies and auditors are integrated in different countries and apply IFRS, particularly to enhance consistency in the measurement of assets and liabilities for the purposes of financial reporting purposes (IVSC, 2014).

Despite the existence of financial reporting standards and valuation standards, the large challenge faced by countries that have transferred to adopting International Financial Reporting Standards (IFRS) is the difference in interpretation and then in application . If preliminary studies were found in European countries (for example) that adopted (IFRS). As of 2005, allows companies to subsequently measurement choose between the fair value model and the cost model for investment property. Although the entity is must use a single model for all of its investments, but if the fair value cannot be determined reliability and on a continuous basis, the investments are measured using the cost mode (IAS40.para.32-A), Thus, the entity can maintain investment property, some of which are measured at fair value model and others are based on the cost model. The researchers found that the measurements were clearly different, and the main reason of this difference is that there are multiple references to the valuation of (up to ten references in the European countries) (IVSC 2007) . On the other hand, the application of fair value has resulted in significant fluctuations in the amounts of assets and liabilities, and then effected on relevant and reliability of accounting information provided to users (Abdulluhi & Maaji, 2016) (Gokcen & Teraman, 2018), and that different valuation practices may provide different results because of the different inputs used and the adjustment to this inputs (Aurora & Bontes,2013) . However the (IASB) believes that financial reports are not designed to show the value of a entity; but they provide information (indirectly) to help existing and potential investors, lenders and other creditors to assess the value of the entity (IASB, Framework 2018:para.1-7), in the other words Accounting provides information as input to users' own decision models, rather than providing a decisive valuation (Whittington, 2010:104). Thus, we need to make additional improvements towards application consistency of valuation and financial reporting standards. .The core questions that this chapter attempts to answer are: Is there a relationship between (IVS) and (IFRS) ? Or are (IVS) a prerequisite for adoption of IFRS? And whether their use together serves to valuation the business, assets and liabilities of the entity in real values?

BACKGROUND AND PRIOR STUDIES

(IVSC) founded in 1981, is a non-governmental, non-profit organization working in cooperation with other international bodies such as the World Bank, the Organization for Economic Co-operation and Development (OECD) and the (IASB). The main purpose of (IVSC) is to standardize valuation standards around the world by creating a set of bases and approaches that apply in all countries, and that support transparency for international investors. The IVS basis is therefore broader in comparison to domestic standards such as the United States valuation standards (Spies & Wilhelm, 2005: 6) If we consider that the valuation corresponds to the measurement in financial reporting, the roots of the bases of valuation exist in accounting as there are several themes within literatures on current/ cost value based accounting .One theme calls for adjusting historical cost data (general purchase power accounting) to reflect change in general price level . This theme has its root in the work of German theorists,(Mahlberg, Schmalenbach, and Schmidt). This theme also developed in U.S.A by Sweeny (1933). Another theme adopting a current replacement cost approach, also has roots in the work of Schmidt, and was subsequently popularized by Edward & Bell (1961) . The current value theme was advocated by Chambers (1966), Sterling (1970), and others (Lawrence et al, 1995: 173). On the professional side, the (IASB) has set out in its conceptual framework included bases of measurement issued in (1989), then through the joint project with FASB in the (2010), and finally the revised version of (2018). This framework categorized the bases of the measurement in two groups: historical cost and current value. This chapter also described these bases and factors must be takes into consideration in selecting the basis of measurement. The current value Included: fair value, value in use (for assets), fulfillment value (for liabilities), and current cost . (IASB Framework, 2018.6). These bases were adopted in the IAS and IFRS (issued by the Board itself) that based to conceptual framework.

The transition to various bases of measurements is in accordance with International Financial Reporting Standards (IAS & IFRS) creates new accounting measurement problems: Is the fair value concept itself the market value (value at exchange) or value from management's point of view (value in use) ? or replacement value (entry price) or all of these concepts? .Then are these concepts consistent with the concepts included in the International Valuation Standards (IVS) issued by the International Valuation Standards Council (IVSC)? . These are other questions that this chapter is trying to answer.

in the aspect of prior studies, as for the methods (approaches) of valuation Pagourtzi et al (2003) classified them into two groups, as traditional approaches and advanced approaches. Spies & Wilhelm (2005) test the requirements for valuation approaches in accordance with the IFRS and what probable conflicts may be arise between the IFRS and the US valuation approaches..The research showed that the US valuation approaches are very similar in their bases and approaches to the IVS, which mainly result from the origin of the (IVS). However, the authors' analysis and conclusion preceded the issuance of (IFRS 13) Fair Value Measurements issued by the (IASB) in 2011 which expanded the concept of fair value and input levels. Ilsjan &Kask (2014) attempted to explore practical problems in the implementation of the income approach in the valuation for financial reporting. The authors have found that some of the concepts required in the standards are very general and need some specification to harmonize the behavior of the valuers in practice.

Abdulluhi & Maaji (2016) review the effect of fair value measurement on financial statements, and consistency of its with financial instruments . Then attempt to demonstrate that fair value has a clear advantage through its ability to reflect the reality of current financial and economic conditions. Gokcen & Teraman (2018) studied how to determine the synergistic value by which the difference between market value and fair value was explained, The results show that if an IFRS is adopted to determine the fair value of the acquired assets and liabilities the goodwill of the business will be shown. But when the IVS is adopted, this goodwill is not appear even probable business combination is realized . Because the values represent a combination of market value and synergistic value. Therefore, the need to expand and deepen the study of all the foundations and approaches of valuation in this chapter, especially after the issuance of the revised version of the conceptual framework of the (IASB) and the factors that determine the selection of the bases and approaches of measurement (valuation).

THE NEED AND PURPOSES OF VALUATION AND ACCOUNTING STANDARDS

With the emergence of multinational companies, the opening up of global markets, and the expansion of foreign investment, required the need for so-called international harmonization, which means increasing compatibility by reducing or delineating differences in international practices (Nobes & Parker, 2008:75). The best strategy for achieving this harmonization is to produce internationally accepted standards by specialists from the profession in a particular field of business. Examples of these standards are (IVS) issued by (IVSC) and the (IAS-IFRS) issued by (IASB). In general, the standard is intended as a predetermined model that measures the weight, length, or quality of a particular object (Diaionu& Coman, 2006:3). And as defined by the International Standards Organization (ISO) as a document prepared unanimously and endorsed by a recognized body that gives repeated common uses, outlines or specifications for activities or outcomes to ensure optimal implementation in a specific context (Hatto,2010: 5) In the same context, the (IASB) defines the standard as a guiding rule for professionals to support their judgments, develop their opinions, and sets out their practices (but does not eliminate judgment and personal opinion). It also aims at reducing differences in accounting practices for the same circumstances. Moreover, the standards are adopted as a general framework for assessing the quality and efficiency of technical work, depth of professional responsibility (IASB.2010). Thus, the board sought to standardize practical practices in accounting to eliminate the differences in these practices among countries because these differences would negatively affect the comparisons between the performance of companies and between countries and adverse selection of investment decisions taken by domestic and foreign investors.

For its part, the (IVSC) believe that its main objective is to build confidence and public trust in the valuation process by producing standards and ensuring its adoption and implementation internationally to valuation assets around the world, along with the application of those standards with a high level of professionalism. The council also believes that these standards are part of the international financial system, (IVSC Framework: 1)

While emphasizing the need for valuation standards and financial reporting standards domestically and internationally. As a result of the multiplicity of bases and approaches of valuation (measurement) in each and the interdependence between them, we can set common objectives as follows:

- The existence a frameworks that ensures balance and fairness between the interests of groups (users) of financial statements and valuation reports.
- To regulate and organize the disclosure process in the financial statements and valuation reports to its users by relying on specific and clear procedures.
- Provide a clear understanding for international investors of the financial statements and valuation results contained in those statements.
- The existence of professional references such as (IVSC) and (IASB) are based on them by the local accounting standards and valuation setters when the emergence of new problems of application and the search of solutions .
- To enhance the reliability and objectivity of information provided to financial markets.

THE RELATIONSHIP BETWEEN IVS AND IFRS

The challenge for any entity is to produce financial statements that meet need of users and are useful for decision-making. Thus many professional accounting bodies have adopted a main objective of financial reporting which is to provide financial information about the entity that is useful to users to making rational decisions relating to providing resources to the entity that related to investment, credit, and similar other decisions (FASB, 2000:16), (IASB,2018: para.1-2) Other sub-objectives are derived from this main objective the objective is to provide information about the company's financial position, which is information about the company's economic resources and claims. This information helps the users valuate the company through the use of asset-based approach for valuation. The other sub-objective is that financial reporting provides information on cash flows (inflows and outflows). This information assists users in assess the entity's ability to generate future net cash flows and through it they can assess the entity using the income approach for valuation .

To achieve the usefulness of information in decision-making, international professional organizations have sought to issue a single set of high quality standards, understandable, enforceable and globally accepted. The significant change in these standards is the adoption of a different valuation basis in determining the amount of the financial statements in addition of traditional accounting measure is based on the historical cost. These measurement bases have included fair value, value in use for assets, fulfillment value for liabilities, current cost . The purpose of allowing the use of different measurement bases is to make accounting information more useful to its users and to achieve the qualitative characteristics of accounting information (relevance and faithfulness representative). Financial reporting standards have also allowed different approaches to measure fair value or consistent with the market approach, income approach and cost approach. The selection of a specific approach to measure fair value is to be based on its relevant to the asset or liability being measured and in (especially the adequacy and observably of inputs available (Alibhai et.al 2018: 765)

On the other hand the (IVSC) believes that valuers should have an understanding of the nature of the accounting definitions (carrying amount, cash generating unit, fair value, net realizable value, residual value etc.) and principles underlying IFRS issued by the (IASB) .as well as the adherence to market-based concepts, objectivity, and full disclosure of relevant matters within pertinent and user-friendly format are fundamental to the requirements of valuation for financial reporting (IVA1.1) .Therefore, the IASB has shifted from a **Rule-based accounting standards setting approach** to **principles -based accounting standards setting approach**, with a view to making these standards understandable and interpretable by users of financial statements, reduces judgment in interpreting standards, and provides special requirements for recognition, measurement and reporting that demonstrate the actual activities of an economic unit. Unlike a Rule-based approach, that is based on a set of strict rules that can sometimes be arbitrary.As well as the accounting standards include special conditions for recognition, and specific timing to be measurement as an asset or liability in the accounting records and are then reflected in the financial statements. The element for which these conditions are not applicable is not recognized. So many elements of intellectual capital and intangible assets are not inclusion in the financial statements. Because it do not meet requirements of measurement and disclosure despite their large values and may be a basis for generating income for the company. Accordingly In 2013 The trustees of (IVSC) and (IASB) recognized that interaction and exchange of information on how to measure fair values would be relevant and useful in developing standards and guidance on fair value measurement, which should improve the financial statements prepared in accordance with (IFRS) (www.ifrs.org) .

In practice, those interested in valuation practices believe that in some cases there is a need to follow a set of procedures as required in the financial reports, particularly approaches for accessing non-observable value in the market (to be used) to assist the auditors in the entity or to revaluation the financial statements such as "value in use" or allocation of purchase price in a business combination and acquisition transactions. In this context, they believe that they need to find a range of procedures and adopt (IVS) wherever possible in the preparation of financial statements.

Market Value, Fair Value, and Bases of Valuation

For over decades, professional bodies have attempted to establish a specific definition of value (investments value, assets value, assets value etc) or differentiating them from one to another. But the different valuation objectives and the different environments in which they are issued have prevented agreement on this subject, for example Pagourtzi et al (2003) finds that the definition of market value is merely an attempt to clarify assumptions to make an estimate of the exchange price of a property when it is sold in the open market. These assumptions include the legal nature of the interests, the physical circumstances of the property, the nature and timing of the market, and assumptions related to possible purchasers in the market. Thus, the IVSC has developed a comprehensive definition of market value, including most the circumstances surrounding the valuation of the market:

Market Value is the estimated amount for which a property should exchange on the date of valuation between a willing buyer and a willing seller in an arm's-length transaction after proper marketing wherein the parties had each acted knowledgeably, prudently, and without compulsion (IVS1.4).

The IVS104 explained the assumptions contained in the definition in details:

Estimated amount the price payable for a transaction in a market transaction on a neutral basis. **For which the property should exchanged** the value of the asset is an estimate rather than a pre-determined amount or an actual sale price. **On the date of valuation** requires that the value be determined as of a specific date because markets and market conditions may change. **Willing buyer** refers to the person who has the motives of the purchase and is not forced to, As well as the **Willing seller** "is not enthusiastic nor a seller ready for sale at any price. **After proper marketing** "means that the asset is being offered on the market in the best possible way to be sold at the best reasonable price to be obtained. **Each *party had each acted knowledgeably, prudently*** "it is knowledgeably assumed that both the willing buyer and the willing seller are reasonably aware of the nature and characteristics of the asset, its actual and potential uses, and the state of the market at the valuation date..**Without *compulsion*** "proves that each party is motivated to do the treatment, but is not forced or coerced to do so. Accordingly, when estimate the market value, the valuer should examine the circumstances surrounding the valuation process, in other words estimate the highest and best use or most probable use of property.

Fair value accordance IASB: is the price that would be received to sell an asset or paid to transfer a liability in an orderly transaction between market participants at the measurement date (IFRS13.9).

Fair value is a market-based measure, not an enterprise-specific measure. For certain assets and liabilities, transactions may be available Marketable or observable market information. For other assets and liabilities, observable market transactions may not be available And observable market information. However, the objective of measuring fair value in both cases is the same The price at which a transaction is made under normal circumstances to sell the asset or to convert the obligation between the market participants on a date Measurement under current market conditions i.e. the exit price on the date of measurement from the perspective of a market participant retains the asset Or owe the obligation). (IFRS13.2) As a result, an entity's intention to hold an asset or to settle or otherwise fulfill a liability is not relevant when measuring fair value (IFRS13.3) . That the assumption of market-based measurement rather than the enterprise – specific measure penetrates the entity theory to determine the fair value of assets and liabilities, and makes the asset or liability and it related markets the focus of that input rather than entity conditions at the measurement date. Accordingly, fair value is based on the assumption that there is orderly transaction between market participants (as specified) at the current measurement date and market conditions, from the perspective of a market participant who holds the asset or who has the liabilities and, in other words, the exit price. IASB believes that the exit price is always an appropriate definition of the fair value of the asset, regardless of whether the entity intends to use or sell the asset. Furthermore, the exit price is always an appropriate definition of the fair value of the liability, regardless of whether the entity intends to meet the obligation to Time or transfer to another party that meets them over time (Alibhai et al, 2018:) .The standard also requires that the fair value be based on observable price to the maximum extent possible, however this may not be available and therefore will depend on the use of valuation approaches which should have a strong bias towards the use of observable inputs rather than unobservable inputs, which are more objectivity and likely to be taken into account by market participants rather than unobservable inputs.

IASB in recognizes that active market may not always exist in order to identify a market price for a specific asset or liability. Instead the standard established a hierarchy that prioritizes the reliability of the inputs that may be used in valuating fair value (Abdullahi & Maaji, 2016: 85). The hierarchy for fair value measurement purposes is to increase consistency and comparability in these measurements between companies in the same sector, starting with definition of input according IFRS13:

Inputs: The assumptions that market participants would use when pricing the asset or liability, including assumptions about risk, such as the risk inherent in a particular valuation technique used to measure fair value (such as a pricing model) and the risk inherent in the inputs to the valuation technique. Inputs may be observable or unobservable.

Observable input are either directly observable or indirectly observable, As stated above the IFRS13 emphasizes bias in the use of observable inputs rather than unobservable inputs. In other words, a hierarchy gives priority to unadjusted prices in active markets and for similar assets and liabilities. An active market is a market in which transactions involving assets and liabilities are carried out frequently and at a reasonable transaction volume and price information is continuously available.

The first level of input (Level 1 input) to fair value are the quoted prices that traded in the active market for similar assets and liabilities. The entity can access this market on the measurement date, as the quoted prices in this market provides a more reliable guide to measuring fair value without having to adjust it (with limited exceptions)), Where an entity that has an asset or liability is traded in an active market, the price in that market is used to measure the fair values of the asset or liabilities owned by the entity even if the market does not absorb the size of the asset or liability through a single transaction. The second level of input (Level 2 input) to fair value are the quoted prices other than first level inputs, which can be observed for assets and liabilities, either directly (i.e., as prices) or similar prices, or indirectly (i.e., derived from prices) through various methods such as interest rates, rate of return etc. The third level (Level 3 input) is inputs that are not available in the market (not observable) of the assets and liabilities, but the entity is based on the information available to it and based on the nature of the asset or liability to estimate their fair values. From the previous presentation of the definitions of market value and fair value, there is a clear difference between these concepts. Although the assumptions included in the definition of market value meet the requirements of fair value definition but do not cover the three hierarchical levels of inputs provided by IFRS because they relate only to market participants without reference to inputs which unobservable and estimates of management, on the other hand, the definition of the fair value itself does not match with the hierarchical levels, which confirmed the definition of orderly transaction between participants in the market, even if this transaction is expected (not actual) . However, IVSC recognized this problem by giving other concepts of values and a different perspective of fair value, trying to compare it with the fair value definition from the perspective of IFRS (Figure 1). Second problem relates to both definitions of how close they are to the bases of valuation that contained in the (IVS) and the accounting measurement techniques contained in IFRS, simply stating that they are unable to achieve such a relationship despite the existence of the excuses provided by the two parties.

The third problem relates to the concept of highest and best use. Which means the actual use of the non-financial asset by market participants maximizes the value of the asset individually or group of assets and liabilities (eg business unit). This depends on the physical characteristics of the origin (location and size of the buildings for example), the legal license for the available use, and the availability of financial feasibility for the use of the asset. When we return to definitions of market value and fair value we see that it is closer to the (value in exchange) while the concept of higher and better value refers to the (value in use), yet it remains the concept of higher and best use of open endings and place of judgment and subjective opinion.

Figure 1. Comparative fair value under (IVS) and (IFRS)
Source: (IVSC) (2016) Illustrative, Examples chapter1 –Based of value:p6

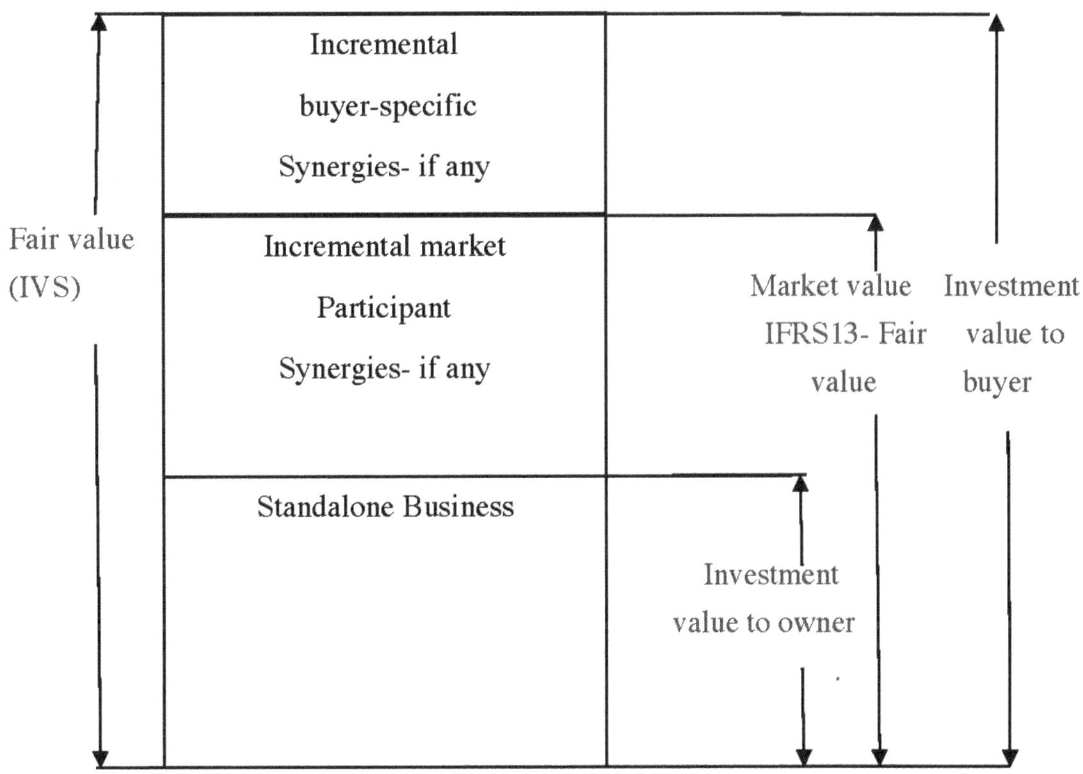

APPROACHES AND METHODS OF VALUATION

Bases of valuation describe the fundamental premises on which the reported values will be based. It is important that the basis of value be appropriate to the terms and purpose of the valuation agreement, as a basis of value may influence or dictate a valuer's selection of approach, inputs and assumptions, and the ultimate opinion of value (IVS104:10.1). (IFRS13) does not specify a particular technique in estimating fair value, but it emphasizes that the technique used should be appropriate to the circumstances of the measurement process and that the data are available. This means that any of the three approaches detailed in this chapter, the accountants and auditors of financial statements recognize that there is a clear difference between fair value concept and market value concept as presented above, and the managements makes sure that the values used to identify the elements of financial statements are consistent with the fair value measurement requirements of (IFRS 13) (E&Y, 2013:8). All approaches based on the economic principles of price equilibrium, expectations of benefits or substitution. Therefore, we must know the conditions and circumstances surrounding the use of any of the following approaches:

Market Approach

This approach provides an indication of value by comparing the asset with compare or similar assets for which price information is available. It shall be applied when the following conditions are met (IVS 105) the standard set out special procedures and considerations for each of these conditions (IVS105:20.1):

- A similar asset was recently sold in an appropriate value-based transaction
- The underlying asset is traded in the market.
- There are frequent or recent transactions of similar observable assets.

This approach is defined in accordance with IFRS 13 (B5) as an valuation approach that uses prices and other relevant information resulting from market transactions involving similar or comparable assets, liabilities or a group of assets and liabilities (i.e. business). While the intellectual framework of the (IASB) identified two types of techniques to implement this approach (IFRS Foundtion: 2012:15)

- Transaction price paid for an identical or a similar assets of an investee (para:28–33)
- Comparable company valuation multiples (para: 34–69).Valuation techniques within the market approach are based on the concept of comparables, assuming that the value of an asset (or line of business or company etc) can be measured by comparing it to similar assets (or lines of businesses or companies etc) for which a market price is available.
  To illustrate how to use this approach

Assume that (X) company invested a sum of money on 1/1/2018 in the purchase of 1000 shares of (Y) company shares for $ 10 per share. and on 31/12/2018 shows that the closing price of (Y) shares is $ 12 per share: However, the fair value of the Company's investments can be valued using the market approach $ 12,000(1000×12) because the closing price represents the exchange transactions made in the capital market of a similar asset and the inputs are observable (the same approach can be applied to investments in equity instruments or debt instruments) for companies listed in the financial markets.

Income Approach

The one reason of uses this approach as not all of the assets owned by the company are invested by the company itself, they may be leased to another party and this property has no a market price, in this case, the amount of rent represents the return on investment to the owner, and income generated from the rent is simply cash flows. The value of the property is determined by discounting these flows at present value (Pagourtzi et al 2003: 388). Accordingly the (IVSC) defined as approach provides an indication of value by transferring future cash flows to a single present value, by reference to revenue or cash flows or reducing cost, according to specific considerations: when the asset ability original ability to generate income (revenue) is the fundamental element affecting the value, and in the reasonable expectations of the future revenue amount of the asset (IVS105.40). In the same dimension (IASB) defined this approach as technique classified as income approaches measure fair value based on current market expectations about future amounts (such as cash flows or net income) and discount them to an amount in measurement date dollars (Alibhai,2018: 757). There are a number of techniques used under this approach: (IFRS Foundation 2012:35) (Ilsjan & Kask, 2014: 84).

- Discounted cash flow (DCF) method (para:71–114) method, investors are required to estimate the future expected cash flows of an investee
- Dividend discount model (DDM)(Para: 115–116)
- Constant-growth DDM(Gordon Model) (para:117–121)
- Capitalization model (para:122–124)

But the most commonly recognized are (DFC) and capitalization models (E&Y, 2013:9). This is because cash flows represent real and real amounts, unlike income flows that may include estimated amounts that the management interferes with in quantity and timing using (earnings management). The same can be said on the (DDM) dividend depend on management distribution policy of income, the choice of a particular policy may be intended to affect stock prices. The dividend can be used as a mechanism for referring to the external parties (non-insiders) with the possibility of growth and stability in the company's dividend (Dividend Signaling Model). The third model is based on a previous assumption abandoned by adopter due to rapid changes in the business environment, at last it is possible to conclude that the first and fourth model are the best for use as well as being the most used.

To illustrate how to use this approach:

Assume on December 31, 2017, (X) company bought a machine for $ 200,000. This machine produces copper wire and achieves net annual cash flow of $ 60,000, the machine's life is five years, and its salvage value is $ 5000. Assume no price of machine markets of this machine. Then the appropriate way to valuation it at December 31, 2018 is the **Discounted Cash Flow (DCF) method**, by discount the net annual cash flows at an appropriate discount rate (present value of cash flows) over its remaining life (4 years) plus the present value of the salvage value at the end of the life (assume the discount rate is 10%):

The present value of annual cash flows: Present value of $ 60000 receivable annually for 4 years at 10% (PVF-OA4, 10%): $60000 ×3.16986) = $190192

Plus: The present value of cash flows from salvage value of machine (PVF4, 10%):

$ 5000 × .68301 = 3415
Then: Fair value of the machine at 31/12/2018 = $193607

Cost Approach

Cost approach using the common economic principle that a buyer will pay for asset no more than the cost to obtain an asset of equal utility .When used this approach, some critical factors need to be taken into consideration:availability of comprehensive cost data, replication to current depreciated state, inflation etc. The method used for valuation technique in this approach is Depreciated Replacement Cost (DRC). (Aurora & Bonts,2013:100). This approach is applied when the market participants can reproduction the asset with the same characteristics of the asset being valuation, and the asset does not have the ability to generate revenue directly. The unique nature of the asset makes the market approach and income approach inefficient. In most cases, and is con n all cases, the basis of the value used reflects the replacement cost (IVS105). The IFRS 13 adopted this approach in a manner that approximates the international valuation standards and considers it to be one of the measurement techniques that related to fair value.

To illustrate how to use this approach:

Assume that (X) Power Company has manufactured a giant machine for the production of electric power. It takes two years to complete manufacture this machine. The raw materials costs for two years amounted to $ 40,000, $ 50,000 respectively, and labor costs $ 20,000, $ 30,000 respectively. The company used 5% of its production capacity to manufacture machine (overhead costs charged to the machine costs for two years $ 10,000, $ 15,000 respectively). Assuming there is no market value for the machine because there is no similar machine in the market, and no separate annual cash flows can be determined because its work integrates with other machines, so the appropriate approach to the valuation of the machine is the cost approach, and therefore the fair value of the machine:

First year costs = 40,000+ 20,000+ 10,000 = $ 70,000
Second year costs = 50,000 + 30,000+ 15,000 = $ 95,000
The fair value of the machine = $ 165,000

RELATIONSHIP BETWEEN BASES AND APPROACHES OF EVALUATION

The (IVSC) considers that all valuation approaches are based on market value basis.. If the market-based derivative is used to compare sales to the same asset, it leads to the use of the market value. Then if cash flows are determined by using the income method, the discounted cash flow analysis will be based on the market value because the discount rate will be derived from the market. When using the cost approach to determine the cost of an asset and determine its depreciation, that determination should be based on the market. Although data availability and circumstances relating to the market or the property itself will determine which valuation methods are most relevant and appropriate, the outcome of using any of the foregoing procedures must be market value if each approach a is based on market-derived data.(IVS1:4.2)

The (IASB) distinguishes between measurement techniques (approach) and value bases, for example one way to estimate the measure is by using cash-flow-based measurement technique (income approach).

Table 1. Valuation Bases & Approaches under IFRS and IVS

<table>
<tr><th>Valuation Approaches</th><th colspan="2">Bases of Value (IFRS)</th><th colspan="2">Bases of Value (IVS)</th></tr>
<tr><td rowspan="3">• Market approach
• Income approach
• Cost approach</td><td>Fair value</td><td rowspan="3">• Input level1
• Input level 2
• Input level 3</td><td>Market-derived criteria</td><td rowspan="3">Market value</td></tr>
<tr><td>Value in use</td><td>Market-derived rate</td></tr>
<tr><td>Depreciated Replacement Cost (DRS)</td><td>Market- based estimated cost & depreciation</td></tr>
</table>

Such technique is not measurement basis. This is technique used in applying a measurement basis. Hence, when using such a technique, it is necessary to identify which measurement basis is used and the extent to which the technique reflects the factors applicable to that measurement basis. For example, if the measurement basis is fair value, the applicable factors are considering (IASB framework: 6.14). As for as cash flow –based measurement technique can used in applying a modified measurement bases, this bases my result in information that is more relevant to users of financial statements, despite more difficult to understanding for them(IASB Framework:9.41)

Application of Valuation Standards

Real Estate Valuation

Valuers shall obtain from the management of the entity a list of assets to be valued, classifying them as operational assets, i.e. assets requisite to the operations of the entity, or non-operational assets, being properties held for future development, investment, or assets surplus to the operations of the entity (IVA1.5). The purpose of this is to know which accounting or financial reporting standards apply to the asset under valuation. The need for valuation real estate derives from two major aspects these are:

(1) Unharmonious of real estate in its natural unlike shares and bonds. Due to its unharmonious real estate needs to be valued by professional valuers, who collect and Interpret relevant market information of all possible characteristics describing the property.
(2) Incomplete information in markets about real estate, real estate markets are not effective and therefore, the need for a formal valuation theory arises (Ilsjan& Kaskm,2014:76).

The real estate asset owned by an entity can be classified according to IFRS into three categories:

- Property, plant and equipment in case of owner-occupied real estate according to IAS 16.
- Investment property (in case of non owner-occupied real estate, held mainly to earn rental income or for capital appreciation or both) according to IAS 40.
- Long term leases according to IAS 17, and follow IFRS 16

Since the International valuation Application for financial reporting (IVA1) is primarily for property, plant and equipment (IAS16), the Standard for investments Property (IAS 40) and the Standard for leases (IAS17) we will focus also the valuations in this chapter on the assets covered by these standards.

According to IAS 17, the lessee is to record a finance lease as an asset and an obligation (liability) at an amount equal to the lesser of (1) the fair value of the leased property at the inception of the lease, net of grants and tax credits receivable by the lassoers, or (2) the present value of the minimum lease payments.

1. Valuation of Property, Plant, and Equipment

(IVS300) provides that the valuer should choose the appropriate value basis for the valuation of the plant and equipment. This is a critical point in the valuation process to assess, because the value item of asset varies under different valuation circumstances, which the asset is valued under an in used, orderly liquidation or forced liquidation of (IVS300.30). As well as his standards allowance using the three approaches to the valuation of plant and equipment according to the nature of the asset, the available information, and the factors and circumstances surrounding the valuation process (IVS300.40). On the other hand, the (IAS16) permits the revaluation of assets if there is an increase in value (IAS16.39), and the measurement is at fair value and where there is a market-based evidence. In the absence of evidence because of the particular nature of the asset or the asset is rarely sold, the entity has the right to use the income approach or cost approach (DRC) (IAS16.33). In all cases, the valuation process is preferred by a professional and independent valuer.

2. Valuation of Investment Property

The international valuation standards does not distinguish between the investment property invested for trading purposes and the investment property invested for rental purposes, as well as not distinguish between operating leases and finance leases, (The Council calls it a real property interest) is a right of ownership, control, use or occupation of land and buildings (IVS400.2). Unlike the accounting standards that emphasize the asset, it is probable that an asset will be recognized when (and only when) future benefits from the investment property will flow and the cost of the property can be measured reliably (IAS40.16). When measuring the fair value of an investment property in accordance with (IFRS 13), Because of the difference between the broad concept of property interests and the specific concept of property investment, international valuation standards have allowed the three valuation approaches, while the financial reporting standards have been confirmed on, an entity must ensure that the fair value reflects, among other things, the rental income from current leases and other assumptions that market participants use when pricing an investment property under the current market conditions (IAS 40.40). Which means that the financial reporting standards call for the use of the income approach in the valuation of investment properties, although not clearly indicated.

3. Valuation of Property for Leased Assets

(IAS17) and subsequently (IFRS 16) (effective from 1 January 2019) classified leases contracts into operating leases and finance leases based on the time period and the significant of the asset. In all cases, if the leases are classified as finance, the lessee should assess the lessee should valuation the assets and liabilities in fair value, which means that the financial reporting standards focus on the lessee rather than on the lessor because the benefits and risks of the asset are transferred to him. The lessee uses the asset measure (right of use) to apply the cost model, However, if the fair value of the IAS40 is applied

Table 2. Basis of valuation for accounting purposes according to IAS 16, IAS 40, and IFRS16

Asset class	Accounting measurement	Basis of valuation	Valuation approach(focus)
Property, plant and Equipment(IAS16)	Fair value Depreciated replacement cost (DRS)	Marker value	Market approach Cost approach
	Value in use	Value in use	Income approach
Investment Property(IAS40)	Fair value	Market Value	Income approach
Leases (Finance lease) (IFRS16)	Fair value	Value in use	Cost approach

to its investment properties, it should also apply the fair value model to the assets (right of use) that meets the definition of the investment property(IFRS16.34), and if the asset relates to the category of property, plant and equipment in which the revaluation is carried out IAS 16, the lessee may choose to apply the revaluation model to all assets (right of use) related to that class of property, plant and equipment(IFRS16.35). On the other hand, the lessee must measure the liabilities of the lease contract to the present value of the unpaid rent payments on that date, and the implicit interest rate should be used to discount such payments if it can be easily determined(IFRS16.26)

Valuation of Intangible Assets

An intangible asset is a non-monetary asset evidenced by its economic characteristics, and has no physical characteristics. But it gives economic rights and benefits to its owner, which known through its characteristics such as ownership, function, market status, and reputation (IVS210: 2.1). The financial reporting standards do not give a clear definition of intangible assets. But they specify a certain conditions for recognition of the asset as an intangible asset: firstly identifiable (by distinguishing it from goodwill, sold, transferred, leased or exchanged either individually or with a contract) (IAS38.12), secondly controlled as a result of past events (the entity has the ability to obtain the future benefits flowing from the intangible asset (IAS38.13), and thirdly, that economic benefits are expected to flow from them. In terms of classification of intangible assets, the (IVS210) has classified intangible assets into five groups: first, market-related assets such as trademarks and trade names; secondly intangible assets related to customers such as customer lists and contracts; third, related to works of art such as plays, books, films and music, froth related to contracts such as licensing contracts, and five related to technology such as patents, databases, and software (IVS210: 2.3), while the financial reporting standards presented examples of intangible assets without classifying them. n terms of value, IVSC considers that valuations of intangible assets are carried out using the value bases determined by organizations other than the council, that's mean when the purpose of the valuation for financial statements is to use the value bases specified in the financial reporting standards. In general, however, the council considers that the three approaches (market, income and cost) can be used to valuation of intangible assets. On the other hand, the financial reporting standards allow either the cost model or the fair value model. However, if the second model is used, it should be applied to all intangible assets of the company and fair value should be estimated by reference to the active market (IAS38.75) The analysis of the above concepts shows that (IVS) have expanded to include all concepts of intellectual capital (human capital, structural capital and customarily capital) while the concept of intangible assets in financial reporting standards is determined by the rules of measurement and recognition. Which means that many items of intangible assets are not reflected in the financial statements. Therefore, the future calls for the benefit from (IVS) to include a greater number of items of intangible assets in order to arrive at a more accurate value of the assets of the entity

CONCLUSION

Fair value measurements have provided new measures for company's assets and liabilities, and generally have been given higher values than before the adoption of this concept. Because these values are based on many of them to market prices, this concept to make accountants closer to the market than before and open the prospect of cooperation between them and the professional valuers who have more knowledge of those markets. And although the (IVS) was not adopted by the (IASB), but it have become a main source to valuation for financial reporting purposes, It also requires accountants to distinguish between the market based valuation (value in exchange) conducted by external valuers, and the cash flow –based valuation (value in use). However, the definitions of market value and fair value covered the related approaches in the mark – market (market derived data) reasonably, but did not cover the areas that need inputs unobservable in the market, nor those related to the entities of a special nature or small or large monopoly activity that operates outside primary or secondary markets. As well as the use of prices as a function of value represents an intellectually challenge for standards setters for valuation and financial reporting, as the price reflects the value in limited cases also considered the concept of market value synonymous with the concept of fair value Is not yet proven . thus there is a need to modify and develop the two concepts to make them closer, or to find a common concept for them. Despite, the use of the market value is more useful for financial reporting purposes because it implicitly implies the concept of fair value as well as other concepts that make the valuation process more realistic and more accuracy. It is therefore expected that the convergence projects and joint ventures between the (IVSC) and (IASB) will continue .The analyzes presented in the chapter show the need to adopt the (IVS). It is an urgent necessity to prepare financial statements for financial markets or tax authorities or for other purposes because the valuers are more familiar with the nature of the markets, their classification and location than the accountants and auditors as well as having specialized professional qualification. In the absence of external valuers inside the companies, these standards are intended to become a suitable guide for financial statements preparers and auditors in the valuations and measurements contained in (IFRS) .in addition the (IVS) are expected to increase confidence in the business results of the companies and financial positions shown in their financial statements because they are based on their compliance with standards issued by specialized professional legal bodies. On the other hand, (IVS) can become an important guide for potential investors and investment institutions who want invest in companies before making investment decisions.

REFERENCES

Brown, L. D., Huefner, R. J., & Sanders, J. R. (1995). A test of the reliability of current cost disclosures, accounting theory: A contemporary review. Orlando, FL: Harcourt Brace.

Bezant, M. & Rogers, D. (2016). *Asset – based valuation floor or flawed valuation?* An FTI Consulting White Paper, Dec. 2016. Retrieved from www.fticonsulting.com

Bunea-Bontas, C. A. (2013). *Valuation techniques used in fair value* (pp. 97–104)., Retrieved from www.strategicmanagerial.ro/pdf

Diaconu, P. & Coman, N. (2006). *Accounting research from the globalization perspective*. Available at https://ssrn.com

Ernst & Young. (2013). Appling IFRS in real estate. Retrieved from www.eyjapan.jp

Financial Accounting Standards Board (FASB). (1999-2000). Statement of financial accounting concepts. Hoboken, NJ: John Wiley & Sons.

Goken, G., & Teraman, O. (2018). Importance of synergistic value in the context of business combination: A case study from Turkey. *Economics*, *6*(1), 49–60.

Hatto, P. (2010). Standards and standardization handbook. *European Research Area.* Retrieved from https://www.iec.ch

Hemphill, L., Lim, J. L. C., Adair, A., & McGreal, S. (2014). *The Role of International Valuation Standards in Influencing Valuation Practice in Emerging & Established Markets*. Retrieved from www.rics.or/research

Hong Kong Institute of Certified Public Accountants. (2018). *Conceptual Framework for Financial Reporting 2018*. Hong Kong. International Valuation Standards (IVS). Retrieved from www.ivsc.org and http://www.iasplus.com/standard/ias40.htm

Ilsjan, V. & Kask, K. (2014) *Practical issues in the valuation of real properties with special references to income approach & financial reporting purpose.* Retrieved from https://www.researchgate.net/publication/29137708

International Financial Reporting Standards (IFRS). (2012). Measuring the Fair Value of Unquoted Equity Instruments (Updated in February 2013). Retrieved from http:www.ifrs.org/use-around-the –world/Education

International Valuation Standards Council (IVSC). (2014). Illustrative Examples Chapter 1 – Bases of Value, Exposure – Draft – Jan – 14-0%.pdf.

International Valuation Standards Council (IVSC). (n.d.). International Valuation for Financial Reporting (IVA1). Retrieved from www.anzvps.api.org.au

International Valuation Standards Council (IVSC). (n.d.). International Valuation Standards 1 Market value –Basis of valuation, 4.1.

International Valuation Standards Council (IVSC). (2007). *International Valuation for Financial Reporting Valuation Under International financial reporting Standards*. Retrieved from wwwanzvps.api.org.au

Millington, A. (2000). *An introduction to property valuation* (5th ed.).

Nobes, C., & Parker, R. (2008). *Comparative international accounting* (10th ed.). USA: Prentice Hall.

Pagourtzi, E., Assimakopoulos, V., Hatzichristos, T., & French, N. (2003). Real estate appraisal: A review of valuation methods. *Journal of Property Investment & Finance*, *21*(4), 383–401.

Rabiu, S., & Ma'aji, M. M. (2016, April). A critical evaluation of measurement & effects of fair value in financial statements. *Innovation Research in Social Science & Strategic Management Techniques*, *3*(3), 81–90.

Spies, F. F. & Wilhelm, D. B. (2005) *A critical analysis of.... when used for financial reporting according to IFRS*. Retrieved from www.prres.net

Statement of Protocols for Co-operation on International Financial Reporting Standards (IFRS) and International Valuation Standards (IVS). (2014). Retrieved from www.ifrs.org

Whittington, G. (2010). Measurement in financial reporting, overview of the central thesis. Journal of Accounting, Finance, and Business Studies, ABACUS, 46(1).

Wiley, I. F. R. S. (2017). *Interpretation and Application of IFRS Standards*. PKF International Ltd.

Chapter 3
Optimal Capital Structure for Maximizing the Firm Value

Rumeysa Bilgin
Istanbul Sabahattin Zaim University, Turkey

ABSTRACT

Capital structure decisions of management affect the value of a firm. This fact leads to the creation of an extremely rich capital structure literature over the last 60 years. This chapter explains main theories of capital structure and discusses the concept of target leverage which maximizes the firm value. The roles of tax payments, profitability, firm size, asset tangibility, growth opportunities, income volatility, and non-debt tax shields are examined as determinants of capital structure. The current status of capital structure research and some important empirical issues are discussed. Considerations for future research are presented.

INTRODUCTION

The main objective of the managers should be maximizing the firm value. Since a firm can be considered as a combination of its investment projects, the value of a firm is merely a function of its future cash flows and weighted average cost of capital. Thus, in order to increase the firm value, it is necessary to either increase free cash flows, or reduce the weighted average cost of capital. Free cash flows are related to sales revenues, operating expenses, taxes and operational investments. Therefore, it is not affected by the financing decisions. On the other hand, weighted average cost of capital is directly related to the capital structure, in addition to market interest rates and the firm's riskiness.

The main objective of the capital structure research is to investigate whether or not the firm value can be increased by changing the capital structure. In other words, is there any importance of capital structure decisions? When the answer to this question is negative, the studies on capital structure do not have any meaning (Rajan, 2012). Modigliani & Miller (1958) showed that the value of a firm is independent from its capital structure under certain assumptions. Their assumptions can be summarized as the inexistence of transaction costs, taxes, bankruptcy costs and information asymmetry between managers and investors. Besides, the firm's pre-tax profit is assumed to be unaffected from the use of debt and investors should

DOI: 10.4018/978-1-7998-1086-5.ch003

be able to borrow from the same interest rate as firms. Theoretical and empirical studies, conducted in the first 20 years following Modigliani and Miller's paper, focused on whether the firm value is related to capital structure and showed that it is impossible to satisfy all of these assumptions in real life. Thus, it is concluded that capital structure affects the firm value. Once the causal relationship between a firm's capital structure and its value is recognized, a following up question becomes what is the optimal capital structure for maximizing the firm value. As a result of half a century's diligent research, various capital structure approaches (trade-off theory, pecking order hypothesis and free cash flow hypotheses, market timing, signal hypothesis etc.) were developed in order to answer this question.

These approaches differ based on the emphasis each gives to tax advantages of debt, asymmetric information problems and agency theory.

Trade-off theory emphasises the importance of tax advantage of debt and the bankruptcy costs of debt (Modigliani & Miller, 1963). Besides, there are other versions of trade-off theory, which deals with other costs and benefits of capital structures (Frank & Goyal, 2009). All of these versions predict an optimal level of capital structure, which maximizes the firm value. This optimal level is the leverage ratio where the marginal increase in the firm value because of the benefits of debt use (i.e. tax shield of interest) is equal to the marginal decrease of the firm value due to the bankruptcy costs.

On the other hand, pecking order hypothesis argues that there is not an optimal leverage ratio. Firms make their capital structure decisions based on a financing hierarchy (Myers & Majluf, 1984). Market timing and signaling approaches reach similar conclusions.

However, recent literature reveals that managers have target (optimal) capital structures and make their financing decisions in order to reach it (Bancel & Mitto, 2004). An extensive literature with related to the determinants of target capital structure and speed of adjustment in case of deviations from the target is emerged over the recent years (Hovakimian et al., 2004; Drobetz & Wanzenried, 2006; Zhou et al.,2016; Elsas & Florysiak, 2015).

This chapter explains the aforementioned theories of capital structure and the determinants of target leverage which maximizes the firm value. The roles of tax payments, profitability, firm size, asset tangibility, growth opportunities, income volatility and non-debt tax shields are examined as determinants of capital structure. Besides, the current status of capital structure research and some important empirical issues are discussed. Lastly, some considerations for future research are presented.

Background

Firms often need external funds to finance their investments. In such a case, a firm has two main options: borrowing from a bank or issuing equity. The present value of a firm, which uses all its assets in its operations, is estimated by discounting its expected future free cash flows with its weighted average cost of capital. Weighted average cost of capital is estimated as the weighted average of the high cost of equity financing and the relatively lower cost of after tax debt financing. The main goal of the management is to maximize the firm value. Thus, in order to increase the firm value, it is necessary to either increase free cash flows, or reduce the cost of the average capital. Free cash flows are related to sales revenues, operating expenses, taxes and operational investments. Therefore, it is not affected by the capital structure. On the contrary, weighted average cost of capital is directly related to the financing decisions, in addition to market interest rates and the firm's risk. The capital structure literature, which is one of the cornerstones of financial theory, deals with the effect of changes in leverage ratio (financing preferences) on the value of the firm.

Capital structure research starts with the basic question of whether or not the value of a firm can be increased by changing its external financing mix. In other words, is there any effect of capital structure decisions on firm value? If the firm value is affected by capital structure decisions, what should be the optimal capital structure to maximize the it?

The answer to the first question was given by Franco Modigliani and Merton H. Miller in 1958. According to their value irrelevance proposal, value of a firm is not related to its capital structure decisions under a number of assumptions. These assumptions aimed to define a perfect market where, a single buyer or seller cannot determine prices (full competition), there are not any transaction costs, bankruptcy costs, taxes or asymmetric information. Besides, investors are rational, individual investors can borrow from the same interest rate as firms and cash flows from the firm's assets are independent of its capital structure. By showing that the firm value is independent from the capital structure under some assumptions, they actually showed that capital structure decisions affect value of the firm when these assumptions are not valid (Miller, 1988). Empirical and theoretical literature studies following the seminal paper of Modigliani and Miller (1958) immediately proved that most of their assumptions are not valid in the real world (Harris and Raviv, 1991). These efforts have led to the development of a very rich empirical literature and a number of well-known capital structure theories. This section provides a detailed discussion of these capital structure theories and focus on their explanation of how firms should determine their capital structures.

Trade-Off Theory

A few years after the publication of their influential study, Modigliani and Miller (1963) demonstrate that when there are taxes, firm value is affected from financing structure. This result is the base point of trade-off theory of capital structure.

According to trade-off theory, advantages and disadvantages of the debt financing are the only determinants of capital structure (Parson and Titman, 2009). Firms determine their capital structures at the point where the marginal benefit of using more debt is equal to its marginal cost. In the early versions of trade-off theory, it is assumed that the firm's optimal capital ratio is equal to the tax advantage of debt financing and the marginal effects of the bankruptcy costs resulting from the use of debt (Myers, 2001). At this point, the concept of bankruptcy costs must be defined before proceeding with the explanation of trade-off theory.

Bankruptcy Costs

If a firm fail to make debt service on periodic interest and principal money installments, creditors may request the bankruptcy of the firm. The amount of interest and principal installments to be paid periodically increases with increased indebtedness. The Firm may face bankruptcy costs if it experiences problems in creating the cash flows required to make its debt service. The bankruptcy costs can be divided into two sub-groups as direct and indirect costs.

Direct bankruptcy costs refer to costs incurred during the legal process following a firm's bankruptcy, such as attorneys' and accounting costs. In addition, in the case of liquidation, the decrease in the market price of the firm should also be considered as a direct cost.

Indirect costs, on the other hand, are the costs resulting from the loss of confidence in the eyes of their stakeholders, especially their customers and suppliers, with the possibility of bankruptcy. The cases where suppliers do not want to make sales on credit and customers face the risk of not being able to use their warranty rights due to a potential bankruptcy can be given as examples of indirect costs. The fact that the creditors demanded collateral to lend money and keep the interest rates quite high is another one of the costs that firms with a high risk of bankruptcy often encounter. Although the existence of bankruptcy costs is a generally accepted fact, it is not possible to measure these costs quantitatively.

Static Trade-Off Theory

According to static trade-off theory, the leverage ratio of a firm is determined by establishing a one period balance between the tax advantage and bankruptcy costs of the debt (Kraus and Litzenberger, 1973). In real life, however, the tax structure is too complex to explain with a static model. In addition, dynamic capital structure models should be preferred since firms operate in more than one period. However, static models are good starting points to explain the theory.

Static trade-off theory is explained by Bradley et al. (1984) under the following assumptions;

1. Investors exhibit a risk-neutral attitude. (This assumption allows investors to choose the investment tool with the highest post-tax return).
2. Investors' interest income is taxed at a gradual tax rate, while dividends and capital gains are taxed at a fixed tax rate.
3. The earnings of the firm are taxed at the end of each period with a fixed marginal tax rate.
4. Since all taxes are collected at the end of the period, interest and principal payments can be deducted from tax and creditors should pay taxes at the end of the period.
5. There are non-debt tax shields such as accumulated depreciation and investment incentive. However, they cannot be transferred to another firms by means of leasing and mergers.
6. The firm faces financial distress costs (bankruptcy costs) if it does not make periodic interest and principal payments.
7. The value of the firm as of the end of the period is a random variable. Financial distress costs will decrease this value.

According to the model, the capital structure of the firm is determined at the trade-off point of the marginal tax advantage provided by the debt and its marginal bankruptcy costs. Inferences from the model are as follows (Frank and Goyal, 2009):

1. There is a negative relationship between bankruptcy costs and optimal debt ratio.
2. There is a negative relationship between the non-debt tax shield and optimal debt ratio.
3. There is a positive relationship between tax rate the individuals pay on stock returns and optimal debt ratio.

Static trade-off theory implies that capital structures of firms should be equal to their optimal levels provided that there are no transaction costs. Since the bankruptcy costs used in the model cannot be observed and the firms in real life continue their activities in more than one period, it is difficult to test the model. In addition, retained earnings are not mentioned in the model. Besides, it does not allow firms to have a capital structure ratio other than the optimal capital ratio ignoring the target adjustment arguments. Since all these shortcomings limit the practical usability of the model, dynamic versions of trade-off theory are developed.

Dynamic Trade-Off Theory

According to the dynamic trade-off theory, each firm has a target capital structure and it may change over time. Firms try to reach this optimal leverage by continuous adjustments. Unlike static trade-off theory, this theory considers multiple periods. The leverage ratio is allowed to be different in each period. The dynamic structure acknowledges that the firm's financial decisions in a period are affected by future factors. The current optimal capital structure depends on what is the optimal structure in the next period. It may be necessary to find financing or distribute dividends in the coming period. There are two options for external funding; to issue debt or to issue equity. Which option is preferred will affect the capital structure in this period.

In the first modeling of dynamic trade-off theory, transaction costs were not taken into consideration. Fischer et al. (1989) included the costs of recapitalization in dynamic trade-off theory when firms changed their capital structure. Due to the recapitalization costs, firms allow capital structures to deviate slightly from the target structure. In other words, firms have lower and upper limits for leverage ratio. When a firm makes a profit in a period, it decreases its leverage ratio. When the debt falls down to the lower limit, it borrows again. If the firm cannot make enough profit, it borrows more. If this continues until the upper limit is reached, the leverage ratio is reduced again by equity issuance. In this way, the leverage ratio is kept between the lower and upper limits.

Graham and Harvey (2001) found that 64% of the firms in their sample had a certain target leverage ratio or specific lower and upper leverage ratio limits. This result supports the dynamic capital structure theory.

Target Capital Structure

Modigliani and Miller (1963) proved that the firm value will increase with increasing leverage ratio when there is a corporate tax but no bankruptcy costs. A linear and positive relationship between firm value and leverage ratio is implied in this framework. The value of the firm is maximized with 100% debt usage when there are corporate taxes but no bankruptcy costs. In real life, firms prefer to keep leverage rates at more reasonable levels (Graham 2000).

Firms increase their leverage ratios and values until a certain threshold debt ratio is reached. At this period, bankruptcy costs resulting from the use of debt are too small to have an impact on the firm value. When this threshold debt ratio is exceeded, bankruptcy costs have a growing negative impact on the firm value with increasing indebtedness. However, debt utilization continues to increase the value of the firm during this period since the bankruptcy costs of the debt are smaller than the tax advantage of the debt. As the amount of debt financing increase, the marginal increase in firm value decreases gradually. When the leverage ratio reached to a certain level, the marginal bankruptcy costs of debt exceeds the marginal tax advantage of it and the firm value begins to be negatively affected by the use of extra debt. For this reason, this certain leverage ratio is accepted as the "optimal capital structure ratio" for the firm (Brigham and Daves, 2014).

Trade-off theory states that the optimal capital structure ratio that maximizes the firm value at the point where the marginal benefit and the marginal cost of debt financing is equal. However, since it is not possible to measure all the benefits and costs arising from the use of debt, the optimal ratio cannot be determined precisely (Ehrhardt and Brigham, 2016).

Criticisms for Trade-Off Theory

Trade-off theory is based on Modigliani and Miller (1958) value-irrelevance proposal and has a strong theoretical background. In particular, it is successful in explaining why most firms avoid excessive use of debt. However, this theory cannot explain the fact that many successful firms, which are not likely have any financial difficulties, do not fully utilize their interest-based tax shields. These firms use surprisingly little debt financing. Besides, it fails to explain the negative relationship between the profitability and leverage ratio observed in the empirical studies (Myers, 2001).

Deviations from The Target Leverage

Trade-off theory provides an excellent framework for capital structure research. It implies a target leverage ratio for each firm on the trade-off point between the marginal benefit and cost of debt financing. However, empirical support for this explanation is not as strong as it is expected. Instead, a number of factors which cause deviations from the target capital structures are detected as a result of empirical research. These findings led scholars to look for alternative explanations for capital structures decisions. The resulting approaches are explained in this section.

Pecking Order Hypothesis

Pecking order hypothesis was developed by Myers (1984) based on the earlier work of Donaldson (1961). This theory explains the financing decisions of firms in the context of asymmetric information problem.

The present value of a firm, which distributes all of its earnings to its shareholders as dividends, can be calculated by discounting its earnings before interest and taxes of the future periods at weighted average cost of capital. However, most firms will prefer to evaluate their growth opportunities instead of distributing their entire earnings as dividends. In this case, the firm value can be calculated the present value of the future earnings before taxes plus the net present value of the firm's growth opportunities (Ross et al., 2013). Thus, the net present values of the projects that are seen as growth opportunities (investment opportunities) should be positive in order to increase the value of the firm. Managers who aim to maximize the value of the firm cannot be expected to invest in projects with negative net present values. How to obtain the necessary financing to invest in projects with positive net present vales is one of the main financial decisions that managers need to make.

The dividend payout ratios of firms are not supposed to change in the short term. Therefore, the funds required to seize new investment opportunities cannot be obtained by reducing the amount of dividends paid. If the firm's retained earnings (i.e. the remaining portion of the operating profits after interest, tax and dividend payments are made) are not enough to finance its investments, the firm proceeds to obtain cash by using cash and marketable securities. A firm that finances its investments in this way only uses internal financing. However, if internal funds (retained earnings) are not sufficient, external financing option is employed.

When external financing is needed for capital investments, firms follow a financing hierarchy. They prefer debt financing before financing with hybrid securities such as changeable bonds and preferred stocks. Equity financing is preferred only as a last resort if all of the other options are not sufficient to finance capital investments fully.

To sum up, according to the pecking order hierarchy, firms first use retained earnings to finance their capital investments, and in case of insufficient internal resources, firstly they prefer to finance with debt, then with hybrid securities and, finally, with equity. The tax advantage provided by the debt is of secondary importance.

The most important determinant of the leverage ratio is the profitable (non-negative) investment opportunities facing the firm and its ability to meet the necessary financing with its own internal resources. Leverage ratios of firms which do not have many profitable investment opportunities or can provide the necessary financing without resorting to external sources will be low.

There is asymmetric information problem in the background of the hypothesis. Asymmetric information is the existence of information, but not a fair distribution of it (Douma and Schreuder, 2008). This leads to problems of opportunistic behavior. The problem of adverse selection / hidden information is the main starting point of pecking order hypothesis. In the case of adverse selection, one of the parties to a possible transaction is more aware of the variables in the transaction than the other party.

Asymmetric information problem in the knowledge economy is adapted to the capital structure literature by Myers and Majluf (1984). This approach draws attention to the asymmetric information problem between managers and investors. Managers are considered to know the intrinsic value of firm's assets and its growth opportunities. However, investor's information set includes the market value of the firm rather than the intrinsic value. Therefore, investors do not know whether the intrinsic value of the securities issued by the firm is above or below their market value. However, the managers know exactly whether the securities issued by their firm are overvalued or undervalued. Once it is accepted that the purpose of the managers is to maximize the firm value, when the firm's intrinsic value is lower than the market value (i.e. when the stock is undervalued), managers will issue equity. Likewise, when the firm's intrinsic value is higher than the market value (i.e. when the stock is overvalued), managers will prefer debt financing. Pecking order hypothesis can be explained with the help of Myers and Majluf (1984) models in the context of asymmetric information problem.

Agency Theory

Another approach that is closely related to pecking order hypothesis is the agency theory. Agency costs are among the reasons why the value-irrelevance proposal of Modigliani and Miller (1958) is not valid in real life. All the theories of capital structure mentioned so far are based on the assumption that the purpose of the managers is to maximize the firm value (i.e. the stockholder wealth).

The agency relationship can be defined as the fact that one or more agents give power to a principal to make decisions on their behalf. In such a relationship, it will be costly for the agents to make principal to decide only to protect the interests of the agent. These costs, referred to as agency costs, have been studied in detail by Jensen and Meckling (1976). The problem of agency costs in firms can be divided into two parts: agency costs of equity and agency cost of debt.

Managers may aim to maximize their personal benefits instead of maximizing the stockholder wealth. Managers may prefer to do their own personal activities rather than spend time and effort to fulfill their responsibilities in the firm. They can use resources of the firm for their personal benefit. Expenses such as unnecessary travels, club memberships or excessive luxury offices can be evaluated in this group. In order to protect the interests of their friends and allies within the firm, they can make incompatible decisions with the aim of maximizing the value of the firm. They may take unnecessary risks or prefer an excessively riskless approach. In order to avoid the risk of failure in capital budgeting decisions, they may choose not to invest in a project with a positive net present value. Or they may decide to invest in a project that is too risky in order to close the failure of an earlier project. Managers of profitable firms may choose to keep their positive cash flows from the operations as marketable securities instead of distributing them to shareholders. In this way, it reduces the risk of the firm and prevents it from shrinking. (The payments made to the shareholders reduce the value of the firm.) In this case, shareholders lose the opportunity to obtain higher returns by seeking the investment opportunities outside the firm. Executives may be reluctant to disclose the information that investors need or apply manipulations to prevent the announcement of facts. In this case, investors increase the risk of the expected rate of return and decrease the value of the stock (Ehrhardt and Brigham, 2016).

Therefore, shareholders have to use various monitoring methods and control mechanisms to prevent undesired results arising from the agency problem. Perhaps the most important of these mechanisms is that the managers in badly managed firms are either dismissed by the board of directors with the efforts of the major shareholders, or as a result of the hostile takeover (threat of removal). Another commonly used mechanism is performance-dependent payment systems. In this system, the salary and/or bonus of the manager's salary can be determined according to the accepted indicators related to firm success such as the market price of the stock or the profit of the period. Besides, the payments to be made to the manager can be in the form of stock or stock options. However, since it is not possible to fully measure manager's performance, all these arrangements cannot fully eliminate the agency costs (Myers, 2001).

Representation problems may also arise between stockholders and lenders (creditors). When firms face the risk of bankruptcy, they can transfer funds from lenders to shareholders. In the event of bankruptcy, the assets of the lenders are paid first. The residual claims on the remaining assets belong to the shareholders. Therefore, in the case of bankruptcy, the lower the value of the firm's debt, the greater the amount the shareholders will have.

In the case of bankruptcy, managers can transfer resources from lenders to shareholders. Due to limited liability regulations in the corporations, the probable losses of the shareholders are limited only by their investment in the firm. Therefore, if the liquidation value of a firm cannot meet the debts, its shareholders do not have to pay the remaining portion of debt.

When a manager of a near bankrupt firm invests in projects with a high return but a high risk, the shareholders will obtain a high return if the project is successful. However, if the project fails, their return will not change because they are shareholders of a firm that is already in bankruptcy. Lenders, on the other hand, do not increase their returns in case of success but may not be paid in case of failure. In other words, the risk of high-risk investments made by a firm in a bankruptcy situation is undertaken by the lenders. If the executives of a firm in bankruptcy pay dividends, the market value of the old debt will decrease as the firm's risk exposure increases.

The lenders make highly covenants to protect themselves which includes the return of bonds in case of leveraged buyout, limitation of dividend payments and the limitation of new borrowing. The Agency theory helps to explain the importance of financial distress and bankruptcy costs in trade-off theory by drawing attention to the conflict of interest between lenders and shareholders.

Signal Hypothesis and Market Timing

In the perfect markets where Modigliani and Miller (1958) value irrelevance proposal is valid, all participants have the same set of information (symmetry of information). However, in real life, manager's information set is much broader than the information set of investors (asymmetry of information). The signal hypothesis draws attention to the impact of financing decisions on firm value under the assumption of information asymmetry. Managers who aim to maximize the wealth of the current shareholders will prefer to meet their financing needs by borrowing while they have positive expectations about the future cash flows of the firm. In this way, the future increase in the firm value will be transferred to current shareholders only. However, if the managers expect that the value of the firm will fall in the future, they prefer to issue equity. Then, the current shareholders will share the future losses with the new shareholders. Under these conditions, the market decrease the value of a firm in case of equity issuance and increase it in case of borrowing. In other words, managers send signals to the market through financing decisions. Debt issuance is perceived as a positive signal, while stock issuance is considered as a negative signal.

Market conditions may also be influential on firms' capital structures. Under/overvaluation of stocks is possible in inefficient markets. According to behavioral finance, sometimes investors can collectively conduct an over-evaluating behavior with an optimist perspective (bull market). At some other times, they undervalue stocks in the market with a pessimistic perspective (bear market). Firms tend to issue shares when they think that their shares are overvalued in the market. Similarly, they refrain from equity issuance during the bear market. Unlike the signal hypothesis, this situation is not caused by asymmetric information between managers and investors, but only by the difference in opinion about the stock market in general. Market timing explains the periodic increases in the issuance of shares in real-life capital markets.

Free Cash Flow Hypothesis

Jensen (1986) defines free cash flow as an excess amount of cash after investing in all positive net present value projects. It is the amount of cash remaining after all the fixed assets and net working capital investments are made and the taxes are paid for the firm to continue its activities. It is called "free" because it is distributable to the firm's creditors and shareholders. For firms with large amounts of free cash flows, this excess cash should be transferred to shareholders through increased dividends or share repurchases.

Given the fact that free cash flow is an excess cash after making all positive net present value projects, it is clear that using it in investment projects will not increase the firm value. However, managers ignore this fact when they aim to maximize their economic interests rather than the wealth of shareholders. Therefore, there is a need for a mechanism to encourage managers to transfer the free cash flows to the investors instead of investing to projects with return rates lower than their weighted average cost of capital or wasting unnecessarily. Jensen argued that this mechanism is the firm's borrowing. The free cash flow hypothesis argues that debt use can solve the agency problems arising from free cash flow. When the principal and interest payments are not made, the creditors have the right to demand the bankruptcy of the firm and managers can be fired. Thus, the use of debt will prevent managers from wasting resources. The disciplining effect of the debt on managers cannot be denied, especially for high-income firms (cash cows). However, it would be wrong to say that this effect exists for all firms.

IMPORTANT ISSUES RELATED TO THE OPTIMAL CAPITAL STRUCTURE FOR MAXIMIZING FIRM VALUE

Determinants of Capital Structure

As a general definition, target capital structure is the leverage ratio where marginal costs of debt is equal to marginal benefit of debt. Some firm characteristics are accepted as proxies for costs and benefits of leverage. These characteristics are known as determinants of capital structure. In this part, the determinants of capital structure are discussed in the light of well-known capital structure theories explained above.

Tax Payments

The tax deductibility of interest payments is the starting point of trade-off theory. A straightforward implication of these tax benefits is that, ceteris paribus, firms with higher taxable income levels should have higher leverage ratios. Immediately after the development of trade-off theory, researchers tried to support it with empirical findings. However, there are a number of obstacles in testing the existence of a relationship between the tax benefits of debt and leverage ratio. Thus, it is no easy to detect tax effect in empirical studies (Frank and Goyal, 2009).

Early attempts have not reported any relationship between tax payments and leverage ratios (Breadley 1984; Titman and Wessels, 1988). Later, Graham (1996, 1998, 1999) found out a positive relationship between marginal tax rate and leverage ratios. However, later empirical studies which uses less complicated proxies for tax advantages of debt than Graham did, usually do not find any tax effect on leverage at all (Antoniou et al., 2008; De Jong et al., 2008; Fan and Titman, 2012; Kayo and Kimura, 2011; Faff et al., 2016; Venanzi and Naccarato 2017; Faccio and Xu,2015).

Profitability

Since the bankruptcy probability is relatively low for more profitable firms, they can borrow more and can enjoy the increase in their value without any negative effect of debt such as financial distress. Thus, interest tax shields will be more attractive for them. Therefore, trade-off theory implies a positive relation between leverage and profitability (Frank and Goyal, 2009). Similarly, free cash flow hypothesis emphasis the disciplinary effect of debt in reducing the agency costs of free cash flows. The hypothesis, which advocates debt utilization in profitable firms to eliminate agency costs, also foresees a positive relationship between leverage ratio and profitability (Jensen 1986). The profitable firms increase their leverage to prevent executives from making unnecessary expenditures with excessive amounts of cash. This policy enforces management to maximize shareholder wealth instead of pursuing their personal objectives.

On the other hand, pecking order hypothesis argues that firms prefer to finance their investments with retained earnings instead of external financing because of the information asymmetry between managers and investors. Firms use external financing only if the retained earnings do not meet their financing needs. For this reason, profitable firms use less debt to finance their investments. Thus, pecking order hypothesis implies a negative relationship between leverage ratio and profitability (Myers, 1984; Myers and Majluf, 1984). Negative relationships between leverage ratio and profitability were also observed in empirical studies (Harris and Raviv, 1991; Rajan and Zingales, 1995; Booth et al., 2001; Utrero-González, 2007; De Jong et al., 2008; Antoniou et al, 2008; Pereira-Alves and Ferreira, 2011; Fan et al., 2012; Kieschnick and Moussawi, 2018).

Asset Tangibility

The asset tangibility can be considered as an indicator that reflects the financial distress probability. In the event of bankruptcy, tangible assets can be liquidated to satisfy the claims of the creditors since, their value will not decrease significantly. For this reason, according to trade-off theory, tangible assets reduce the financial distress costs and facilitates more debt financing. In case of financial distress or bankruptcy, unlike intangible assets which will lose their value, tangible assets can be converted to cash without a huge loss in their value. Therefore, they are accepted as collaterals in debentures. Also, cost of debt is lower for firms with tangible assets since they decrease the risk premium for lenders.

According to the agency theory, as the ratio of fixed assets to total assets increases, the possibility of the firm's borrowing increases and the cost of debt arising from the agency problem decreases. In addition, agency costs of debt are also lower for these firms because asset substitution is not easy with more tangible assets. Therefore, a positive relation between leverage and asset tangibility is implied by both trade-off and agency theories.

On the other hand, pecking order theory implies that tangible assets make equity issuance easier by reducing information asymmetry problem. Fixed assets facilitate the financing with equity issuance as they reduce the asymmetric information problem. Therefore, there is a negative relationship between leverage ratio and asset structure. When the maturity of the debt is taken into consideration, it is stated that there may be a positive relationship between the asset structure and long-term indebtedness and a negative one between asset structure and short-term indebtedness. Thence, pecking order theory does not have a clear argument about the sign of the relationship. However, a significant positive relationship between leverage ratio and tangibility is found in the literature (Harris and Raviv, 1991; Rajan and Zingales, 1995; Booth et al., 2001; Utrero-González, 2007; De Jong et al., 2008; Antoniou et al, 2008; Pereira-Alves and Ferreira, 2011; Fan et al., 2012; Kieschnick and Moussawi, 2018).

Firm Size

Firm size can be accepted as a negative proxy for the possibility of bankruptcy. The likelihood of bankruptcy for large firms is lower than that of small firms. According to trade-off theory, large firms pay lower risk premiums because they have diversified their investments more. They have been operating for many years and have a certain recognition in the debt market. Therefore, the agency cost of these firms is low. As the probability of bankruptcy of large firms is very low, they take advantage of the tax-shield by taking a large amount of debt. As a result, trade-off theory argues that there should be a positive relationship between firm size and leverage ratio.

On the other hand, asymmetric information problem between managers and investors is not very serious for large firms. Thus, their cost of equity is affordable and their stocks are demanded in the stock market. On the other hand, they can easily access to the debt market and raise funds cheaply (Cheng and Shiu, 2007). As a result, the projection of pecking order hypothesis regarding the relationship between firm size and leverage ratio is unclear. According to the results of empirical studies, this relationship is positive (Harris and Raviv, 1991; Rajan and Zingales, 1995; Booth et al., 2001; Utrero-González, 2007; De Jong et al., 2008; Antoniou et al, 2008; Pereira-Alves and Ferreira, 2011; Fan et al., 2012; Kieschnick and Moussawi, 2018).

Growth Opportunity

Market-to-book value ratio is accepted as a proxy of the firm's growth capacity and is negatively correlated with leverage ratio according to trade-off theory. The larger portion of the market value for a firm with high growth capacity comes from its intangible assets. In the case of financial distress, as the value of these assets will be destroyed, investors are much more likely to lose money when they go bankrupt. Thence, the cost of debt is higher than the cost of equity for firms with high growth capacity. Since growth capacity increase financial risks, managers have to decrease their use of debt in order to decrease their financial distress probability. Similarly, agency theory predicts a negative relationship between leverage rate and growth capacity.

On the other hand, according to pecking order hypothesis, holding profitability fixed, leverage should be higher for growth firms, since they need more external financing. Thus, there must be a positive relation between growth opportunities and leverage. Previous empirical findings are conflicting. Some studies report a negative relationship between the leverage ratio and growth opportunities (Rajan and Zingales, 1995; Booth et al., 2001; De Jong et al., 2008; Antoniou et al, 2008; Fan et al., 2012; Kieschnick and Moussawi, 2018). Others document a positive relationship (Utrero-González, 2007; Cheng and Shiu, 2007).

Earnings Volatility

The change in net profit was used as an indicator of operational risk. According to static trade-off theory, firms with high operational risk may not be able to meet the debt service. Consequently, they have a high cost of indirect bankruptcy. Therefore, firms with high earnings volatility must prefer low leverage ratios.

Results of empirical studies are far from consensus. There are studies that report a negative relationship (Antoniou, 2008; Graham and Leary, 2015), while other says no relationship at all (Titman and Wessels, 1988). One of the reasons why the expected negative relationship between earnings volatility and leverage ratio is not observed in empirical studies is the endogeneity problem. There is a two-sided relationship between income volatility and leverage ratio. Therefore, it is difficult to make a causal deduction by using one way econometric models.

Non-Debt Tax Shield

Static trade-off theory emphasis that firms prefer debt to take advantage of the tax shield of interest. However, there are other non-debt tax shields such as depreciation and investment incentives. De Angelo and Masulis (1980) argued that non-debt tax shields like amortization and investment incentives may decrease the importance of tax benefits of debt financing. The larger the non-debt tax shield, the lower the attractiveness of the tax advantage of interest. Therefore, static trade-off theory implies a negative relationship between non-debt tax shield and leverage ratio.

Harris and Raviv (1991) promoted the non-debt tax shield as one of the most widely accepted determinants of capital structure in the literature. However, Titman and Wessels (1988) have argued that there is not enough evidence to suggest such an effect. Previous empirical studies support both views (Antoniou et al., 2008; Leary and Roberts, 2005).

Industry Effects

There is a near consensus in the literature about the explanatory effect of industry dummies in capital structure research (Mac Kay and Phillips, 2005). Total explanatory power of firm level determinants of capital structure discussed above is not high enough to be content with them only. Assuming the existence of some common factors for the firms operating in the same industry is a reasonable. Firms generally accept industry mean leverage ratio as their target leverage ratio and adjust theirs towards it (Hovakimian et al., 2001). Some researchers try to cover the industry effect by using some proxies for industry characteristics (Kayo and Kimura, 2011). Others prefer to include industry dummies to capture industry-level variability of leverage ratios (Antoniou et al., 2008).

Determinants of Capital Structure: Estimation Issues

In the last 60 years, many empirical studies have been carried out on the determinants of capital structure. The difficulty in accessing data of firms operating in other countries has led to the focus on the US (and several developed countries) markets in the first studies in the literature. Hence, theories on capital structure have been tested within the framework of capital structure decisions of firms in developed countries. The resulting determinants and their relationships with capital structure are mostly based on the inferences from US firms.

In the last two decades, capital structure studies have gained a new dimension with the establishment of global data sets containing firm level panel data from many countries. In the first international studies conducted during 1990s, it was investigated whether the results from some European countries support the US results (Rajan and Zingales, 1995). Later, global data sets were used to investigate whether the determinants of capital structure were different in other developed and developing countries.

With the popularity of large scale datasets, the estimation methods gained importance. Initially panel random or fixed effects regression models are employed. Then, dynamic panel models are estimated using more advanced approaches like System GMM or structural equation modeling (SEM). Recently three serious issues are discussed in the empirical capital structure literature.

The first issue is the correct estimation of the leverage ratio. In empirical studies conducted to investigate the determinants of capital structure, leverage ratio is used as an independent variable. This ratio has been estimated in several different ways in the literature. One of the most frequently used formula is dividing the financial (interest-bearing) debt by total assets. As Welch (2011) proved, this ratio is not only for firms with low financial debt amounts but also for firms with a high level of non-debt liabilities such as account payables. Therefore, it does not reflect the real indebtedness of the firm. It would be more accurate to calculate the leverage ratio as the ratio of the total financial debt to the total investment or the ratio of total debt to total assets.

The second important issue is the zero-leverage phenomenon, which was recently introduced by Strabulaev (2007) and Strabulaev and Yang (2013). This phenomenon can be explained as some firms do not prefer to use debt. In the last few years, studies have shown that zero-leverage phenomenon exist in many countries around the world (Bessler et al., 2013; Ramalho and Silva 2009); Dang, 2013; El Ghoul et al., 2017). Although zero leverage is an empirically proven phenomenon, modern theories of capital structure fail to explain its reasons (Strabulaev, 2007; Strabulaev and Yang, 2013). This situation leads to the possibility that the factors affecting the initial debt decision of an unleveraged firm may be different from the decision of how much debt an already leveraged firm should utilize.

The last issue is related to the probability distribution of the leverage ratio variable. Since it is estimated by dividing the financial debt to the total investment, it is a fractional variable that is valued between 0 and 1. It is clear that the conditional expectation of fractional variables will be a non-linear function of the explanatory variables (Papke and Wooldridge, 1996). Therefore, using linear models in studies of capital structure will cause inaccurate model specification problems. Ramalho and Silva (2009) proposed the use of a quasi-maximum likelihood-QML estimator developed by Papke and Wooldridge (1996) to solve this problem. This model, called Fractional Regression Model (FRM), can also be used in panel datasets (Papke and Wooldridge, 2008).

SOLUTIONS AND RECOMMENDATIONS

Considering the current situation of the capital structure studies, it can be said that there is a consensus on a set of firm-level capital structure determinants. These are profitability, asset tangibility, firm size and growth opportunity (Harris & Raviv, 1991; Rajan & Zingales, 1995; Booth et al., 2001; De Jong et al., 2008; Antoniou et al., 2008; Frank & Goyal, 2009; Alves & Ferreira, 2011; Fan et al., 2012; Kieschnick & Moussawi, 2018). Moreover, there are some studies which found a relationship between leverage ratios and some other firm level factors such as non-debt tax shield, liquidity, firm age and corporate structure in the literature DeAngelo & Masulis, 1980; Antoniou et al., 2008; González & González, 2008; Ramalho et al., 2016; Kieschnick & Moussawi, 2018). Even though there are statistically significant relationships between leverage ratios and these generally accepted firm-level determinants of capital structure, the explained portion of cross-sectional variability in capital structures is still very low. Besides, the results of the cross country studies show that macro-economic variables are even less important in capital structure decisions of firms. To sum up, firm specific effects are the most important determinants of capital structures which are detected until now.

In order to understand the capital structure decisions of firms locally and globally, a few step must be followed in empirical studies. First of all, correct proxies of the capital structure determinants must be selected and data on these proxies must be collected without any measurement error. Secondly, correct estimation methods must be employed. In order to achieve this step, data must be analyzed in detail using descriptive methods instead of implementing the estimation methods of the previous similar studies. Especially, methods such as multilevel models or random coefficient models which allows the estimation of separate slope coefficients for each cross-sectional unit can be used with panel data sets.

Besides the dynamic nature of the capital structure decisions must be taken into consideration. When firms have target leverage ratios, they change their capital structures at each period until it is equal to the target ratio. Even after a firm reached to its target capital structure ratio, it can change. In this case, firm has to adjust its capital structure towards the new target. Thus, there is a close relationship between the current and past leverage ratios of a firm. This dynamic structure must also be included in the models. Dynamic estimation methods such as System GMM can be employed.

Lastly, the fractional nature of a correct proxy of the capital structure must be taken into consideration during the method selection process. Since the expected value of a fractional model cannot be a linear function, a nonlinear method or Papke and Wooldridge (1996) quasi-maximum likelihood estimator can be employed.

FUTURE RESEARCH DIRECTIONS

Capital structure is one of the most diligently researched areas of the modern corporate finance. But the current situation of the literature is somewhat disappointing. Even though empirical research promotes some firm level variables as the proxies of capital structure determinants, their total explanatory power is extremely low considering the unexplained variability in leverage ratios. Thus, further researchers may focus on modelling this unexplained variability with the help of state-of-the-art econometric techniques such as panel data estimators and non-linear models. While doing this, the suggestions of Welch (2011), Starbulaev (2007) and Ramalho and Silva (2009) must be taken into consideration.

Another improvable area of the capital structure research is the survey studies. These studies may provide the opportunity of understanding why managers make their capital structure decisions in the way they did. Cross-country surveys can be conducted to understand the motives behind the leverage choices of managers all around the world.

Lastly, meta analyses may be conducted to summarize the overall results of the capital structure research.

CONCLUSION

This chapter is based on the relationship between capital structure and the firm value and discuss the concept of optimal capital structure. It presents an overview of the capital structure research and discuss the current situation of the literature. It starts with the discussion of the main theoretical approaches to the capital structure. Trade-off, pecking order, free cash flow, market timing and signaling approaches are explained in detail. Besides, related subjects like agency theory and information asymmetry are mentioned.

The current status of empirical capital structure is analysed in two parts. In the first part, the state of the art finding of the capital structure research, the so-called firm level determinants are mentioned. The relationships between the leverage ratio and tax payments, profitability, firm size, asset tangibility, growth opportunities, income volatility and non-debt tax shields are explained in detail within the light of capital structure theories. In the second part, the estimation issues in empirical capital structure research are discussed and some recommendations are made for a better research quality.

REFERENCES

Antoniou, A., Guney, Y., & Paudyal, K. (2008). The determinants of capital structure: capital market-oriented versus bank-oriented institutions. *Journal of Financial and Quantitative Analysis*, *43*(1), 59–92. doi:10.1017/S0022109000002751

Bancel, F., & Mittoo, U. R. (2004). Cross-country determinants of capital structure choice: a survey of European firms. *Financial Management*, 103–132.

Bradley, M., Jarrell, G. A., & Kim, E. H. (1984). On the existence of an optimal capital structure: Theory and evidence. *The Journal of Finance*, *39*(3), 857–878. doi:10.1111/j.1540-6261.1984.tb03680.x

Brigham, E. F., & Daves, P. R. (2014). *Intermediate financial management*. Cengage Learning.

Cheng, S. R., & Shiu, C. Y. (2007). Investor protection and capital structure: international evidence. *Journal of Multinational Financial Management*, *17*(1), 30–44. doi:10.1016/j.mulfin.2006.03.002

De Jong, A., Kabir, R., & Nguyen, T. T. (2008). Capital structure around the world: the roles of firm- and country-specific determinants. *Journal of Banking & Finance*, *32*(9), 1954–1969. doi:10.1016/j.jbankfin.2007.12.034

DeAngelo, H., & Masulis, R. W. (1980). Optimal capital structure under corporate and personal taxation. *Journal of Financial Economics*, *8*(1), 3–29. doi:10.1016/0304-405X(80)90019-7

Demirguc-Kunt, A., & Maksimović, V. (1994). *Capital structures in developing countries: evidence from ten country cases* (Vol. 1320). World Bank Publications.

Donaldson, G. (1961). *Corporate debt capacity: a study of corporate debt policy and the determination of corporate debt capacity*. Boston, MA: Division of Research, Harvard University.

Douma, S. W., & Schreuder, H. (2008). *Economic approaches to organizations*. Pearson Education.

Drobetz, W., & Wanzenried, G. (2006). What determines the speed of adjustment to the target capital structure? *Applied Financial Economics*, *16*(13), 941–958. doi:10.1080/09603100500426358

Ehrhardt, M. C., & Brigham, E. F. (2016). *Corporate finance: A focused approach*. Cengage Learning.

Elsas, R., & Florysiak, D. (2015). Dynamic capital structure adjustment and the impact of fractional dependent variables. *Journal of Financial and Quantitative Analysis*, *50*(5), 1105–1133. doi:10.1017/S0022109015000496

Faccio, M., & Xu, J. (2015). Taxes and capital structure. *Journal of Financial and Quantitative Analysis*, *50*(3), 277–300. doi:10.1017/S0022109015000174

Faff, R. W., Gray, S., & Tan, K. J. K. (2016). A contemporary view of corporate finance theory, empirical evidence and practice. *Australian Journal of Management*, *41*(4), 662–686. doi:10.1177/0312896216632032

Fan, J. P., Titman, S., & Twite, G. (2012). An international comparison of capital structure and debt maturity choices. *Journal of Financial and Quantitative Analysis*, *47*(1), 23–56. doi:10.1017/S0022109011000597

Fischer, E. O., Heinkel, R., & Zechner, J. (1989). Dynamic capital structure choice: Theory and tests. *The Journal of Finance*, *44*(1), 19–40. doi:10.1111/j.1540-6261.1989.tb02402.x

Frank, M., & Goyal, V. (2009). Capital structure decisions: which factors are reliably important? *Financial Management*, *38*(1), 1–37. doi:10.1111/j.1755-053X.2009.01026.x

González, V., & González, F. (2008). Influence of bank concentration and institutions on capital structure: new international evidence. *Journal of Corporate Finance*, *14*(4), 363–375. doi:10.1016/j.jcorpfin.2008.03.010

Graham, J., & Leary, M. (2011). A review of empirical capital structure research and directions for the future. *Annual Review of Financial Economics*, *3*(1), 309–345. doi:10.1146/annurev-financial-102710-144821

Graham, J. R. (2000). How big are the tax benefits of debt? *The Journal of Finance*, *55*(5), 1901–1941. doi:10.1111/0022-1082.00277

Graham, J. R., & Harvey, C. R. (2001). The theory and practice of corporate finance: Evidence from the field. *Journal of Financial Economics*, *60*(2-3), 187–243. doi:10.1016/S0304-405X(01)00044-7

Graham, J. R., Leary, M. T., & Roberts, M. R. (2015). A century of capital structure: the leveraging of corporate America. *Journal of Financial Economics*, *118*(3), 658–683. doi:10.1016/j.jfineco.2014.08.005

Harris, M., & Raviv, A. (1991). The theory of capital structure. *The Journal of Finance*, *46*(1), 297–355.

Hovakimian, A., Hovakimian, G., & Tehranian, H. (2004). Determinants of target capital structure: The case of dual debt and equity issues. *Journal of Financial Economics*, *71*(3), 517–540. doi:10.1016/S0304-405X(03)00181-8

Jensen, M. C. (1986). Agency costs of free cash flow, corporate finance, and takeovers. *The American Economic Review*, *76*(2), 323–329.

Jensen, M. C., & Meckling, W. H. (1976). Theory of the firm: Managerial behavior, agency costs and ownership structure. *Journal of Financial Economics*, *3*(4), 305–360. doi:10.1016/0304-405X(76)90026-X

Kieschnick, R., & Moussawi, R. (2018). Firm age, corporate governance, and capital structure choices. *Journal of Corporate Finance*, *48*, 597–614. doi:10.1016/j.jcorpfin.2017.12.011

Kraus, A., & Litzenberger, R. H. (1973). A state-preference model of optimal financial leverage. *The Journal of Finance*, *28*(4), 911–922. doi:10.1111/j.1540-6261.1973.tb01415.x

Leary, M. T., & Roberts, M. R. (2005). Do firms rebalance their capital structures? *The Journal of Finance*, *60*(6), 2575–2619. doi:10.1111/j.1540-6261.2005.00811.x

MacKay, P., & Phillips, G. M. (2005). How does industry affect firm financial structure? *Review of Financial Studies*, *18*(4), 1433–1466. doi:10.1093/rfs/hhi032

Miller, M. H. (1988). The Modigliani-Miller propositions after thirty years. *The Journal of Economic Perspectives*, *2*(4), 99–120. doi:10.1257/jep.2.4.99

Modigliani, F., & Miller, M. (1958). The cost of capital, corporation finance and the theory of investment. *The American Economic Review*, *48*(3), 261–297.

Modigliani, F., & Miller, M. (1963). Corporate income taxes and the cost of capital: A correction. *The American Economic Review*, *53*(3), 433–443.

Myers, S., & Majluf, N. (1984). Corporate financing and investment decisions when firms have information that investors do not have. *Journal of Financial Economics*, *13*(2), 187–221. doi:10.1016/0304-405X(84)90023-0

Myers, S. C. (2001). Capital structure. *The Journal of Economic Perspectives*, *15*(2), 81–102. doi:10.1257/jep.15.2.81

Papke, L. E., & Wooldridge, J. M. (1996). Econometric methods for fractional response variables with an application to 401 (k) plan participation rates. *Journal of Applied Econometrics*, *11*(6), 619–632. doi:10.1002/(SICI)1099-1255(199611)11:6<619::AID-JAE418>3.0.CO;2-1

Papke, L. E., & Wooldridge, J. M. (2008). Panel data methods for fractional response variables with an application to test pass rates. *Journal of Econometrics*, *145*(1-2), 121–133. doi:10.1016/j.jeconom.2008.05.009

Parsons, C., & Titman, S. (2007). Empirical capital structure: A review. *Foundations and Trends in Finance*, *3*(1), 1–93. doi:10.1561/0500000018

Rajan, R. G. (2012). Presidential address: The corporation in finance. *The Journal of Finance*, *67*(4), 1173–1217. doi:10.1111/j.1540-6261.2012.01745.x

Rajan, R. G., & Zingales, L. (1995). What do we know about capital structure? Some evidence from international data. *The Journal of Finance*, *50*(5), 1421–1460. doi:10.1111/j.1540-6261.1995.tb05184.x

Ramalho, E. A., Ramalho, J. J., & Coelho, L. M. (2016). Exponential regression of fractional-response fixed-effects models with an application to firm capital structure. *Journal of Econometric Methods*, *7*(1). doi:10.1515/jem-2015-0019

Ramalho, J. J., & da Silva, J. V. (2009). A two-part fractional regression model for the financial leverage decisions of micro, small, medium and large firms. *Quantitative Finance*, *9*(5), 621–636. doi:10.1080/14697680802448777

Ross, S. A., Westerfield, R., Jaffe, J. F., & Jordan, B. D. (2013). *Corporate finance* (pp. 353–354). McGraw-Hill/Irwin.

Strebulaev, I. A. (2007). Do tests of capital structure theory mean what they say? *The Journal of Finance*, *62*(4), 1747–1787. doi:10.1111/j.1540-6261.2007.01256.x

Strebulaev, I. A., & Yang, B. (2013). The mystery of zero-leverage firms. *Journal of Financial Economics*, *109*(1), 1–23. doi:10.1016/j.jfineco.2013.02.001

Titman, S., & Wessels, R. (1988). The determinants of capital structure choice. *The Journal of Finance*, *43*(1), 1–19. doi:10.1111/j.1540-6261.1988.tb02585.x

Venanzi, D., & Naccarato, A. (2017). The capital structure choice of European firms: The role of financial system and institutional setting. *International Business Research*, *10*(12), 22–47. doi:10.5539/ibr.v10n12p22

Zhou, Q., Tan, K. J. K., Faff, R., & Zhu, Y. (2016). Deviation from target capital structure cost of equity and speed of adjustment. *Journal of Corporate Finance*, *39*, 99–120. doi:10.1016/j.jcorpfin.2016.06.002

ADDITIONAL READING

Hang, M., Geyer-Klingeberg, J., Rathgeber, A. W., & Stöckl, S. (2018). Measurement matters—A meta-study of the determinants of corporate capital structure. *The Quarterly Review of Economics and Finance*, *68*, 211–225. doi:10.1016/j.qref.2017.11.011

Miglo, A. (2016). Capital structure in the modern world. Springer. Eckbo, B. E. (Ed.). (2008). Handbook of empirical corporate finance set (Vol. 2). Elsevier. Constantinides, G. M., Harris, M., & Stulz, R. M. (Eds.). (2003). Handbook of the Economics of Finance: Corporate finance. Elsevier. doi:10.1007/978-3-319-30713-8

Ramalho, E. A., Ramalho, J. J., & Murteira, J. M. (2011). Alternative estimating and testing empirical strategies for fractional regression models. *Journal of Economic Surveys*, *25*(1), 19–68. doi:10.1111/j.1467-6419.2009.00602.x

Ramalho, J. (2014). FRM: Stata module to estimate and test fractional regression models.

Strebulaev, I. A., & Whited, T. M. (2013). Dynamic corporate finance is useful: A comment on Welch. Available at SSRN 2194680.

Venanzi, D. (2017). How Country Affects the Capital Structure Choice: Literature Review and Criticism. *International Journal of Economics and Finance*, *9*(4), 1–11. doi:10.5539/ijef.v9n4p1

KEY TERMS AND DEFINITIONS

Capital Structure: The ratio of debt financing to the total external financing of a firm.

Determinants of Capital Structure: Some firm characteristics which are empirically proved to be proxies for costs and benefits of leverage.

Market Timing: An approach of capital structure which suggests that market conditions may also be influential on firms' capital structures. Firms tend to issue equity during bull markets refrain from it during bear markets.

Optimal Capital Structure Ratio: The capital structure ratio which maximizes the firm value at the point where the marginal benefit and the marginal cost of debt financing is equal.

Pecking-Order Theory: A theory of capital structure which suggests that firms first use retained earnings to finance their capital investments, and in case of insufficient internal resources, firstly they prefer to finance with debt, then with hybrid securities and, finally, with equity.

Signal Hypothesis: An approach of capital structure which suggests that managers send signals to the market through financing decisions. Debt issuance is perceived as a positive signal, while stock issuance is considered as a negative signal.

Trade-off Theory: A theory of capital structure which suggests that firms decide their capital structure only taking into consideration the advantages and disadvantages of debt.

Chapter 4
Challenges in Valuation by Using Discounted Free Cash Flow Method

Orhan Goker
Galatasaray University, Turkey

Sinem Derindere Köseoğlu
Independent Researcher, Turkey

ABSTRACT

It is generally believed that, in determining the real value of a company, the best results are obtained by using the Dicounted FCF method. The overall value of the firm itself or the value of equity is determined by discounting the "appropriate" cash flows by "appropriate" discount rates. We basically need to determine three major parameters: free cash flows, cost of capital, and the terminal value. All these three parameters have sub-parameters within themselves. Because all these parameters and their sub-parameters are to be future values, many factors like the riskiness of the firm in question, its leverage ratio, whether it is a profitable firm, newly-established or public company will not only influence the calculation of these parameters/sub-parameters but will also make it more difficult for the analyst. This chapter explains what variables are needed for company valuation, how they are determined, and what problems may be faced in calculating these values. Finally, authors propose solutions to all the problems analysts will likely face.

INTRODUCTION

Many business valuation models and methods from very simple to highly complex ones are used in finance literature and practice. Discounted Free Cash Flow Method (Discounted FCF Method) is one among them, which is mentioned under income-based approach. According to income-based valuation approach, the value of a business is equal to the present value of the future cash flows of the company discounted at the appropriate rate of return. In the income-based valuation approach, the value of the company depends on the cash flows that the company can create and the risk level of these cash flows.

DOI: 10.4018/978-1-7998-1086-5.ch004

The discounted cash flow method is one of the most widely used methods by both the experts and investors who are interested in the company valuation. Taking into account the future cash flows, the risk level of these cash flows and the risk level of the company are the main reasons for the common use of this method. However, the fundamental variables of the method; the free cash flows that the company will create in the future, company's cost of capital and its terminal value are highly sensitive to assumptions. This sensitivity can also prevent realistic results in determining the value we aim to determine.

Therefore, although this method is considered as one of the best methods, it is important to examine this method with many challenges and to offer solutions to these problems. This chapter explains the cash flow analysis and discusses the problems facing the analyst while applying this method and tries to give solutions to these problems.

In this work, the details of the Discounted Cash Flow Valuation methodology are discussed. Although different approaches include various discounted cash flow models, three valuation model are examined in this chapter; namely Dividend Discount Model, Free Cash Flow to Equity (FCFE) and Free Cash Flow to Firm (FCFF). Author of this document attempted to see the problems and concepts related with the subject from the eyes of a valuation analyst. While the Dividend Discount Model is also mentioned in the chapter, the main concentration of the chapter will be on FCFE and FCFF valuation models. Three sub-subjects taken into account are the fundamental variables of the Discounted FCF model; "Free Cash Flow", "Cost of Capital (Appropriate Discount Rate)" and "Terminal Value". The estimation methodology, problems and solutions related to these variables have been explained under following headlines.

Discounted Free Cash Flow (FCF) Method

In this method, first the future cash flows are estimated and then discounted by the "appropriate rate of return'' to find the firm or the equity value. Therefore, according to this method the value of a business or the value of the equity of the business is the present value of the expected cash flows over its expected life.

$$Value = \frac{E(FCF)_1}{(1+k)} + \frac{E(FCF)_2}{(1+k)^2} + \frac{E(FCF)_3}{(1+k)^3} + \ldots + \frac{E(FCF)_n}{(1+k)^n} \quad (1)$$

where; *E(FCF)* represents expected free cash flow the firm will generate in the future, k; is required rate of return.

The full expression of the above formula is as shown below. If we discount the FCFF by WACC we will get the overall value of the firm, and if we discount the FCFE by the required rate of the shreholders (required rate of equity, cost of equity) we will get the value of equity of the firm. The FCFF or FCFE in the formula below are assumed to be constant.

$$Business\ Value = \sum_{t=1}^{t=n} \frac{FCFF}{(1+k_o)^t} \quad (2)$$

$$Equity\ Value = \sum_{t=1}^{t=n} \frac{FCFE}{(1+k_e)^t} \tag{3}$$

k_0=WACC (overall cost capital)
k_e=required rate of equity

Theoretically, the value of the firm determined by discounting the FCFF is equal to the value of the equity determined by discounting the FCFE plus the present value of the long-term debt.

Business Value=Equity Value+PV of Debt

$$Business\ Value = \sum_{t=1}^{t=n} \frac{FCFF}{(1+k_o)^t} = \sum_{t=1}^{t=n} \frac{FCFE}{(1+k_e)^t} + PV\ value\ of\ long\ term\ debt \tag{4}$$

Assuming the company has an infinite life, the t value will go to infinity, and also assuming cash flows are constant and the t is infinite, the formula will be as follows:

When "constant FCF's" and "t" approach infinity the formula will be as follows;

$$Business\ Value = \sum_{t=1}^{t=\infty} \frac{FCFF_t}{(1+k_o)^t} \tag{5}$$

$$Equity\ Value = \sum_{t=1}^{t=\infty} \frac{FCFE_t}{(1+k_e)^t} \tag{6}$$

However, the cash flows generated by the company are not usually constant; but they may increase at a constant rate.

When "t" goes to infinity and FCFs grow at a constant rate; the formula will be as such;

$$Business\ Value = \left[\sum_{t=1}^{t=\infty} \frac{FCFF_0 * (1+g_{EBIT})^t}{(1+k_o)^t}\right] = \left[\frac{FCFF_0 * (1+g_{EBIT})}{k_o - g_{EBIT}}\right] \tag{7}$$

$$Equity\ Value = \left[\sum_{t=1}^{t=\infty} \frac{FCFE_0 * (1+g_{EPS})^t}{(1+k_e)^t}\right] = \left[\frac{FCFF_0 * (1+g_{EPS})}{k_e - g_{EPS}}\right] \tag{8}$$

g_{EBIT}=future growth rate of EBIT (Earning Before Interest and Tax)
g_{EPS}=future growth rate of EPS (Earnings Per Share)
Valuation with terminal value formula;

Even if the companies grow, this growth will not be usually steady and long-term; the firms mostly grow at a relatively high rate in early years and then at a slower rate.

In the light of the assumption that companies have infinite lives, firm valuation consists of two stages: in the first stage, the cash flows of the company are determined and estimated for a certain period called "horizon of analysis" (e.g. 5 years, 10 years). At the end of this period, the company's outgoing cash flows are forecasted. This is called terminal value of the company which is usually estimated by a growth rate after the 5-years or 10-years estimated period.

According to the FCF approach the company or equity value is reached by taking the present value of free cash flows for the 5-years or 10-years estimated period and the present value of the terminal value.

$$BV = \left[\left[\sum_{t=1}^{t=n} \frac{FCFF_t}{\left(1+k_o\right)^t} \right] + Terminal\ Value_{business} \right] \tag{9}$$

$$Terminal\ Value_{business} = \frac{FCFF_n * \left(1+g_{EBIT}\right)}{k_o - g_{EBIT}} * \frac{1}{(1+k_o)^n} \tag{10}$$

$$EV = \left[\sum_{t=1}^{t=n} \frac{FCFE_t}{\left(1+k_e\right)^t} + Terminal\ Value_{equity} \right] \tag{11}$$

$$Terminal\ Value_{equity} = \frac{FCFE_n * \left(1+g_{EPS}\right)}{k_o - g_{EPS}} * \frac{1}{(1+k_e)^n} \tag{12}$$

where; n: estimated period (e.g. 5-years, 10 years); terminal value period: from n to infinity.

Two Stage FCFF and FCFE Valuation Formula

Sometimes instead of estimating individual cash flows in the initial stage, FCF for period 0 is estimated and then a constant growth rate is used to determine the other cash flows in the horizon of analysis, and then a second growth rate is used to determine the remaining cash flows beyond the horizon of analysis. This two stage valuation models utilize different growth rates in a presupposed relatively high growth period and a stable period with relatively low growth rate.

$$BV = \left[\sum_{t=1}^{t=n} \frac{FCFF * (1+g_{1EBIT})^t}{\left(1+k_o\right)^t} \right] + terminal\ value_{business} \tag{13}$$

$$\boldsymbol{Terminal\ Value_{business}} = \frac{FFCF_0 * (1+g_{1EBIT})^n * \left(1+g_{2EBIT}\right)}{k_o - g_{2EBIT}} * \frac{1}{(1+k_o)^n} \tag{14}$$

$$EV = \sum_{t=1}^{t=n} \frac{FCFE*(1+g_{1EPS})^t}{(1+k_e)^t} + \left[\left[\sum_{t=1}^{t=\infty} \frac{FCFE*(1+g_{1EPS})^n *(1+g_{2EPS})^t}{(1+k_e)^t} \right] * \frac{1}{(1+k_e)^n} \right] \tag{15}$$

$$\textbf{\textit{Terminal Value}}_{equity} = \frac{FCFE*(1+g_{1EPS})^n *(1+g_{2EPS})}{k_e - g_{2EPS}} * \frac{1}{(1+k_e)^n} \tag{16}$$

where;

g_1= growth rate for horizon of analysis
g_2 =growth rate for terminal period

WACC (k_o) Weighted Avarage Cost of Capital Formula:

$$WACC(k_o) = \left[\frac{E}{V} * k_e\right] + \left[\frac{D}{V} * k_d * (1-t)\right] \tag{17}$$

where; k_d; cost of debt, *E*; weight of market value of the company's equity, *D* ;weight of market value of the company's debt, *V*; (E + D); total market value of the companies all financing, t; corporate tax rate

k_e=required return to equity formula:

$$E(k_e) = r_f + \beta_{equity} * (E(r_m) - r_f) \tag{18}$$

where; r_f risk free rate of return, $E(r_m)$ expected market risk premium, β_{equity}; systematic risk measure.

As it is seen from the above formulas, the most important variables that determine the value of the firm or equity in the valuation process based on DCF method is the "free cash flows that the company will create in the future" and "the cost of capital for discounting those cash flows". The terminal value can also be added to those two fundamental variables. In order to calculate these fundamental variables, determining some sub-variables within themselves is needed. In the case of using the discounted FCF method to realize valuation, it is necessary to calculate and determine many variables such as the free cash flows expected to be created in the future, the estimated time period of the cash flows, the growth rates after this estimation period, the weighted average capital cost, the cost of equity, cost of debt, beta as the systematic risk measure, retention ratio, market risk premium and weights of capital structure components.

In the Tables 1, 2 and 3 shown below, these fundamental variables and sub-variables for Dicounted FCF Method are indicated.

All inputs in the table are important in firm valuation and therefore will be discussed in detail.

An investor or analyst has to come up with estimates for (a) the company's free cash flows over the forecasted period, (b) a terminal value to account for cash flows beyond the forecast period, and (c) the discount rate.

Table 1. Sub-Variables of Free Cash Flows

<table>
<tr><th>Method</th><th>Fundamental Variables</th><th>Sub-variables</th></tr>
<tr><td rowspan="2">Free Cash Flow</td><td>FCFF
(entire firm valuation)</td><td>Revenue
Operating Costs
Working Capital Investments
Fixed Capital Investments
Taxes</td></tr>
<tr><td>FCFE
(equity valuation of the firm)</td><td>Revenue
Operating Costs
Working Capital Investments
Fixed Capital Investments
Taxes
Financing
Interest Payments</td></tr>
</table>

Table 2. Sub-variables of Discount Rate

<table>
<tr><th>Method</th><th>Fundamental Variables</th><th colspan="2">Sub-variables</th></tr>
<tr><td rowspan="3">Discount Rate</td><td rowspan="3">WACC</td><td>Cost of Equity</td><td>Beta
Rf (risk free rate of return)
Market Risk Premium</td></tr>
<tr><td>Cost of Debt</td><td>Tax rate
Interest rates</td></tr>
<tr><td>Weights</td><td>Market Value Weights</td></tr>
</table>

Table 3. Sub-variables of Terminal Value

<table>
<tr><th>Method</th><th>Fundamental Variables</th><th>Sub-variables</th></tr>
<tr><td rowspan="2">Expected Growth rate
(for terminal value estimation)</td><td>Net Income</td><td>retention ratio b=(1-Dividends/Net Income)
Return on Equity (=Net Income/Book Value of Equity)</td></tr>
<tr><td>Operating Income</td><td>Reinvestment Rate
Return on Capital</td></tr>
</table>

CHALLENGES IN DETERMINING FREE CASH FLOWS AND SOLUTIONS

When applying the income approach, the value of a business is determined by assessing the present value of its future cash flows. So, in general terms, the value of a business is the present value of the expected cash flows of the company. According to this method, the company is worth a value as long as it can create cash flows. Considering the time value of money, the cash flows of the following years are discounting to present value by a required rate of return. Discounted FCF analysis belongs to the "**income approach**" and is one of the theoretically most sound valuation methods as the value depends on the expected income one can achieve with a business. Discounted cash flow (DCF) valuation views the **intrinsic value** of a business as the present value of its expected future cash flows

What is the future cash flow of a business? It can be dividends or free cash flows (FCF). When the expected cash flows taken into account are dividends, the DCF model is called the **discounted dividend approach** or **dividend discount model**. When the expected cash flows taken into account are Free Cash Flow, the DCF model is called the **discounted free cash flow (FCF) model**. The Discounted FCF method can give us the overall value of the company or the value of its equity by discounting Free Cash Flow to Firm (FCFF) and Free Cash Flow to Equity (FCFE) respectively Whereas dividends are the cash flows actually paid to stockholders, free cash flows are the cash flows *available* for distribution to shareholders. Unlike dividends, FCFF and FCFE are not readily available data, it is necessary to estimate these quantities from the available financial data/information, which requires a clear understanding of free cash flows and the ability to interpret and use the information correctly.

Comparing the Free Cash Flow to Firm (FCFF) and Free Cash Flow to Equity (FCFE) Approaches to Valuation

Free Cash Flow Concept

In this method, the cash flows are referred as "Free Cash Flows" (FCF). FCF is the cash left over after paying operating expenses and capital expenditures of the company. It is used **"free"** term due to paying operating expenses, capital expenditures and also tax. Cash flows that are free from all expenses and taxes. There are two approaches to Discounted FCF valuation method. The first approach is to value the equity in the company. The second approach is to value the entire company. Free cash flows to the firm (FCFF) and free cash flows to equity (FCFE) are the cash flows available to, respectively, all of the investors in the company and to common stockholders. The FCFF concept refers to expected cash flows left to shareholders and long-term lenders, who are main financial source providers of the firm. They shape the capital structure of the company. FCFF expresses cash flow left to all beneficiaries of the company apart from government. The beneficiaries of a firm are stockholders, bond holders and government. Because FCF is calculated by deducting tax payments, it refers to the remaining cash to other beneficiaries after government. On the other hand, The FCFE concept refers to expected cash flows left to shareholders only in the future. Because, FCFE is calculated by deducting interest payments and other commitments.

Business Value vs. Equity Value Concepts

The main principle of applying Discounted FCF method is the need to match free cash flows to discount rates: equity cash flows to the cost of equity (required rate of equity) and firm cash flows to the cost of capital (weighted average cost of capital). While determining present value of FCFF by using WACC (k_o) gives the entire company value, determining present value of FCFE by using cost of equity (k_e) gives equity value of a company.

FCFF → WACC (k_o) → *Entire Business Value*
FCFE → Cost of equity(k_e) → *Equity Value of a Business*

Business Value (Firm Value, Enterprise Value, Company Value) = Equity Value + Debt Value

According to the empirical studies conducted by Copeland et al. (1996), if the discounting rates are estimated correctly to reflect the risk of the cash flow source, the firm value found in both methods should give the same result. In other words, the entire firm value that is estimated by FCFF will be equal to the total of equity value, which is estimated by FCFE, and present value of debt.

Estimating FCFF and FCFE

In order to forecast the future cash flows of the company, the cash flows created in the past period should be examined. The company's previous financial performance should be analyzed. The analyst, who wishes to perform a sound analysis during the valuation process, should examine in detail the past factors such as the return on capital, the growth rate and the cash flows. In addition, it is necessary to examine the sector of the firm, to forecast the capital expenditures and taxes to be paid in the future as well as investigating past data of the company. FCFF or FCFE are forecasted after all those examinations and estimations.

Table 4. FCFF and FCFE estimations

FCFF	FCFE
I-Cash Flow From Operations	**I- Cash Flow From Operations**
Sales Revenue	Sales Revenue
-Cost of goods sales	-Cost of goods sales
=Gross Profit	=Gross Profit
-Operating expenses	-Operating expenses
=Operating Income (EBIT)	=Operating Income (EBIT)
-Tax	-Tax
+Depreciation	+Depreciation
+/- Net Working Capital Change	+/- Net Working Capital Change
=total cash flow from operations	=total cash flow from operations
II- Cash Flow From Investments	**II- Cash Flow From Investments**
-Capital Expenditures	-Capital Expenditures
Free Cash Flow to Firm (FCFF)	**Free Cash Flow to Firm (FCFF)**
	III-Free Cash Flow From Financing
	New Debt Outstanding
	Dept Capital Payment
	-interest*(1-t)
	Free Cash Flow to Equity (FCFE)
	-Dividend Payment
	=Net Change in Cash

A firm realizes cash inflows or cash outflows from three ways: its operations, its investments or its financing.

- **Cash Flow from Operations:** Indicates changes in operations and working capital.
- **Cash Flow from Investments:** Indicates the capital expenditures, net results of companies' mergers and acquisitions activities
- **Cash Flow from Financing:** Indicates the net position of the companies related to financing activities.

The total net change of these three cash flows gives net changes in the cash of the company (cash and cash equivalents). FCFF and FCFE measures are different from net changes in the cash of the company.

The FCFF is calculated by making adjustments on the depreciation and other accounting practices that do not require cash outflow on the profit figure, and the changes in working and investment capitals are taken into consideration. In other words, FCFF is the amount of cash flow a company generates (net of taxes) after taking into account non-cash expenses such as amortization and depreciation, changes in operating assets and liabilities (net working capital), and capital expenditures. In the FCFF calculation, cash flows from operations and investments are taken into consideration but, the cash flow from financing is not included.

FCFE is a measure of how much cash is available only to the equity shareholders of a company after considering all expenses, taxes, working capital investments, capital expenditures and debt are paid.

The FCF estimation period varies depending on the sector of the firm. In general, although the estimated period is 5-years to 10-years, it can be decreased and increased according to the sector.

When the company is stable and the total error margin is low forecasted period can be shortened in parallel with the data related to the sector of the company. However, when a company operates in a sector with relatively more uncertainty, cash flows need to be forecasted for longer periods of time.

Problems and Solutions in Estimating FCFF and FCFE

As stated above, in the valuation process cash flows are estimated for a certain period of time ("horizon of analysis"- 5 years, 10 years) by taking into consideration the past cash flows of the firm and the economic conditions. Then, because the economic life of a firm is infinite, a representative value called the terminal value is determined by assuming that the future cash flows will increase until infinity by a constant growth rate. One of the main problems in determining the cash flows during this 5- to 10-year period is a situation where the company to be valued is a "startup or young company'' and/or it is a "company with negative earnings''. In determining the future cash flows of the company to be valued, we normally take into consideration the past cash flows of the company as well, but in a startup company we do not have such data available. Similarly, we have the same problem for companies with negative earnings as well. In addition, determining the growth rate of the future cash flows of such companies is rather difficult. Thus, this situation creates a serious setback for the valuation of such companies.

Therefore, it is conceivable to say that in valuing startup, young firms or companies with negative earnings, the use of cash flows approach will have major pitfalls in determining the FCFs needed for the valuation process.

Valuing Startups and Young Companies

This type of companies does not have any historic data. As a result, as the analyst, we do not have the chance to determine their past cash flows and the growth rates related to these cash flows. This situation makes it more difficult to estimate the future cash flows of such companies. Since we do not have any past date of these companies, it becomes questionable to say that they will be commercially viable or even to keep their existence in the future. The valuation of start-up companies will be discussed in detail in another chapter of this book (see Chapter 8: *"Startup Valuation: Theories, Models and Future"*), but here we try to emphasize only the important points to be considered in the FCF method:

- In start-up companies the future cash flows are estimated for shorter periods, 3-5 years; because, the future cash flows will be more difficult to determine properly.
- Cash flows are determined on a separate basis for each asset of the company. In determining the cash flows of individual assets, the cash flows of similar assets in the industry can be/are taken into account. This will give the analyst the chance to determine the past data for such companies. After determining the value of each individual asset by using those cash flows, we can get the overall value of the firm by summing up these values. The reasoning in this approach is that the sum of the NPV's of all the projects of the firm will give the total value of the firm itself.
- In determining the value of such companies, the relative valuation approaches are used as a supplement to the discounted FCF approach.

Valuing Companies with Negative Earnings

If a company incurs negative earnings, it does not necessarily mean that the company is less valuable; in fact, some studies indicate that companies with negative earnings can become more valuable. For example, Study of Zörgiebel (2016) results indicated that *"IPO's with negative earnings are higher valued compared to IPO's with positive earnings and already listed companies"*.

In valuing the companies with negative earnings, the first step to do should be to determine why these companies have negative earnings. There may be numerous reasons for a company to make a loss. Once the reasons are determined, then remedies to solve that problem are taken into consideration. In some companies, negative earnings can be of short-term nature (Short-term Problems-for Firms with Temporary Problems) and in others negative earnings can be of long-term nature (Long-term Problems). In this book the situation of companies with negative earnings is analyzed in a separate chapter (see Chapter 7: *"Valuation of Negative Earning Firms*); here we emphasize only certain points related to DCF approach.

In situations where negative earnings of the firm are considered temporary, it is expected that the company will have positive earnings once the problem is solved. Or if the firm is in a cyclical situation, it is conceivable to assume that the firm will have positive earnings after a period with negative earnings. In valuing such firms, we should determine the future cash flows by "normalizing" earnings. There are a number of ways used today to normalize earnings:

- The first approach is to get the average of the earnings.
- Or we can get the average of ROE or ROC of the firm in the past.

- However, if the company with negative earnings is a newly-established firm in this case it will not be possible to normalize the earnings by using past data: instead of using company's own ROE or ROC, similar companies' ROE or ROC values are used to determine the earnings of the company in question.

On the other hand, if the problems are of long-term nature or if they are of operational or structural nature, we should then use the operating margins of the industry, not the firm. However, some authors (Russel 2007) suggest that the DCF approach should not be used in such situations.

Challenges in Calculating the Weighted Average Cost of Capital and Solutions

In using the DCF approach to determine the overall value of a company, we use the estimated/future FCFF and discount them by the WACC of the firm in question. WACC gives the weighted average cost of all the long-term financing alternatives of the firm. In this approach all the cash outflows are deducted from the cash inflows generated by the firm and thus the residual (net or free) cash inflows are determined. The second important element in this approach is the discount rate WACC itself. We know that WACC is determined by taking into account both the weights and the after-tax costs of long-term capital components. But we should emphasize that there are many sub parameters used in determining the WACC and each one of these parameters are worth analyzing. The formula for WACC is given in equation 17. The parameters and subparameters used in the formula are stated below.

Weights

In determining the WACC we take into consideration the weights of all the long-term capital components. The debt ratio in the capital structure is also known as leverage ratio. The weights used in calculating WACC can be determined at book values or at market values. However, because the cash flows used in valuing and the WACC are based on future values, the weights used in the determination of the WACC should also be used at market values, not at book values. But at this point we face a real challenge: How can one determine the future market values of the capital components in question?

Weight of Equity=Market Value of Equity/Total Market Value of Equity and Debt
Weight of Debt = Market Value of Debt/ Total Market Value of Equity and Debt

Required Rate of Equity (Cost of Equity)

Equity is in general considered to be riskier than debt, because in a situation of bankruptcy first the creditors will get their claim and the rest will be shared by shareholders. Because equity is riskier than debt, its cost is also higher as compared to that of debt. The cost of debt is an actual cost and it is usually the interest rate on the debt. The cost of equity on the other hand is an opportunity cost. Therefore, a number of models are used to determine the cost of equity. Like CAPM, APT, Fama-French 3-Factor Model or multi-factor models etc. However, in practice the most commonly used one among the models is CAPM. The cost of equity formula according to this model is given in equation 18.

In the CAPM, in order to determine the cost of equity a risk premium is added to the risk-free rate of return. Naturally, risk premium will be higher for investments with higher risk and vice versa. In this model, the risk premium of a firm will be equal to the multiplication of the market risk premium with the Beta of the equity of the firm in question, which measures the sensitivity of the shares of that firm to the changes in the market portfolio. To sum up, we can state:

Required Rate of Equity=Risk Free Rate+Company Risk Premium

*Company Risk Premium=Beta*Market Risk Premium*: As can be seen here, the risk premium of the company is affected both by the company beta and the market risk premium.

Market Risk Premium= Return of Market Portfolio - Risk Free Rate

Beta

Beta is the measure of the systematic risk of the equity of the firm. Almost all of the risk-return equilibrium models in finance assure that the investors do good diversification, eliminate non-systematic risk and therefore expect to get a return for the systematic risk they take.

In practice Beta is calculated by measuring the sensitivity of the returns of the shares of the firm to the market portfolio with the use of regression analysis. In other words, the returns of the shares of the firm to be valued are regressed to the returns of the market portfolio, and the slope of the regression line gives us the Beta of the shares in question, and it shows the riskiness of the share. However, the Beta calculated as such may have the following pitfalls:

- Highly sensitive to data frequency; for example, Betas determined according to daily, weekly or monthly returns may vary from one another,
- may have a high standard error,
- may show different results according to the period taken; for instance, Betas calculated for the last 1, 5 or 10 years may easily vary from each other,
- if the company's financial leverage changes in time the Beta's in the future may also vary,
- Beta may vary according to the market return calculated

Since the Beta problem is a highly detailed subject, it is discussed under two separate chapters in this book. (See Chapters 5 and 6: titled *"Challenges in Estimation of Beta: Market Models used for Risk Estimation" and "Estimating the CAPM Beta for Public and Private Firms: Challenges and Solutions"*)

Market Risk Premium

This premium is also known as equity risk premium. Market risk premium signifies the risk premium of all the risky assets making up the portfolio, not the risk premium of a single firm or single asset. (''Risk premium for the portfolio of all risky assets''.) When we say market risk premium, we are faced with historic or expected market risk premium. Historical risk premium is calculated by deducting the risk-free rate of return from the historic returns from the historic returns of all the risky assets in the market portfolio. In other words, this difference will give us the risk premium of the market portfolio. Similarly, expected market risk premium is determined by deducting the expected risk-free rate of return from the expected return of the portfolio consisted of all risky assets.

Expected Market Risk Premium=Expected Return of Market – Expected Risk Free Rate of Return

In order to determine the expected market risk premium, we usually use the historic market risk premiums. We use the price indexes of the markets the companies operate in to determine the return of the market portfolio and the riskless interest rate to be deducted from the average market rate of return calculated will be the interest rate of the long-term treasury bonds in the same markets. However, there are a number of questions to be answered in this calculation:

- **Time Period:** How long a period should we take to use historical data? The average return of the market portfolio can be determined for a period of 5, 10, 15 years or even longer. Because of the risk perception and even changing market conditions, short-term can be preferred to reflect the near future, but taking longer terms reduces the standard error. In order to get an "optimal'' result it may be suggested to take a rather long period with an emphasis given to the last periods and calculate the average return of the market portfolio as such.
- **Market Portfolio:** Which market index should we use? In theory, most calculations are based on stock exchange indexes, because the portfolio mentioned in theory is the market portfolio consisting all risky assets.
- **Average Technique:** Which averaging technique should we use? In determining the return of the portfolio should we use arithmetic or geometric average? In arithmetic average we calculate, but in geometric average what is calculated is the compound return! If there is no correlation between the returns over the time analyzed, and if our aim is to forecast the next period, then the arithmetic average is a better measure. However, there is not always a random walk between the returns: for example, Fama and French (1988) have proven empirically that there is a negative correlation between the returns. In addition, Fama and French (1992) have shown that the correlation is rather low in one-year returns and high in 5-year returns. As a result, in situations like this, the arithmetic average will tend to show the risk premium higher than what it really is or should be. Therefore, we should prefer to use the arithmetic average in determining the average return from short-term data, but use the geometric average if we use long-term data. In practice we see that the arithmetic average is more widely used.

Risk Free Rate of Return

Risk-free rate of return assumes a situation in which the expected return and the actual return are always the same. Risk-free rate is the lowest rate of return an investor can get in a market in which the firm to be valued prevails. This rate embodies the inflation rate and symbolizes the expected rate of return of the investments with no default risk or reinvestment risk. Normally, Treasury Bills (TBills) with shortest maturity are considered risk-free investments, and thus the return of 3-month TBills is typically considered ''risk-free'' rate of return, because they have a very wide market. But this rate may vary according to the purpose of the analyst, for example, in company valuation the interest rte of Treasury Bonds with longest maturity (30 years or longer) is taken as the risk-free rate. This is surely an understandable practice, because the economic life of firms is assumed to be infinite. In this case, the rate used includes the country risk as well.

- Whatever currency the valuation process is carried in, Treasury Bonds must have been issued in the same currency as well.
- Because firm valuation represents a long-term analysis, the return of long-term Treasury Bonds should be used as the riskless rate of return. However, in certain situations, no Treasury Bonds are issued in the currency which the valuation process is carried on; in such situations foreign currency discount rate should be converted to the ''local'' currecy discount rate by using the inflation rates.

Cost of Debt

The cost of debt of a company is the return that the firm provides to its lenders or creditors. The interest rate of a loan is an important indicator of the actual cost of a debt, and therefore it is easier to determine its cost as compared to determining the cost of equity. In terms of riskiness, company bonds are different than Treasury Bills or Bonds; in company bonds, there is default risk. Therefore, investors buying company bonds expect an additional return on their investments as compared to investing in treasury bills or bonds. This additional return is required to meet the additional risk of company bonds. The higher the risk of the company, the higher will be that additional risk premium. In general, the cost of debt for a firm can be expressed as follows:

Cost of debt= (Riskfree Rate+ Default Spread)(1-corporate tax rate)*

Even though a company is not listed on stock exchange, various rating agencies disclose their default spreads. Companies like S&P, Moody's and Fitch calculate default spreads of most companies, and their default spreads are added to the riskless rate of return and thus their cost of debt is determined.

However, it may be difficult or even impossible at times to determine the credit ratings of some companies. In such situation, we should look into their cost of borrowing in recent years. Secondly, the analyst himself/herself may calculate the riskiness of the company in question and thus determine its default spread.

Corporate Tax Rate

In the DCF method the free cash flows to be used are determined on an after-tax basis; in fact, this is why they are called "free" cash flows. Similarly, the discount rate used is also on after-tax basis. On the ather hand, the interest paid in the borrowing is tax-deductable and thus it will create a tax benefit to the company. Therefore, in calculating the WACC for the firm in question, the cost of debt should also be as an after-tax cost.

Challenges in Calculating Terminal Value and Solutions

In using the discounted FCF approach, we assume that the cash flows beyond the horizon of analysis grow at a constant rate and determine the terminal value accordingly; because after the companies reach a saturation point their growth rate usually levels off. By using the standard perpetuity formula, we determine the terminal value as of the end of the time horizon by using a constant growth rate. Therefore, the growth rate of the cash flows is significant in the determination of the terminal value.

On the other hand, we can determine growth rate of the cash flows of a firm in a number of ways:

Historical growth rate: We can determine the future growth rate by analyzing the past growth rates. Here we can use the arithmetic or geometric average of the past growth rates. Of course, the growth rates will change according to the cash flows we use. If we take FCFE to determine the value of the equity we can determine the growth rate based on EPS (or net income). If we take the FCFF to determine the overall value of the firm, we can determine the relevant growth rate based on the EBIT growth rate. However, we should also state that historic growth rates may be sensitive to the time length taken into consideration. In addition, it may be difficult to determine the growth rates in situations where the company incurs a loss.

Relative growth rate: We can use the growth rate of EBIT or EPS of similar companies in the industry.

Fundamentals growth rate: We can calculate the growth rate of the company in question by taking into consideration its fundamentals. Growth is primarily based on two major factors: How much will the company spend on new investments and what return will these investments yield? We show below a number of examples regarding the growth rates o net income and EBIT based on these fundamentals:

Net Income (or EPS) growth rate (for FCFE)

g_{EPS}=ROE * (b)

where b is equity reinvestment rate, and ROE return on equity

Equity reinvestment rate (b) = [(Net Capital Expenditures+Change in Working Capital)*(1-debt ratio)] / Net Income

ROE= Net Income / BV of Equity

EBIT growth rate (for FCFF)

g_{EBIT}=ROC * (b)

where b is reinvestment rate, and ROC return on capital

Reinvestment Rate (b) = [(Net Capital Expenditures+Change in Working Capital)] / EBIT (1-t)
ROC=EBIT (1-t) / Book value of (debt + equity)

FREE CASH FLOW AND BUSINESS VALUATION HYPOTHETICAL EXAMPLE

A hypothetical company's actual 2018 and projected 2019 balance sheets and income statements are as given in Table 5. The long-term liabilities of the company all consist of long-term bonds. The company has 2.500.000 shares outstanding with $100 nominal (par) value. If we assume that firm's earnings are expected to grow 10% forever and the WACC of firm is 12%. According to this information it has been calculated the FCFF, FCFE for the company and estimated the value per share of common equity as of 01/01/2019.

FCFF and FCFE are calculated according to Table 4. Starting from net income or EBIT does not change the result when calculating the FCFF and FCFE as long as necessary adjustments are made. It can be seen FCFF and FCFE calculations in Tables 6 and 7 starting from both net income and EBIT.

SUMMARY

In this chapter, it is tried to give all details about discounted FCF method which is accepted the most important method in business valuation for finding intrinsic value. This method is based on the future free cash flows that the firm expects to generate in the coming years. Both cash flows and the relevant discount rates as expected values, not as historic ones. In the model, the cash flows are estimated for a certain length of time called "horizon of analysis" and the further cash flows are usually assumed to be changing at a constant rate until infinity, because economic lives of firms are considered to be infinite.

Table 5. The company's actual 2018 and projected 2019 balance sheets and income statements

Balance Sheets (millions of dollar)	**2019**	**2018**	**INCOME STATEMENT**	**2019**	**2018**
Cash	70,0	67,5	Net sales	1325	1250
Marketable securities	172,5	165,0	Cost of sales	-1000	-950
Accounts receivable	210,0	200,0	**Gross Profit**	**325**	**300**
Inventories	280,0	265,0	Depreciation	-75	-62,5
Total Current Assets	732,5	697,5	**EBIT**	**250**	**237,5**
Net plant and equipment	702,5	662,5	Interest	-57,5	-52,5
TOTAL ASSETS	**1435,0**	**1360,0**	Earnings before taxes	192,5	185
			Taxes (%20)	-38,5	-37
Accounts payable	140,0	130,0	**Net Income**	**154**	**148**
Notes payable	345,0	325,0			
Accruals	70,0	70,0			
Total Current Liabilities	555,0	525,0			
Long Term Bonds	432,5	410,0			
Commen Stock	250,0	250,0			
Retained earnings	197,5	175,0			
Common Equity	447,5	425,0			
TOTAL LIABILITIES&EQUITY	**1435,0**	**1360,0**			

Table 6. Calculating FCFF and FCFE starting by EBIT

I-Free Cash Flow from Operations	
EBIT	250
-Taxes	(50)
NOPAT	200
+Depreciation	75
ΔAccounts receivable	(10)
ΔInvertories	(15)
ΔAccounts payable	10
ΔAccruals	0
ΔNet Working Capital	(15)
Total Cash Flow from Operations	260 (NOPAT+Depreciation+/-Net Working Capital)
II-Free Cah Flow from Investments	
ΔMarketable Securities	(7,5)
ΔCapital Expenditures	(115) (Ending Fixed Asset+Depr.-Beginnig Fixed Asset)=
	702.5+75-662.5 = 115
Total Cash Flow from Investments	(122.5)
Free Cash Flow to Firm (FCFF)	**= 137.5 I+II** = (260 – 122.5)
III-Free Cash Flow from Financing	
Notes Payable	20
Long Term Liabilities	22.5
- Interest * (1-0.20)	**(46)** Interest expenses *(1-tax rate of company)
Total Cash Flow from Financing	(3.5)
Free Cash Flow to Equity (FCFE)	=134,137.5-3.5=134

There are three basic inputs of finding business value by using Discounted FCF; "Free Cash Flows", "Weighted Average Cost of Capital" and "Terminal Value". All these three inputs have also sub-parameters within themselves. There are some difficulties to estimating all of these parameters and sub-parameters. It is tried to explain what variables are needed for company valuation, how they are determined and what problems we may face in calculating these values. And finally, it has been proposed possible solutions to all these problems that analysts are likely to face. In addition, it has given a hypothetical business valuation calculation to give general insights about the issue.

Table 7. Calculating FCFF and FCFE starting by net income

I-Free Cash Flow from Operations	
Net Income	154
+Depreciation	75
ΔAccounts receivable	(10)
ΔInvertories	(15)
ΔAccounts payable	10
ΔAccruals	0
ΔNet Working Capital	(15)
Total Cash Flow from Operations	214 (Net Income+Depreciation+/-Net Working Capital)
II-Free Cah Flow from Investments	
ΔMarketable Securities	(7,5)
ΔCapital Expenditures	(115) (Ending Fixed Asset+Depr.-Beginnig Fixed Asset)=
	702.5+75-662.5 = 115
Total Cash Flow from Investments	(122.5)
+ Interest * (1-0.20)	**46** Interest expenses * (1-tax rate of company) **[(57.5*(1-0.20)]**
Free Cash Flow to Firm (FCFF)	**= 137.5 I+II+ Int. exp. *(1-tax rate)** = (214-122.5+ 46)
III-Free Cash Flows from Financing	
Δ Notes Payable	20
Δ Long Term Liabilities	22.5
- Interest * (1-0.20)	**(46)** Interest expenses *(1-tax rate of company)
Total Cash Flow from Financing	(3.5)
Free Cash Flow to Equity (FCFE)	**=134** (137.5-3.5)
Dividend Payment	(131.5) (Beginning Ret. Earn+ Net Income-Ending Ret. Earn.)=
	175+154-197.5
Total Cash Flow	2.5 ΔCash= 70 –67.5 =2.5
According to equation 7, business value has been estimated as below: $Business\ value = \frac{FCFF}{WACC-g} + cash = \frac{137.5}{0.12-0.10} + 67.5 = 6875 + 67.5 = \$6942.5 million$	
PV of Debt = 325 +410 = $735million	
Equity Value = 6,942.5 – 735 = $6,207.5million	
Value Per Share = $\frac{6,207,500,000}{2,500,000} = \$2,483$	

REFERENCES

CFA Institute. (2019). *Free Cash Flow Valuation*. Retrieved from https://www.cfainstitute.org/membership/professional-development/refresher-readings/2019/free-cash-flow-valuation

Copeland, T., Koller, T., & Murrin, J. (1996). *Valuation: Managing and measuring the value of companies*. New York, NY: John Wiley & Sons.

Damodaran, A. (2008). What is the riskfree rate? A search for the basic building block. Stern School of Business, New York University, December.

Damodaran, A. (2009). Valuing young, start-up and growth companies: estimation issues and valuation challenges. Stern School of Business, New York University, May.

Damodaran, A. (2018). Equity risk premiums (ERP): Determinants, estimation and implications. Stern School of Business, New York University, March.

Damodaran, A. (n.d.). Growth rates and terminal value. *DCF Valuation.*

Demuth, A. (n.d.). *Income approach and the discounted cash flow methodology.* Retrieved from https://globalarbitrationreview.com/chapter/1151372/income-approach-and-the-discounted-cash-flow-methodology

eFinancial Models. (2016). *Discounted cash flow model.* Retrieved from https://www.efinancialmodels.com/2016/12/28/dcf-model-calculating-discounted-cash-flows/

Fama, E. F., & French, K. R. (1988). Dividend yields and expected stock returns. *Journal of Financial Economics*, 22.

Fama, E. F., & French, K. R. (1992). The Cross-Section of Expected Returns. *The Journal of Finance*, 47.

Fernandez, P. (2013). WACC: definition, misconceptions and errors, IESE Business School, University of Navarra, November.

Motley Fool, Foolish Fundamentals: Free Cash Flow.

Value-Based Management.net. (n.d.). Earnings before interest, taxes, depreciation and amortization.

Mills, J., Bible, L., & Mason, R. (2002). Defining free cash flow. *The CPA Journal.*

Russell, P. J. (2007). Valuation of imaging centers: alternative methods and detailed description of the discounted cash flow approach. *Journal of the American College of Radiology*, *4*(1), 53–64. doi:10.1016/j.jacr.2006.08.019 PMID:17412225

Tarter, J. (n.d.). EBITA a useful cash-flow tool, but no substitute for good judgment. Federal Reserve Bank of Cleveland. *Supervision & Regulation Department.*

Zörgiebel, S. (2016). Valuation of IPOs with negative earnings, Goethe University Frankfurt. doi:10.2139srn.2698281

Chapter 5
Challenges in Estimation of Beta:
Market Models Used for Risk Estimation

Tarana Azimova
https://orcid.org/0000-0001-6951-5844
Nisantasi University, Turkey

ABSTRACT

Capital asset pricing model (CAPM) brings deep intuitive understanding of the relationship between expected return and risk. Unfortunately, the empirical record of the CAPM has not been satisfactory since its commencement. The empirical testing of CAPM is void in most cases due to the use of an inefficient index as a proxy for market portfolio. Plausible tests require a well-diversified market portfolio which so far has been unfeasible to obtain. Lack of validity in empirical records has been caused by complexity in exerting valid estimations of the beta coefficient. This chapter judges which of the indices provides investors the best beta forecast and questions which time period should be selected for beta calculation. This chapter reveals that the choice of return intervals causes variations in beta estimation of the security. Applying higher frequency has an advantage in that it increases the number of observations, but a shortfall is that beta tends to have substantial bias with shorter return intervals used.

INTRODUCTION

To present date, the CAPM remains one of the most popular models in finance, the model is straightforward and uses only one factor yet powerful and widely applicable. The CAPM builds on Harry Markowitz's earlier work on modern portfolio theory and was introduced by William Sharpe (Markowitz, 1952). The CAPM shows a linear expected return-risk relationship that exactly defines the expected return given the systematic risk of a security. In doing so the CAPM makes the conversion from total risk to systematic risk, the main determinant of expected return.

DOI: 10.4018/978-1-7998-1086-5.ch005

The model affirms that the expected return of securities changes only by their systematic risk which is represented by beta (Fama & French, 2004). According to the CAPM, investors should create a portfolio which is a combination of the market portfolio and the risk-free asset. The model is not only essential from a conceptual perspective but is also applied broadly in practice (Brown & Walter, 2013). Investors use the model's expected rate of return to calculate the value of assets such as bonds, stocks, mortgages and other similar assets. Businesses on the other hand use the required rate of return obtained from the CAPM in capital budgeting for evaluating economic feasibility of the projects and decision-making processes. Moreover, investors use different ratios such as Sharpe ratio, Treynor ratio and Jensen's alpha that are derived from the CAPM to measure the performance of mutual fund managers, pension fund managers and institutional money managers (Jensen, 1968; Jensen, 1972).

Even though the CAPM is a model that simplifies an intricate investment environment by introducing the relationship between security's risk and return, unfortunately the empirical record of the CAPM has not been satisfactory ever since its commencement (Johnstone, 2013; Merton, 1973). In addition, the model is subject to theoretical limitations. Theoretical constraints that are intrinsic in the structure of the model are as follows:

- A number of unrealistic assumptions about investors: investors are risk-averse, utility maximizing, rational individuals and investors are price takers; about markets: markets are frictionless, including no taxes and no transaction costs; about holding period: investors plan for the same single holding period; about investors beliefs: investors have homogeneous beliefs or expectations; about investments: all investments are indefinitely divisible. These assumptions mean that all investors give the same value to all securities therefore all investors will choose the same optimal risk portfolio, which is the market portfolio.
- Limited number of investment characteristics such as systematic risk of the asset.
- Application of the model for one period only. A single-period model is incapable to encompass parameters that change over time.

Empirical concerns in CAPM implementation can be summarized as follows:

- Using a market portfolio that includes all assets existing in the economy. The market portfolio however is not yet observable.
- The empirical testing of CAPM is void in most cases due to the use of inefficient index as a proxy for market portfolio opposite to what the hypothesis put forward that the benchmark should be efficient. Plausible tests require well diversified benchmark that is the world market portfolio which has been unfeasible to obtain so far. In fact, the theory suggests that the CAPM is not testable unless we can find out the precise composition of the market portfolio.
- In addition, lack of validity in empirical records has been caused by complexity in exerting valid estimations of the beta coefficient.

Our objective in this reading is to identify and discuss the main challenges that analysts and investors face while estimating beta. The foundation of this reading is to define beta that would maintain an exact fit between the data and econometric model. Based on the theoretical and practical applications our aim is to obtain the beta for a plausible comparison that could also be used to reflect future investment decisions.

BACKGROUND

To construct a diversified portfolio, an investor will put together various securities listed in the market. Any investor aims to reach an optimum portfolio, therefore the process of adding new assets can continue by following the impact on the portfolio's risk and return. The process lasts until addition of another security doesn't have substantial impact on portfolio performance. We have to estimate the return and risk level of a portfolio in order to understand whether including additional asset influence an overall portfolio performance. We estimate the return a portfolio by applying risk-generating models. On the other hand, for individual assets, the investors are mostly interested in the systematic risk, because the market pays off for non-diversifiable risk only, which is beta.

The notion of beta to evaluate risk is a main component of Modern Portfolio Theory. The beta that is used in various risk and return models has two distinctive features. Firstly, beta defines a risk appended to the diversified portfolio. Therefore, there is a great probability that an asset is categorized as low risk in terms of market portfolio risk and high risk in terms of individual investment. Secondly, beta of an asset is determined by regressing the returns against the market portfolio, over a time span. Therefore, all betas have a tendency to move toward market portfolio and thus standardize around one. We are able to estimate a realized return by applying the single-index model as following:

$$R_i = (1-\beta_i)R_f + \beta_i R_m + e_i \quad (1)$$

We can further rewrite the equation by taking the covariance of both sides as follows:

$$Cov(R_i, R_m) = Cov(\beta_i \times R_m + e_i, R_m) \quad (2)$$

$$Cov(R_i, R_m) = \beta_i Cov(R_m, R_m) + Cov(e_i, R_m) \quad (3)$$

$$Cov\left(R_i, R_m\right) = \beta_i \sigma_m^2 + 0 \quad (4)$$

The first term in this equation is beta multiplied by the variance of market returns. The second term is the error term; because the error term is not correlated with the market we are able to further omit it. We can solve the formula in terms of beta as follows:

$$\beta_{i,} = \frac{Cov\left(R_i, R_m\right)}{\sigma_m^2} = \frac{corr_{i,m}\sigma_i\sigma_m}{\sigma_m^2} = \frac{corr_{i,m}\sigma_i}{\sigma_m} \quad (5)$$

The beta is calculated as the covariance of the return on an individual security and the market return divided by the variance of the return on the market. The term is equivalent to the product of the security's correlation with the market divided by the standard deviation of the market return. This equation shows an important result that is if the correlation between a security and the market increases then the systematic risk of the asset would also increase. For example, if the correlation between a security and the market is 0.80 and a security and market have standard deviations of return of 0.20 and 0.10, respectively, the assets beta would be (0.80) (0.20)/0.10=1.6. On the other hand, if the correlation is 0.90, then beta of the asset would be (0.90) (0.20)/0.10=1.8.

It can be seen from the equation, that beta is a measure of how responsive a security's return is to the overall market. Therefore, beta captures a security's risk that cannot be eliminated through diversification or asset's systematic risk. We generally use historical returns to measure variances and correlations needed for the calculation of beta. A positive beta shows that the security's return follows the market, or moves in the same direction with the market portfolio. On the other hand, a negative beta indicates that the security's return follows a trend that is reverse to that of the market or moves in the opposite direction to the market. We can estimate the beta of the market portfolio by replacing σ_m for σ_i in the numerator. Because the correlation of the market portfolio with itself is one, the beta of the market can be measured as follows:

$$\beta_{i,} = \frac{corr_{i,m}\sigma_i}{\sigma_m} = \frac{corr_{m,m}\sigma_m}{\sigma_m} = 1 \tag{6}$$

The beta of the market portfolio equals to one, therefore the average beta of securities in the market is one. Any non-market return generating assets by definition has zero risk. The beta of the risk free asset equals to zero, for example a short-term government bill has zero risk, therefore its beta equals to zero. The risk free asset has no correlation with the market. Most assets, for both developing and developed countries tend to be highly correlated with the market portfolio. The correlation coefficients between different stock pairs are also high, indicating that the different industries have identical responses to the similar economic and market movements. As a result, finding an asset that will be negatively correlated and that will serve as insurance to overall portfolio is not quite common. The table 1 shows correlations between different pair stocks of Turkish companies with the market. For Turkish economy ISE 100 index (Istanbul Stock Exchange) serves as a proxy for market portfolio and includes 100 biggest companies.

The data shows that correlations coefficients are generally positive and high. Most of the assets in our sample except for Kartonsan Karton Sanayi and Ticaret Company display high correlation with market portfolio (ISE 100).

We can also estimate beta by using a more practical approach which is the market model. The market model is measured by applying regression analysis:

$$R_i = \propto_i + \beta_i R_m + e_i \tag{7}$$

Table 1. Correlations between different pair stocks and ISE 100

Company	Correlation
Akbank	0.943
Aselsan	0.721
Cemas	0.364
KartonsanKartonSanayiveTicaret	-0.383
Turk HavaYolları	0.475
Vestel	0.742

Figure 1. Security Characteristic Market Line, Beta Estimations Using a Market Returns and Asset's Return

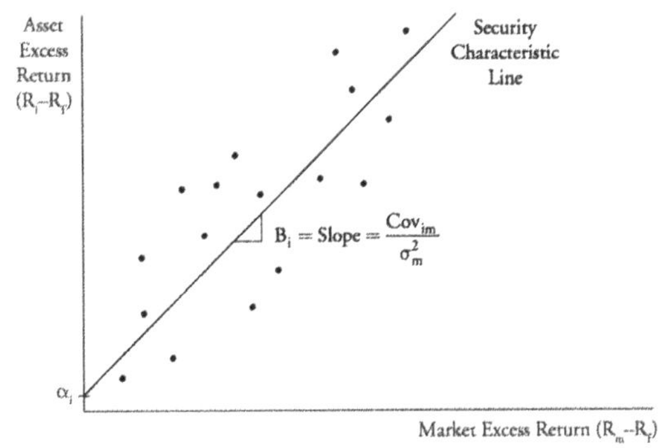

Regression analysis is a statistical technique that measures the relationship between the dependent variable and independent variable or variables. In beta estimations we use raw security return and raw market return figures for measuring the two parameters $\propto_i$ andβ_i. Regression analysis is analogous to plotting all connecting points of the market return and the security's return (R_m, R_i) and the designing a line through all points such that it lessens the sum of squared linear deviations from the line. The Figure 1 shows the market model and the two parameters of the regression model, $\propto_i$ which the intercept term and β_i which is the slope term. The line that is obtained from the market model and used to estimate the beta coefficient is called the security characteristic line (SCL).

The SCL is a straight line that shows the excess return of the asset on the excess return on the market portfolio.

The security market line applies to all individual assets in the market. On the other hand, the security market line also applies to a portfolio. Consider a portfolio consisting of two assets, with certain weights in it such as w_1 and w_2. We can write the return for the portfolio as follows:

$$R_p = w_1R_1 + w_2R_2 \tag{8}$$

The returns on the two assets can be stated as follows:

$$ER_1 = R_f + \beta_1(ER_m - R_f) \tag{9}$$

$$ER_2 = R_f + \beta_2(ER_m - R_f) \tag{10}$$

By substituting the returns into the return for the portfolio equation we get the extended formula for expected return of a portfolio for two securities.

$$ER_p = w_1ER_1 + w_2ER_2 = w_1\left(R_f + \beta_1\left(ER_m - R_f\right)\right) + w_2\left(R_f + \beta_2\left(ER_m - R_f\right)\right) \tag{11}$$

$$ER_p = R_f + \left(w_1\beta_1 + w_2\beta_2\right)\left(ER_m - R_f\right) \tag{12}$$

From this equation we can conclude that the beta of the portfolio is a weighted average of all security's betas.

$$\beta_p = \sum_{i=1}^{n} w_i \beta_i \quad (13)$$

where $\sum_{i=1}^{n} w_i = 1$

Example:

If the investor puts 30 percent of her funds in the government bill, 20 percent in the ISE 100 and 50 percent in Aselsan Company that has a beta of 0.69. Given the risk-free rate of 8 percent and the market return of 18 percent, what are the portfolio's systematic risk and expected return?

Solutions:

The beta of the government bill is zero, the beta of the ISE 100 is one and the beta of Aselsan Company is 0.69.

The beta of a portfolio is:

$$\beta_p = w_1\beta_1 + w_2\beta_2 + w_3\beta_3 = 0.30 \times 0.0 + 0.20 \times 1 + 0.50 \times 0.69 = 0.545$$

The return of the portfolio given by the CAPM equals

$$ER_p = R_f + \beta(ER_m - R_f)$$

This formula exhibit that there is a positive relationship between the expected return of a portfolio and the systematic risk of the portfolio estimated by β_P.

$$ER_p = 0.04 + 0.545 \times (0.18 - 0.08) = 0.0945 = \%9.45$$

MAIN FOCUS OF THE CHAPTER

Issues, Controversies, Problems

The notion of beta to evaluate risk is a main component of Modern Portfolio Theory. The beta that is used in various risk and return models has two distinctive features. Firstly, beta defines a risk appended to the diversified portfolio. Therefore, there is a great probability that an asset is categorized as low risk in terms of market portfolio risk and high risk in terms of individual investment. Secondly, beta of an asset is determined by regressing the returns against the market portfolio, over a time span. This study aims to show challenges in beta estimation and define beta that would maintain an exact fit between the data and econometric model.

Selection of a Market Portfolio

A market portfolio is a hypothetical bundle of investments that involve every type of asset existing in the world financial market. Individual assets included in a portfolio weighted in proportion to its total value in the market, characterized by its market capitalization. The expected return of a market as a whole is therefore identical to the expected return of a market portfolio. Because the market portfolio includes all assets it is completely diversified by nature, eliminating all kind of unsystematic risk and is therefore subject to systematic risk only. Since commencement of the capital market model economists arguing intensely on possibility of creating truly diversified portfolio in practice that contain not only any kind financial assets but also commodities, collectibles and essentially any asset that has a price and salable (Roll, 1977; Adler & Dumas, 1983).

The market portfolio is a primary element of the capital market model (CAPM). However, in real financial world, there are no comprehensive benchmarks that can represent the market portfolio. In practice, analysts use fixed income market indices and equity market indices as a proxy for market portfolio. Benchmarking an a fixed-income or equity is comparatively straightforward. Market indices include only listed securities and represent each market separately. For instance, S&P 500 is a commonly used index to measure beta for US companies, but it includes only 500 equities of the thousands of equities existing in the US financial market. In developing countries, the indices tend to be even narrower and contain only a number of large companies. S&P U.S. aggregate bond index is a widely used index to calculate the performance of publicly issued U.S. dollar denominated bond. This contains government treasuries, corporate, residential mortgages, taxable municipal binds etc.

Can a selection of a market portfolio make a distinction? The table below provides a summary of betas calculated for Aselsan Company, using three different indices. The data provided in the table 2 is obtained from investing.com as of April 1 2019.

The statistical data shows that the choice of the market portfolio doesn't have significant impact on beta estimations for a company. This can be explained by the fact that in developing countries, the indices tend to be constricted including only limited number of securities. As a result, moving from one index to another doesn't cause greater variability of systematic risk as it can be in the case of developed market's indices which include greater number of assets.

In terms of making a judgment as to which of indices provides the most accurate beta measurement, Damodaran (2010) suggests passing it through the "market portfolio" test. Because market portfolio is broad and represent an entire market, indices that hold greater number of assets will provide more accurate estimates compared to indices that include less. Thus, justification for the use of the ISE 100 (Istanbul Stock Exchange) by all analysts becomes obvious. The ISE 100 is a market-capitalization-weighted and a broad index and includes 100 largest companies operating in Turkey.

Table 2.

Index Used	Beta Estimated
BIST 100	0.69
BIST 50	0.69
BIST 30	0.69

On the other hand, the use of the right index depends on the type of marginal investor. If marginal investor is in Turkey, it is logical to use a well-diversified Turkish index, which is ISE 100. However, if the marginal investor is an overseas investor, a more appropriate measure of market portfolio will be usage of the multi-market indices. There are market indices that designed to represent different security markets simultaneously. Multi-market indices are of great significance to investors who follow a global approach to equity investing without any bias toward a particular geographic region. In case of multi-market indices, index providers weight the assets within each country by market capitalization weights and then weight individual country in the world index in proportion to its relative gross domestic product (GDP). Over time the number of global investors can increase outweighing the number of local investors. This rationale can be explained by the fact that single Aselsan Company's security will be less risky to a global investor who possesses a multi-market portfolio than to an investor in Turkey with all of her wealth in Turkish securities.

The companies increasingly spread their operations across multiple countries and regions. Their exposure to risk will therefore be determined by political and economic situations in their home countries as well as beyond their home countries. The table 3 shows a global index that is widely used by overseas investors. MSCI ACWI provides two basic indices for both developing and emerging countries in different geographic regions. The index is constructed applying MSCI's Global Investable Market Index (GIMI) methodology, which is designed to take into consideration fluctuations reflecting conditions across regions, market fields and market-cap segments. The MSCI ACWI market coverage classifies indices into MSCI World Index and MSCI Emerging Market Index. The two indices categorize countries based on two dimensions: on economic development and geographic region.

The figure 2 shows variations on global indices for the time period between 2003 to 2018. The figure indicates that a co-movement or correlation pattern of the global indices gross returns has increased over time. In fact, during 2008 financial crisis the set of global indices declined in unison. An important conclusion is that although overseas investment expansion generally diminishes the risk significantly, it doesn't necessarily provide the same level of risk reduction during times of economic crises.

Table 3. MSCI ACWI Index

MSCI WORLD INDEX			MSCI EMERGİNG MARKETS INDEX		
Americas	Europe and Middle East	Pacific	Americas	Europe, Middle East and Africa	Asia
Canada United States	Austria Belgium Denmark Finland France Germany Ireland Israel Italy Netherlands Norway Portugal Spain Sweden Switzerland United Kingdom	Australia Hong Kong Japan New Zeeland Singapore	Brazil Chile Colombia Mexico Peru	Czech Republic Egypt Greece Hungary Poland Qatar Russia South Africa Turkey United Arab Emirates	China India Indonesia Korea Malaysia Pakistan Philippines Taiwan Thailand

Source: MSCI Barra (https://www.msci.com/acwi)

Figure 2. MSCI Emerging and Developed Markets Index Performance Chart (Gross Return) in USD

Source: MSCI Barra (https://www.msci.com/acwi)

Figure 3. MSCI Emerging Markets Index Country Allocation

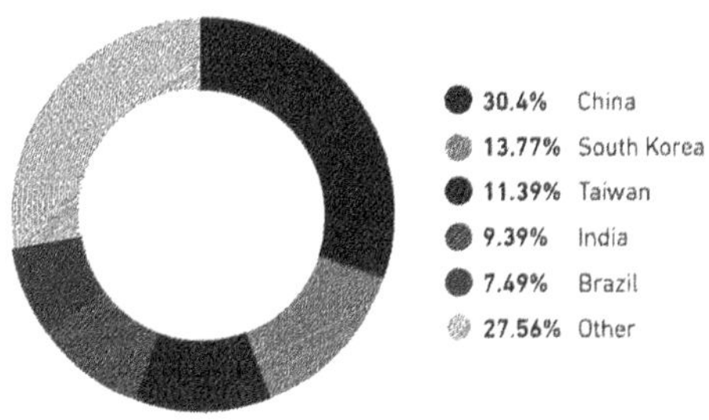

Source: MSCI Barra (https://www.msci.com/acwi)

MSCI Emerging Markets Index weights the assets within each country by market capitalization and then weights the individual country in the world index in proportion to its relative gross domestic product (GDP). Thus, the rationale for the biggest proportion of weight in the index allocated to China becomes clear. China is currently the world second biggest GDP country in nominal terms.

Choice of a Return Interval

Selection of data frequency is another significant choice that can influence systematic risk calculations. Depending on the periodicity of returns, matching susceptibility to price variations is a key point for selecting the appropriate investment. Despite to the availability of an abundant academic literature, there is no consensus with regard to data frequency that should be applied in beta calculations. Historical return frequencies are presented in different time intervals such as annually, quarterly, semiannually, monthly, weekly, and daily. Moreover, return frequencies for intra-day transactions can be as short as fifteen minutes.

Can a selection of data frequency make a difference for beta calculations? Using the example of Aselsan Company, we estimate beta for different return intervals. We calculate beta using shorter return intervals such as daily, weekly return data and longer return data such as monthly and yearly. The table 4 demonstrates the systematic risk estimations for the time period from 2009 to 2018.

Table 4. Beta estimated using different return intervals

Return periodicity used	Systematic Risk Estimated
Daily	0.72
Weekly	0.67
Monthly	0.69
Yearly	0.75

These calculations show that the choice of return intervals causes variations in beta estimation of the security of Aselsan Company. Applying higher frequency has an advantage in that it increases the number of observations in the regression analysis; however, it does come with a shortage as well. That is, betas tend to have substantial bias with shorter return intervals used. This can be explained by the fact that assets do not trade on a regular basis and performing calculation on a time interval when assets are not traded lead to deviations in calculations of beta.

Moreover, using high frequency stock return data such as daily and weekly in measuring the systematic risk of a company often causes considerable distortions. The distortions occur due to the presence of microstructure noise in the market which is the lag of the observed price to the underlying price due to the frictions in the market (Borch, 1969).

The noise in the time series can be reduced in one of two ways: firstly, by using longer return intervals of the time series such as annual. On the other hand, longer investment horizons are generally not affected by the noise, but can be affected by the trend in the time series. Another potential shortcoming that can arise here is the scarcity of financial data of the companies. Data scarcity has emerged as one of the major difficulties in beta calculations of the companies. Some companies simply don't possess quality input data while other companies are listed for only short period of time.

Alternatively, we can measure the systematic risk using short return interval returns, and then modify these parameters for the extent of the non-trading. As a result of distinct selections in time intervals and time periods, different professional beta estimation services often end up with various systematic risk parameters for the same company. Therefore, to approximate these values the services apply simple tools such as adjusting company's regression betas towards one. For example, one of the most common techniques used by professional service companies is the tool developed by Bloomberg. This technique is quite simple in terms that it only uses the historical beta, market beta and certain weights attributed to both raw beta and market beta.

The justification can be traced to researches that point out that, there is a trend on the part of betas of all companies to incline towards one, over time. This result squares up with common logic. Because the companies that continue their operations in the market tend to grow over time. The growth of the companies will push their systematic risk toward the average beta of an overall market. We describe this technique in more details in the following sections.

Choice of a Time Period

The choice of a time frame is very important determinant of beta estimation. Studies and professional beta estimators question which time period should be selected for systematic risk calculation (Klemkosky & Martin, 1975). The main objective is to obtain the best time frame used in beta estimations for a plausible comparison that could also be used to reflect future investment decisions.

Table 5. Beta estimations for Aselsan Company with time frames

Time Period	Beta Measured
2 years	0.778
4 years	0.703
7 years	0.740

What is the optimum period to use in calculation systematic risk? The risk and return models don't explicitly state the time frame that the investor should use to calculate beta. Moreover, risk and return models doesn't even provide a point of reference with regard to the timeframe an investor needs to use to measure systematic risk and as described by the quote below, this condition does not make difference among professional service companies.

A commercial provider of betas once told the authors that his firm, and others, did not know what the right period was, but they all decided to use five years in order to reduce the apparent differences between various services' betas, because large differences reduced everyone's credibility! (Brigham & Gapenski, 1997)

We estimate betas of Aselsan Company using daily prices for periods ranging from 2 years to 7 years and compare them. We compute daily returns based on straightforward holding period rates of return between days. Following table provides systematic risk calculations based on the different timeframes.

The beta estimations for Aselsan Company show that the choice of time period makes insignificant difference in systematic risk estimation. The time period of 4 years corresponds to beta of 0.703 which is close to the beta estimated by professional service companies. The systematic risk data for Aselsan Company obtained from investing.com as of April 1 2019 equals to 0.69.

Professional beta providers use periods ranging from one year to five years, with different beta outputs. In general, greater number of observations is required for more reliable regression output. Using granular daily or weekly returns increase the number of observations but may give rise to time variation bias in systematic risk estimations. Thus to reach a tradeoff, the time period should be selected for each company, taking into consideration the firm's characteristics. In fact, beta calculations can be quite sensitive to changes in time periods, because the companies change over time. Most of the studies apply periods ranging from six months to five years. Companies experience change over time in terms of economic texture, capital structure and business mix:

- The companies are influenced by changes in economic conjecture. That is the companies adjust their businesses to reflect shifts in macroeconomic parameters such as interest rates or exchange rates which will change their beta.
- The companies can change their business mix and invest in new business areas which can involve company purchases. In the process of expanding their businesses they change their business structures, which will change their beta.
- On the other hand, the firms can shrink their business mix through divesting their current business textures that will change beta.

- Moreover, the companies can also change capital structure, by rolling over or adding debt. Actions such as split ups, bond or equity calls and dividend payments will also influence the capital mix leading to changes in beta.

These changes can cause beta to change substantially over short time span, let alone for future periods. For instance, consider the company which has remained relatively stable for let's say 3 years and then the company has undergone major changes for the last 5 years. We should measure systematic risk for the time frame of 3 years and 5 years separately. As a result, we should investigate the company and use estimation periods for beta calculations based on the changes of the company's operations. We can fulfill this process by asking the following questions:

- Is the time frame used to calculate systematic risk taking into account as representative of the moderate range of volatility of macroeconomic parameters?
- Is the company's operation leverage and financial leverage being representative of company's current and future leverage? (Bhandari,1988).
- Is the firm operating in the similar or same market segments?
- Is the growth rate or growth rate expectation being consistent?
- Are there any significant firm-specific or industry-specific events that affect the firm's operations?

In overall, in beta calculation an investor should not only consider the statistical approach which itself has certain assumptions and limitations but also should focus on firm operations and its variability over time. As a result, raw betas are not reliable unless calculated using methods that adjust beta combining both statistical modeling, company or industry specific and macroeconomic events. The process of modifying and adjusting the beta to fit the current state of the firm can significantly decrease the standard error and lead to a more precise systematic risk calculation.

Decomposition of Total Risk for a Return Generating Models

While calculating beta in practice another problem arises with this apportionment. With the introduction of risk and return models, we break down total risk into systematic and non-systematic variances. The total variance is therefore equal to the sum of systematic and nonsystematic variances. For a single index model, therefore the variance of historical returns can be shown with the following equations:

$$R_i = (1 - \beta_i)R_f + \beta_i \times R_m + e_i \quad (14)$$

The systematic risk, by definition, depends on the correlation between the security and the market. We can show the folmula by referring to covariance between R_i and R_m.

$$Cov(R_i,R_m) = Cov(\beta_i \times R_m + e_i,R_m) \quad (15)$$

$$Cov(R_i,R_m) = \beta_i Cov(R_m,R_m) + Cov(e_i,R_m) \quad (16)$$

$$Cov\left(R_i, R_m\right) = \beta_i \sigma_m^2 + 0 \quad (17)$$

Or

$$\sigma_i^2 = \beta_i^2\sigma_m^2 + \sigma_e^2 + 2Cov\left(R_m, e_i\right) \tag{18}$$

We are able to eliminate the covariance term in this formula because, by definition, any kind of non-market parameter or return is not correlated with the market. Therefore, we can break down total risk into systematic and non-systematic risks as follows:

$$\sigma_i^2 = \beta_i^2\sigma_m^2 + \sigma_e^2 \tag{19}$$

Total variance can be shown as follows:

$$\sigma_i = \sqrt{\beta_i^2\sigma_m^2 + \sigma_e^2} \tag{20}$$

For well-diversified portfolios, such as market portfolio, non-systematic risk equals to zero. Thus, the total variance of a market portfolio and other well-diversified portfolios consist of systematic risk only, which is $\beta_i\sigma_m$.

We can further simplify the formula above in terms of beta as follows:

$$\beta_{i,} = \frac{Cov\left(R_i, R_m\right)}{\sigma_m^2} = \frac{corr_{i,m}\sigma_i\sigma_m}{\sigma_m^2} = \frac{corr_{i,m}\sigma_i}{\sigma_m} \tag{21}$$

All financial assets normally include both systematic and nonsystematic variances. While making investment decisions, investors generally prefer those assets that contain a large portion of nonsystematic risk and insignificant amount of systematic risk. This is due to the fact that once investor has bought the assets with a large amount of nonsystematic risk; they would reduce the risk, through adding other assets that are not highly correlated with the assets in a portfolio. This process minimizes nonsystematic risk and ultimately remove it altogether from the portfolio. Because all investors have incentive to accept more of diversifiable risk, the demand for nonsystematic risk keeps increasing until its expected return falls to zero. This means that in the efficient markets investors are compensated for systematic risk only. Because no incremental compensation can be earned for undertaking diversifiable risk investors try to eliminate nonsystematic risk from their portfolios. By investing in different industries, different regions and various asset classes' investors offset poor return movements, thereby reducing the total risk of the portfolio. Theil (1971) initially show a single index model with the following equation:

$$r_{it} = \alpha_i + b_i r_{mt} + w_{it} \text{ for } t=1, 2,\ldots,n \tag{22}$$

According to Theil (1971), the third term in this equation comprises the error term, the beta coefficient and mean beta coefficient for an individual security.

$$w_{it} = (b_{it} - b_i)r_{mt} + e_{it} \text{ and } E(w_{it}) = 0 \tag{23}$$

The last term in the equation can be shown with the following equation:

b_{it} beta coefficient for an individual security in a given period t
b_i mean beta coefficient for an individual security, which equals to E(bit) over n different periods.

The systematic risk in the return-generating models changes randomly from period to period and around the mean beta parameter, b_i. We are able to take the variances of both sides of equation and decompose total variance into diversifiable and non-diversifiable variances with the equation below:

$$var(w_{it}) = var(b_{it})var(r_{mt}) + var(e_{it}) \tag{24}$$

The first term is the variance of the security's beta around the mean beta for each period. The greater the volatility of the first term, the greater the variation in b_{it} beta coefficient for an individual security will be from period to period. We can justify the common assumption of stability of a beta coefficient over a certain period of time if the beta's variance is very small. However, empirical investigation shows that the beta varies significantly from period to period. Fabozzi and Francis (1978) examined 700 stocks listed in the New York stock exchange and concluded that for the most stocks' betas varies from period to period rather than remain constant as the ordinary least squares model assumes. The study, therefore suggest that the equation is econometrically flawed if the beta is a random parameter.

$$var\left(r_{it}\right) = b_i^2 var\left(r_{mt}\right) + var\left(e_{it}\right) \tag{25}$$

Solving the formula (24) for $var(e_{it})$ and substituting this residual variance into formula (25) results in the following equation:

$$var\left(r_{it}\right) = b_i^2 var\left(r_{mt}\right) + \left(var\left(w_{it}\right) - var\left(b_{it}\right) var\left(r_{mt}\right)\right) \tag{26}$$

According to Fabozzi and Francis (1978) if $var(b_{it})$ is other than zero, decomposition of the total risk will be confounded with noise from the random movement of beta coefficient. In other words, it is not possible to measure empirically individual effects of diversifiable and non–diversifiable risk in the estimation of the prices of market securities. This result therefore undermines too many empirical investigations. Besides confounding the risk decomposition, variations in beta coefficients can make the residual errors from the ordinary least squares model heteroscedastic. The authors demonstrate these changes by restating the following equation in terms of the error term

$$w_{it} = (b_{it} - b_i)r_{mt} + e_{it} \text{ and } E(w_{it})=0 \tag{27}$$

$$e_{it} = w_{it} + (b_{it} - b_i)r_{mt} \tag{28}$$

That is if the beta moves randomly the second term, will be other than zero, and will be added to diversifiable variance term w_{it}. Consequently, the residual will sum systematic and nonsystematic variances and will be heteroscedastic due to changes in beta coefficient. Heteroscedasticity diminishes the efficiency of the ordinary least squares model result.

Systematic and nonsystematic variances are closely interrelated in one security, partitioning the total risk into systematic and unsystematic will be bewildered with deviations in beta. Since separating the risk is biased with the increase in the standard error empirical estimations of the individual effects of market risk will be very challenging if not impossible. Consequently, if changing in beta coefficient has been ignored, the econometric interpretation of beta coefficients using historical data results into deviations. To cope with the possible fallacious results, professional beta estimating companies generally apply models to form adjustments for changing in beta and use this beta to estimate the expected risk for the security.

Standard Beta Estimations

Generally accepted way of calculating beta is using ordinary least squares regression (OLS). The slope resulting from the OLS can be shown as

$$\beta = \frac{corr\sigma_i}{\sigma_m} \tag{29}$$

where the σ_i and σ_m are the standard deviations of the security and market rate of returns respectively. This way of beta calculation is generally referred as standard beta or theoretical beta. An important assumption used in this technique is that the market portfolio return doesn't contain any error term. Because analysts don't really use the market portfolio and use the market index as the proxy for the market, there will be error term present in estimation. Possible error term in the proxy measurement is characterized by unpriced variation and residual risk. The error term therefore captures the noise and random behavior of the market index returns'. This risk exists even in a well-diversified global portfolio. In a well-diversified global portfolio, the error term includes alteration from country weights.

We shall refer to this as the benchmark errors or variables errors. In any period, noise and random variation of dependent variable can make it difficult to model the factors that drive returns. This problem doesn't diminish though by selecting indexes with greater number of assets. As the matter of fact, Roll's (1977) states that the CAPM is not testable unless the correct constitution of the market portfolio is known. While there are statistical tools for tracking an error term in independent variable, we need the variance of the error term which is not known.

SOLUTIONS AND RECOMMENDATIONS: A WAY FORWARD

Defining betas is significant and the central focus of the finance. Even though there are an obvious set of methods or practices that can be used in beta calculations we have seen that traditional approaches have shortcomings. That is beta estimated purely on historical data is unadjusted risk estimator. These betas are not sound indicator of the future. In the literature this situation referred to as beta instability problem.

To overcome these deficiencies, professional services generally apply models to form an adjustment estimation for the historical beta and use this beta to estimate the expected risk for the security. Historical beta, also known as raw beta is based on the historical relationship between the security's return and the index return. The modified beta is a prediction of a security's future beta. The modified beta is firstly derived from raw beta, but adjusted by the assumption that an asset's real beta over time will move towards the market beta, of one.

The generalized equation for modified beta can be shown as below:

$$\beta = w_1\beta_m + w_2\beta_{i;t-1} \tag{30}$$

where, $w_1 + w_2 = 1$

Because betas tend to converge back to the average of market beta, the modified beta will move toward one. One important conclusion that can be drawn here is that if the historical beta is less that one, then the modified beta will be higher than unmodified beta and closer to 1. To illustrate, professional service such as Bloomberg calculate a modified beta by using fairly simple technique:

Adjusted Beta, $B = B_{i,t-1}(0.67) + 1.00\ (0.33)$

Most other analysts use analogues methods, with little differences in the weights attributed to each parameter. An important question that arise within this concept as why adjust betas toward one. The justification can be traced to researches that point out that, there is a propensity on the part of betas of all firms to converge towards one, over time. This result squares up with common logic. Companies that survive in the market are inclined to grow over time. The companies will grow in size over time to reach their objectives, including increasing sales, possessing assets in place, increasing cash flows and maximizing their profits. The companies can increase their market shares through external expansion such as mergers or acquisitions. All these progresses should push betas toward the market average of one.

The analytical tool for beta estimation applied by the professional services brings about certain clarification to the overall model. The main advantage of using the modified beta technique is the simplicity in application of this method. Because the simplicity is highly desirable feature of any tool, this technique is quite widespread among analysts.

Professional estimation services adopt far more sophisticated adjustments to bring about the understanding of the how major components can be used together to increase the quality of estimations of systematic risk. In order to provide the best estimations analysts, modify regression betas based on the firm's current fundamental position. That is financial fundamentals such as income statement, balance sheet and cash flows can serve as important predictors of systematic risk. For example, cyclicality of revenues is an important predictor of beta. The earnings of some firms change with the business cycles. The company's earnings increase during the expansion of the business cycle and decrease during its contraction. Financial assets with highly cyclical revenues have high betas. On the other hand, the change in income statement parameters such as the earnings before interest and taxes is also a good predictor of the systematic risk. Because variable costs vary in direct proportion with sales figure, volatility in earnings before interest and tax is mainly induced by fixed costs. High variability in fixed costs is predictive of high systematic risk. High dividend payout is generally predictive of low beta, however high interest payout on debt which is considered as fixed payment irrespective of company's earnings is predictive of high systematic risk. The companies can change their business models through external acquisitions, investing in new businesses and new markets. The combination of different types of business activities that an individual company engaged in can significantly change over time, leading to even more complex business mix and sophisticated financial structures. On the other hand, firms' degree of financial leverage can change over time. The companies change their financial leverage by rolling over or issuing debt. Actions such as bond calls, dividend payments and changes in the market-value of debt will also change the financial structure. A large variability of the degree of company's dissemination among industries and markets will change the companies' beta. Therefore, a dynamic approach to implementation of constant weights over longer period of time can increase the accuracy of estimations.

FUTURE RESEARCH DIRECTIONS

The shortage of formal statistical methods to test the presence of error term and to solve other complex problems of the model discussed earlier in this chapter is presently a significant drawback. Therefore, further research should focus on developing appropriate statistical tools. On the other hand, beta predictive and estimating tools and practices should be developed on an individual company basis, reflecting the firm's fundamentals.

CONCLUSION

Forecasting betas is major and the central focus of the finance. Even though there are an obvious set of methods or practices that can be used in beta calculations we have observed that traditional tools have shortcomings. That is beta estimated purely on historical data is unadjusted risk estimator. These betas are not sound indicator of the future. This situation referred to as beta instability problem.

Researchers have made a number of attempts to provide superior predictors of future betas and conducted studies examining the determinants of betas (Abell & Krueger, 1989; Bornholt 2013). Most researchers demonstrate that fundamental information about a company can be used together with raw beta estimates to provide more accurate predictors of future betas (Bowman, 1979). Empirical results from these investigations indicate on a relationship between beta and fundamental variables such as asset size, dividend payout ratio, liquidity, standard deviation in percentage change in operating income over some time period, market capitalization etc. Once target variables have been identified and model data requirements have been met, the modified systematic model can be accurately measured and precisely forecasted. At each successive analytical stage, this technique can be updated and generalized to calculate adjusted betas for all companies operating in economy. Even though the beta in capital asset pricing model doesn't reveal the returns adequately and the model itself has limitations and in overall ineffective in asset's returns modeling the CAPM is still widely applied in the practice. The recently developed techniques still based on a raw beta which is estimated using the CAPM.

REFERENCES

Abell, J., & Krueger, T. (1989). Macroeconomic influences on beta. *Journal of Economics and Business, 41*(2), 185–193. doi:10.1016/0148-6195(89)90016-7

Adler, M., & Dumas, B. (1983). International portfolio choice and corporation finance: A synthesis. *The Journal of Finance, 38*(3), 925–984. doi:10.1111/j.1540-6261.1983.tb02511.x

Aswath, D. (2010). *Estimating risk parameters*. Stern School of Business.

Bhandari, L. (1988). Debt/equity ratio and expected common stock returns: empirical evidence. *The Journal of Finance, 43*(2), 507–528. doi:10.1111/j.1540-6261.1988.tb03952.x

Borch, K. (1969). A note on uncertainty and indifference curves. *The Review of Economic Studies, 36*(1), 1–4. doi:10.2307/2296336

Bornholt, G. (2013). The failure of the capital asset pricing model (CAPM): An update and discussion. *Abacus, 49*(S1), 36–43. doi:10.1111/j.1467-6281.2012.00382.x

Bowman, R. (1979). The theoretical relationship between systematic risk and financial (accounting) variables. *The Journal of Finance, 34*(3), 617–630. doi:10.1111/j.1540-6261.1979.tb02129.x

Brown, P., & Walter, T. (2013). The CAPM: Theoretical validity, empirical intractability and practical applications. *Abacus, 49*(S1), 44–50. doi:10.1111/j.1467-6281.2012.00383.x

Fabozzi, F., & Francis, J. C. (1978). Beta as a random coefficient. *Journal of Financial and Quantitative Analysis, 13*(1), 101–115. doi:10.2307/2330525

Fama, E., & French, K. (2004). The capital asset pricing model: theory and evidence. *The Journal of Economic Perspectives, 18*(3), 25–46. doi:10.1257/0895330042162430

Grinblatt, M., & Titman, S. (1992, December). The persistence of mutual fund performance. *The Journal of Finance, 47*(5), 1977–1984. doi:10.1111/j.1540-6261.1992.tb04692.x

Harry, M. (1952). Portfolio selection. *The Journal of Finance, 7*(1), 77–91.

Jensen, M. (1968). The performance of mutual funds in the period 1945-1964. *The Journal of Finance, 23*(May), 389–416. doi:10.1111/j.1540-6261.1968.tb00815.x

Jensen, M. (1972). Optimal utilization of market forecasts and the evaluation of investment performance in mathematical methods in investment and finance. In G. P. Szego & K. Shell (Eds.), Mathematical methods in finance. North-Holland, 1972, 311-335.

Johnstone, D. (2013). The CAPM debate and the logic and philosophy of finance. *Abacus, 49*(S1), 1–6. doi:10.1111/j.1467-6281.2012.00378.x

Klemkosky, R., & Martin, J. (1975). The adjustment of beta forecasts. *The Journal of Finance, 30*(4), 1123–1128. doi:10.1111/j.1540-6261.1975.tb01027.x

Merton, R. (1973). An intertemporal capital asset pricing model. *Econometrica, 41*(5), 867–887. doi:10.2307/1913811

Roll, R. (1977). A critique of the asset pricing theory's tests part 1: on past and potential testability of the theory. *Journal of Financial Economics*, *4*(2), 129–176. doi:10.1016/0304-405X(77)90009-5

Theil, H. (1971). *Principles of Econometrics. New York, NY*: John Wiley & Sons.

ADDITIONAL READING

Blume, M. (1974). On the Assessment of Risk. *The Journal of Finance*, *3*(6), 1–10.

Cooley, T., & Prescott, E. (1973). Tests of an Adaptive Regression Model. *The Review of Economics and Statistics*, *1*(55), 248–256. doi:10.2307/1927000

Francis, J. (1977). Analysis of Equity Returns: A Survey with Extensions. *Journal of Economics and Business*, *3*(12).

Michailidis, G., Tsopoglou, S., Papanastasiou, D., & Mariola, E. (2006). Testing the Capital Asset Pricing Model: The Case of the Emerging Greek Securities Market. *International Research Journal of Finance and Economics*, *4*, 78–91.

Partington, G. (2013). Death Where is Thy Sting? A Response to Dempsey's Despatching of the CAPM. *Abacus*, *49*(S1), 69–72. doi:10.1111/j.1467-6281.2012.00386.x

Reilly, F., & Wright, D. (1988). A Comparison of Published Betas. *Journal of Portfolio Management*, *14*(3), 64–69. doi:10.3905/jpm.1988.409155

Roll, R. (1988). The Stochastic Dependence of Security Price Changes and Transaction Volumes: Implications for the Mixture-of-Distributions Hypothesis. *The Journal of Finance*, *43*(3), 541–566.

Rosenberg, B., & Guy, J. (1976). Beta and Investment Fundamentals. *Financial Analysts Journal.*

Ross, S. (1976). The Arbitrage Theory of Capital Asset Pricing. *Journal of Economic Theory*, *13*(3), 341–360. doi:10.1016/0022-0531(76)90046-6

Swamy, P. (1971). Statistical Inference in Random Coefficient Regression Models. Berlin: Springer-Verlag, 15(1), 41-55. doi:10.1007/978-3-642-80653-7

KEY TERMS AND DEFINITIONS

Beta Instability Problem: Beta estimated based on traditional estimation model is not sound indicator of the future, due to inner shortcomings of the model.

Empirical Record: The model constructed based on the use of statistical analysis and techniques.

Fundamental information: Creating or serving as a primary component of a system or structure.

Liquidity: The capability to buy or sell a security quickly and readily at a value close to market price. The ability to roll over or meet short-term obligations using mostly securities that are easily converted into cash.

Portfolio Planning: The process of constructing a plan for creating a portfolio that will satisfy investment objectives of the client.

Position: The amount of asset that a company possesses.

Sharper Ratio: A measure of the average return in excess of risk-free rate earned per unit of standard deviation.

Variance: The probability-weighted average (expected value) of squared deviations from an expected value of a random variable.

Volatility: The standard deviation of the asset's continuously compounding returns.

Chapter 6
Estimating the CAPM Beta for Public and Private Firms:
Challenges and Solutions

Luis Javier Sanchez-Barrios
Universidad del Norte, Colombia

Benedicto Kulwizira Lukanima
Universidad del Norte, Colombia

Natalia Hernandez-Vargas
https://orcid.org/0000-0002-1942-6402
Universidad del Norte, Colombia

Luis Ricardo Almanza Herazo
Universidad del Norte, Colombia

ABSTRACT

This chapter presents solutions to some challenges when calculating CAPM Beta. Three methods for calculating traditional beta are presented and illustrated through the case of Facebook. Different choices of market index, data frequency, and sample size result in different values of beta; however, in all cases beta was greater than one. The chapter explores ordinal beta as an alternative measure to treat outliers in both developed and thin markets. Using a sample of 84 US stocks, there was no statistical difference between median traditional and ordinal betas. This was not the case for a sample of 47 Colombian stocks, which questions the usefulness of traditional beta in thin markets. In contrast with median traditional beta, median ordinal beta did not change significantly as a result of irregular data series. The contrary occurred when the observation (sampling) period was reduced; this leaves open the question of subjectivity when defining such period. Finally, the process of valuing a private company was illustrated through the case of Palmoil Ltd., a Colombian company.

DOI: 10.4018/978-1-7998-1086-5.ch006

INTRODUCTION

Beta is one of the vital variables in company valuation. It is a component to calculate the cost of equity within the Capital Asset Pricing Model (CAPM). However, estimating beta has become among the challenging issues due to lack of universal criteria in determining the estimation variables such as: historical sample size, data frequency, outliers and portfolio market returns. In this chapter, an attempt is made to outline and discuss these challenges and suggest some possible remedies for both public and private companies.

The chapter does not intend to reach conclusions about solutions to the challenges. Instead, it extends the existing debates in the literature on practical issues to be considered in order to overcome the estimation challenges. Specifically, these practical challenges are addressed contextually, utilizing real company cases as well as taking into account contrasting circumstances between developed markets and thin markets (emerging markets or infant markets). The chapter focuses on the following specific aspects:

1. It gives a brief theoretical background of the CAPM, its practical limitations and the role of beta.
2. Second, it describes the general procedure in estimating CAPM beta, with specific emphasis on data requirements, challenges and possible solutions. On this aspect a clear distinction is made between practical problems in developed markets and emerging markets. Here, the US is used to represent developed markets, whereas Colombia represents thin markets.
3. It addresses the issues of outliers by introducing an alternative beta estimate, hereafter referred to as ordinal beta. In this aspect, a contrasting analysis is made between the traditional CAPM beta and the ordinal beta, focusing on their suitability in developed markets and thin markets.
4. It presents a method of estimating beta for private companies based on beta of comparable public companies, while highlighting limitations and solutions.

Background

In company valuation, one of the crucial ingredients in estimating the value of equity is the cost of equity, which is usually calculated using the CAPM. The CAPM, which is nested on the risk-return trade-off hypothesis (Markowitz, 1959; Sharpe, 1964; Lintner, 1965; French et al., 1987, Fama & French, 2004), contends that an investor is expected to earn higher than 'normal' returns for investments with higher risks, following the finance principle of "the higher the risk the higher the return". Therefore, return on equity depends solely on the risk that cannot be eliminated through diversification (i.e.: systematic risk, which is measured by beta).

The CAPM is based on the following assumptions: First, investors are well diversified on individual assets (unsystematic risk) though portfolio investments. Therefore, their expected rate of return depends only on the systematic risk (beta) of their portfolios. Second, there is a Single-period transaction horizon because all investors are myopic: they have only one and the same holding period. Third, investors can borrow and lend at the risk-free rate of return. Fourth, capital markets are perfect. Hence, all securities are priced correctly.

However, CAPM has some limitations, which contradict its assumptions. First, the perfect market assumption cannot truly apply in real-world capital markets, even in advanced and well-developed stock markets. Moreover, as pointed out by Reilly and Brown (2003), transaction costs in the real world do not allow investors to correct all the mispricing because transaction costs tend to offset any potential excess returns in some instances. Second, the estimation of beta depends on the holding period sample that an analyst used; whereas CAPM assumes that investors have a single-period transaction horizon. In reality, investors do not rely only on returns generated at the end of a single period because their intention is to earn returns for long time in life. Third, CAPM inputs are derived from historical data, whereas investment analysis is based on future expected returns from future cash flows. Fourth, beta is the only risk factor that determine the estimated cost of equity. In real world, however, several firm's factors and macroeconomic factors tend to influence investors' expected returns (see Fama and French, 1992 and 2004). A number of studies suggest that the variability in expected return is not related to market beta (see for example Basu's, 1977; Banz, 1981; Bhandari, 1988; and Chan et al., 1991). Whereas CAPM considers only one-period risk and return, investors in the real world consider how their portfolio return is linked with their income and future investment opportunities as a whole.

Despite several limitations, the CAPM is still a prominent model in real world application for estimating equity rate of return. There are theoretical and practical reasons to explain the prominence of CAPM.

First, CAPM is based on the diversification concept. In real world, investors are assumed to be risk-averse and they tend to manage their investment risk through portfolio diversification. The assumption that investors hold diversified portfolios means that all investors prefer to hold a portfolio that reflects the stock market as a whole. Realistically, it is almost impossible for an investor to own the market portfolio itself. However, it is possible for an investor to diversify away unsystematic risk and to construct portfolios that align to the stock market. Therefore, it is quite reasonable for CAPM to assume that investors are concerned only with returns that provide compensation only for systematic risk.

Second, practical evidence in favour of CAPM is either weak or mixed. Hence, CAPM is applicable only based on beliefs that it really works. After all, neither there is sufficient evidence against it nor a substitute model that is practically better than CAPM. For these reasons CAPM serves as a standard (or benchmark) model the estimation of stock expected returns. Financial analysts, managers and investors apply it as a true standard model for investment analysis.

Third, CAPM is applicable on specific circumstances that suit it: not in every kind of analysis. This means, users of the model should only apply it after taking into account its practical usefulness in estimating the cost of capital.

Fourth, unlike a number of other alternative methods, a principal advantage of CAPM nests on its objectivity in estimating costs of equity, despite its simplicity.

CHALLENGES AND SOLUTIONS IN ESTIMATING BETA (β)

1. Estimating Beta (β) of Public Firms

a. Developed Markets

i. Obtaining Market Data

Estimation of beta requires availability of two sets of historical data: close prices of a respective stock and an appropriate stock market index. For publicly traded stocks in developing markets, these sets of data are readily available from different online sources like Yahoo Finance, Bloomberg, Reuters, Investing.com, and the like.

The main challenge, however, is the choice of a suitable index because stock markets tend to have several indices for different purposes. For example, indices in the US market include S&P500, NYSE Composite, Dow 30, NASDAQ Composite, and others. Moreover, there are some global stock indices like Morgan Stanley Capital International (MSCI) and Global Dow. Here, we do not aim at giving details about these indices, but it is worth noting that none of these indices actually measure the entire market portfolio either US or globally. Let us look at the following two examples. The S&P500 includes only 500 stocks: a fraction of thousands of publicly traded stock in the US market. The MSCI World Index (for 23 developed countries) measures the market performance of 4,500 large and mid-cap companies that have a global presence. Indeed, it is almost practically impossible to find an index that represents an entire market portfolio either in a particular country or globally. Therefore, in choosing an index, the aim is simply to have something that somehow represents the respective stock. Other issues relate to data frequency and sample selection.

ii. Methods of Estimating Beta

In this section, we show and illustrate different approaches for estimating CAPM beta. All of these methods should yield the same result. The estimation is based on returns of the two data sets: stock prices and market index, whereby the return is a percentage change in prices and can be calculated as follows:

$$Return = \frac{P_t}{P_{t-1}} - 1, \tag{1}$$

which is equivalent to

$$Return = \frac{P_t - P_{t-1}}{P_{t-1}}, \tag{2}$$

where: P_t and P_{t-1} denote the current and previous close stock price (or index), respectively.

Method 1: Regression or scatters

In this method, beta is estimated as a coefficient in a regression of stock returns (dependent variable) against market returns (independent variable), such that:

$$SR_t = c + \beta MR_t + \varepsilon_t, \tag{3}$$

where: SR_t and MR_t denote stock returns and market returns for the sample period in each a given time (t), respectively; β is the estimated coefficient for stock beta; c is a constant; and ε_t is a random error term.

This regression equation can also be easily estimated through a plot of correlation scatters of the two variables.

Method 2: Covariance-variance

This method estimates beta as a ratio of the covariance (between stock returns and market returns) to the variance of market returns, such that:

$$\beta = \frac{Cov\left(SR_t, MR_t\right)}{Var\left(MR_t\right)}, \tag{4}$$

where: $Cov\ (SR_t,\ MR_t)$ represent the covariance between the two stock returns for a given time, while $Var(MR_t)$ is the variance of market returns for that time.

Method 3: Slope

This is the proportional change in stock returns to change in market returns, and can be presented as follows:

$$\beta = \frac{\Delta SR_t}{\Delta MR_t}, \tag{5}$$

where: ΔSR_t and ΔMR_t denote changes in stock returns and market returns over time, respectively.

iii. Case of Facebook

Facebook stocks are listed at NASDAQ since 2012. The company provides services through social networks such as Facebook, Instagram, Messenger and WhatsApp.

In this illustration we show how beta varies according to three key aspects: the choice of index, data frequency and sample selection. Regarding the *choice of index*, although the S&P500 is considered favourable for US stocks, we include two other major US indices (NYSE Composite and NASDAQ Composite) in order to explain the challenge of index selection. Since different analysts use different data frequencies, we estimate beta on daily, weekly and monthly frequencies. Similarly, we show the impact of sample selection with beta estimates for 2-years and 3-years samples. A 2-year sample (with weekly frequency) is a replica of Bloomberg, whereas a 3-year sample (with monthly frequency) replicates Yahoo Finance estimation method.

Step 1: Collect data from a reliable source

In this case data sets include Facebook close stock prices and three different indices (S&P500, NYSE Composite and NASDAQ Composite). Historical data were obtained from Yahoo Finance spanning from 9th May 2016 to 10th May 2019 (for a 3 years' sample) and from 9the May 2017 to 10th May 2019 (for a 2 years' sample). Specifically, three different frequencies were used: daily, weekly and monthly as indicated in Table 1. Data set returns were calculated using the formula described earlier.

Step 2: Calculate returns - For each data set, returns were calculated as indicated in (2).
Step 3: Calculate Beta (β)

Table 1. Data samples

Frequency	2 Years Sample Period	3 Years Sample Period
Daily	9th May 2017 – 9th May 2019	9th May 2016 – 9th May 2019
Weekly	8th May 2017 – 6th May 2019	8th May 2016 – 6th May 2019
Monthly	1st May 2017 – 1st May 2019	1st May 2016 – 1st May 2019

Source: Yahoo Finance (2019)

Table 2. Beta estimates

Sample	Index	Data Frequency		
		Daily	Weekly	Monthly
2 Years	S&P500	1.29	1.24	1.43
	NYSE Composite	1.24	1.18	1.34
	NASDAQ Composite	1.20	1.24	1.41
3 Years	S&P500	1.22	1.19	1.30
	NYSE Composite	1.10	1.11	1.18
	NASDAQ Composite	1.15	1.19	1.35

Any method of calculating beta can be used because they all give the same result. Summary results are shown in Table 2 compared to estimates from other analysts as shown in Table 3. An example for the use of scatter graphs and regression is depicted in Figure 1 for 3-years monthly data. This is a replica of Yahoo Finance, which also uses the same data frequency on three years.

Overall, the estimates in Table 2 are consistent on one aspect: that is, beta is greater than one, suggesting that the stock returns are more volatile the market. However, there are marginal differences across indices, data frequencies and sample sizes. Table 3 compares beta estimates from other analyst sources. Clearly, our estimates are consistent with those from NASDAQ, Yahoo Finance and Market Watch. In contrast. According to the Financial Times and Reuters, Facebook stock returns are less volatile then

Table 3. Beta estimates from other analysts

Source	Beta on 10th May 2019
NASDAQ	1.32
Financial Times (FT)	0.94
Yahoo Finance	1.30
Reuters	0.95
Market Watch	1.19

Sources: Yahoo Finance (2019): https://finance.yahoo.com/quote/FB/;
Market Watch (2019): https://www.marketwatch.com/investing/stock/fb;
NASDAQ (2019): https://www.nasdaq.com/symbol/fb;
Reuters (2019): https://www.reuters.com/finance/stocks/overview/FB.OQ
Financial Times (2019): https://markets.ft.com/data/equities/tearsheet/summary?s=FB:NSQ

Figure 1. Beta estimates with scatter graphs

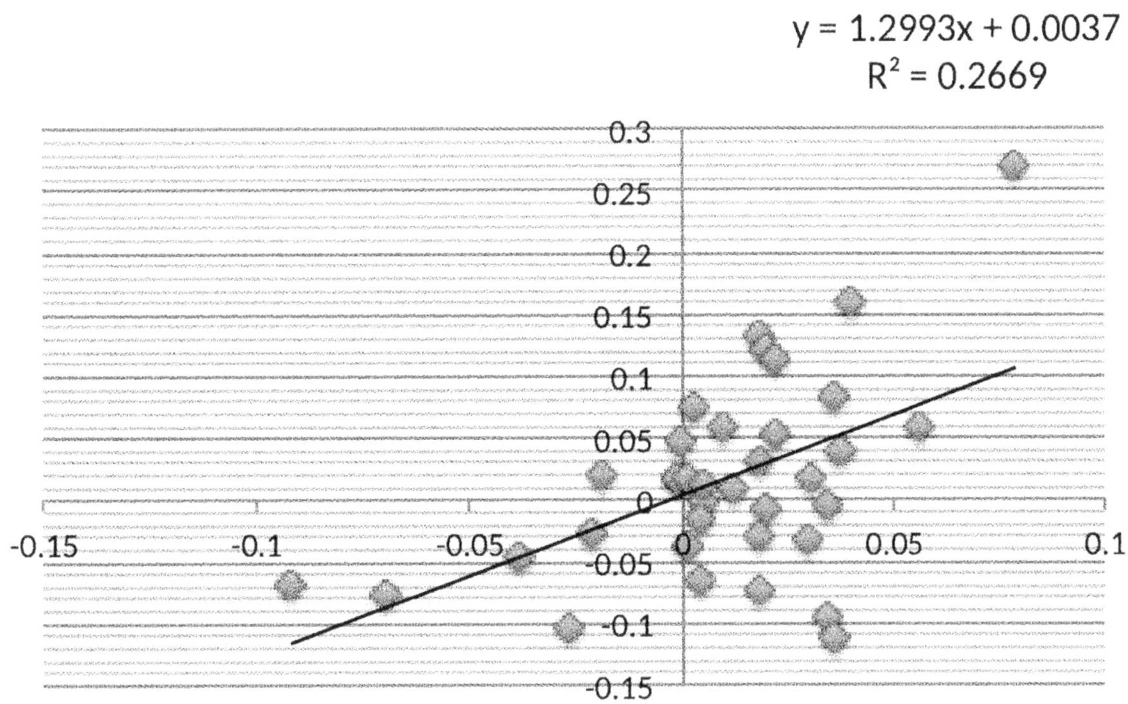

market returns. It is this contrast that makes beta estimation and its application to be a challenging issue that tends to be solved through subjective judgements of analysts.

b. Thin Markets: The Colombian Case

Traditionally Beta is calculated following the approaches described before, which assume normality of data (i.e.: the response variable in Multiple Linear Regression is expected to follow a normal distribution; covariance and variance ratio can be transformed into a correlation and standard deviation ratio, which assume that returns follow a normal distribution). Such assumption makes sense based on the Central Limit Theorem (Sullivan, 2007) for large data sets such as those from developed markets.

Betas in thin markets are usually calculated under the traditional approach, including further adjustments in the CAPM for country and company size among others (Damodaran, 2019). Yet data are different to those in developed markets in terms of outliers, market indexes, data frequency and time coverage. These challenges to the calculation of Beta are described and tackled in this section.

i. Outliers

Usually returns are treated as interval variables, which makes sense as they are by definition numerical variables. Under the covariance-variance traditional approach in (4), Beta can be restated as:

$$\beta = \frac{r_{MR,SR}\sigma_{SR}}{\sigma_{MR}}, \tag{6}$$

where:

$r_{MR,SR}$ = Pearson correlation between market and stock returns,
σ_{SR} = Standard deviation of stock return, and
σ_{MR} = Standard deviation of market return.

Abnormal values (outliers) can largely affect covariances and correlations between returns and variances of returns which ultimately result in under or overestimated Betas, which increases the cost of equity and impacts the value of companies; this is a major issue in thin markets with few observations that are more likely to be affected by outliers.

The challenge here is how to detect any possible outliers and treat them. Outliers are defined as:

$$\begin{cases} Outlier = 1 & \text{if } return_i \le Q_1 - 1.5 \times IQR \text{ or } return_i \ge Q_3 + 1.5 \times IQR; \\ Outlier = 0 & \text{otherwise} \end{cases}, \tag{7}$$

where:

Q_1= First quartile,
Q_2= Second quartile, and
IQR= Interquartile range.

Some analysts trim and ignore outliers; this is not correct because outliers are genuine observations that reflect an actual pattern of the data. Another approach is winsorising (Barnett and Lewis 1994): replacing outliers for a threshold previously defined; this approach relies heavily on subjectivity, which does not solve the issue.

An alternative approach is to treat returns as ordinal variables and hence restate (2) accordingly:

$$\beta_{ord} = \frac{\rho_{MR,SR} MAD_{SR}}{MAD_{MR}}, \tag{8}$$

where:

β_{ord}= Ordinal Beta
$\rho_{MR,SR}$= Spearman correlation between market and stock returns.

$$MAD_{SR} = median_i \left| Stock\ return_i - median_j \left(Stock\ return_j \right) \right| \tag{9}$$

is the median absolute deviation of stock return and

$$MAD_{MR} = median_i \left| Market\ return_i - median_j \left(Market\ return_j \right) \right| \quad (10)$$

is the median absolute deviation of market return.

Several reasons justify the use of (8). The median is identified as the observation that splits an ordered distribution in equal proportions; it is not calculated using the values of observations. Therefore, it is not biased by outliers (Leys et al., 2013) as is the case for averages. Median absolute deviation is an alternative to standard deviation (Hampel, 1974; Huber, 1981); it is the median of the absolute deviation from the median of the original dataset, which still captures the variability of data and solves the issue of biased central and dispersion measures. Consequently, no observations are excluded for the calculation of Beta, which will be referred as Ordinal Beta, β_{ord}, from here onwards.

In contrast with Pearson correlation ($r_{MR,SR}$). Spearman correlation ($\rho_{MR,SR}$) does not require normality of variables and does not compare values against averages. Instead, observations are ranked based on their values; differences in ranks are then used to calculate the degree of correlation between variables (Triola, 2008).

Prior to exploring the adequacy of β_{ord} in thin markets it is useful to analyze results in a developed market such as the US Stock Exchange. A random sample of n=84 stocks was obtained. Monthly returns per stock were calculated and compared against those of the market: Standard & Poor´s (S&P) index between May 1st, 1990 and March 1st, 2019.

Stock returns varied between -16.94% and 11.16%, whereas market returns varied between -63.57% and 159.8%. For illustration purposes, three stocks were chosen: Apple (Figure 2), Google (Figure 3) and Fortive Group (Figure 4). Outliers were also explored for each stock; given that the observation period of each stock varied depending on issue date and frequency of trading, a percentage of outliers within the observation period of each stock was calculated. It varied between 0% and 17.1%.

Figure 5 depicts returns of S&P. Returns beyond/below the upper/lower dotted lines were classified as outliers, based on (7).

Figure 2. Apple returns

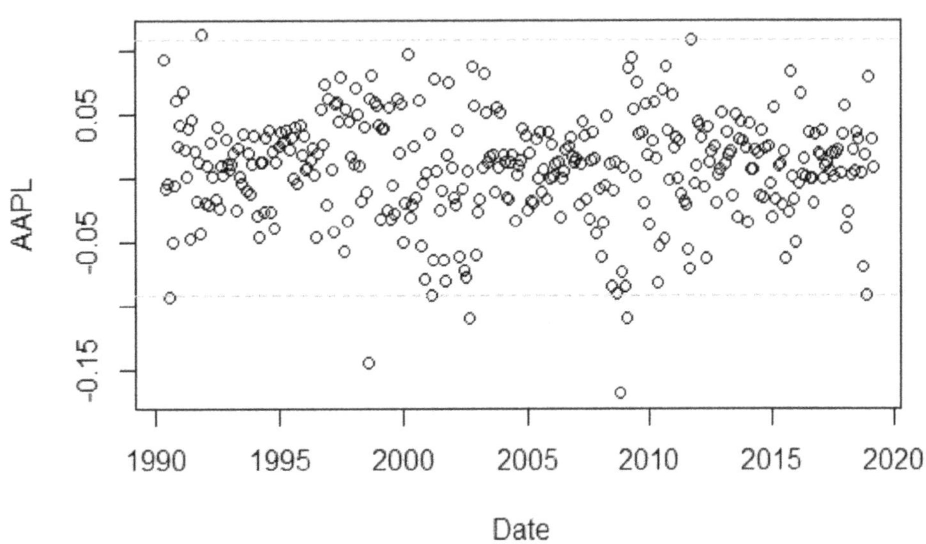

Figure 3. Google returns

Figure 4. Fortive Group returns

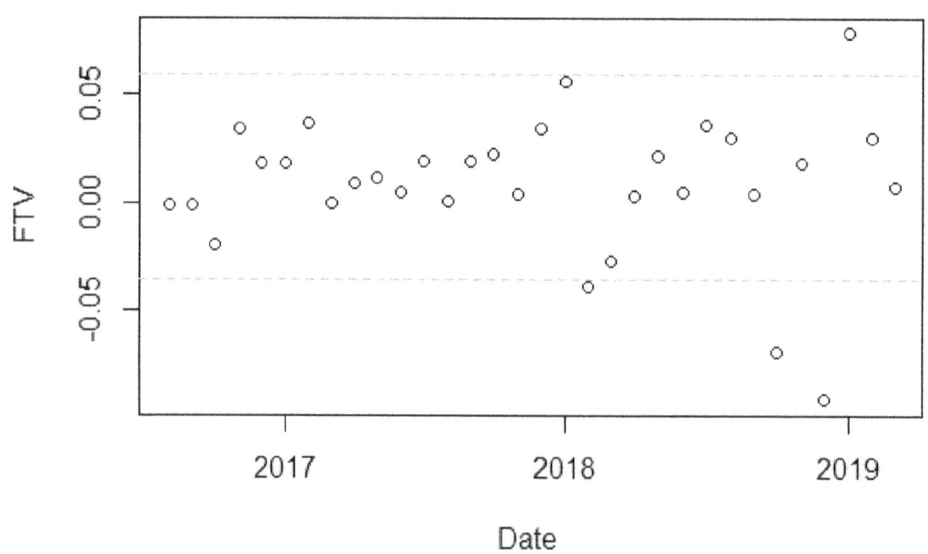

In order to infer about the normality of data, the Kolmogorov-Smirnov test was run for market returns: Ho: Market returns follow normal distribution (D= 0.4562, p<0.000001). Hence, it cannot be inferred that data follow the normal distribution and therefore it is not adequate to calculate Pearson correlation ($r_{MR,SR}$) instead Spearman correlation was used to calculate β_{ord} in (8).

For comparison purposes in the US market, β and β_{ord} were calculated per stock. An initial exploration of the boxplot in Figure 6 suggests that $Median_{\beta\text{-}\beta ord}$ is close to zero; a distinctive feature of the distribution is a pronounced right tail that evidences overestimation of risk when using β in comparison

Figure 5. S&P returns

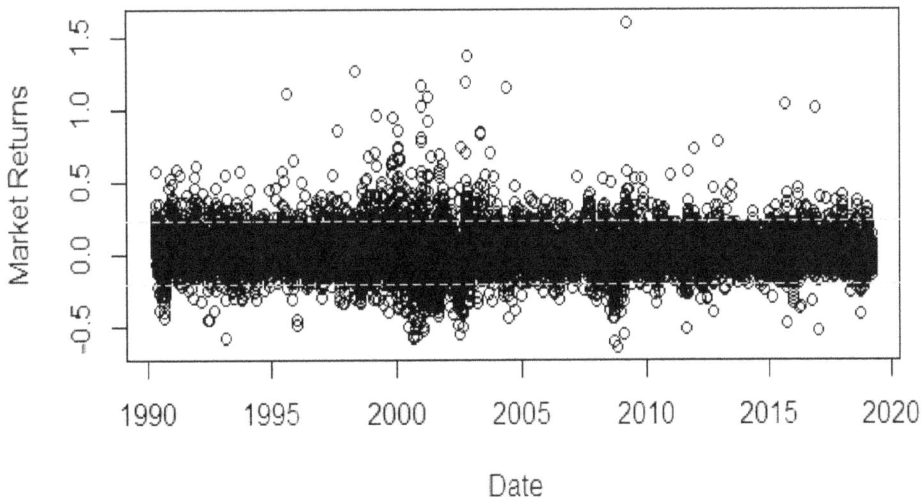

with β_{ord} two extreme cases of overestimation are depicted as outliers. Figure 7 shows early signs of consistency of both measures, as both increase in the same direction. Again, two outliers are clearly identified in the graph. The Kolmogorov-Smirnov test was run for (β-β_{ord}): Ho: β-$\beta_{ord} \sim N(\mu_{\beta\text{-}\beta ord}, \sigma_{\beta\text{-}\beta ord})$; data does not follow the normal distribution (D=0.46331, p<0.000001). For normal distributions with equal variances, the t test has a power advantage. This is not the case for non-normal distributions with outliers, in which the power of Mann-Whitney-Wilcoxon test is greater.

Results presented above confirm that (β-βord) does not follow a normal distribution, which justifies the use of the Wilcoxon signed rank test of matched pairs (Pallant, 2007) to properly assess the usefulness of β_{ord} versus β and hence infer if it makes a difference or not to use either measure. Specifically: Ho: $Median_{\beta}= Median_{\beta ord}$ (W = 3533, p-value=0.9886); hence it does not make a difference to use either measure in a developed market such as the United States. Consequently, the ordinal measure suggested in this chapter performs and is consistent with traditional Beta; either measure could be used to calculate the cost of equity in the US market.

In order to assess the adequacy of β_{ord} for the Colombian market, we used a sample n= 47 stocks between July 15th, 2002 and March 28th, 2019. The sample included 28 stocks in COLCAP to capture a good proportion of the liquidity of such a thin market and 19 stocks chosen randomly. Returns were calculated using first observation per month; given the characteristics of this market, frequency was not monthly as was the case of the US market.

Returns for the whole sample of stocks varied between -83.97% and 906.67. The following stocks were chosen for illustration purposes: Marly (Figure 8), Promigas (Figure 9) and Bancolombia (Figure 10). Percentage of outliers during observation period varied between 0% and 20%, with a lower proportion of stocks without outliers compared with the US market. This confirms the high volatility of the Colombian market due to its infant nature.

Figure 11 corresponds to COLCAP returns which varied between -35% and 208.81%; it can be inferred from the Kolmogorov-Smirnov test that data do not follow the normal distribution (D=0.43647, p<0.000001).

Figure 6. (β-β$_{ord}$), US Market

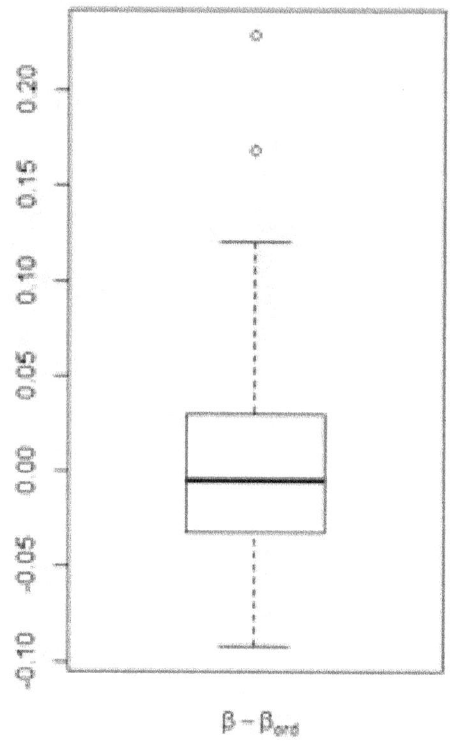

Figure 7. βord vs. β, US Market

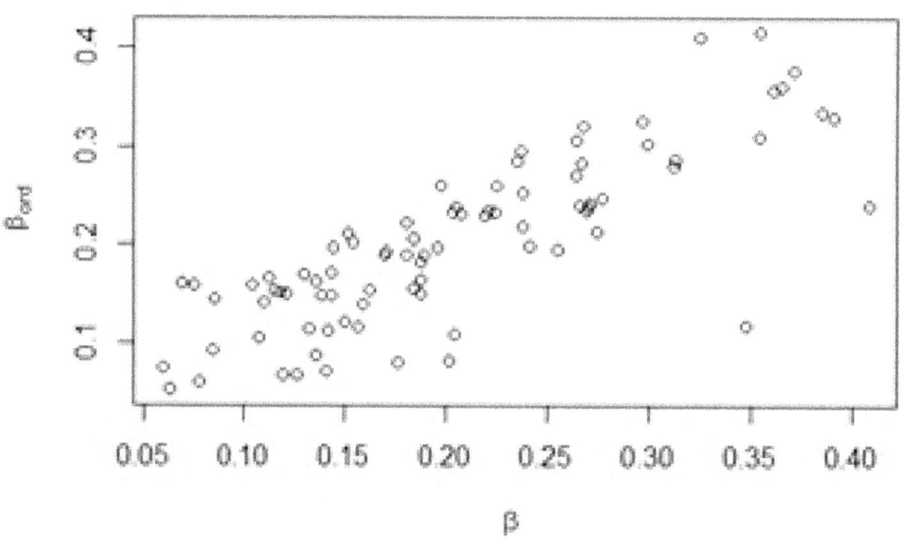

Figure 8. Marly returns

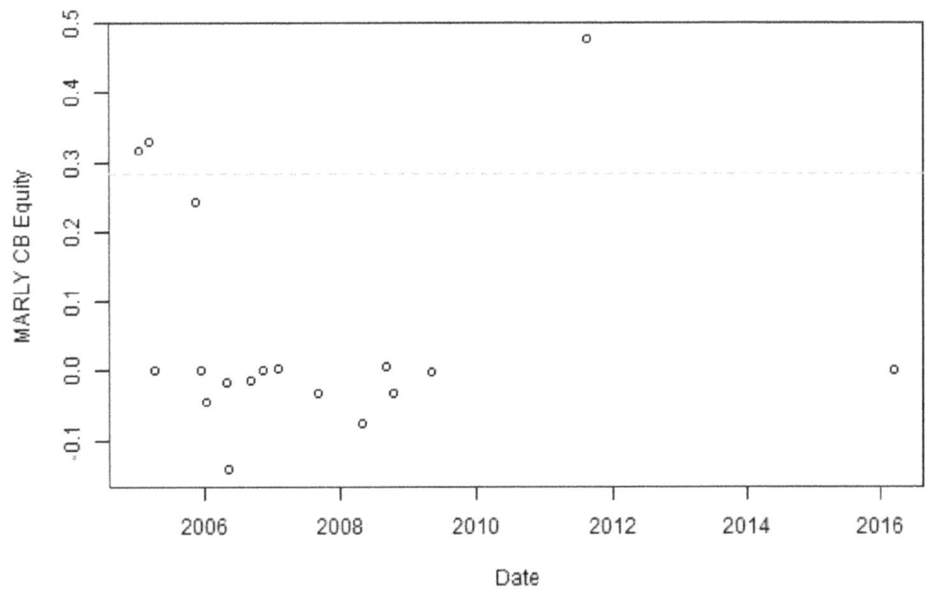

Figure 9. Promigas returns

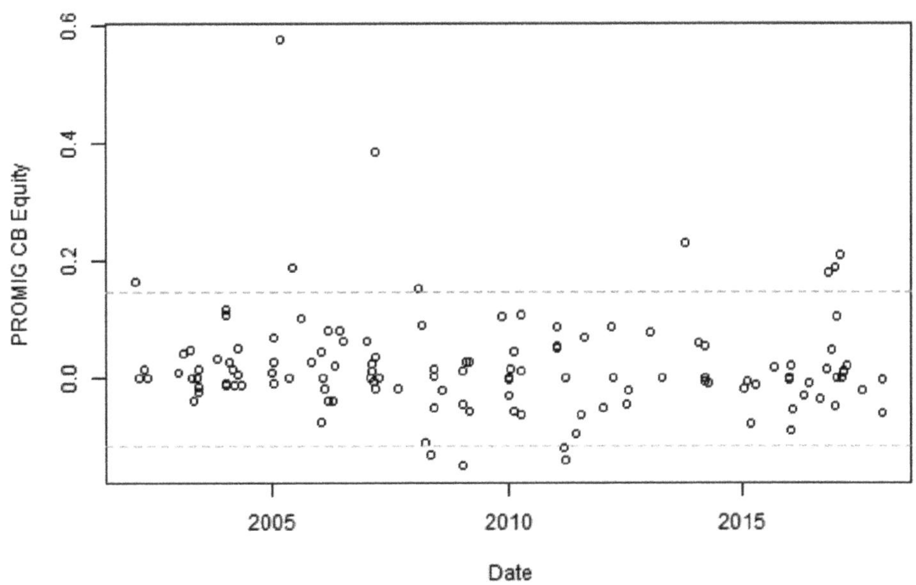

Figure 10. Bancolombia returns

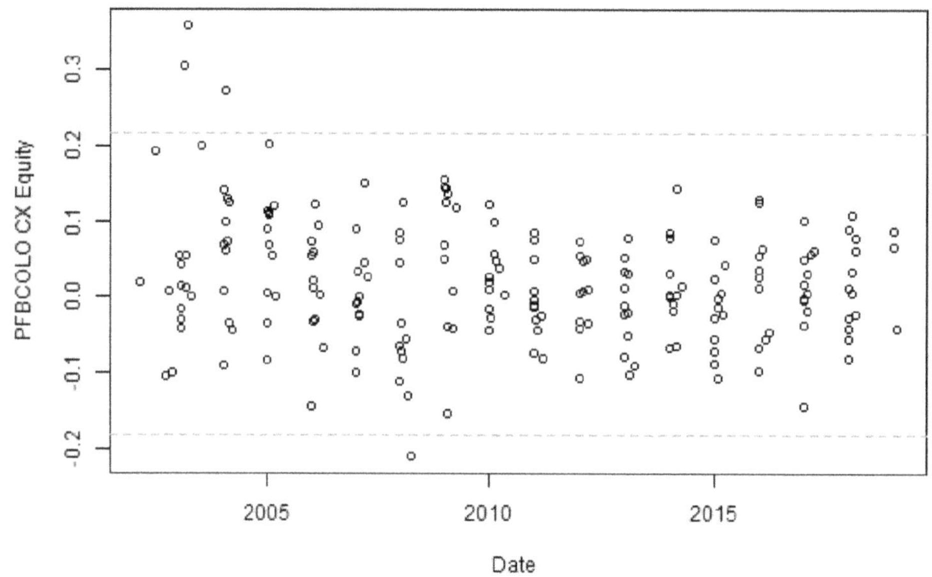

Figure 11. COLCAP returns

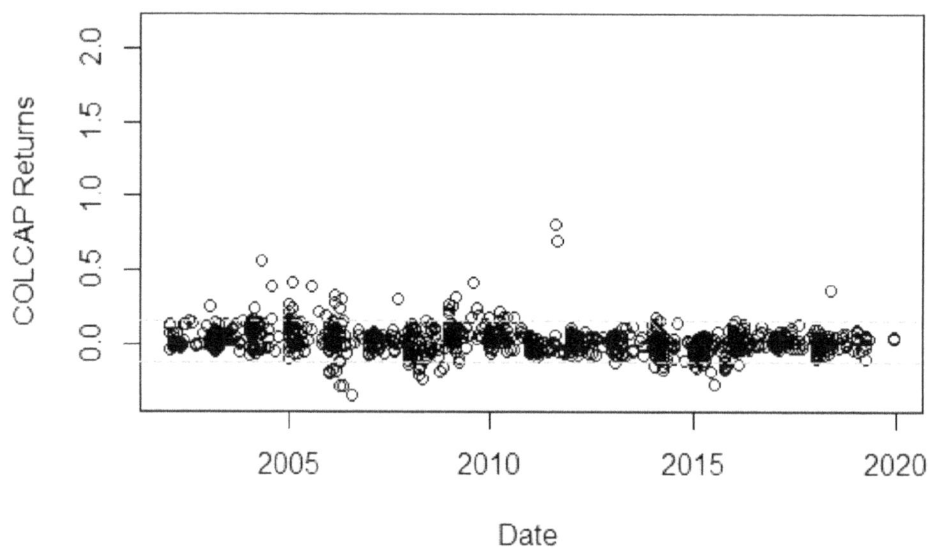

ii. Market Index

Some stock markets have several indices, specific for particular segments of companies (e.g. large corporations, financial services, energy sector, etc.). The challenge here is how to determine the appropriate market index for the stock to be valued. A common practice is to use a broad stock index that includes all stocks in the market. However, due to challenges that may be caused by thin trading in some markets, some popular indices (like S&P 500, Dow Jones Composite, FTSE, etc.) tend to be used. However, there should be evidence that the chosen index is linked to the stock returns in which beta is being estimated. We tackle this issue by calculating correlations between the returns of Colombian stocks and the returns of two market indices: COLCAP and S&P.

Figure 12 shows graphically the relationship between the full sample of Colombian stock returns and COLCAP returns; likewise Figure 13 plots Colombian stock returns versus S&P returns. Results show that stock returns are more correlated with COLCAP returns than S&P returns; a good proportion of stocks do not react to S&P in contrast with COLCAP, which somehow exhibit a pattern. In terms of correlations,

$$\rho_{Stocks,COLCAP} = 0.5095498\left(s = 1.3261*10^{10},\ p < 0.000001\right);$$

$$r_{Stocks,COLCAP} = 0.26749\left(t = 20.498,\ d.f. = 5{,}452,\ p < 0.000001\right).$$

This confirms that Colombian stocks are correlated with COLCAP, the local index that not only includes some of those stocks but also, reflects context conditions of the Colombian market. Additionally, Spearman correlation is stronger than Pearson correlation, indicating then that there is a monotonic relationship between both variables that is not necessarily linear. This follows also from the non-normality of COLCAP returns. Hence, the market index that should be used to calculate β_{ord} in Colombia is COLCAP.

Regarding the use of β or β_{ord} for the Colombian market, a similar rationale to that used for the US market was followed. Not surprisingly, (β - β_{ord}) does not follow the normal distribution (D= 0.39472, p<0.000001). Ho: $Median_{\beta-\beta ord}= 0$; according to the results, it makes a statistically significant difference to use either measure in the Colombian market (W = 955, p<0.000001). This is a result of particular features of such market as explained below.

Figure 12. COLCAP$_{returns}$ vs Colombian stock$_{returns}$

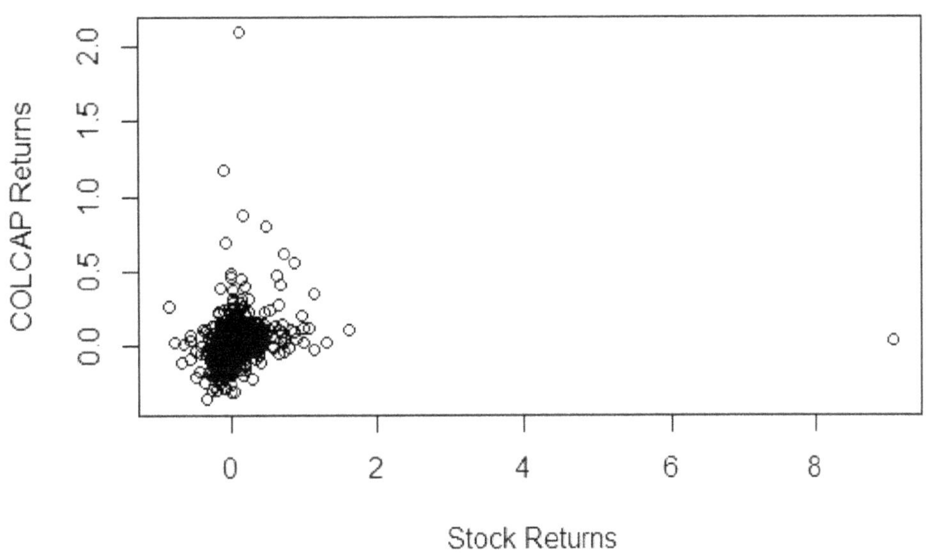

Figure 13. S&P$_{returns}$ vs Colombian stock$_{returns}$

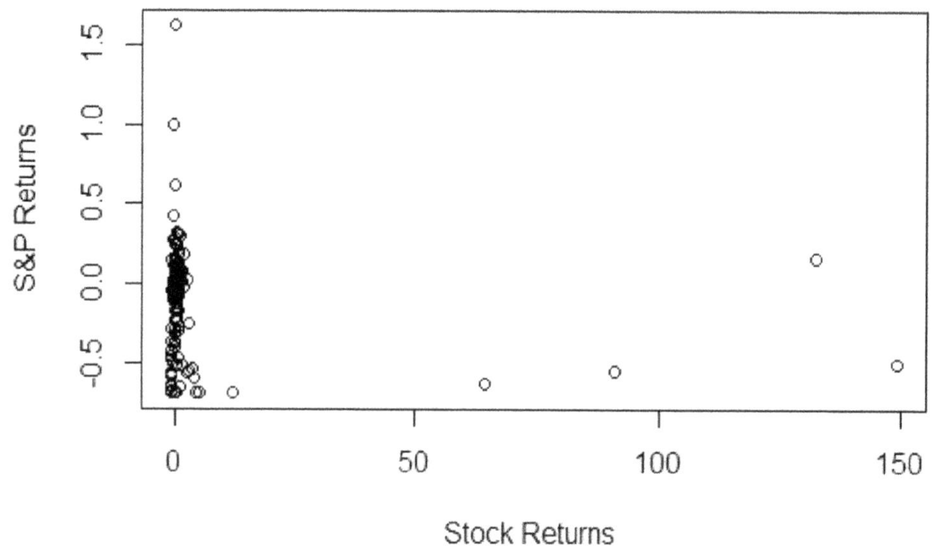

Overall, the Colombian market is more volatile than the US market in terms of greater values of β and β_{ord}. More extreme outliers in Figure 14 in contrast with Figure 6 confirm this. Additionally, scatterplots also suggest that there is a proportional relationship between both measures in the US market (Figure 7) whereas in the Colombian market (Figure 15) for β>0.5, β_{ord} increases at a greater rate than that for lower values of β. This indicates that β_{ord} underestimates systematic risk of companies with low β´s whereas the contrary occurs otherwise.

iii. Data Frequency

The choice of data frequency depends on data properties and the trading pattern of stocks to be estimated. In active stock markets, where stock prices are quoted almost continuously on daily basis, beta can be estimated better from daily data because it can easily capture most of the microstructure effects (see for example Scholes and Williams (1977), Dimson (1979), and Cohen *et al.* (1983a,b)). Nevertheless, obtaining high frequency observations is a limiting factor in some markets with thin trading, which are found in some emerging and infant stock markets. Hence, low frequency data (e.g. monthly) is an alternative. Some analysts suggest the use of intra-day data, but it is practically difficult to implement.

As stated in i., Colombian stock returns were calculated using first observation of month. This was done to use a common rule in a market that is not regular in terms of trading. In order to tackle with the data frequency issue stated above, returns were also calculated for all dates in the data sample. The former approach led to the calculation of β and β_{ord} presented before and the latter to β' and β'_{ord}.

Figure 16 shows that for a set of companies β´ is greater than β, however median>0 and the right tail of the distribution suggest that using data series with a more consistent trading pattern tend to overestimate systematic risk when the traditional approach is used. On the other hand, β´ord is less sensitive to data frequency with a case that shows underestimation of systematic risk. $(\beta - \beta')$ and $(\beta_{ord} - \beta'_{ord})$ do not follow a normal distribution either (D=0.44877, p<0.000001 and D=0.47796, p<0.000001, respectively). Therefore, Wilcoxon signed Rank tests are implemented in order to test the median differences.

Figure 14. (β-β_{ord}), Colombian Market

Figure 15. β_{ord} vs. β, Colombian Market

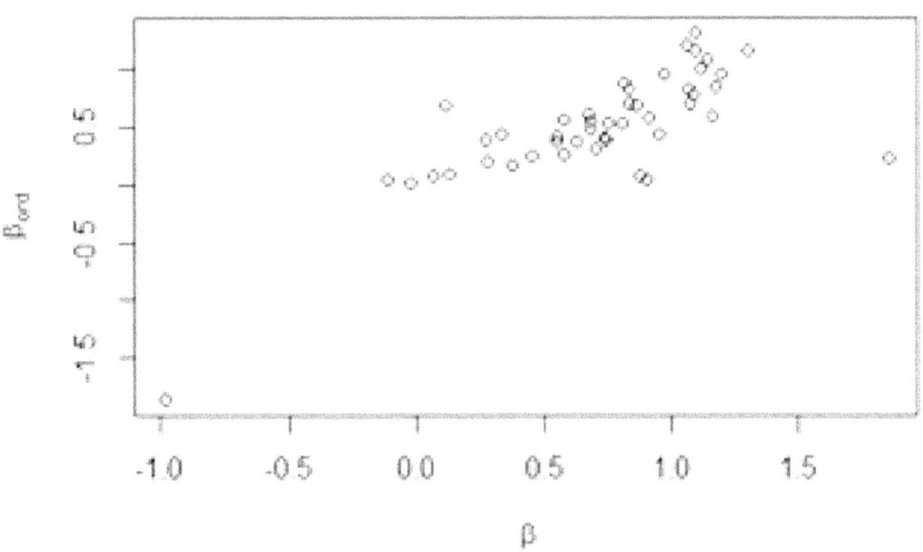

Figure 16. (β-β´); (βord-β´ₒᵣ𝒹), Colombian Market

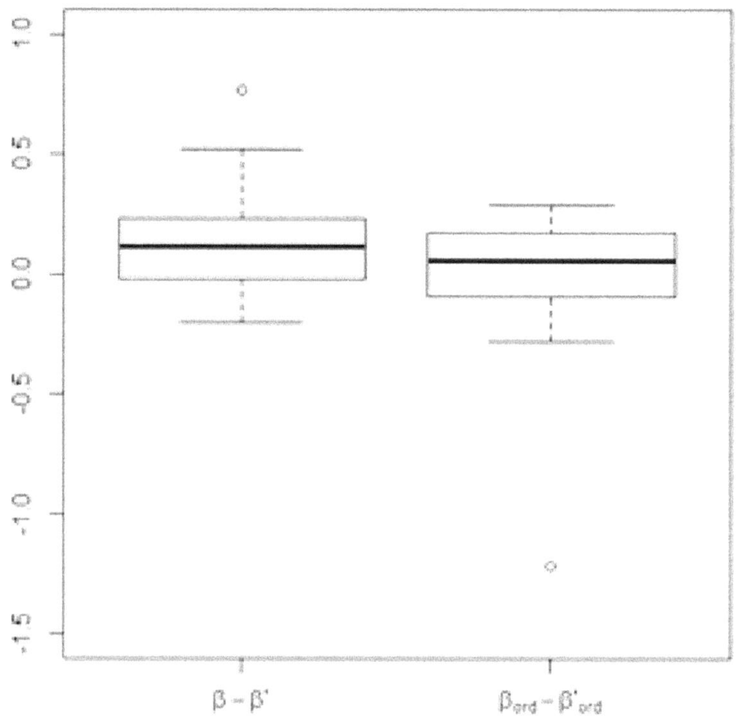

Results show that traditional betas are significantly different (W = 931, $p<0.000001$) and depend on data frequency considerations; this is not the case for ordinal betas (W = 694, p =0.1721). Given that traditional betas are more sensitive to trading frequency, β_{ord} should be preferred to β for thin markets.

iv. Time Coverage

Beta is sensitive to the sample size and time coverage. Therefore, the main challenge is that different betas can be given for the same stock because there is no standard way of determining the sample size. For example, Yahoo Finance estimates beta using monthly returns covering three years, whereas Bloomberg uses weekly returns covering two years. But for markets with thin trading, larger samples may be appropriate even with monthly data (probably between 4 to 6 years).

Observations per stock in the Colombian market varied between n=7 and 201 dates. In order to assess the effect of sample size on Beta calculations, another sample = n/2 was obtained from the original sample and used to calculate β'_{ord}, β_{ord} and β''_{ord} do not follow a normal distribution either D=0.48751, $p<0.000001$ and D=0.509398, $p<0.000001$, respectively). Results for the Wilcoxon signed rank test (Ho: Median β_{ord}, β''_{ord} =0) suggest that there is a difference between ordinal betas calculated for different observation periods (W=302, p=0.00492). This is useful for practitioners, as it suggests that for stocks with very few observations, results vary significantly. See Figure 17.

Figure 17. (β_{ord}-β''_{ord}), *Colombian Market*

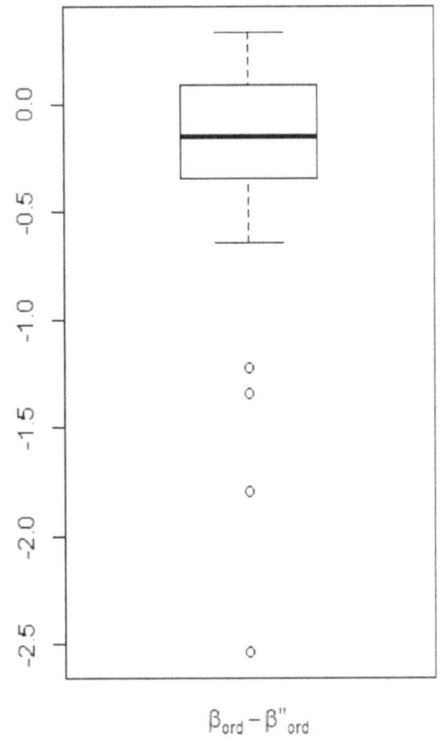

2. Estimating Beta (β) of Private Firms in Thin Markets

As stated earlier, CAPM involves the estimation of Beta and two additional parameters: Risk free rate and market return. Two parameters (risk-free rate and market return) can be applicable to private firms without significant limitations. The only parameter that creates complications in estimating the cost of equity in private firms is beta. This is because private firms do not have observable market information (historical prices) that is required for the estimation beta (the risk parameter). However, the beta of a private firm can be estimated by using the comparable Beta approach. This section explains this approach and illustrates it through the valuation of a private Company in Colombia.

a. Comparable Beta Approach

This approach involves the estimation of an average beta of comparable public firms. The estimated average beta is then used as a proxy beta of a comparable private firm. The main challenge to be addressed is on how to determine comparable publically traded firms. This entails 4 aspects as explained below.

Step 1: Identify the industry/business line of the private firm and determine a group of public comparable firms

Knowledge about the nature of a private company is vital in determining a peer group of public companies. The main challenge is difficulties in obtaining data for private companies. Usually, information about private companies is limited due to the fact that they are not obliged to disclose it publically, except when required for a specific purpose. However, it is important to ensure a proper definition of industry or business line in order to avoid inaccurate estimation beta for the private company. For countries with developed capital markets (most of them are western countries), it is not a big challenge to obtain a reasonable number of comparable companies in a particular sector. In some countries, however, where capital markets are infant, it is difficult or even impossible to apply this approach due to lack of comparable firms.

It is useful to identify more than one comparable company in a single market in order to have a wider vision of the market; it is not advised to choose companies in different markets as betas may capture conditions of various markets and hence distort calculations.

Regarding multiple business lines, in some cases it is difficult to determine a specific industry in which a private firm belongs because it operates in multiple business lines. For example, a company operates in a range of companies in different lines of business and sectors such as food and beverage, packaging, logistics, marine passenger services, petroleum and entertainment.

Analysts could identify a comparable company after conducting a thorough analysis of integrated reports and verifying their main economic activity is similar to that of the private company under analysis. Depending on data availability, an alternative is to identify similar revenue streams of comparables in their Profit and Loss (P&L) Statement. It should be noted, however, that these figures might be subject to creative accounting practices and hence distort figures. This is a limitation that analysts must deal with.

EBIT or EBITDA should not be used as bases to identify comparables as those figures are consequences of the business model in place; unveiling this is not always a straightforward exercise, which makes comparison cumbersome and difficult. Additionally, costs and expenses are more prone to be manipulated, if applicable, to creative accounting practices. Finally, in thin markets as Colombia, private firm owners may manage them as well; this poses challenges to their financial management as personal and company finances intertwine and hence operational expenses are overestimated.

Size is another issue when defining comparables of private firms in thin markets. In reality, and in most cases, it is a practical fact that private firms tend to be smaller in size than public firms. A common practice is to account for this by adjusting the risk premium in the CAPM, which does not affect Beta (Damodaran, 2019). This size premium is not only a result of market capitalization of the company. Since private companies do not trade in stock markets, they are not usually audited by state agencies or private audit firms, resulting in higher risk for the stockholders who in turn demand greater rewards.

Step 2: Determine the average beta of public comparable companies

Once comparables are chosen, different central measures are available to calculate the industry Beta. A first alternative is the arithmetic mean of Beta; this approach does not consider differences in sizes between comparables in terms of market cap. Another option is to calculate a weighted average of Betas, which tackles with the flaw explained before. This is calculated as follows:

$$\bar{\beta}_P = \sum_{i=1}^{n} \beta_i \times X_i , \tag{11}$$

where: β_i=Levered beta of public company *i* and X_i=Proportion of market cap of company *i*.

Depending on data availability and number of comparables, median Beta can be identified to solve issues with outliers.

Step 3: Convert the average beta into unlevered beta

Debt-equity ratio, it is a key variable in estimating beta; it is a unique feature of each company, either private or public. A common practice is to assume that the private firm belongs to the industry in which the companies are operating at an optimal capital structure; hence, its debt-equity ratio should be consistent with the industry average leverage ratio. For valuation purposes, it makes sense to use the optimal capital structure of industry comparables because potential investors usually have access to significant amounts of capital and aim for an optimal capital structure that minimizes WACC and does not restrict the company´s cash flows.

Unlevered Beta for the group of public companies is calculated as follows:

$$\beta_U = \frac{\beta_L}{1+\left(1-T_c\right)\left(\frac{D}{E}\right)}, \qquad (12)$$

where: β_U and β_L are the unlevered and levered betas, respectively; T_c is the average corporate tax rate and D/E is the average debt to equity ratio.

Step 4: Calculate the levered beta of a private firm

A levered beta of the target private company is obtained by adjusting the average unlevered beta of comparable public companies by the leverage ratio of the private company. Therefore, beta of the private firm is calculated as follows:

$$\beta_{L(p)} = \beta_U\left[1+\left(1-T_c\right)\left(\frac{D_P}{E_p}\right)\right], \qquad (13)$$

where: β_U is the unlevered beta from comparable firms, and $\beta_{L(p)}$ is the beta of the private firm. T_c is the corporate tax rate that the private company is subject to, and D_p/E_p is the target debt to equity ratio of the private company. It follows then that size of private companies impacts leverage and hence beta; greater leverage results in a greater beta.

b. The Case Under Analysis: Palmoil Co

The company is a private Colombian-based exporter of palm oil and its derivatives henceforth referred as Palmoil Co. It has been in operation since 2009 and has already reached maturity. Table 4 shows historical income statements between 2015 and 2018.

Table 4. Income Statement 2015-2018: Palmoil Co. Figures in COP millions

	2015	2016	2017	2018
Revenue	57,243	70,127	72,292	74,677
Costs	50,803	63,252	63,320	66,283
Gross Profit	6,440	6,875	8,972	8,393
Operating expenses	4,138	5,638	5,187	5,823
EBIT	2,303	1,236	3,786	2,571
Other income	2,754	4,559	2,777	3,633
Other expenses	2,795	4,690	2,798	4,029
Profit before taxes	2,263	1,106	3,765	2,175
Taxes	440	643	1,743	809
Net Profit	1,822	463	2,022	1,366

As this is a trading company, gross profit is not heavily impacted by the international fluctuation of palm oil prices. Average gross profit margin during the last 4 years was 11.18%; during 2018 gross margin was 11.24% despite the fluctuations of the palm oil prices. Therefore, forecasting commodities was not required to project profits.

Likewise, operating expenses were stable across years. They mostly include personnel and consulting expenses which are not expected to vary significantly in the near future. Due to its trading business, Palmoil Co. requires minor investment in fixed assets. Thus, depreciation is relatively low as shown in Table 5.

Other income and expenses include effects such as exchange rate and interests associated with financial obligations. They were not considered for valuation purposes, as they are not related with the core business.

Step 1: Identify the industry/business line of the private firm and determine a group of public comparable firms

Palmoil Co. is a trading company within the agricultural industry for food processing. Comparables should also engage in trading activities of similar products such as soy oil, canola oil, olive oil, etc.

For the case under analysis, Bunge Ltd. and ADM were used as comparables for Palmoil Co. Both are publicly listed with more than 20 years of trading story. Their mission is also to commercialize agricultural products including palm oil and its derivatives. In contrast, other companies engaged in ad-

Table 5. Operating expenses 2015-2018: Palmoil Co. Figures in COP millions

	2015	2016	2017	2018
Expenses excluding depreciation and amortizations (D&A)	3,850	5,207	4,917	5,591
D&A	288	431	270	232
Operating Expenses	4,138	5,638	5,187	5,823

Table 6. Average beta of public comparable firms

Company	Beta	D/E
ADM	0.81	1.46
Bunge	1.44	3.11
Weighted Avg	0.96	1.86

Source: Yahoo Finance

ditional activities were not deemed as comparable to Palmoil Ltd.: Glencore PLC also operates mines through subsidiaries (additional activities); Trafigura is mainly concerned with energy commodities (same activity but different segment) and Wilmar Group is similar to Bunge Ltd. but is traded in Singapore Exchange (different market).

Step 2: Determine the average beta of public comparable companies

Table 6 shows company betas and D/E as of December 2018, estimated using monthly data for a 3-year sample period.

Step 3: Convert the average beta into unlevered beta

According to the corporate tax calculator at Market Watch (2019), sector's median tax rate for the past 11 years was 29.6%. For the case under analysis:

$$\beta_U = \frac{0.96}{1+(1-0.296)(1.86)} = 0.416$$

Step 4: Calculate the levered beta of a private firm

Beta of Palmoil Ltd. was calculated using Tc= 40% (average rate between 2015 and 2018); β_u =0.42; and target D_p/E_p =8.32:

$\beta_{L(p)}$ = 0.416[1 +(1 – 0.40)(8.32)] = 2.49

c. Company Valuation

Given that Palmoil Ltd. is a mature company, its growth can only be achieved through large capital investments required to expand to other market segments. The company was valued using forecasted discounted free cash flows, in particular, through its terminal value. Only free cash flow for year 2019 (FCF_{2019}) was forecasted and used to calculate the terminal value (TV) as no medium or long term plans were provided to assume variations of existing cash flows:

FCF_{2019} = EBIT×(1-T) + D&A- ΔKTNO – CAPEX (14),

where:

T= Tax Rate= 40%,
D&A = Depreciation and amortization,
ΔNOWK= Δreceivables + Δinventories - Δpayables (9), and
CAPEX = Capital Expenditures.

FCF_{2019} calculations are presented in Table 7.

$$TV = \frac{FCF_{2019} \times (1+g)}{(WACC-g)}, \tag{15}$$

where: g = perpetual growth rate=1% and WACC= Weighted Average Cost of Capital.

$$WACC = k_e \times \frac{E}{(D+E)} + k_d \times (1-T) \times \frac{D}{(D+E)}, \tag{16}$$

where: k_e= Cost of Equity, k_d = Cost of debt, E = Value of equity, D = Value of structural debt and T = Income tax rate.

$$K_e = R_f + \beta i \times MP + CRP \tag{17}$$

where: Rf= Risk-free return (US T-Bonds yield for 10 years) plus inflation differential between United States and Colombia, βl = Levered Comparable Beta, MP = Market Premium adjusted for emerging markets and CRP = Country Risk Premium of Colombia.

Table 7. Forecasted Free Cash Flow: Palmoil Co. Figures in COP millions

		2019
	Revenue	76,917
(-)	Costs	68,272
(=)	Gross Profit	8,645
(-)	Expenses	5,997
(=)	EBIT	2,648
(-)	Taxes	1,059
(+)	D&A	232
(-)	Δ NOWK	13
(-)	CAPEX	0
(=)	Free Cash Flow	1,808

Therefore, *ke* equals 24.8% as shown below:

Ke Palmoil= 4.7% + 2.49x 7% + 2.64% = 24.8% and

$WACC_{Palmoil}$= 24.8% x 10.73% + 7.8%*89.27% = 9.62%.

Finally, terminal value calculation was obtained by using (15). Best practices for the industry usually place this value below 1% to prevent overvaluation:

TV = COP 1.808M x (1+1%)/ (9.62%-1%) = COP 21.177 million.

A sensitivity analysis was conducted to show the impact of g on the value of Palmoil. See Table 8.

FUTURE RESEARCH DIRECTIONS

Results presented in this chapter shed light on challenges and solutions that academics and analysts face when calculating Beta for company valuation purposes. Yet further research would be useful to continue expanding on this topic.

First, alternative definitions for Beta that capture the variability of market and stock returns could be explored. Second, the formulation of traditional Beta (β) and ordinal Beta (β_{ord}) need to be statistically validated when using different market indices, data frequency and time coverage need to be tested in different markets. This will provide guidance to practitioners and to some extent, reduce subjectivity when deciding on those aspects prior to valuating companies. An open question is if it makes sense to consider β_{ord} an estimator of β or if both indices capture systematic risk in a different way. Third, calculations for β_{ord} can be replicated and used to value private companies in developed and thin markets that have been previously valuated using β. The impact of using β_{ord} on company value can then be compared against actual values negotiated as a result of corporate mergers and acquisitions. Fourth, portfolio betas under

Table 8. Terminal value, Palmoil Ltd. Figures in COP millions

g	Terminal Value (COPM)
0.10%	19,005
0.20%	19,226
0.30%	19,451
0.40%	19,682
0.50%	19,917
0.60%	20,158
0.70%	20,404
0.80%	20,656
0.90%	20,914
1.00%	21,177

the perspective of β_{ord} is a novel topic that could be further explored in both developed and thin markets. Finally, another challenge for the valuation of private companies is to define comparables using portfolio β and/or β_{ord} when revenue streams are not clearly defined.

CONCLUSION

Outliers are a common feature of time series in both developed and thin markets. Instead of overseeing outliers, they can be statistically treated and hence acknowledged when quantifying systematic risk. Obviously, this results in under/overestimation of traditional beta.

β_{ord} is an alternative to β that tackles adequately with outliers. For time series with a low percentage of outliers (a common feature in developed markets) the difference between β and β_{ord} is insignificant. In contrast, β and β_{ord} tend to have significant differences in the presence of outliers (a common feature in thin markets). β_{ord} is more robust than β in thin markets with irregular data frequencies. Additionally, it does make a difference to use β or β_{ord} when sample size in thin markets changes. Consequently, special care should be taken when using β_{ord} in thin markets.

Two competing forces are present in the calculation of β_{ord}: Spearman correlation and Median Average Deviation. The former is greater than Pearson correlation, whilst the latter smoothes data variability in contrast with standard deviation. These effects result in the differences explained above.

Subjectivity, knowledge and experience are common features additional to technical competences of analysts when valuing companies. Deciding on market indices, data frequency and sample size result from personal choice. This is the case for both developed and thin markets. The same applies when identifying comparables to valuate private companies.

REFERENCES

Banz, R. W. (1981). The relationship between return and market value of common stocks. *Journal of Financial Economics*, *9*(1), 3–18. doi:10.1016/0304-405X(81)90018-0

Barnett, V., & Lewis, T. (1994). *Outliers in statistical data*. Chichester, UK: Wiley.

Basu, S. (1977). Investment performance of common stocks in relation to their price-earnings ratios: A test of the efficient market hypothesis. *The Journal of Finance*, *12*(3), 129–156.

Bhandari, L. C. (1988). Debt/equity ratio and expected common stock returns: Empirical evidence. *The Journal of Finance*, *43*(2), 507–528. doi:10.1111/j.1540-6261.1988.tb03952.x

Chan, L. C., Yasushi, H., & Josef, L. (1991). Fundamentals and stock returns in Japan. *The Journal of Finance*, *46*(5), 1739–1789. doi:10.1111/j.1540-6261.1991.tb04642.x

Cohen, K. J., Hawawini, G. A., Maier, S. F., Schwartz, R. A., & Whitcomb, D. K. (1983a). Estimating and Adjusting for the Intervalling-Effect Bias in Beta. *Management Science*, *29*(1), 135–148. doi:10.1287/mnsc.29.1.135

Cohen, K. J., Hawawini, G. A., Maier, S. F., Schwartz, R. A., & Whitcomb, D. K. (1983b). Friction in the trading process and the estimation of systematic risk. *Journal of Financial Economics*, *12*(2), 263–278. doi:10.1016/0304-405X(83)90038-7

Damodaran, A. (2019). Damodaran online. Available at http://pages.stern.nyu.edu/~adamodar/

De Winter, J. C., & Dodou, D. (2010). Five-point Likert items: T test versus Mann-Whitney-Wilcoxon. *Practical Assessment, Research & Evaluation*, *15*(11), 1–12.

Dimson, E. (1979). Risk measurement when shares are subject to infrequent trading. *Journal of Financial Economics*, *7*(2), 197–226. doi:10.1016/0304-405X(79)90013-8

Fama, E. F., & French, K. R. (1992). The cross-section of expected stock returns. *The Journal of Finance*, *47*(2), 427–465. doi:10.1111/j.1540-6261.1992.tb04398.x

Fama, E. F., & French, K. R. (2004). The capital asset pricing model: theory and evidence. *The Journal of Economic Perspectives*, *18*(3), 25–46. doi:10.1257/0895330042162430

French, K. R., Schwert, G. W., & Stambaugh, R. F. (1987). Expected stock returns and volatility. *Journal of Financial Economics*, *19*(1), 3–29. doi:10.1016/0304-405X(87)90026-2

Hampel, F. R. (1974). The influence curve and its role in robust estimation. *Journal of the American Statistical Association*, *69*(346), 383–393. doi:10.1080/01621459.1974.10482962

Huber, P. J. (1981). *Robust statistics*. New York, NY: John Wiley. doi:10.1002/0471725250

Leys, C., Ley, C., Klein, O., Bernard, P., & Licata, L. (2013). Detecting outliers: Do not use standard deviation around the mean, use absolute deviation around the median. *Journal of Experimental Social Psychology*, *49*(4), 764–766. doi:10.1016/j.jesp.2013.03.013

Lintner, J. (1965). Security prices, risk, and maximal gains from diversification. *The Journal of Finance*, *20*(4), 587–615.

Marketwatch. (2019). Corporate tax calculator. Available at https://www.marketwatch.com/graphics/2017/sp-500-company-tax-rates/#/

Markowitz, H. (1959). *Portfolio selection: efficient diversification and investments*. New York, NY: John Wiley & Sons.

Pallant, J. (2007). *SPSS survival manual* (3rd ed.). Open University Press.

Scholes, M., & Williams, J. (1977). Estimating betas from nonsynchronous data. *Journal of Financial Economics*, *5*(3), 309–327. doi:10.1016/0304-405X(77)90041-1

Sharpe, W. F. (1964). Capital asset prices: a theory of market equilibrium under conditions of risk. *The Journal of Finance*, *19*(3), 425–442.

Sullivan, M. (2007). *Statistics: Informed decisions using data* (2nd ed.). Upper Saddle River, NJ: Pearson Prentice Hall.

Triola, M. (2008). *Essentials of statistics* (3rd ed.). Boston, MA: Pearson Addison Wesley.

Chapter 7
Valuation of Negative Earning Firms

Faisal Usmani
Aligarh Muslim University, India

Atif Ghayas
Aligarh Muslim University, India

Mohd Sarim
Aligarh Muslim University, India

ABSTRACT

This book mostly concentrates on firms with positive earnings, but this chapter focuses on the negative earnings firms or firms with very low earnings. It is easier to value a positive earning firm than a company with negative earnings. Analyzing negative earning firms has always created problems for researchers and analysts. In case of a negative earning firm, growth rates cannot be predicted or used in the valuation of firms. When current income of the firms is negative, growth rate will make it more negative. Tax computation becomes more complicated and the Going Concern Assumption does not apply properly. Authors start with complications in valuing negative earning firms, discuss the causes of negative earnings, and whether the problem is short-term, long-term, or cyclical in nature. Finally, authors provide the appropriate valuation technique for each case.

INTRODUCTION

Start-ups and early-stage companies with negative earnings, and experiencing seasonal or structural financial problems, do not allow use of traditional valuation concepts as it is unclear how and when the company will produce positive cash flow for their investors. To value such companies, it is critically important to have a more in-depth analysis and understanding of external and internal forces that affect a firm's ability to generate positive cash flow. It is quite clear, zero positive cash flow eventually equals

DOI: 10.4018/978-1-7998-1086-5.ch007

no value! The dot-com bubble at the turn of 21st century clearly demonstrated that when the business hype finally ends, start-ups and early-stage companies must produce a financially successful business and revenue model that can generate cash flow.

Start-up and early-stage companies are generally valued on a prospective basis, with the underlying managerial assumption that the business model of the company being valued will eventually succeed (and hence, generate positive cash flow). As far as a firm is predicted to survive, negative profitability is, by definition, a transitory state since investors have an abandonment option and will not allow losses to continue indefinitely (Jenkins, 2003). Therefore, this study elucidates the model of mean-reversion of profitability to reflect the expected future profitability of loss firms. That is in fact what investors are betting on, especially for a company like Uber.

One of the keys to success and to achieving the valuation placed on a start-up and early-stage companies is the ability to raise sufficient capital to cover the operating losses until profitability is reached. One of the most significant issues in valuing a start-up or an early stage company is sufficiency of capital to achieve the business plan. Undercapitalized start-ups and early-stage companies by their nature are doomed and the valuations placed on them are subject to scrutiny. (Joos and Plesko, 2005).

Valuation and Complications of Negative Earning Firms

A valuation is a method of calculating the true worth of a business or of a firm for a number of reasons. One of the most important reasons can be associated with providing information to the investors who are looking for return on their investments made, or on the investments that will be made in future.

A business valuation process involves varying data such as value of inventory, equipment and property, liquid assets in hand, share price, market capitalization, and projected earnings, among others. There are several methods of business valuation and the choice of method adopted is contingent upon a number of factors such as the purpose of valuation, size of business, etc. A valuation of a business or a company may be conducted by adopting different approaches such as valuation using market value of business, valuation using return on investment of a business, valuation using the value of assets of a firm, valuation by applying discounting of cash flows, etc. (David, 2018).

It is easier to value a positive earning firm than a company with strangely low or negative earnings. Analyzing negative earning firms have always created problems for researchers and analysts. One of the main causes of negative earnings may be attributed to the overall deterioration in the wealth of the company. A newly established firm also faces the problem of negative earnings in initial years of business. Also, seasonal impact on business may also result in a negative earning for various forms of businesses.

Companies that are losing value lead to many issues for analysts who are endeavoring to evaluate them. However, none of these issues are theoretical, they are critical from an estimation perspective. Generally, it is simpler to take an existing profitable business on a higher profitable growth but it is very difficult to convert an unprofitable business into profitable one. The risk to lose, or total failure, is very high in the negative earning firms. It is advisable to normalize the abnormally high expenses of negative earning firms by comparing it to the previous year figures. In such a case a clear distinction should be made between losses and expenses.

In case of a negative earning, growth rates cannot be predicted or used in the valuation of firms. When current income of the firms is negative, growth rate will just make it more negative. Tax computation becomes more complicated and the Going Concern Assumption does not apply properly because running losses for long time exposes the firm to ultimate bankruptcy.

A general way of valuation of a firm, irrespective of its type and nature, is by using expected cash flows and scale it with by using suitable methods of time vale of money (Damodaran, 1999). However, in case of negative earning firms, the first step before initiating the valuation process of a negative earning firm, it is important to identify the causes of negative earnings that may be classified as short-term or long-term causes, affecting a firm or an industry or the economy as a whole, on a temporary basis or on a permanent basis (Sandra, 2014). A short-term problem is expected to resolve in near future and the company will be able to recover soon. A temporary problem is expected to affect a firm alone, or the entire industry or the economy as a whole. Such firms expect to recover earnings soon. If such temporary factors remain affecting a firm or an industry or the entire economy as whole, consistently over a period of time, are referred to as long-term problems that may demonstrate a permanent nature, leading to continuous deterioration in earnings. In some of the cases the life cycle of a firm may also be responsible for the negative earnings.

Gopalan et al. (2007) investigated the functioning of internal capital markets in Indian Business Groups and shown the importance of intragroup loans to support financially weaker firms. Findings suggests that an important reason for extending such support may be to avoid default by a group firm and resulting negative spillovers to the rest of the group leading to significant drops in external financing, investments, and profits of other firms in the group and an increase in their bankruptcy probability. In another study Matsumoto (2002) reported that managers take actions to avoid negative earnings surprises. The author hypothesizes that certain firm characteristics are associated with greater incentives to avoid negative surprises. Also, the firms with higher transient institutional ownership, greater reliance on implicit claims with their stakeholders, and higher value-relevance of earnings are more likely to meet or exceed expectations at the earnings announcement. On the contrary, Skinner (1994) believed that managers willingly disclose information that led to large negative surprises that ultimately bring a large stock price reaction.

This study has classified negative earning firms based on prominent study in firm valuation conducted by Damodaran (2012). The complications related with each type of causes of negative earnings are discussed below:

1. Short-term or Medium-term Problems
2. Long-term Problems
3. Cyclical Problems

1. Short-Term Problems

Short term problems can be the reason of negative earning for some firms, these problems can be related to a specific firm, a particular Industry or the entire economy. Firm specific reasons may include a strike by employees, delay in product release or a product recall which will negatively affect the earnings. Example of a sector-wide reason can be a spike in the prices of raw material, change in consumer preferences will result in negative earnings of majority of the forms in the sector. And lastly, decline in the economic activities in can be an example of economic reason which will affect all the firms in the economy. In all the above cases, we expect earnings to turn green sooner or later once the problem disappears.

2. Long-Term Problems

In some cases, the financial problems faced by a firm are much deeper and long-term in nature. For e.g. A firm can have low or negative earning just because it employs more debt in the capital structure than required which lead to excessive cash outflows. The earnings of firm may be negative owing to its wrong selection of options for marketing policy or product mix. Such firm needs a crucial and substantial planning and, often, new management. A firm can have negative earnings due to incompetent and unproductive operations. For e.g. the firm's plant and equipment may be outdated or its employees may not be properly trained. In all such cases, serious attention and significant time is needed for financial health of a firm to improve.

3. Cyclical Problems

Sometimes, the negative earnings are related to the product life cycle or economic cycle and not due to its operations. Such firms that need big investments initially will lose value until these investments start paying off. Once the firm start generating revenues its earnings turn from negative to positive. For e.g. Pharmaceutical firms invests huge amount of funds initially in research and development expenses, and continuously reports negative earnings. Once they get approval for a promising drug they developed, their earnings turn to positive.

BACKGROUND OF THE STUDY

Valuation of firms with negative earning is a complicated subject in the field of valuation that has confounded many investors and academicians. The need for a business valuation can arise for several reasons: incoming investors, lawsuits, inheritance, business sale, partner exit, public offering, or net worth certification.

Business valuation provides various valuable information to business owner related to real worth or value of the firms in terms of market competition, value of assets, and value of expected cash flows.

The study (Zhang, 2000) demonstrated the relative significance of earnings versus book value by explaining equity value varies cross-sectional with operating efficiency and growth capabilities. As far as, low-efficiency firms are concerned, book value is predicted to dominate earnings for negative earning firms. Whereas, for regular firms earnings are considered to be more important than book value. Growth firms, earnings and book value together explain equity value. The study further states that there is negative association between equity value and negative earnings. Firms reporting losses regularly poses main challenge for financial statement users who primarily rely on accounting earnings for numerous decisions.

Before selecting the method of valuation, it must be ascertained that why the firm's earning is negative. As discussed earlier, generally negative earning firms are classified into three categories. The firms that are incurring losses for several years are classified as a long-term negative earning firm while the firms that incurred in loses for a short period of time are classified as short-term negative earning firms. Some firms incurred losses regularly in some specific time period repeatedly are classified as seasonally negative earning firms. During their business cycle, they repeatedly incurred losses with seasonal variation. In those specified periods there earning becomes negative otherwise they there earning is non-negative in another period of their business cycle.

There are few more factors that are also equally important in valuation of firms and selecting proper method for valuation. Among those factors, suitability of the method to the firm's condition, industry, business and availability of details desired for valuation are significant considerations in valuation of firms with unprofitable cash flow. According to (Nanavati, 2019) one rule to remember is that invariably, perception, and adequacy will outplay difficulty, ample data in valuation of firms with negative earnings.

IMPORTANCE OF THE STUDY

This study aims to explore and offer description for the negative earnings firms and provide three different method of valuation. Latest studies in accounting has documented that considerable number of loss firms are operating. Existing theories on the valuation of negative earning firms are based on adaptation/abandonment options or limited liability, assuming that these firms are operationally distressed (Darrough and Ye, 2007). This increase in the incidence of negative earnings makes it imperative to understand how these firms should be valued by the market. However, because the information content of losses is likely to be different from that of profits, the valuation of loss firms is not straightforward.

A firm Value (FV) is an economic concept that indicates firm's value. It is the value that a business is worthy of at a particular date. Generally, the valuation of firm is conducted on the basis of enterprise value, operating free cash flows, market value, and book value. However, firm with negative earning is more complex and need to take into consideration several other things.

The main reason behind a valuation is to assess the success of your strategic decision-making process and provide the ability to track performance in terms of estimated change in value. The negative earnings complicate the use of earnings-based valuation models, since a loss reduces the ability of reported earnings to provide information about the earning power of a firm's assets. Given the increase in the frequency of negative earning firms, the demand of how investors perceived negative earnings has gain considerable relevance.

METHODS OF VALUATION

Before selection of negative firms' valuation method, we must ascertain that why the firms have negative earning. It should be determined whether negative earning period is temporary or long-term issue. Many firms sometimes go into negative earning period due to some major investment or write-off and they become profitable after that phase are termed as short-term negative earning firm. It the firms are incurring losses in one phase of business cycle repeatedly and become profitable after those periods are termed as cyclical or seasonal negative earning firm. Valuation concept and techniques can be applied around the world irrespective of business and trade environment. Undoubtedly, Investment can be affected by many pull and push factors. But same valuation techniques can be used across many diverse and different business scenarios.

Long-Term Negative Earning Firms

"Firms can sometimes make mistakes in terms of the product mixes they offer, the marketing strategies they adopt, or even the markets that they choose to target. They often end up paying a substantial cost in terms of negative or lower earnings and perhaps a permanent loss of market share."

"Firms have low or negative earnings that can be traced to strategic missteps, you have to determine whether the shift is a permanent one. If it is, you will have to value the firm on the assumption that it will never recover lost ground, and scale down your expectations of revenue growth and expected margins. If, on the other hand, you are more optimistic about the firm's recovery or its entry into new markets, you can assume that the firm will be able to revert to its traditional margins and high growth (Damodaran, 2012)"

1. Long Term or Permanent Problem

Firm Z borrowed huge sums to finance for its extension until the late 2000s. At the end of 2010, Debt outstanding of firm Z is \$400 million and market value of equity \$80 million, causing a debt to capital ratio of 83.33%. Due to overleverage:

a. The bottom-up beta for the firm is 2.50. Risk-free rate is 7% and the risk premium is 5% (3% as the mature market premium and 2% for country risk:

Cost of equity = 7% + 2.5(5%) = 19.5%

b. Due to the high default risk, the pretax cost of borrowing is 12.5%; the tax rate for the firm is 25%.
c. The operating income before tax was \$45 million, but the interest expenses of the firm was \$50 million, leading to loss for the firm.

It is assumed that the operating income will grow 10% a year for the following six years and 8% a year afterwards. During that period, it is further assumed that the firm's capital expenditures (which are currently 6 million), depreciation (which is currently 2 million), and noncash working capital (which is currently 170 million) will increase at the same rate as operating income, yielding the following assessments for the cash is shown in Table 1.

In next six years onwards, it is assumed that the firm Z will decrease its debt ratio from 83.33% to 50%, which will result in the beta decreasing from 2.50 to 1.00 and the pretax cost of debt from 12.0% to 10.0%. The costs of capital for Firm Z are assessed each year for the succeeding six years (Table 2).

For estimating the terminal value, it is assumed that growth rate is 8% in perpetuity, after year 6, and a return on capital of 16%. Reinvestment rate at the end of year 6:

Reinvestment rate = 8%/16% = 50%
Terminal value = 59.79(1.08)(1 – .50)/(.096 – .08) = 2,017.91

Table 1.

	1	2	3	4	5	6
EBIT(1-t)	37.13	40.84	44.92	49.41	54.35	59.79
+Depreciation	2.20	2.42	2.66	2.93	3.22	3.54
-Capital Spending	6.60	7.26	7.99	8.78	9.66	10.63
-Change in working Capital	18.70	20.57	22.63	24.89	27.38	30.12
=FCFF	14.03	15.43	16.97	18.67	20.53	22.59

Table 2.

	1	2	3	4	5	6
Beta	2.5	2.2	1.9	1.6	1.3	1
Cost of Equity	19.5	17.94	16.38	14.82	13.26	11.7
Cost of Debt (After Tax)	9	8.7	8.4	8.1	7.8	7.5
Debt ratio	83.33	76.66	70.00	63.33	56.67	50
Cost of Capital	10.75	10.86	10.79	10.56	10.17	9.60

Short-Term Negative Earning Firms

"When earnings are negative because of temporary or short-term problems, the expectation is that earnings will recover in the near term." "A firm can have a bad year in terms of earnings, but the problems may be isolated to that firm, and be short-term in nature." "If the loss can be attributed to a specific event—a strike or a lawsuit judgment, for instance—and the accounting statements report the cost associated with the event, the solution is fairly simple."

Several firms document a one-time loss due to write-offs from restructuring but are neither financially nor operationally distressed (Darrough, M., & Ye, J. (2007).

2. Short Term Problems

In 2015, Firm X reported their operating loss of $200 million and a net loss of $500 million due to firm specific problem. In order estimate normalized earnings at firm X, we estimated a pretax operating income of $500 million. For the purpose of valuation, following additional assumptions were made:

- We assumed that the long-term growth rate would be 5% in both revenues and operating income, as the firm had been growing at 5% a year prior to 2015.
- The firm had a book value of capital invested of $4000 million at the beginning of 2015, and was expected to maintain its return on capital (based on the adjusted operating income of $500 million).
- The firm's tax rate is 30%

In order to value firm X, we first estimated the return on capital at the firm, using the adjusted operating income:

Return on capital = EBIT(1 – t)/Book value of capital invested
= 500(1 – 0.30)/4000 = 8.75%

Based on the expected growth rate of 5%, this would require a reinvestment rate of 57.14%:

Reinvestment rate = g/ROC = 5%/8.75% = 57.14%

After making these assumptions, we were able to compute Firm X's expected free cash flows in 2016:

EBIT(1 – t) = 500(1.05)(1 – 0.30) $367.5 million
- Reinvestment = 500(1.05)(0.5714) $299.9 million

Free cash flow to firm $67.6 million

To figure out the cost of capital, we estimated a bottom-up beta of 0.90 for the industry. The long-term bond rate in the host country was 5%, and Firm X could borrow long-term at 5.1%. We assumed a market risk premium of 3%. The market value of equity as $5000 million, and there was $2500 million outstanding debt at the end of year 2015.

Cost of equity = 5% + 0.90(3%) = 7.7%
Cost of debt = 5.1% (1 – .30) = 3.57%
Debt ratio = 2500/ (5,000 + 2500) = 33.33%
Cost of capital = 7.7% (.6666) + 3.57% (.3333) = 6.31%
Value of operating assets at end of 2015 = Expected FCFF in 2016 / (Cost of capital – Expected growth rate)
= 67.6 / (.0631 – .05) = 5160.30 million

Adding to this the value of the cash and marketable securities ($1200 million) held by Firm X at the time of this valuation, and netting out the market value of debt ($2500) yields an estimated value of $28,006 million for equity, significantly lower than the market value of $50,000 million.

Value of equity = Value of operating assets + Cash and marketable securities – Debt
= 5160.30 + 1250 – 2500 = $3910.3 million

Cyclical or Seasonal Negative Earning Firms

Cyclical valuations of a firm can be significantly affected by the level of base year earnings. There are two potential solutions: One is to adjust the expected growth rate in the near periods to reflect cyclical changes, and the other is to value the firm based on normalized rather than current earnings (Damodaran, 2012)

Table 3.

Year	Revenues	Operating Income	EBITDA	Operating Margin	EBITDA/ Revenues
2009	150000	10000	19995	6.5	13.33
2010	180000	12000	24300	7.2	13.5
2011	220000	13500	30800	8.1	14
2012	250000	17500	36250	8.9	14.5
2013	300000	20000	45000	9.5	15
2014	180000	12200	16200	7.3	9
Average		14200		7.91	

1. Cyclical Problem

Firm Y was reporting stable growth till the year 2013. The currency crisis of 2013 due to slow down in world economy lead to the Firm Y reporting a substantial decrease in profits in the year 2014. To normalize Firm Y's operating income, we looked at its operating performance from 2009 to 2013 in the table 3.

Averaging the operating margin before tax from the year 2009 to 2014 produce an average operating margin of 7.91%. Multiplying this margin with the revenues in 2014 yields a normalized operating income of $14238 million (7.91% of $180000 million), this value will be used for our normalized operating income.

Following assumptions were made to value the firm:

To estimate Firm Y's cost of equity, we used a bottom-up beta of 1.10 for this industry. Using the 10-year government bond rate of 4% as the risk-free rate and an equity risk premium of 6.5%. we computed a cost of equity of 11.15%.

Cost of equity = Risk-free rate + Beta × Equity risk premium
= 4% + 1.10 (6.5%) = 11.15%

In 2014, Firm Y's Debt to Equity ratio was 3:2. The cost of the debt of Firm Y is 6% and the marginal tax rate for the firm in 2014 was 35%. With the given information, we calculate the cost of the capital.

Cost of capital = 11.15%(.4) + 6%(1 − .35)(.6) = 6.8%

Assuming that firm is stable and its growth rate is 2% in perpetuity. We further assume that the firm will produce return on capital identical to its cost of capital on its investments.

Reinvestment rate g/ROC = .02/.068 = .2941

Using normalized operating income ($14238 million), the marginal tax rate for the economy (35%), the reinvestment rate (29.41%), the stable growth rate of 2% and the cost of capital of 6.8%, we estimated the value of the operating assets at Firm Y:

Value Operating assets = Operating income (1 + g)(1 – tax rate) (1 – Reinvestment rate)/(Cost of capital – g)
= 14238 (1+.02)(1 – .35)(1 – .2941)/(.068 – .02)
=$1,38,823

DISCUSSION

This study addresses the problem of valuing firms that report negative earnings or losses. We have categorized the negative earning firms in three categories. The firms that are making losses continuously year after year are long-term negative earning firms.

The way we treat negative earnings firms will be determined by the reason why the firm has negative earnings in the first place. Valuation technique used for each of the case will be different according to the firm in question. Investing in negative earning firms is a high-risk proposal (Picardo, 2018). Considering these aspects, using a suitable valuation method and evaluating reward-risk, assessing management capability, and using a portfolio approach could reduce the risk of investing in negative earning firms and make it beneficial and advantageous to the investors.

The sharp rise in the incidence of firms reporting losses in many economies makes the valuation of loss firms a significant concern. Although abandonment and adaption options are available for loss firms, many of the loss firms are not necessarily a candidate for abandonment or adaptation. Therefore, we have focused this study on negative earnings firms that are likely to stay in business for many years.

Investors consider information beyond aggregate earnings cash flow and accruals. Investors do not consider losses to be persistent and homogenous. In fact, they consider the causes and nature of the losses to evaluate its long-term implications for firm value.

CONCLUSION

With the advent of start-up culture and various branches of entrepreneurship, financing and evaluating negative earning firms have become an important aspect of business valuation. As it has been already mentioned above that the negative earning firms cannot be evaluated in the same fashion as positive earning firms. The financial crisis of 2008 has thrown many companies out of business and many into heavy losses. Therefore, this issue has again attracted the attention of researchers, academicians, and policymakers. After exploring various existing literature on the subject, this chapter has tried to present it in a more simple and presentable way.

Financing companies with negative earnings is a risky investment. Nevertheless, applying a proper valuation method such as Discounted Cash flow (DCF) or Enterprise Value to Earnings before Interest, Taxes, Depreciation and amortization (EV to EBITDA), and following usual safeguards, such as evaluating risk-return trade off and assessing management capability can mitigate the risk of investing in such companies.

We have attempted to examine three of the most important valuation techniques to value negative earning firms in this study. There are many other valuation methods that might also be considered while valuing the negative earning firms. Apart from core valuation methods, the behavioral aspects of managers may also by studied in future researches.

REFERENCES

Barnes, S. A. (n.d.). *The Uber dilemma: Valuing startup and early stage companies with negative earnings.* Retrieved from https://files.constantcontact.com/85e69272601/1234ed1a-3764-40fc-9ff5-fbdce61aa83b.pdf

Damodaran, A. (1999). The dark side of valuation: firms with no earnings, no history and no comparables.

Damodaran, A. (2012) Valuing firms with negative or abnormal earnings. 3rd Edition. Investment valuation: Tools and techniques for determining the value of any asset. In A. Damodaran (Ed.), Investment valuation: tools and techniques for determining the value of any asset, University Edition. iBooks.

David, S. (2018, Dec. 5). 7 business valuation methods all entrepreneurs should know [Web log post]. Retrieved from https://www.fundera.com/blog/business-valuation-methods

Gopalan, R., Nanda, V., & Seru, A. (2007). Affiliated firms and financial support: Evidence from Indian business groups. *Journal of Financial Economics*, *86*(3), 759–795. doi:10.1016/j.jfineco.2006.09.008

Jenkins, D. S. (2003). The transitory nature of negative earnings and the implications for earnings prediction and stock valuation. *Review of Quantitative Finance and Accounting*, *21*(4), 379–404. doi:10.1023/B:REQU.0000004784.30694.0c

Joos, P., & Plesko, G. A. (2005, July). Valuing loss firms. *The Accounting Review*, *80*(3), 847–870. doi:10.2308/accr.2005.80.3.847

Matsumoto, D. A. (2002). Management's incentives to avoid negative earnings surprises. *The Accounting Review*, *77*(3), 483–514. doi:10.2308/accr.2002.77.3.483

Sandra. (2014, Feb. 5). *How to value companies with negative earnings.* Retrieved from http://www.financeninvestments.com/banking/companies-negative-earnings.html

Skinner, D. J. (1994). Why firms voluntarily disclose bad news. *Journal of Accounting Research*, *32*(1), 38–60. doi:10.2307/2491386

Valuing Firms with Negative Earnings. Retrieved from http://pages.stern.nyu.edu/~adamodar/pdfiles/valn2ed/ch22.pdf

Chapter 8
Startup Valuation:
Theories, Models, and Future

Murat Akkaya
https://orcid.org/0000-0002-7071-8662
T.C. İstanbul Arel University, Turkey

ABSTRACT

This chapter analyzes startups and methods for valuing them. Startup means a process for activating a job or action. Startup as a young innovative company has a dominant and key role in modern economies. Startups are newborn or young companies struggling to achieve their potential and growth. One of the most challenging issues in corporate finance is to decide on firm valuation. It is even more difficult to evaluate companies that do not generate income. Deciding the value of a Startup is similar to valuing a specific table. The valuation at this stage is very important. Since startup is a company, it is necessary to look at the methods developed specifically for Startups. Nasser (2016) determines 9 different valuation methods to determine Pre-Money Valuation; Berkus Method, Risk Factor Summation Method, Scorecard Valuation Method, Comparable Transactions Method, Book Value Method, Liquidation Value Method, Discounted Cash Flow Method, First Chicago Method, and Venture Capital Method. Traditional valuation methods are also applicable in valuation.

INTRODUCTION

Recently, the impact of globalization has increased due to the rapid change and progress in the fields of information, communication and technology, and this has enabled new business ideas and business models to grow in a short time. These business models are financial technology firms (FinTech) and startups. Startup word means a process for activating a job or action. Startup as a young innovative company has dominant and key role in modern economies. Startup is early stage company which has unique characteristics and new innovative idea, product or service to succeed market potential and grow. Startups turn ideas into businesses. Entrepreneurial founder has a new innovative idea and tries to capitalize this idea by a startup.

DOI: 10.4018/978-1-7998-1086-5.ch008

The aim of this study is to analyze startups and the methods for startup valuation. With the increasing number of incubators, venture capital funds and angel investors, people are becoming more and more aware of the presence of more startup companies. The entrepreneurs, who usually set out with their own limited resources or with the support they get from their immediate surroundings, aim at investing in a venture capital or angel investor at this stage. Following this, new investors or existing investors are following second, third round investments. It is even more difficult to evaluate companies that do not generate income such as startups. Traditional valuation methods and specific methos have been used in startup valuation. The most important criteria in the evaluation of startup are as follows; market forces in the sector, money supply and demand balance in the sector, the size of sales or sales in the same sector recently and the appetite and risk limit of the investor.

STARTUP

Startups are newborn or young companies struggling to achieve their potential and growth. Startups create opportunity for new jobs. Moreover, small innovative and technology companies have increased the growth of world economy in recent years.

Newborn companies have some common characteristics despite diversity in their forms. These are (Damodaran, 2009):

- They don't have histories or they have very limited history with one or two years of data.
- They have small or no revenues and they result in operating losses
- They need private equity.
- Most of them don't survive and fail.
- Multiple claims on equity.
- Illiquid investments ocur.

Common characteristics of startups are analyzed by many studies. According to these studies, most of startups fail especially in the very early stages. There is high rate of failure in theese companies. Less than one third of young companies survive (Vesper, 1990). Lack of finance, business knowledgeand technology, team management problems, lead to startup problems.

Startups which can survive have a significant role in economies and they create success stories (Martinsons, 2002). Blank & Dorf (2014) define startup as a enterpreuners searching repeatable and scalable business model under extreme uncertainty.

A startup is (Oliveira & Zones, 2018):

- Business model in which a startup searches oppotunities to increase customer's values and /or transform this value as a revenue for the startup.
- Repeatable as an ability of making products constantly available to the end-user regardless of demand and with little need for customization and adaptation.
- Scalable as an ability to increase scale by customers, and growing. Thus, operating costs decrease comparing to income.
- A company that appears under extreme uncertain conditions.

The Lifecycle of Startups

Startups are diversified in an economy. They own a lifecycle (Figure 1) and different stages in their life. These stages are shown in Figure 1 (Salamzadeh & Kawamorita, 2015);

- **Bootstrapping Stage:** Bootstrapping is defined as highly creative ways of acquiring the use of resources without borrowing (Freear et al., 2002). This is early stage of a startup. In this stage, entrepreneurial founder has a new innovative idea and tries to turn this idea into a profitable business. High risk and uncertainty take place in this stage. He/she needs a team. This stage aims to position the startup for growth by demonstrating product feasibility, cash management capability, team building and management, and customer acceptance (Brush et. al., 2006). Thus, angel investors discover startups in this stage and they invest on them.
- **Seed Stage:** This stage covers different activities such as teamwork, prototype anlysis, market entrance, valuation, support mechanisms search such as accelerators and incubators. Then, the startups grow by average investments. This stage is complex and includes high uncertainty. The main characteristics of this stage is the initial capital to create product and/or service (Manchanda & Muralidharan, 2014). Startup owners look for accelerator or incubators, small medium enterprise development (SME) centers, and hatcheries to accelerate this process. Most of them do not attain such support mechanisms. Consequently, they have low profit. Thus, most of them fail. Who succeeds in this stage will survive and be a profitable company. *Valuation* is the main concern by this stage.
- **Creation Stage:** This stage starts by market entrance, product sell and first employee hire. Company will be formed in this stage. Moreover, corporate finance is mainly used to finance startup. This stage includes high investment. Thus, venture capitals finance the startups to facilitate the creation stage.

The development of a startup can be summarized in four stages (Figure 2).

Figure 1. Lifecycle of Startups

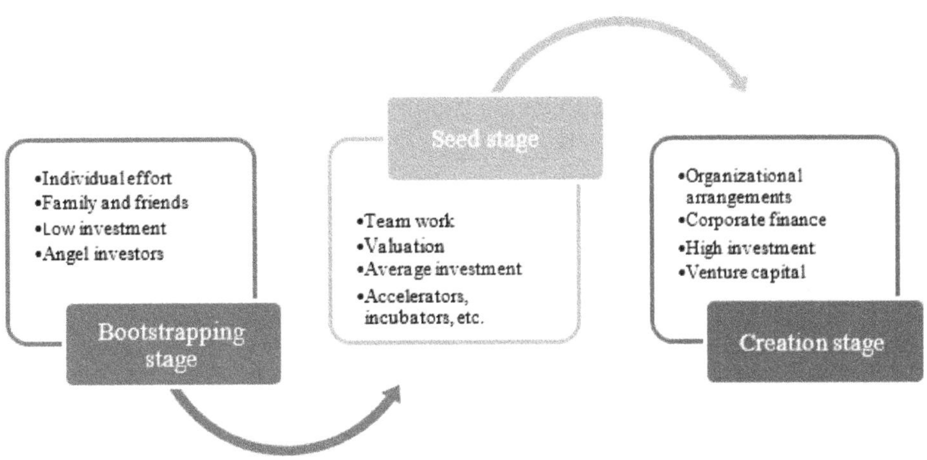

Source: Salamzadeh & Kawamorita, 2015

Figure 2. The stages of Startups

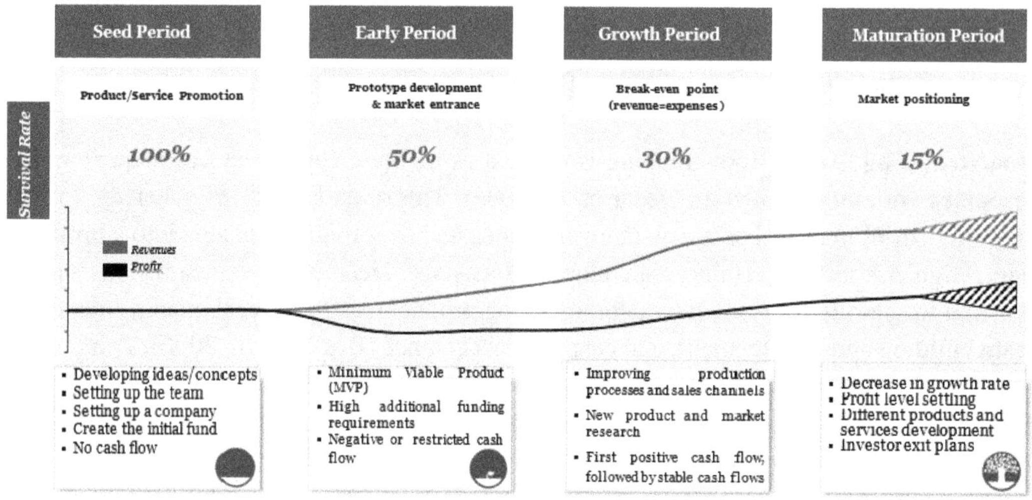

Source: PwCplatform, 2019

STARTUPS THEORİES

The theories considered as “startup theories” in the literature are in three main areas: organization, management, and entrepreneurship (Salamzadeh & Kawamorita, 2015).

- **Organization Theories**

Van de Ven et al. (1984) first considered three main approaches for startup creation. These approaches are entrepreneurial, organizational and ecological. The organizational approach focuses on:

- Conditions under which an organization is planned
- The processes followed in initial development
- Consequences of theses processes on firm’s performance

There are also relevant studiesin organizational approach: Contingency Theory (Tosi & Slocum, 1984), Gartner (1985), Katz & Gartner (1988), Organizational Configurations (Miller, 1990), Uncertainty Theory (Kamps & Pólos, 1999), Organizational Ecology Theory (Scholz & Reydon, 2009) and Resource Dependence Theory (Davis & Cobb, 2010).

- **Management Theories**

Management means relations with people. Management theories focus on individuals or teams coordinating their efforts to achieve goals. They have less attempt to explain startups in an organizational sense. The management theories mainly are: human resource management, small business governance, strategic management, complexity theory and team management.

- **Entrepreneurship Theories**

Van de Ven et al. (1984) argues that the entrepreneurial approach explains the characteristics of the entrepreneur or promoter of a new entity. But this approach has problems in explaining startups. Salamzadeh (2015) categorizes entrepreneurship theories on startups in two: macro level theories (Schumpeter, 1934) and micro and meso level theories.

Eentrepreneurship theories focuses on the early stages of business or organization. Because entrepreneur has a new idea, creativity and innovation sense which are paramount and integral parts of startups.

Startup Challenges

The startup challenges are unique. Hovewer, they differ due to factors affecting startups lifecycle. The main common challenges are (Salamzadeh & Kawamorita, 2015):

- **Financial Challenges:** Finance plays important role in a startup process and it is an integral part of this process. Startups may face financial problems in any stage of lifecycle. In bootstrapping stage, entrepreneur has a new innovative idea and tries to convince relatives and friends to invest in this idea in this early stage. Thus, he or she needs extra money to achieve his/her idea. Angel investors provide finance by reasonable valuation plans in the seed stage. Finally, venture capitals are the finance provider in the creation stage.
- **Support Mechanisms:** Support mechanisms have an important role in startups. Venture capitals angel investors, accelerators, incubators, technoparks, SME centers, are examples of these support mechanism. Support mechanisms decrease the risks in startups' lifecycle.
- **Human Resources:** Each startup has a founder and/or some cofounders at the beginning. Then, as startups grow, they need qualified persons or experts to develop the prototype. That's why, they try to find people and make a team. Consequently, they hire employees. This process is important. Otherwise, startup might fail due to lack of knowledge and human resource management.
- **Environmental Factors:** Environmental factors such as customer choices, trend changes, market and legal issues affect startup's success. Enviroment might be supportive or destructive. The environmental factors for a startup are very crucial. They are more difficult than an existing company.

STARTUP VALUATION

One of the most challenging issues in corporate finance is to decide on firm valuation. It is even more difficult to evaluate companies that do not generate income. Deciding the value of a Startup is similar to valuing a specific table. The valuation at this stage is very important. A bad appraisal at the beginning affects the next rounds negatively. So firm valuation method should be examined in detail.

The most important criteria examined in startup valuation are;

- Global/local economical factors
- Financial conditions
- Market forces involved in sector
- Money supply and demand balance in the sector

- The size of sales or sales recently in the same sector
- The investor's appetite and risk limit
- Investor sentiment and confidence

Also, some difficulties that appear in the startup valuation are (Kotova, 2014):

- High degree of uncertainty in efficiency. It is the result of new markets or by new business models,
- Information about cash flows and the amount of reinvestments is complex,
- Uncertainty in valuation.
- There is no income at the beginning of startup valuation,
- Risks in valuation.

Thus, startups investors/analysts need to use different methods to deal with the difficulties in the cash flow and valuation by focusing on similar indicators about startups. They define a discount rate including risks associated with investment. Finally, they correct the necessary share for investors and owners.

The valuation methods of a startup in different stages are shown in Figure 3.

Some authors describe early-stage valuation as an art, not a science. But this is no real. Because there are factors influencing valuation (Borsa İstanbul, 2016):

- *Traction*: Traction is the first to convince investors. Investors are convinced when they see the users,
- *Reputation*: Reputation leads high valuation.
- *Revenues*. They make the startup easier to value and are important especially for the Business to Business startups.
- *Distribution Channel*
- *Industry Hotness.*

Achleitner and Nathusius (2003) classify the valuation methods as in figure 4.

Startup is a box and very special box. Each box has a value. The value of a box increases by putting more things in such as patents, management, team, innovative ideas. What is the value of startup? The answer depends on the Pre-Money Valuation and Post-Money Valuation. Nasser (2016) determines 9 different valuation methods to determine Pre-Money Valuation.

1. The Berkus Method
2. The Risk Factor Summation Method
3. The Scorecard Valuation Method
4. The Comparable Transactions Method
5. The Book Value Method
6. The Liquidation Value Method
7. The Discounted Cash Flow (DCF) Method
8. The First Chicago Method
9. The Venture Capital Method

Figure 3. The Startup Valuation Methods by PwC

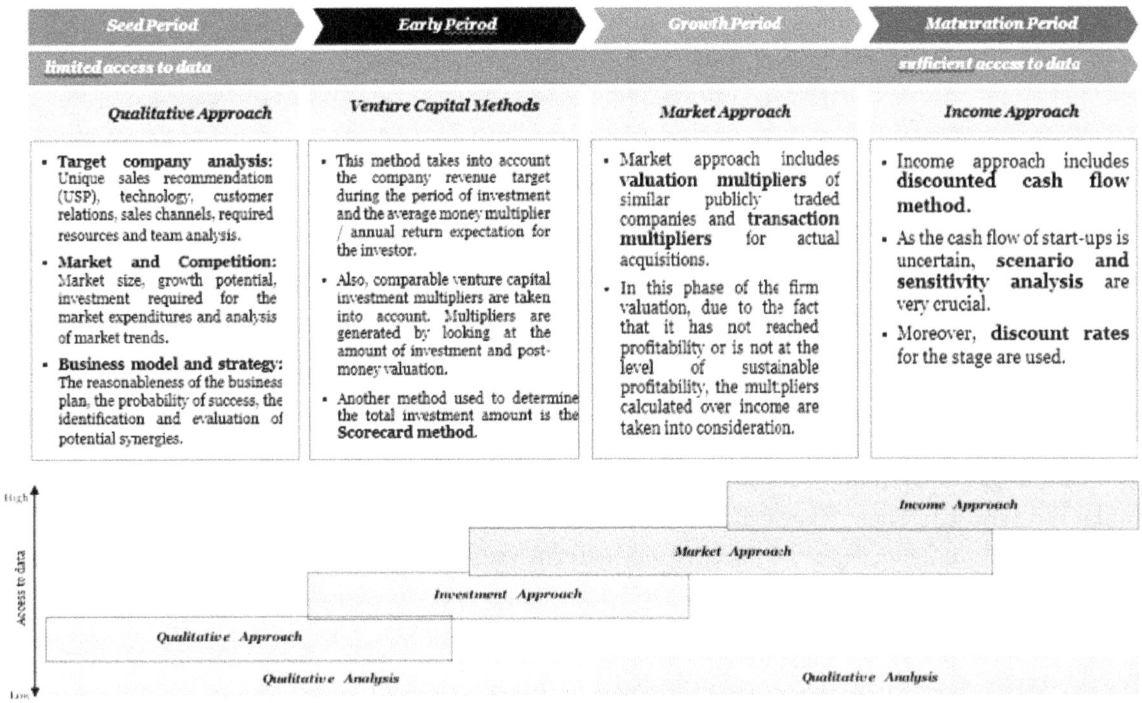

Figure 4. The Startup Valuation Methods by Achleitner and Nathusius

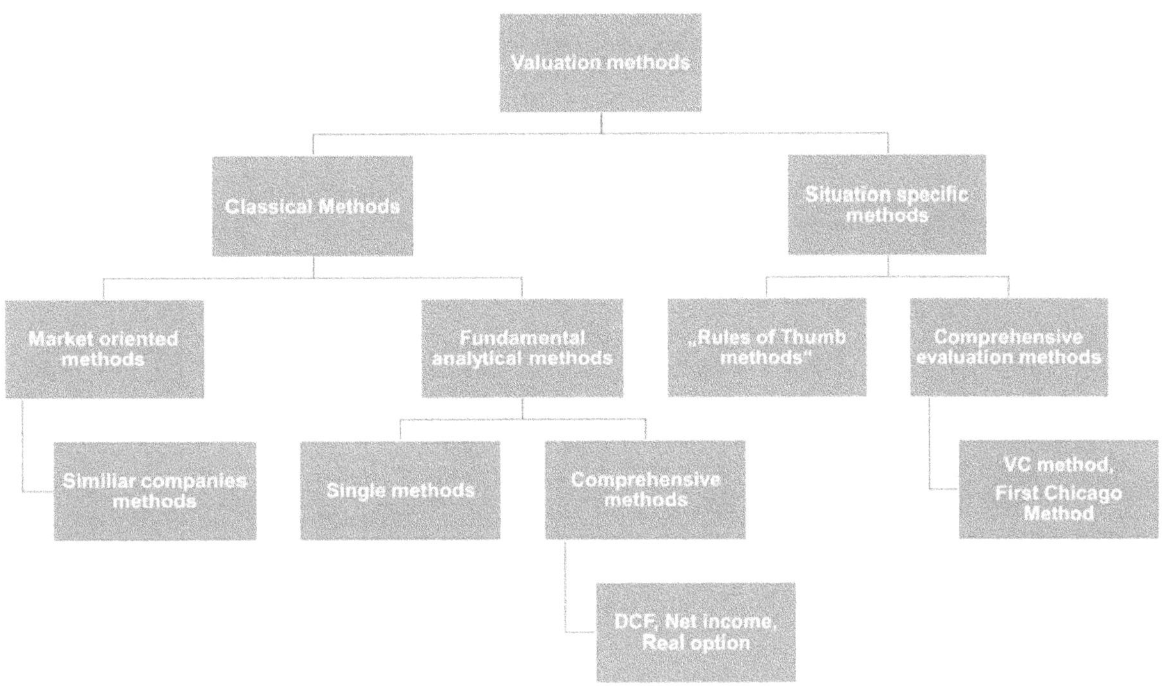

Figure 5. The Berkus Method Valuation

Given a max. value of $2M for a similar box

1.	Sound idea (basic value)	**$300k**/$400k
2.	Prototype (technology)	**$100k**/$400k
3.	Quality management team (execution)	**$300k**/$400k
4.	Strategic relationships (go-to-market)	**$200k**/$400k
5.	Product rollout or Sales (production)	**$100k**/$400k
	BOX VALUATION	**$1,000,000**

1. The Berkus Method: Dave Berkus develops flexible and simple method in 2009. This method has also convenient rule of thumb. To estimate the startup value, investor should know at first how much a similar box is worth. Then, 5 key criteria are assesed in building boxes (Figure 5).

The amounts in figure 5 are maximum earned to form a valuation. The Berkus Method is a pre-revenue valuation and allows up to $2 million or up to $2.5 million as a post rollout value. The Berkus Method values startups below the actual amount. Also, this method is not applicable after revenue creation in any time.

2. The Risk Factor Summation (RFS) Method: This Method evolves from the Berkus Method that has a narrow set of important criteria in valuation. This method defines the various types of risks. First step in this method is to determine an initial value of startup box that is the average value for a similar box in same sector. Then, there are 12 risk factors risk factors modelled as multiples of $250k, to value box. Risk factors range from very low risk $500k to very high risk -$500k. The highest risk is management risk (Figure 6).

The most difficult part in RFS and other valuation methods is to find actual data about similar startups.

Figure 6. The Risk Factor Summation Valuation

INITIAL VALUE				**$1,500,000**
1.	MANAGEMENT RISK	*Very low*	*+$500,000*	$2,000,000
2.	STAGE OF THE BUSINESS	*Normal*		
3.	LEGISLATION/POLITICAL RISK	*Normal*		
4.	MANUFACTURING RISK	*Normal*		
5.	SALES AND MANUFACTURING RISK	*Normal*		
6.	FUNDING/CAPITAL RAISING RISK	*Normal*		
7.	COMPETITION RISK	*Very high*	*-$500,000*	$1,500,000
8.	TECHNOLOGY RISK	*Low*	*+$250,000*	$1,750,000
9.	LITIGATION RISK	*Very low*	*+$500,000*	$2,250,000
10.	INTERNATIONAL RISK	*Normal*		
11.	REPUTATION RISK	Very low	+$500,000	$2,750,000
12.	POTENTIAL LUCRATIVE EXIT	Normal		
BOX VALUATION				**$2,750,000**

Table 1. The Scorecard Valuation Method Valuation

COMPARISON FACTOR	RANGE	TARGETCOMPANY	FACTOR
Strength of Entrepreneur and Team	30% max	125%	0.3750
Size of the Opportunity	25% max	150%	0.3750
Product/Technology	15% max	100%	0.1500
Competitive Environment	10% max	75%	0.0750
Marketing/Sales/Partnerships	10% max	80%	0.0800
Need for Additional Investment	5% max	100%	0.0500
Other factors (great early customer feedback)	5% max	100%	0.0500
		SUM	1.0750

Source: Payne, 2011

3. The Scorecard Valuation Method (SVM): This Method posted by Bill Payne (2011) is a way to value prerevenue startups and very popular among angel investors. SVM is same with RFS method at beginning. First step is to determine a base value of startup comparing with companies in the same region and sector of the target company. Then, factors depending on the investor's perception wil have different weights considering their impact on the success. Factors and weights are strength of the management team (30%), size of the opportunity (25%), product/technology (15%), competitive environment (10%), marketing/sales channels/partnerships (5%), need for additional investment (5%) and others (5%). The startup whose score is 17,5% will be better than an average similar startup (Table 1).

Valuation for the target company = the Sum of Factors (1.075) X the average pre-money valuation of $ 2.0 million at a pre-money = $2.15 million.

4. The Comparable Transactions Method (CTM): CTM is for pre and post-revenue startups and indeed a rule of three. The Comparable Transactions Method finds approximate the market price of the target. CTM uses informations about assets same or similar to startup to value (Figure 7). First step is to identify the relevant comparable transactions. Then, the key valuation metrics are calculated such as EBITDA, gross margin or specific indicators related to the sector.

5. The Book Value Method (BVM): Book value is the value of the owners' equity in the balance sheet (capital and reserves). The book value (net book value) corresponds to the amount calculated by deducting the payables from the total assets. This is the difference between total assets and liabilities. The Book Value Method focuses on tangible assets and tangible value of a firm. However, startups focus on intangible assets. Thus, BVM is not applicable for startups.

The book value is sometimes insufficient to reflect the real values of assets. Investors use Adjusted Book Value. Adjusted book value is used to calculate the price in holding property or assets such as securities, liquidation facilities or assigning value to companies faced by companies. Adjusted book value method can be used as a determining method in evaluating:

- Relatively new enterprises,
- Enterprises whose earnings are not stable,

Figure 7. The Comparable Transactions Method

	Sold for	*Revenue multiple*	*WAU multiple*
SIMILAR BOX #1	$957	3,0 x	2,3 x
SIMILAR BOX #2	$647	3,3 x	6,4 x
SIMILAR BOX #3	$327	1,9 x	1,5 x
SIMILAR BOX #4	$737	5,4 x	0,2 x
SIMILAR BOX #5	$6,248	8,6 x	5,7 x
SIMILAR BOX #6	$39,087	7,3 x	4 x
SIMILAR BOX #7	$6,576	12,1 x	31 x
SIMILAR BOX #8	$4,258	8,3 x	3,5 x
SIMILAR BOX #9	$3,798	3,4 x	1,1 x
		...	
		Revenue	*WAU*
MY BOX INDICATORS		$900	1,000
WEIGHTED AVERAGE MULTIPLES		7,6	6,7
BOX VALUATION BASED ON...		**$685**	**$6,736**

- Strikes, legal regulations or the aging of its products predictability make valuation difficult or speculative businesses.

6. The Liquidation Value Method (LVM): The liquidation value is the value of a firm in the event of a definite stopping of the activity. When calculating the liquidation value, it is necessary to consider all costs related to the liquidation of the company. The liquidation value corresponds to the amount obtained from the sale of assets by deducting the taxes paid due to different commission payments, unemployment benefits and the increases in value. The liquidation value differs according to whether a voluntary or compulsory liquidation is considered. Voluntary liquidation is active in order to obtain the best price for each active item the sale of assets within a reasonable period of time. In obligatory liquidation, active assets are sold as quickly as possible, often at a one-time auction. While the historical costs are taken into consideration in the book value method, the current market value of the assets is taken into consideration in this method. However, in case of liquidation of the assets of the company, they may be sold with a value less than the market value. At the same time, the determination of the assets of the liquidated company will be easy if it is traded in the secondary market, if there is no such market. In practice, each enterprise has at least a value equal to the purge value.

7. The Discounted Cash Flow (DCF) Method: The discounted cash flows method in valuation is the process of discounting the future cash flows based on time value of money. The firm assets create a value as long as it can generate cash. Thus, analysts determine the company value by estimating the future cash flows. When estimating cash flows, a certain discount rate is used. With this discount rate, cash flows are discounted to present value considering the time value of money. Discounted cash flows are stated as the difference between cash inflows and cash outflows calculated according to a discount rate.

Advantages (Elmas et al 2017):

- Method provides the scientific value to obtain the true value of the firm,
- It is a method that reflects the future performance of the firm in the most accurate manner to the value of the firm,
- It focuses on the ability to generate cash,

- It is a flexible valuation that allows analysis of different situations
- Many variables such as economic fluctuations and investment policies reflects the impact on firm value,
- It provides possibility to assess the situation in mergers and acquisitions.

Disadvantages:

- Financial projections may be more optimistic or pessimistic,
- Cash flows and weighted average cost of capital which are the main variables of the method are very sensitive to predictions. As a result, it is difficult to reach real results in determining the firm value,
- It is based on subjective assumptions,
- Future uncertainties affect the firm value,
- Method uses only cash flows, cost of capital and ignores some specific issues and strategic factors.

The first difficulty in applying this method to Startups is the estimation of future cash flows. There are many ambiguous factors that affect their work. Because Startups are early stage and fast growth oriented initiatives. In addition, there is often no data for previous years. Therefore, it is almost impossible to make a consistent estimate of future cash flows. The second difficulty relates to the estimate of Startup's growth and discounting rate. Since startups are fast and growth-oriented companies, the growth rates used in financial projection should be well questioned. The terminal value that is the growth rate to be used in the calculation of the total value to be calculated for the years after the fifth year (or the first ten years) will not be easy. In addition, the determination of the rate to be used in discounting the estimated future cash flows to the present value will not be as easy. The startups are risky enterprises due to the uncertainties in their environment and these risks should be placed in the discounting rate in some way. In spite of all these difficulties, analysts can try to find the value of our Startup by applying the DCF method to the data which may give us a starting point to compare with other methods[1].

8. The First Chicago Method: The First Chicago Method is used by venture capital and private equity investors in a situation specific business valuation approach for early stage companies and for companies that have growth potential. Value is the weighted average of these cases. This method combines market-oriented elements and DCF method.

The First Chicago Method is method for post-revenue valuation and has 4 steps[2].

- Define future scenarios for startup: This method makes 3 valuation scenario: a worst case (tiny box), a normal case (normal box) and a best case (big box). Analysts should define financial forecast (including revenues, earnings, cashflows, exit-horizon etc.) for each case. Step 1 is difficult and needs an extensive analytical research.
- Estimate divestment price for each scenario using multiples: After financial-forecast, analysts determine the Terminal Value at the time of the exit (divestment price) by applying multiples. The idea at this stage to compare investment within the same peer group characterized by industry, stage or region. Peer group is critical factor in valuation. Multiples are also important. There are different multiples suitable for different assets such as EBIT, Revenues etc.
- Determine required rate of return and, then calculate value for each scenario: WACC (Weighted Average Cost of Capital) and CAPM (Capital Asset Pricing Model) are used to determine rate of return. But, they have problems. Many Venture Capitals use the required return they determine.

- Estimate probabilities of each scenarios and calculate weighted sum: Last step is to allocate a probability that are naturally correlated to definition of the scenarios and their number. Nobody can estimate precise probabilities of each scenario. After determining probabilities, calculation of the weighted sum of the valuations depending on each scenario takes place (Figure 9).

$$\text{Valuation}^i = \frac{TV^i}{(1+r)^h} + \sum_{t=1}^{h} \frac{CF^i t}{(1+r)^t}$$

i: index of scenario
h: time to exit
T: terminal value
CF: cash flow

9. The Venture Capital Method: Venture capital is a financial method to realize investment ideas of dynamic, creative and innovative entrepreneurs who do not have sufficient financial power by providing capital transfer to share capital and management support when necessary (Ark, 2002). This Method is first described by Bill Sahlman in 1987 and useful in pre-money valuation of pre-revenue startups. Venture capital and private equity are used equally in Europe. However, these two concepts are separated in America. Venture capital investments are long term investments. They are not liquid in the short term and the return period of the investment varies between five and ten years. Basic features are;

Figure 8.. The First Chicago Method Valuation

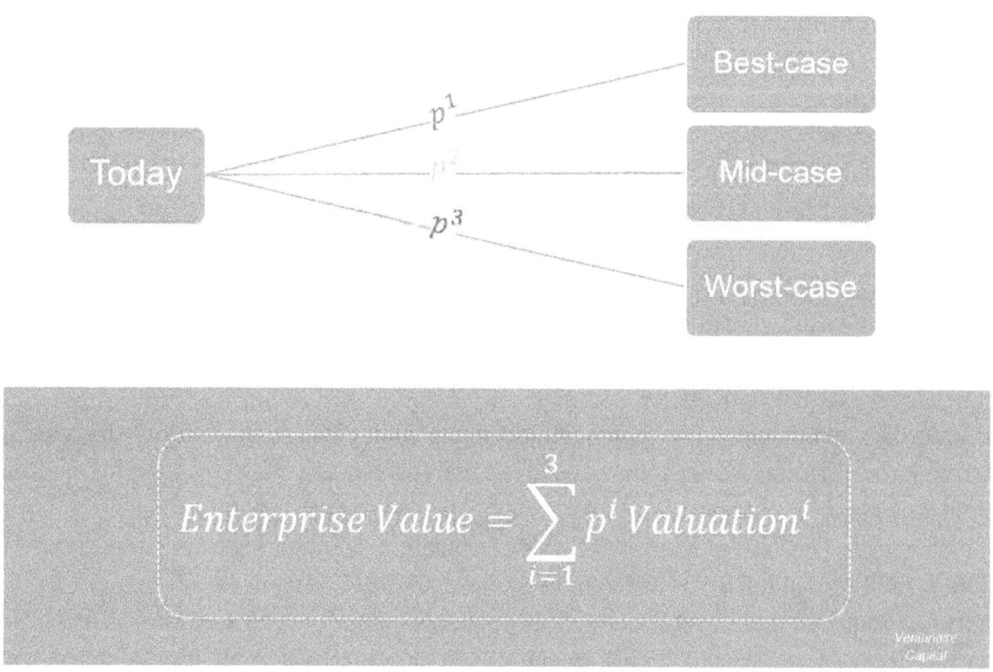

Figure 9. Venture Capital Diagram

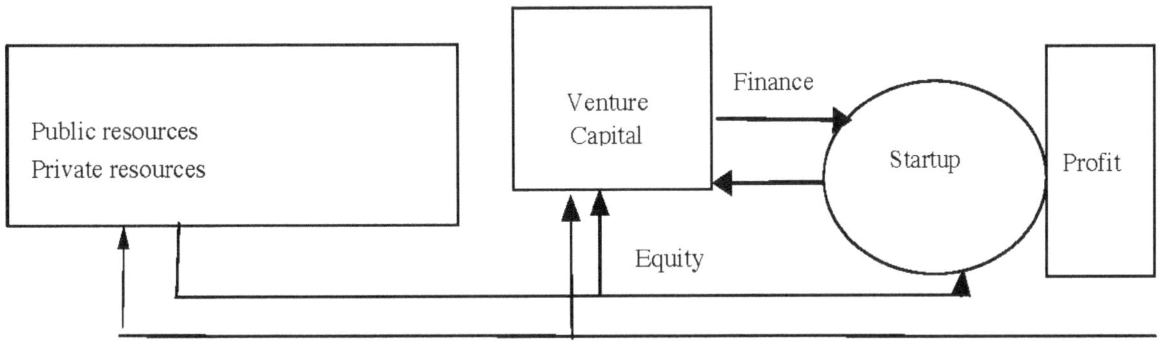

- Financing entrepreneurs who are not supported by banks,
- Making investments in return for stock,
- Long term investment
- Selling the shares after the company has reached a certain level of development.

Venture capitals are interested in a new technological invention to be established or startup in the establishment stage (Figure 9). Therefore, venture capitalist providin funds, does not have the financial data of the past years of the entrepreneurial firm. Thus, it prevents the estimation by making comparisons in the market. This problem causes the venture capitalist to make a decision under uncertainty and increase its risk. The amount of venture capital is not limited to the monetary size of the investment. The venture capitalist can also actively participate in the feasibility studies, establishment and management of the enterprise by using its managerial knowledge and experience (Kuğu, 2004).

Types of Venture Capital Financing are Sead Capital, Start-Up Capital, Early Stage, Gate and Bridge Financing and Management Buy-Out (Çoban & Saban, 2004).

- *Seed capital*: It can be summarized as the financing of the idea stage. This stage is the provision of core capital for the creation of a new product or service. This financing method can be used if the project of the enterprise has a market capacity to produce new products/services and to grow rapidly.
- *Startup capital*: Initial capital creates the general use of venture capital. This financing method is used during the development phase which is the second stage of R & D activities. It is generally used for the financing of companies that have been in the process of establishment or have been in operation for a short time but have not been able to trade their products.
- *Early Stage and Gate Financing*: At this stage, the company has reached a certain size. There are no goods or services available to the market, no brand image and a significant market share that will ensure the superiority of the product in the market. At this stage, the company develops its prototype, but it needs funds for commercial production and marketing. It is difficult to find funds other than venture capital because Firm is insufficient to obtain loans from the banking system and also there is no possibility to provide funds from the capital market. At this stage, the company also has a number of managerial problems. These problems can be overcome by the financial and managerial support of the venture capitalist.

- *Gate and Bridge Financing*: Bridge financing is provided to companies hoping to open to public within 6 months to 1 year. If the company is in a good position for the supply of shares, it is a method used to provide the finance that the company needs in order to continue its activities until it becomes public.
- *Management Buy-Out*: It is s type of financing to enable the company management team to obtain the firm. These investments face little risk and are preferred because they are profitable. Within the scope of financial partnerships, venture capital and private equity funds come into play. Venture capital funds are currently engaged in startup and service-based businesses such as ideas, business plans and product development. Private equity funds are concerned with the development, bridging and management change financing of the more advanced enterprises. Venture capital concept includes only investments in the establishment stages of companies. Investments made during the growth and expansion periods of the companies are called private equity.

The operation procedure of this financing model is as follows (İçerli and Akkaya 2001):

- A professional feasibility report including comprehensive financial and technical research for the product or design developed.
- Project cost at the end of the feasibility report
- A business plan based on the feasibility report is prepared and sent to the venture capital firm.
- The feasibility report is reviewed by the venture capital firm.
- If the report reviewed is promising, the venture capital firm will re-prepare a feasibility report. If the project is not considered sufficient at the end of this report, it is rejected.
- If the project is at the expected profitability level, partnership negotiations are initiated with the entrepreneur company authorities.
- If the agreement is achieved, the establishment of the entrepreneurial company is initiated for the realization of the Project.

Venture capital is a kind of partnership. The venture capital investor calculates that the prices of the shares purchased by the company at a low price level will be highly valued after the growth and development of the enterprise. There are lots of variables effective in determining the share of the partnership: the expected future price/earnings ratio, net profit for the future, tax rates, investment time, discount rate and profitability index of investment. In order for the venture capitalist to support investment, the present value of the investment must be known first by using present value formula. After finding net present value and then the understanding of the feasibility of the investment, it is necessary to determine the partnership share of the entrepreneur and the venture capitalist. The following formula is used to determine the share of the partnership.

$$\text{Requested Share Rate} = \frac{(\text{Profit after tax/capital invested})(\text{Capital invested}) \times (1+\text{IPO rate})}{(1-\text{Capital gain tax rate})(\text{Prince earnings Ratio} \times \text{Net profit})}$$

Venture capital focuses on specific return on investment and selling price. Thus, it is easy for venture capital to determine the maximum price they pay after adjusting for dilution.

Venture Capital Valuation example is shown in figure 10.

Figure 10. Venture Capital Valuation
Source: Nasser, 2016

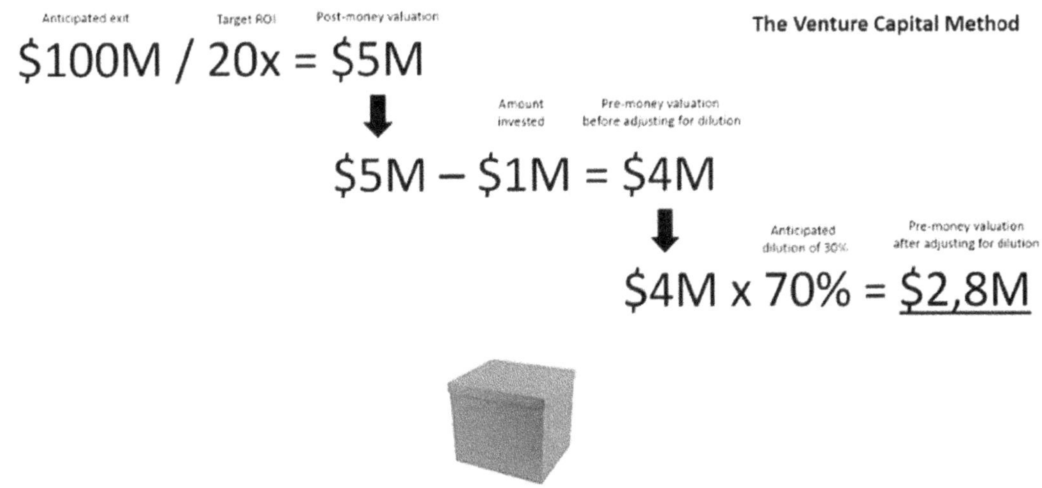

Also, the most commonly used company valuation methods are[3];

- *Comparable Market Value Method:* The previously realized market operations and the value of the companies are examined by comparing to the companies which have similar operations and structures are bought, sold or invested. Access to such information is not easy for non-public enterprises. However, value information on similar companies can still be obtained using a number of resources. In this respect, startups may ask for support from Angel Investors, Angel Investment Networks, entrepreneurs who have already received investments or incubators.
- *Reconstruction Cost Method:* This method calculates the costs that are required to build the current startup as it is from scratch and to bring it to the current location. These costs may be physical investment expenditures. The time spent by Startup founders or employees is also taken into account in the total cost. For example, if the three founders came together and had an early phase of a startup as a result of a year effort, the three founder's one-year alternative costs should also be taken into account when calculating the value of the startup. In other words, instead of being the entrepreneur, the annual earnings will be calculated in the case of their work and this amount is added to the value of the startup.
- *Modified Berkus Method:* This method introduced by angel investor named David Berkus is subsequently modified and used in various ways. In this method, a fixed dollar value range is determined for each criterion set in the table below and their sum is taken into consideration as the value of startup. If there is the following appraisal criterion in Startup, add the following amount to the value of Startup.

According to this table, the value of startup with a good team, completed the prototype and tracktion starts from $ 2 million.

Table 2. Modified Berkus Method

Interesting, high potential, attractive idea	$ 500.000 - $1.000.000
A good management team	$ 500.000 - $2.000.000
Established strategic alliances and market entry barrier	up to $ 500.000
Prototype completed and tested	$ 500.000 - $1.000.000
High quality and advisors board	up to $ 1.000.000
Product sales and tracktion formed	up to $ 1.000.000

Source: Author

- *The Rule of Thumb:* According to this simple method, one-third of startup shares should go to the founders, one-third to managers, and one-third to investors. For example, the investment value of a startup as USD 500.000 million can be considered as USD 1.500.000.
- *Multiples Method*
- *Property Value method*

FUTURE RESEARCH DIRECTIONS

The aim of this study is to explain the methods for startup valuation. In this study, startup valuation models are explained theoretically. Although the partial sample are figured in the study, the valuation samples could not be reached due to the shortness of time. In future studies, data from venture capital companies and valuation companies can be obtained to compare the valuation results and the current values of the startups.

Conclusion

Startup is a young company that has just started developing. Statups are usually small and initially funded and operated by either a number of founders or a single person. They offer a product or service that is not available anywhere else on the market, or even if there are on the market, the founders believe that they are presented in poor quality. They have a huge impact on the today's economy and they increase the growth of each economy.

The costs of Startups tend to exceed their incomes in the initial phase of improvement, testing and marketing. Therefore, they usually need funding. One of the most challenging issues for an entrepreneur is to decide on company valuation. The valuation of startups is difficult. Because, these companies do not generate income. There are different methods in the literature for pre-Money Valuation such as Berkus Method, Risk Factor Summation Method, Scorecard Valuation Method, Comparable Transactions Method, Book Value Method, Liquidation Value Method, Discounted Cash Flow (DCF) Method, First Chicago Method, The Venture Capital Method. The Venture Capital Methos is the most popular and used method.

Since startups do not have a long history and are not yet profitable, investing in them is considered highly risky. Startups have a high failure rate. Thus, investors not only consider an idea, but also take into account the management team's experience. As a result, each startup's specific features and the current stage determine the valuation.

REFERENCES

Achleitner, A. K., & Nathusius, E. (2003). Syndizierung von Venture-Capital-Deals. *Entrepreneur des Jahres–NEWS*, *2*, 8.

Ark, A. H. (2002). Risk Sermayesi: Tarihsel Gelişimi ve Türkiye Ekonomisinin Yeniden Yapılandırılmasında Potansiyel Rolü ve Önemi. *Activefinans, 82vd.*

Blank, S., & Dorf, B. (2014). *Startup: manual do empreendedor.* Alta Books Editora.

Borsa İstanbul. (2016). *Startup Valuation*. https://bfb.az/wp-content/uploads/2016/10/Startup-Valuation.pdf

Brush, C. G., Carter, N. M., Gatewood, E. J., Greene, P. G., & Hart, M. M. (2006). The use of bootstrapping by women entrepreneurs in positioning for growth. *Venture Capital*, *8*(1), 15–31. doi:10.1080/13691060500433975

Çoban, M. & Saban, M. (2006). Türkiye'de risk sermayesi uygulaması ve sorunları. *Muhasebe ve Finansman Dergisi*, (31), 131-140.

Damodaran, A. (2009). *Valuing young, startup and growth companies: estimation issues and valuation challenges*. Available at SSRN 1418687.

Davis, G. F., & Cobb, J. A. (2010). Resource dependence theory: Past and future. *Research in the Sociology of Organizations*, *28*(1), 21–42. doi:10.1108/S0733-558X(2010)0000028006

De Oliveira, F. B., & Zotes, L. P. (2018). Valuation methodologies for business startups: A bibliographical study and survey. *Brazilian Journal of Operations & Production Management*, *15*(1), 96–111. doi:10.14488/BJOPM.2018.v15.n1.a9

Elmas, B., Yılmaz, H., & Yalçın, S. (2017). Firma Değerlemesinde İndirgenmiş Nakit Akımları Yönteminin Kullanımı: Bıst Bilişim Endeksinde Yer Alan Firmalar Üzerinde Bir Uygulama. *Atatürk Üniversitesi İktisadi ve İdari Bilimler Dergisi*, *31*(5), 1221–1238.

Freear, J., Sohl, J. E., & Wetzel, W. (2002). Angles on angels: Financing technology-based ventures- a historical perspective. *Venture Capital: An International Journal of Entrepreneurial Finance*, *4*(4), 275–287. doi:10.1080/13691060220000024923

Gartner, W. B. (1985). A conceptual framework for describing the phenomenon of new venture creation. *Academy of Management Review*, *10*(4), 694–706. doi:10.5465/amr.1985.4279094

İçerli, M. Y., & Akkaya, G. C. (2001). KOBİlerin Finansal Problemlerinin Çözümünde Risk Sermayesi Finansman Modeli. *DEÜ-SBE Dergisi*, *3*(3), 61–70.

Kamps, J., & Pólos, L. (1999). Reducing uncertainty: a formal theory of organizations in action. *American Journal of Sociology*, *104*(6), 1776–1812. doi:10.1086/210223

Katz, J., & Gartner, W. B. (1988). Properties of emerging organisation. *Academy of Management Review*, *13*(3), 429–441. doi:10.5465/amr.1988.4306967

Kotova, M. V. (2013). The theoretical and methodological basis of startups valuation. *Економіка: реалії часу*, 1(11), 107-112.

Kuğu, T. D. (2004). Finansman yöntemi olarak risk sermayesi. *Yönetim ve Ekonomi: Celal Bayar Üniversitesi İktisadi ve İdari Bilimler Fakültesi Dergisi*, *11*(2), 141–152.

Manchanda, K. & Muralidharan, P. (2014, January). Crowdfunding: a new paradigm in startup financing. In *Global Conference on Business & Finance Proceedings* (9, 1, 369-374). Institute for Business & Finance Research.

Martinsons, M. G. (2002). Electronic commerce in China: Emerging success stories. *Information & Management*, *39*(7), 571–579. doi:10.1016/S0378-7206(02)00009-5

Miller, D. (1990). Organizational configurations: Cohesion, change, and prediction. *Human Relations*, *43*(8), 771–789. doi:10.1177/001872679004300805

Nasser, S. (2016). Valuation for startups—9 methods explained.

National Venture Capital Association–NVCA. (2000). Retrieved from http://www.nvca.org.tr/main/index/html

PwCplatform. (2019). *17. Çözüm Ortaklığı Platformu Türkiye Start-up Dünyası, Değerleme Yöntemleri ve Yatırımcı Bakış Açısı*. Retrieved from https://www.pwc.com.tr/tr/Etkinlik/17-platform/sunumlar/turkiye-start-up-dunyasi.pdf

Salamzadeh, A. (2015). New venture creation: controversial perspectives and theories. *Economic Analysis*, *48*(3/4).

Salamzadeh, A. & Kawamorita Kesim, H. (2015). Startup companies: life cycle and challenges. In *Proceedings 4th International Conference on Employment, Education and Entrepreneurship (EEE)*, Belgrade, Serbia. 10.2139srn.2628861

Scholz, M., & Reydon, T. A. (2009). Organizational ecology: No Darwinian evolution after all. A rejoinder to Lemos. *Philosophy of the Social Sciences*, *40*(3), 504–512. doi:10.1177/0048393109348866

Schumpeter, J. A. (1934). *The theory of economic development: An inquiry into profits, capital, credit, interest, and the business cycle*. Transaction Publishers.

Tosi, H. L. Jr, & Slocum, J. W. Jr. (1984). Contingency theory: Some suggested directions. *Journal of Management*, *10*(1), 9–26. doi:10.1177/014920638401000103

Van de Ven, A. H., Hudson, R., & Schroeder, D. M. (1984). Designing new business startups: Entrepreneurial, organizational, and ecological considerations. *Journal of Management, 10*(1), 87–108. doi:10.1177/014920638401000108

Vesper, K. H. (1990). *New Venture Strategies* (2nd ed.). Englewood Cliffs, NJ: Prentice Hall.

ADDITIONAL READING

Davila, A., Foster, G., & Gupta, M. (2003). Venture Capital Financing And The Growth Of Startup Firms. *Journal of Business Venturing, 18*(6), 689–708. doi:10.1016/S0883-9026(02)00127-1

Foster, L., Haltiwanger, J., & Syverson, C. (2008). Reallocation, firm turnover, and efficiency: Selection on productivity or profitability. *The American Economic Review, 98*(1), 394–425. doi:10.1257/aer.98.1.394

Koller, T., Goedhart, M., & Wessels, D. (2010). *Valuation: measuring and managing the value of companies*. John Wiley and sons.

Miloud, T., Aspelund, A., & Cabrol, M. (2012). Startup valuation by venture capitalists: An empirical study. *Venture Capital, 14*(2-3), 151–174. doi:10.1080/13691066.2012.667907

Mongrut, S., & Juárez, N. (2018). Valuation of Start-ups: A behavioral and strategic perspective. *Revista Mexicana de Economía y Finanzas Nueva Época REMEF, 13*(3), 419–439.

Nanda, R., & Rhodes-Kropf, M. (2013). Investment cycles and startup innovation. *Journal of Financial Economics, 110*(2), 403–418. doi:10.1016/j.jfineco.2013.07.001

Ouimet, P., & Zarutskie, R. (2014). Who works for startups? The relation between firm age, employee age, and growth. *Journal of Financial Economics, 112*(3), 386–407. doi:10.1016/j.jfineco.2014.03.003

Zheng, Y., Liu, J., & George, G. (2010). The dynamic impact of innovative capability and inter-firm network on firm valuation: A longitudinal study of biotechnology start-ups. *Journal of Business Venturing, 25*(6), 593–609. doi:10.1016/j.jbusvent.2009.02.001

KEY TERMS AND DEFINITIONS

Angel Investment: Angel investment is a high-risk type of investment that leads entrepreneurs who have a minority share in entrepreneurs with high growth potential.

Startup: Startups are new born or young companies struggling to achieve their potential and growth.

The Discounted Cash Flow: The present value of the future cash flows of a company or a project will be reduced by a discount rate and the cash flows of the company will be deducted from the net cash amount of the company. This value shows us the value of the company or project.

Valuation: Valuation is a determination of how much a transaction can be realized at a price if a company is exchanged with its current form.

Venture Capital: Venture capital is the financing provided by investors for startup companies and small businesses, which are considered to have long-term growth potential.

ENDNOTES

1 http://www.ugurcirak.com/startup-degeri-nasil-hesaplanir
2 www.venionaire.com/first-chicago-method-valuation
3 http://www.ugurcirak.com/startup-degeri-nasil-hesaplanir

Chapter 9
Valuation Challenges in Stranded Asset Scenarios:
A Risk Discourse of Evidence From the UK

Posi Olatubosun
https://orcid.org/0000-0002-5586-3474
King's College London, UK

Sinem Derindere Köseoğlu
Independent Researcher, Turkey

ABSTRACT

This chapter investigates the challenges faced by sell-side analysts in engaging with companies with material stranded assets through the lens of Becksian risk society theory. The research unravels the usefulness of sustainability reports in deriving the intrinsic value of energy companies in the UK, and whether they take Environmental Social and Governance (ESG) factors into consideration in doing so. Qualitative data were collected via dual methods comprising longitudinal participant observation at IR meetings and interview of sell-side analysts and institutional shareholder. Findings indicate dissatisfaction with the existing risk reporting system is a key factor in divestment decisions and asset stranding. The growing Responsible Investment (RI) awareness notwithstanding, the inadequate risk reporting system continues to represent a major source of agitation amongst shareholders and analysts, making the overhaul of the current financial reporting system inevitable.

INTRODUCTION

Some of the world's most valuable and powerful companies, that is energy companies, have a huge problem that may either reduce their intrinsic future value due to the risks and uncertainties attached to their future cash slows, or make the shares to be totally worthless. These companies have substantial billions of dollars' worth of proved reserves made up of coal oil and gas under the heading of 'unsold inventories' in their balance sheets. Owning much of these reserves is the source of massive power and high market

DOI: 10.4018/978-1-7998-1086-5.ch009

value[1]. Power derives from the incidence of the existent 'global technological society' where essentials of such as food, commerce, communication, transportation and industry are driven by these energy mix, whilst their value derives from the intrinsic valuation (commonly based on the present value of future cash flows arising from the sale of energy products). In 2018, $2 trillion in global annual revenue was generated by upstream (exploration and drilling activities) energy companies, and the sector generates up to $90 billion in GDP, representing up to 3% of the global economy[2]. In recent times however, the declining value of these companies has become a source of worry to institutional investors because the future returns accruable to the beneficiaries of institutional investments are linked to the ability of the investee companies to generate future cash flows which is reflected in their respective market capitalisation. As at August 2019, market capitalisation of the top 20 of the world's energy companies is worth $1.7 trillion which reflects a 55% cumulative decline when compared with the highest value ever attained (see table 1). Literature reveals that the declining value is traceable to factors such as stigmatization by environmental campaigners, legislative uncertainties multiple compression arising from weakness in corporate governance, and divergence in the basis for valuation in the investment community. Recent empirical evidence has shown that stigmatisation can influence compression in trading volumes whereby a misalignment exists between ability to generate future cash flow and intrinsic value. For instance, Rosneft produces 2.3 million barrels per day, which is slightly more than ExxonMobil. However, Rosneft is valued at roughly 18% of the value of ExxonMobil. The problem of uncertainty about the future, and the problem of environmental risks have called into question, the validity of the Gordons growth model used in estimating over or undervaluation of shares (Cho, 1988). These uncertainties may lead to lower intrinsic valuation of equities in these companies due to greater worries about their ability to generate future cash flows, or in worst case scenario, inability to finance new projects leading and the inability to generate fresh working capital, therefore making it impossible to continue as a going concern.

Two puzzling problems that have arisen therefore, are the challenge of how to access ESG risk information that would assist equity shareholders and their sell-side analysis analysts in making valuation decisions, and how to quantify them in the valuation of equity shares. Traditionally, business valuation methods such as the capitalisation of future income, asset based, and market-based approaches have been used (Pratt, 2008, Damodaran, 2005). Currently ESG risk information are available on historical basis through the annual publication of sustainability reports which the shareholders and analysts find inadequate. This research is therefore interested in investigating the basis for arriving at risk information for decision making when trading in equity shares.

RESEARCH IN CONTEXT

Stranded Assets

Energy derived from fossil fuel have been fingered in various scientific reports as being a chief source of global warming, and that their continual use would make the earth to be susceptible to catastrophic climate change that may cost trillions of dollars in environmental damages. In order to prevent the occurrence of this environmental damages, these reserves would have to be discarded, which means that they would be 'stranded' in the ground, leading to material diminution in the value of these companies. It is estimated that adherence to the Paris Agreement (2015) adopted as a legal framework by the United Nations Framework Convention on Climate Change (UNFCCC) means that half of all known gas reserves,

Table 1. Market capitalisation of the world top 20 energy companies (in billions of dollars)

Company	Aug 2019	Aug 2017	Highest historical value and date	
Exxon Mobil	286.3	342.1	519.3	October 2007
British Petroleum	125.11	113.6	263.3	May 2006
Chevron Corporation	221.79	197.7	256.1	July 2014
CNOOC	63.85	48.9	120.9	April 2011
ConocoPhillips	57.67	54.4	112.6	June 2008
Eni	53.75	54.6	152.4	May 2008
Enterprise Products	61.77	58	77.2	May 2008
EOG Resources	42.12	52.3	64.5	June 2014
Equinor ASA	56.34	53.6	135.3	May 2008
Halliburton	15.77	37.1	63	July 2014
Kinder Morgan	45.86	42.8	96.5	April 2015
Occidental Petroleum Corporation	38.56	45.8	90.3	May 2011
Petrobras	85.31	52.1	329.9	May 2008
PetroChina	87.81	112.2	472.1	October 2007
Phillips 66	43.14	42.7	50	November 2015
Royal Dutch Shell	223.57	218.7	458.6	January 2013
Schlumberger	43.73	91.5	153.4	June 2014
Sinopec	3.048	95.16	131.2	October 2007
Suncor Energy	44.39	48.7	74.9	March 2011
Total	127.47	121.2	201.1	May 2008
Aggregate	**1727.358**	**1883.16**	**3822.6**	

Source: Researcher's findings.

a third of all known oil reserves and 80% of all known coal reserves will have to stay in the ground. This fear has been further exacerbated by the plan by the EU to be carbon-neutral by 2050. If all these reserves have to stay in the ground, then they would become worthless. Worthless inventories mean the companies would also be worthless except they diversify their portfolio of energy products away from these environmentally-damaging products. This is why economists are beginning to call these worthless reserves "stranded assets." It means that the more these companies discover new reserves of oil, coal or gas, the more they are adding to the stranded assets to their books. It is expected that when economic agents eventually realise the intrinsic value of these assets, the market price of these energy companies is expected to be hit, making the value to go up in smoke. If this carbon bubble scenario plays out as expected, then it is likely to cause premature write-off of equities held in investee companies held by institutional investors, with implications for the realisation of future pensions and other attendant social costs.

The latest analyses (IPCC, 2019; IISD, 2018) suggests that in order to meet the global emissions target of not more than 2° rise in atmospheric temperature, emissions need to remain within the carbon budget of 500 – 900 Giga tons CO_2 by 2050, which is far less than what would be emitted if all the all the worlds current oil coal and gas reserves are burned (that is 2,860 Giga tons), resulting in higher atmospheric temperature. Except there is an accelerate development and deployment of carbon capture technology, the effect would be catastrophic on the environment. New research by carbon tracker shows that just the reserves owned by companies listed on the stock exchanges contain enough carbon to create more than 762 Giga tons of CO_2 and those companies are currently spending $764 billion annually to find yet more reserves. If carbon limits are enforced in the future, then less fuel would be consumed and reserves would become 'stranded assets' which would no longer provide financial returns. If the trend continues, listed companies alone would cause more global warming than all other economic agents.

Another latest research depicts a gory picture. Pfeiffer et al., (2018) took stock of the embodied emissions of all the fleets of power plants installed all over the world (coal, gas, fossil fuel plants). Considering their age, running efficiency, utilisation factor, and anticipated emissions, they are expected to generate 300 $GtCO_2$. This is a problem because in order to achieve the Paris goals of 2°C above the pre-industrial levels, we have a budget 300 $GtCO_2$. This is 60 $GtCO_2$ over budget. In addition to this, there is $7trillion of potential new spent on new plants most of them in Asia, that would be additional 270 $GtCO_2$. That leaves us with a dilemma. Either we build those plants and then we shut down the existing ones, or we install carbon capture storage which is expensive. Or we give up on the climate change goals.

However, in the event of strict adherence to Paris Agreement, it will mean that the amount of gases that we can emit would have to be limited as well as the amount of fossil fuel that we can burn. Therefore, the fossil fuel and coal and gas would have to stay in the ground. All these infrastructures being built to extract them would be stranded. There would be economic and social implications if this happens. There are a few countries that rely on these energy sources as the main means of generating revenue, that is, poor countries like Libya, Venezuela, and Nigeria. These places would have to adapt quickly to reduce social upheavals. Another implication is that it would tear a material hole in public budgets which means that governments would have to do more to compensate for the hole in the overall economy.

Previous evidence from practitioners show that divestment for achieving social purposes is not totally new. History has shown that such trend is not new. For instance, there was a wave of divestment in the 70s and 80s against companies based in South Africa as well as tobacco companies too. However, the current wave of divestment against environmentally damaging companies became rife in 2015 after the Paris Agreement (2015) was signed. For instance, a coalition of institutional investors known as 350.org was formed around the same time to influence institutional investors' freezing of fresh investments in fossil fuel companies in the short term, as well as total divestment from them in the long term (Ansar et al., 2013). In the same vein, Caldecott et al., (2018) have traced the occurrence of stranded asset problem to the natural consequence of the creative destruction which usually typify capitalism. For instance, Metcalfe (2002) demonstrated that the underlying impulse that keeps the engine of capitalism rolling comes from continuous innovation which invariably leads to the demise of the old ones.

Theory of Risk in Valuation

A significant role was played by Beck (1992, 1997) and Giddens (1990, 1991) in deepening our understanding of the sociology of risk in the post-industrial era, especially as it relates to the risks pertaining to environmental risks pertaining to the holding of long-term investment through the concepts of manufactured risks and trusts, which are subsets of the risk society theory. The risk society theory holds that modern society would be preoccupied with the future which generates the notion of risks and how they would be managed (Giddens and Pierson 1998, p209). According to Giddens, risk society springs from the growth of science and technology which is consequences of modernisation. Giddens carefully

Figure 1. Potential impact of stranded assets divestment campaign
Adapted from: *Ansah et al., (2013)*

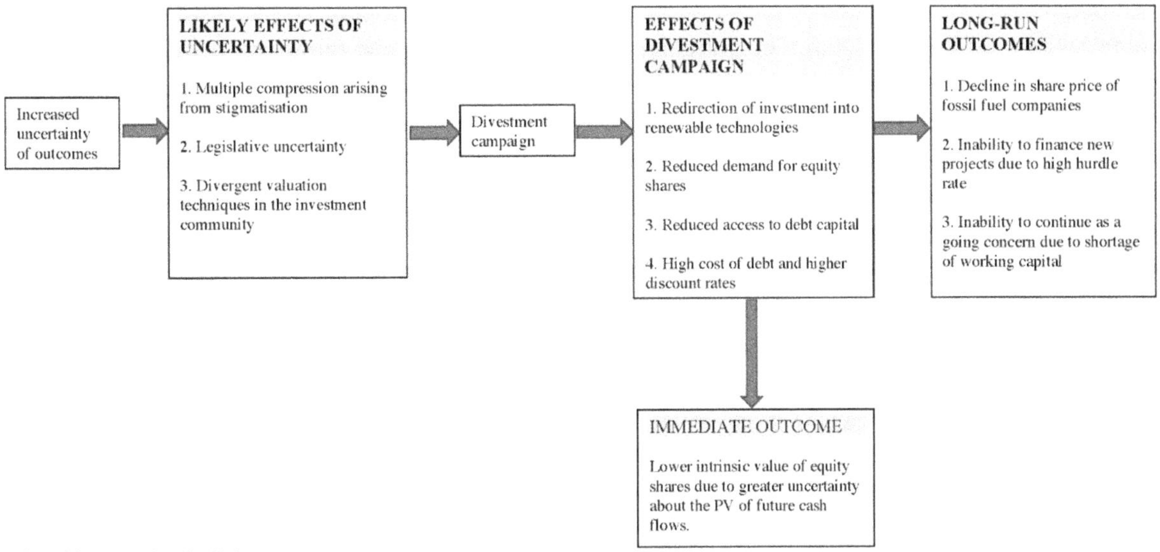

Adapted from: Ansah et al., (2013)

Table 2. Typology of Environmental-related risk

SET	SUBSET
Environmental change	Climate change; natural capital depletion, degradation; biodiversity loss and decreasing species richness; air, land and water contamination; habitat loss; freshwater availability.
Resource landscapes	Price and availability of different resources such as oil and gas, coal and other minerals and metals; e.g. shale gas revolution, phosphate availability, and rate earth metals.
Government regulations	Carbon pricing (via taxes and trading schemes) subsidy regimes (e.g. for fuels and renewables); air pollution regulation; voluntary and compulsory disclosure requirements; changing liability regimes and stricter licence conditions for operation; the 'carbon bubble' and international climate policy.
Technological change	Falling clean technology costs (e.g. solar PV, onshore wind); disruptive technologies; GMO; and electric vehicles.
Social norms and consumer behaviour	Fossil fuel divestment campaign; product labelling and certification schemes; and changing consumer preferences.
Litigation and statutory interpretations	Carbon liability; litigation; damages; and changes in the way existing laws are applied or interpreted.

Source: Researcher's findings

distinguished between 'external risks' which are insurable traditional risks that typified the Middle Ages, and the 'manufactured uninsurable risks' of the modern era. Giddens opined that in the middle ages, social actors fear the losses that the environment could exact on them, whereas in the modern era, social entities are known to exact damages on the environment (1990). The features of the risk society environment include rapid changes in society whereby reforms would almost always lag behind these changes in what Giddens refer to as the juggernaut of modernity (1990). Risk society is characterised by organised irresponsibility (Beck 1994) whereby the social actors who created societal risks are not penalised or held to account due to misalignment in social structures and inability of the law and social order to quickly capture and effect changes. These rapid changes would therefore influence the development of responsibility culture to reduce the incidence of manufactured risk whereby social actors try to differentiate between products or services that carry low elements of uninsurable risks and the others which do not (Giddens 1998, p8). The prevalence of science and technology and the media also increases reflexive risk thinking attitude whereby social agents think about risk reduction or avoidance, and even when all risks have been reduced, attention would be paid to the existence of residual risks (Beck, 1992). In risk society new scientific discoveries will not solve risk problems, but rather exacerbate it because, the more new scientific products are developed, the more society is enmeshed in reflexive risk orientation. The reflexive attitude to risks leads to politics of risks whereby more politics would originate from non-political actors. For instance, each time a product or service is developed, it is backed up politically through effective debate mechanism (Bernstein, 1996). Becks noted that social entities that adopts a 'precautionary principle' as a means of avoiding the politics of risks is likely to burin its fingers when the risk results into actual losses (Beck, 1994). Unfortunately, the risk society is a direct changeover to a new modernity, which means that there is no prior experience for social entities to leverage on.

The above concept of manufactured risks partly explains the reason behind the multiple compression and the stigmatization phenomena that had triggered divestment in the investment community. Unlike the 'external risks', the 'uninsurable manufactured risks' are dynamic, unpredictable and unquantifiable, thereby necessitating the clarification of the concept of trust in a risk society. Trust is central to the issue of valuation of equities as it functions based on the interplay of market forces which social entities rely on without questioning. There is a negative correlation between risk and trust, such that trust reduces when risk increases and vice versa (see Giddens 1990; Ekberg, 2007). There is proliferation of knowledge in risk society. The more new knowledge which invalidates the old ones become available, the more social entities are put on enquiry thereby weakening the level of trust in the system. Since there are no insurance against 'manufactured risks', re-embedding mechanism was suggested by Giddens (1991) as a means of restoring trust in abstract systems which may fail as a result of proliferation of knowledge in risk society. One of such re-embedding mechanisms that had evolved in recent times is the growth of the responsible investment (RI) logic which is premised on long-term ownership, stakeholder perspective, and the consideration of Environmental Social and Governance in appraising institutional investment. Some of the RI embedding mechanisms include divestment from environmentally damaging companies (negative screening), publication of sustainability reports (SR) which is enables shareholders to appraise risks inherent in their investment, and the use of investors' relations (IR) meetings which is an engagement method whereby shareholders are able to meet with management to discuss issues affecting future profits, liquidity and strategy of the company.

Risk Reporting

Conventionally, the published financial report serves as a useful source for the valuation decision-making for analysts and shareholders alike (Gniewosz, 1990). However, they suffer from the inherent limitation of being historical in nature thereby making them limited for projecting into the future, especially when the business operates in a dynamic environment. Nevertheless, many researchers have argued for a radical rethinking of the stewardship perspective upon which the periodic financial reporting is based, so that a new accountability reporting system that takes the views of stakeholders into consideration can become the mainstream (Adam, 2006, Gray et al, 2004). This call has become pertinent due to the awareness of the need to price environmental damages and potential risks emanating therefrom, into

Figure 2. Increasing incidence of environmentalism in reporting (1989-2009)
***SOURCE:** Eccles and Krzuz, 2010*

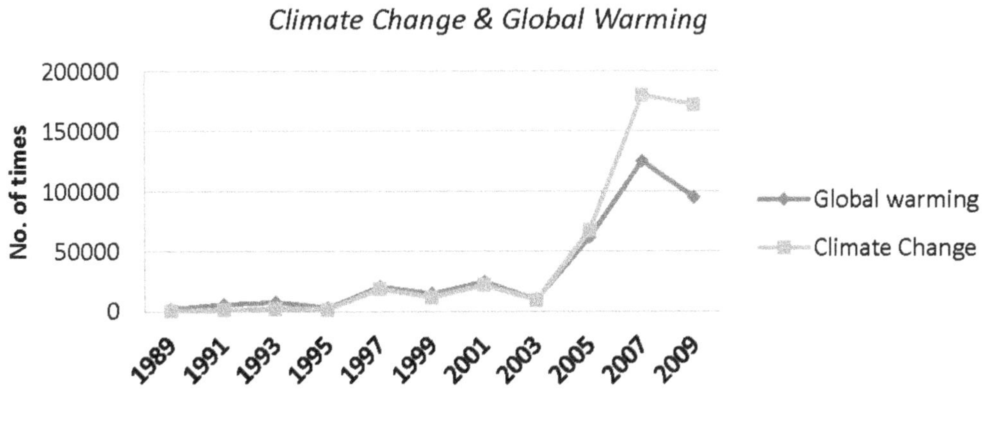

long-term decision-making. This need to ensure *financialisation* of environmental costs in estimating future cash flows has been intensified by researchers who have taken philosophical views which is either deep ecocentric (Rimmel and Jonall, 2013) or anthropocentric (Jones and Solomon, 2013) views on how such accountability reports should look like, especially as the effect of climate change which has cascaded into the consideration of biodiversity, health and going concern fears (Atkins and Maroun, 2018). Figure 2 below shows the increasing importance of environmental risks through the frequency in the use if 'climate change' and 'global warming' from 1989 to 2009, based on publications contained in the Dow Jones Factiva database. These inadequacies in financial reporting have influenced analysts and shareholders to evolve new ways of appraising risks by users of such financial information.

The above inadequacies in financial reporting have influenced analysts and shareholders to evolve new ways of appraising risks by users of such financial information. This research attempts to document the methods used by analysts and shareholders alike in appraising ESG risks in investment. These noticed inadequacies in stewardship have been heightened in the energy and extractive sectors that rely on the use of natural resources for its survival. Since the establishment of the 'Triple Bottom Line' concept (see Elkington, 1997), there has been a noticeable growth in the reporting of the environmental issues to shareholders under various names such as 'CSR' report, 'sustainability reports' and so on, with academic community paying attention to how climate change is reported (Solomon and Darby, 2005), appropriateness of the reporting framework (Gray *et al.,*1996), and their effectiveness (Thomson, 2007) and their usefulness for valuation of stranded assets (Caldecott, 2014). Scientific reports (see IPCC, 2018; IEA2018, World Energy Outlook, 2018) have increased the awareness of the possibility of global warming having negative effect on the ability of extractive companies to generate future cash flows, leading to material diminution in the value of the companies' equity shares.

RESEARCH METHODOLOGY

What are the challenges being faced by sell-side analysts in engaging with companies with stranded assets? What are the bases for arriving at the risk information that they take into consideration in valuing equity shares? How can the existing sustainability reporting system be improved to provide the necessary risk information useful for decision-making? Qualitative data were gathered from longitudinal participant observation at IR meetings and interview of institutional and individual shareholders. This is because valuation is not an exact science which is influenced by access to information and perception (Qu and Dumay, 2011). This work is rooted in interpretive philosophy with the risk society theory (See section 2 above) arrived at based on an inductive approach, and an epistemological premise that realism can be both learnt and self-created.

Longitudinal participant observation was obtained from Investors' Relations (IR) meetings attended in the UK over a 4 year period (2014 – 2017). The attendance at those meetings helped in developing a holistic understanding of the issues involved in issues driving valuation and how it affects shareholders, given that these shareholders are interested in information that would aid them in arriving at buy, sell or hold decisions (DeWalt and DeWalt, 2002). Thirty-three persons were interviewed in total, made up of 20 Individual shareholders and 13 institutional shareholders comprising of 7 pension Funds trustees, 2 hedge funds owners, 2 Sovereign Wealth Funds trustees, and 2 faith-based investors. The interview was both and phenomenological in nature as it helped in confirming or refuting already

These two sources provided us with rich data that helped us to arrive at a balanced picture of the issues involved in risk affecting valuation of shares. This also helped us in cross-checking the authenticity of data coming from diverse sources. This is because a shareholder may say something and do another not related to what had been said (see Arnould and Wallendorf, 1994). All the interviews took place on telephone between 2014 and 2018, and the interview duration was average of 15 minutes each. All the interviewees' anonymity was guaranteed in order to ensure that they are free from bias. The interview was recorded, transcribed and coded via 'NVIVO', before the themes were generated (see Guest *et al,* 2012; and Braun and Clark, 2006).

Table 3. List of interviewees (institutional investors)

Code	Interviewee's position in Pension Fund	Interview duration (minutes)
PF1	Investor Relations Manager	18
PF2	Chief Executive	19
PF3	Head of Finance & Investment	27
PF4	Compliance Manager	29
PF5	Governance Manager	23
PF6	Finance Manager	23
PF7	Head of Finance	23
SWF1	Governance Manager	16
SWF2	Compliance Manager	25
HF1	Managing Director	12
HF2	Managing Director	8
FB1	Head of Investment	27
FB2	Head of Corporate Governance	32

Analysis of IR Meetings

As a member of a shareholders association based in the UK, this analysis is based on participatory observation of investors' relations meetings that took place in extractive companies meetings over a 4 year period, and the analysis of the questions put forward to senior management. The meeting duration is usually for 1.5 hours, made up of 30 minutes presentation by management and an hour for questions and answers. Table 4 shows the cumulative changes over time (CCOT) of shareholders' concerns in the extractive industries between 2014 and 2017. The need to develop new business strategy with reduced emphasis on fossil fuel was a major concern of the shareholders based on the number of questions asked at the IR meetings. However, there was a noticeable decline in the number of questions bothering on strategy from 2017 because the respective companies have started issuing 'Global Outlook' reports showing planned diversification from fossil fuel. For instance, BP plans to achieve 25% revenue from non-oil and gas sources from 2025. This is acceptable to many of the institutional investors, although the social activists and faith-based investors prefer an accelerated diversification.

Aside executive pay, the main ESG concern by shareholders based on questions raised at investors meetings are centred on the need for alternative business strategy and transparency. Traditionally the oil and gas companies in particular have expectations of future cash flows on the expectation that future demand for energy will continue to grow into the foreseeable future. In 2014, the quest for energy companies to diversify was based on the need to avoid disasters similar to the oil spillage which occurred in the Gulf of Mexico in April 2010, which negatively affected share prices and prevented dividend payment. In April 2000, some activist investors had filed a failed shareholder proposal at BP, calling for the stoppage of its planned offshore operations, and asking the company to divert the investment to renewable energy sources. This call was being re-echoed in every meeting, and then dominated questions being asked at investors meetings in 2015 and 2016. However, from 2017, there is a noticeable decline in the ESG concerns arising from business strategy as most of the corporations publish global outlook and sustainability reports indicating material diversification into renewables. For instance, BP plc plans to achieve 25% revenue from non-oil and gas sources from 2025. Nevertheless, the global outlook published by oil majors indicate that the oil and gas business model will remain strong till 2050 as fossil fuel demand will remain strong. Some shareholders believe that enough is not being done to limit temperatures to 2 degrees in fulfilment of the Paris Accord, and move away from low-carbon economy as new technologies in renewables may make their investment in oil and gas redundant sooner than 2040. This arrangement is acceptable to many of the institutional investors, although the social activists and faith-based investors prefer an accelerated diversification.

Questions bothering on transparency in reporting payments to foreign governments and communities was quite high in 2014, which was the time of passing the Act. Since then there has been a decline in the number of questions or concerns perhaps due to the satisfaction of the level of transparency resulting from the publication. Shareholders concerns bothered on the level of compliance expected, the level of inclusion of foreign operations, and the penalties for false declaration or non-compliance. Shareholders also demanded to know the level of compliance of the governments of the countries in which they operate, especially the ones where inadequate progress are being made with a view to divest from them. The ESG concerns of shareholders are now shifting to concerns around unreported embezzlements and bribes paid to government officials, undocumented payments to political parties, non-disclosure of the true beneficial owners, anti-money laundering activities, and the increasing poverty reported in oil producing countries, thereby threatening the 'social licence' or legitimacy of the companies. However, directors are quick to point to the substantial CSR activities that they are engaged in within the local communities where they operate

Fears that anthropogenic rise in GHG attributed to fossil fuel is causing responsible investors to consider negative screening of their oil and gas portfolio. There were claims that almost 600 institutions companies with $3.4 trillion AUM have fully or partially negatively-screened away investments in oil and gas from their portfolios. Neo-Schumpeterian argument that investments are likely to follow the *kondratiev* wave as a result of the coming of age of an existing technological revolution partly explains the gradual stranding of oil and gas assets. There is a suggestion from published financial news, that the process is being accelerated by the planned governmental ban on fossil fuel vehicles between 2040 and 2050. As a direct consequence of the governmental action, all the major oil and gas companies are now projecting a decline in oil exploration and drilling after 2040, although they still project to continue oil exploration in developing jurisdictions thereafter because of expected surge in energy needs which is unlikely to be met via available energy supplies. After 2040, renewables are projected to represent on average, 25% of the world total energy mix which is considered insignificant to accelerate material stranding of oil and gas companies.

Justifications for Risk Reporting

Interview demonstrated growing need for the replacement of the existing reporting system. Based on the observation of the investors' relations meetings, it is clear that investors are dissatisfied with the existing sustainability reports, and they prefer to get a report which captures the risks on a real time, rather than historical basis.

...the sustainability reports are prepared on a boiler plate basis and therefore I waste my time reading it. Mind you, I am not saying that the concept of sustainability reporting is wrong. What I am saying is that the information that I need for active share ownership isn't present, and that is the reason why I come to this meeting, basically to plug the gap.... PF7

Table 4. Shareholders concerns in extractive industries based on the number of questions asked at IR meetings

Shareholder's concerns	2014	2015	2016	2017	CCOT	Typical management's response
Human rights abuse and combating poverty in the local host communities	8	8	4	4	-4	We invest in CSR including training the locals. We partner with civil societies for citizen engagement. We comply with all local laws.
Developing low carbon energy sources and change of business strategy	12	16	18	7	-5	Being addressed, albeit slower than shareholders expected.
Transparency in dealing with governments	8	6	6	5	-3	We support EITI initiative as it is the best way of achieving transparency in the industry.
Excessive pay, and non-linkage of executive pay to carbon emission and allied matters	4	6	7	14	+10	Reporting is sometimes in excess of governments requirements. Pay is linked to performance. We are significantly transforming the business risk, so specialist carbon expert at board level is unnecessary.

Source: researchers' findings

Table 5. Indicators to help assess a company's risk exposure to climate change

<table>
<tr><th>Metric</th><th>Proxy for Climate Change Risk</th><th>Risk Type</th><th>Level of Exposure</th></tr>
<tr><td>Proved oil and gas reserves as a proportion of total assets</td><td>Exposure to stranded assets</td><td>Business strategy risk</td><td>Company exposure</td></tr>
<tr><td>Fossil fuel business as a proportion of the total business</td><td>Exposure to stranded assets</td><td>Business strategy risk</td><td>Company exposure</td></tr>
<tr><td>Vulnerability to climate change of the countries in which the company operates</td><td>Exposure to acute and chronic weather</td><td rowspan="4">Physical exposure</td><td>Country exposure</td></tr>
<tr><td>Revenue arising from fossil fuel sales as a proportion of total revenue</td><td>Revenue vulnerability risks</td><td rowspan="3">Company exposure</td></tr>
<tr><td>Capital requirements from insurance exposure to weather-related catastrophic events as a percentage of total available capital</td><td>Insurance exposure to acute weather</td></tr>
<tr><td>Exploration and drilling (non-current) assets as a proportion of total assets</td><td>Present value of assets exposed to the risk of diminution in value of proved oil/gas reserves</td></tr>
<tr><td>Target for reducing CO_2 emissions in the countries where the oil and gas company operates</td><td>Risk of adverse of environmental tax or regulations</td><td rowspan="3">Regulatory and legal</td><td>Country exposure</td></tr>
<tr><td>Company's carbon footprint</td><td>Risk of adverse additional taxes or increased governmental scrutiny or regulations</td><td>Company exposure</td></tr>
<tr><td>Local litigation and governance activism culture</td><td>Compliance and reputational risk</td><td>Country exposure</td></tr>
<tr><td>Material non-compliance with major industry decarbonisation/sustainability initiatives</td><td>Reputational damage</td><td rowspan="3">Reputational risks</td><td rowspan="4">Company exposure</td></tr>
<tr><td>History of bad "green" publicity</td><td>Reputational damage</td></tr>
<tr><td>Size (by assets)</td><td>Reputational damage (the bigger the company, the more likely it could be targeted by activists)</td></tr>
<tr><td>Quality of disclosure</td><td>Transparency of climate change exposure</td><td>Regulatory and legal</td></tr>
</table>

Source: Adapted from Petkov et al, (2016).

The above statement clearly shows that the investors are interested in SRs but the current reporting system does not meet their requirements. Preparing a real time SR will be expensive, but this demand is understandable in an age where technology has made it possible for reports to be available for viewing online.

....unfortunately it seems like management is not alive to their responsibility as far as adaptive strategy is concerned. I am not proposing that the close shop, but where is the evidence that this company would be around in 25-year time? We need hard evidence but it is shameful that despite the massive capital at their disposal, they are just playing ostrich like everyone else.

From interviews as well as meeting observations, it is obvious that investors are concerned with profits generated now, but more importantly, how future strategies are adapting to new business realities. However, such expectations are not being met as the report is lacks focus on strategy. For instance, a shareholder may be willing to hold equity if there are evidence of diversification thus:

I am delighted to hear today that BP is actively diversifying into renewable such that a quarter of annual profits earned in 7 years' time would be derived from renewables.

Some shareholders believe that SR are inadequate but then, because they are institutional shareholders, they can always obtain the information that guides them for decision-making from other sources from within or outside of the company, whilst others believe that the current reporting system is outdated:

...we do not need such reports (SR) since we can obtain information relating to strategy from other sources. HF2

....information that guides us on whether to buy or sell these shares are no longer available from annual reports, but from newspapers and social media. That ought to be addressed otherwise the accounting and auditing profession would lose their credibility. FB1

Generally, it was noted from these meetings and interviews, that individual shareholders and faith based activist investors desire SR more that the institutional shareholders because they see it as the only way by which they could gauge the strategy and value of the investee company. The desire for more information is indicative of the reduced reliance on historical information which may not be indicative of future performance due to the prevalence of heightened manufactured risks and reduced risks. This view is re-echoed by King and Atkins (2016) thus:

By focusing only on the financial statements, the CFO and the user are ignoring important information about the business of the company. Without the company's long-term strategy being disclosed and showing that the sustainability issues material to the business of the company have been embedded into its strategy, the decision of investing in the equity of that company by just relying on earnings is an uninformed one. (p97)

Three distinct issues became clear from the above. Firstly, there is a dissatisfaction with the existing reporting system. Some shareholders are wary of the sustainability report which is not certified by the auditors, and its 'boiler plate' nature. This calls for the rethinking of the existing reporting system and the training being offered to accountants that prepare and certifies these reports. Arising from the inadequacy of the sustainability is the drive to access risk information by shareholders. Interview data suggests that individual, faith based and social activist shareholders can access relevant risk information from IR meetings from questions asked at such meetings. However, the other institutional investors believe that they can access such information from their representatives on the board. Thirdly is that the shareholders desire a risk reporting system which meets today's requirement of being available online and real time.

Interview data confirms the Giddens (1990) hypothesis on the inverse relationship existing between risk and trust, especially in an environment typified by proliferation of risk knowledge. The narrative nature of the sustainability report makes shareholders to directly juxtapose the information supplied to them via sustainability reports with what they obtain from other sources especially on biodiversity and climate change. As climate change is an uncharted territory for humanity, seeming "organised irresponsibility" and the use of "precautionary principle" of doing nothing is likely to be prevalent (Beck, 1994), making shareholders themselves to develop re-embedding mechanisms such as responsible investment behaviour, which includes divestment from stranded assets.

Discounting Future Cash Flows

Given the concerns of shareholders for diversification from stranded assets based on evidence from IR meetings (see section 6.1), and the growing urge for risk reporting (see section 6.2), it is pertinent that we discuss the effects of the options of the various applicable discount rates on the capitalisation of future projected income from stranded assets. Should we set zero discount rate, constant discount rate or variable rate? From existing literature, setting zero discount rates rate is applicable where economic agents postpone their immediate benefits for the use of future generations by making sacrifices now, which increases future cash flows. For instance engaging in afforestation or developing technology to absorb atmospheric carbon. Under such scenario, zero discounting may be applicable to future economic benefits due to the expectations that they would yield higher PV than the current cash flows (see Maddison, 2001; Lopez et al, 2006). Setting such discount rate is unacceptable as the empirical evidence (see table 1) shows a downward trend in market capitalisation, which evidences decline in underlying future cash flows, and there are no strong evidence of oil and gas companies developing carbon-capture technology. Setting a constant discount rate is equally objectionable in the valuation of income from stranded assets due to the uncertainties attached to the future income.

As a result of the non-plausibility of the discount rate mentioned above, we considered upward discounting of future cash flows whereby higher rates are applied to the cash flows as they approach the set date of the EU-wide ban 2050 and beyond. Since there is growing uncertainty about the future cash flows, some researchers (see Dasgupta, 2001; Pearce et al, 2003) have argued that decreasing weight ought to be attached to the cash flows as they approach 2050, indicating the need to increasing the applicable discount rates. These cash flows would accrue the future benefits minus the expected future payments which may include the *financialisation* of the effects of environmental degradation ($GtCO_2$ and other externalities such as health hazards) together with projected fines and penalties. This may also be applied side-by-side with alternative recommendations (see Gravelle and Smith, 2001; and Brouwer et al., 2005) that benefits accruing from such companies should be segmented and capitalised at different discount rates based on the vulnerability of such earnings to environmental damage. All these shows the effect of factoring the unmitigated 'manufactured risks' on negative outlook in the future of oil and gas industry. Estimating the environmental costs may be particularly problematic as there are no generally accepted metrics for the *financialisation* of ESG costs despite the noticeable rise in the number of ESG rating agencies such as Thompson Reuters, FTSE4GOOD, FTSE Russel, Sustainalytics.

The concept of stranded asset is challenging the traditional basis of valuation due to the availability of new knowledge about the existence of manufactured risks which is putting question mark on streams of future cash flows as well as the existence of material environmental costs which must now be taken into consideration. The misalignment of the risks and benefits on one hand, and the continuous application of previously known cash flow discounting model where the predictability of future cash flows have been altered, is likely to further push back the likelihood of finding a quick solution to the valuation problem, bearing in mind, the "juggernaut nature of modernity" (Giddens, 1990) which we continually experience.

DISCUSSION

The existing financial and sustainability reporting systems are inadequate in helping shareholders to play their actively. This inadequate reporting could be traced to misalignments in the social system which continually evolves, which Giddens (1990) compares to a "runaway engine of enormous power" (p. 139). It is expected that as society continues to evolve, there are likely to be even more changes in the social and financial systems, which makes the development of re-embedding mechanisms such as RI logic imperative. Some (Ramus and Montiel, 2005; KPMG, 2017) have suggested that the existing stewardship system as not supporting proper valuation because it is grounded in the short-termism philosophy, whilst Solomon et al (2013) and Bowen (2014) have noted that these short-term thinking are have egged on greenwashing and impression management rather that RI logic. Some Shareholder view attendance at IR meetings as conferring advantage on attendees as they are able to discuss strategy matters which are not available to the general public. The concern is that by so doing, they can use the information acquired to engage in insider dealings. It is also expected that the same level of detailed attention being paid to quarterly analysis of financial performance ought to be paid to the strategy issues being deliberated at IR meetings in order to generate more useful market information in the spirit of transparency and accountability.

Based on the above, there is a growing desire for risk reporting to replace the existing historical reporting system which places emphasis on past performance and profits rather than the ability of a business to generate future cash flows. Concerns for future expectations are much more now than in the past due to uncertainties attached to the future of the companies in the extractive sector. If this need is sustained, it means that the future of financial and sustainability report is uncertain, as this would also have implications for the training of professional accountants. King and Solomon (2016) have therefore called for the restructuring of the training education being offered to accountants in view of the changing environment. IR meetings showed a divergence between the need of the shareholder and those of the directors. Whilst the directors are interested in stewardship, the shareholders are forward-looking, interested in appraising the effect of the environment on the future value of the firm. This agrees with some views (Adam, 2004; Gray, 2006) stressing the need for an overhaul of the existing reporting system, and the need for new innovative and imaginative ideas where ESG reporting can serve as a proxy for risk management. For instance, biodiversity reporting is a relatively new development, calls are being made to include material biodiversity costs in the annual reports of companies (see Rimmel and Jonall, 2013; Atkins *et al.,* 2015). The usual response from directors of these companies is that there are no accounting standards on this, and that it imposes additional costs on the reporting entity. Nevertheless, the quest for going concern information in this area may quickly transform the reporting landscape in the near future.

Some of the recent developments, like the TCFD has put forward some recommendations for improving climate related disclosures in sustainability reports, whether they be quantitative or qualitative. Again, these disclosures are meant to be voluntary, and they cover issuance of two core disclosures: climate related financial disclosures and climate related scenarios. The climate related financial disclosures cover elements of core ESG issues namely risk management, strategy, governance and KPIs, whilst the scenario report addresses the organisation's climate resilience strategies. They are also recommending scenario analysis that enables companies to think about the future as per climate change with range of outcomes since the effect of climate change is uncertain. The TCFD scenario analysis is similar in concept to the 'what if' model developed by Petkov *et al,* (2016) to report climate change risks indicators. These reports are meant to help investors understand how the organisation assess risks and opportunities relating to climate change. This is likely to help investors to appraise the resilience build into their portfolio. These two reports are also in tandem with Integrated Reporting <IR> which views capital from an accountability rather than a stewardship point of view. In addition, <IR> do not adequately connect financial reporting and environmental risks (Atkins *et al.,* 2015; Carels *et al.,* 2014; Solomon and Maroun, 2012) as there is no incentives for the monetisation of environmental costs. Comparatively, the UK fares better than other jurisdictions in the quest to meet the TCFD requirements, although only four out of seven requirements have been met to date (see table 10.2). However, again these does not meet all the four requirements listed above, especially the need to certify these reports independently by an auditor. In the IR meetings, investors have raised concerns over the non-certification of SRs, and this is confirmed via interviews of UKSA members in chapter 5. The accounting profession and the financial reporting regulators are sluggish in making narrative reporting or <IR> compulsory, which may frustrate any gains made through the TCFD initiative.

With climate change persistently appearing on the agenda of investors, information on the quality of income and assets based on the environmental risks is likely to continue to increase. Unfortunately, the existing accounting standards either on valuation, or the systematic writing off of assets over their economic useful lives, are inadequate as they do not foresee effects of climate change which is able to alter the value income or assets disproportionately. In recent times however, some organisations such as S&P Global Ratings have developed "management and Global" criteria for measuring ESG risks, although such universal criteria capturing income and assets exposure to ESG risks are yet to be applied in reporting by companies. All these are evidences of the transition that the accounting profession is in right now, and climate change is playing an important role.

This paper sets out to investigate the challenges being faced by sell-side analysts in engaging with companies with material stranded assets through the lens of *Becksian* risk society theory. The research seeks to unravel the usefulness of sustainability reports in deriving the intrinsic value of energy companies in the UK, and whether they take Environmental Social and Governance (ESG) factors into consideration in doing so. Qualitative data were collected via dual methods comprising longitudinal participant observation at IR meetings and interview of sell-side analysts. Findings indicate dissatisfaction with the existing risk reporting system is a key factor in divestment decisions and asset stranding. The growing Responsible Investment (RI) awareness notwithstanding, the inadequate risk reporting system continues to represent a major source of agitation amongst shareholders and analysts, making the overhaul of the current financial reporting system inevitable

RESEARCH IMPLICATIONS

This paper sets out to investigate the challenges being faced by sell-side analysts in engaging with companies with material stranded assets through the lens of *Becksian* risk society theory. We found that as the existing financial reporting system is found inadequate, investors are exhibiting adaptive tendencies by placing less reliance on the financial reports, and attending IR meetings in order to get the necessary information which are not disclosed in the financial and sustainability reports. The IR meetings are originally designed to discuss financial reports. However, an evolving trend whereby the issues being discussed in such meeting are much more of strategy and how to reduce going concern risks, have necessitated a proper documentation of the minutes of such meetings, and making them available to all shareholders in order to deepen the risk information available in the market place.

New developments in the field of financial reporting such as the integrated reporting system <IR> are not encompassing a very important information need for valuation, which is risk reporting, and sensitivity to environmental risks in an interactive basis. This will have implications for the future training of professional accounting professionals as well as the auditors. These are manifestations of a risk society where the issue of risk brings about reflexive modernisation. This research focused on the attitude of shareholders and sell-side analysts in the UK. However in order to develop this work further, it is proposed that future research may take a quantitative approach to measuring the effectiveness of the information gathered at IR meetings. Also, future researchers may underpin their work through another theory other than the risk society theory, and they may also apply other methodology other that participant observation at IR meetings as well as semi-structured interviews.

REFERENCES

Adams, C. A., & Whelan, G. (2009). Conceptualising future change in corporate sustainability reporting. *Accounting, Auditing & Accountability Journal*, *22*(1), 118–143. doi:10.1108/09513570910923033

Ansar, A., Caldecott, B., & Tilbury, J. (2013). *Stranded assets and the fossil fuel divestment campaign: what does divestment mean for the valuation of fossil fuel assets? Stranded assets programme. Smith School of Enterprise and Environment.* University of Oxford.

Atkins, J., & Maroun, W. (2018). Integrated extinction accounting and accountability: Building an ark. *Accounting, Auditing & Accountability Journal*, *31*(3), 750–786. doi:10.1108/AAAJ-06-2017-2957

Beck, U. (1992). Risk society: towards a new modernity, London, UK.

Beck, U. (1997). Sub-politics: Ecology and the disintegration of institutional power. *Organization & Environment*, *10*(1), 52–65. doi:10.1177/0921810697101008

Bernstein, P. L. (1996). *Against the gods. the remarkable story of risk*. Chichester, UK: John Wiley.

Brouwer, W. B., Niessen, L. W., Postma, M. J., & Rutten, F. F. (2005). Need for differential discounting of costs and health effects in cost effectiveness analyses. *BMJ (Clinical Research Ed.)*, *331*(7514), 446–448. doi:10.1136/bmj.331.7514.446 PMID:16110075

Caldecott, B. (2018). *Stranded assets and the environment. risk, resilience and opportunity. routledge explorations in environmental studies*. Routledge. doi:10.4324/9781315651606

Cho, D. (1988). The impact of risk management decisions on firms value: gordon's growth model approach. *The Journal of Risk and Insurance*, *55*(1), 118–131. doi:10.2307/253284

CISL. (2014). *The value of responsible investment. The moral, financial and economic case for action*. University of Cambridge.

Damodaran, A. (2005). *Valuation approaches and metrics: a survey of the theory and evidence*. New York, NY: Stern School of Business.

Dasgupta, P. (2001). *Human well-being and the natural environment*. New York, NY: Oxford University Press. doi:10.1093/0199247889.001.0001

Ekberg, M. (2007). The parameters of the risk society: a review and exploration. *Current Sociology*, *55*(3), 343–366. doi:10.1177/0011392107076080

Elkington, J. (1997). Cannibals with forks: The triple bottom line of 21st century business. Capstone.

Giddens, A. (1990). *The consequences of modernity*. Stanford, CA: Stanford University Press.

Giddens, A. (1991). *Modern and self-identity: self and society in the late modern age*. Cambridge: Blackwell Publishing.

Giddens, A., & Pierson, C. (1998). *Conversations with Anthony Giddens: Making sense of modernity*. Cambridge, UK: Polity Press.

Gniewosz, G. (1990). The share investment decision process and information use: An exploratory case study. *Accounting and Business Research*, *20*(79), 233–230. doi:10.1080/00014788.1990.9728880

Gravelle, H., & Smith, D. (2001). Discounting for health effects in cost-benefit and cost-effectiveness analysis. *Health Economics*, *10*(7), 587–599. doi:10.1002/hec.618 PMID:11747043

Gray, R. H., Owen, D. L., & Adams, C. (1996). *Accounting and accountability: changes and challenges in corporate social and environmental reporting*. London, UK: Prentice Hall.

IISD. (2018). Unburnable carbo: Getting the signals right for investors in low- and lower- middle-income countries. Available at https://www.shareweb.ch/site/Development-Policy/Documents/formAttachments/IISD%20for%20SDC%20on%20Unburnable%20Carbon%20copy-edited%2026%20June%202018.pdf

IPCC (2019). Refinement to the 2006 IPCC Guidelines for National Greenhouse Gas Inventories.

Jarret, J., Woodcock, J., Griffiths, U. K., Chalabi, Z., Edwards, P., & Roberts, I. (2012). Effect of increasing active travel in urban England and Wales on costs to the national health service. *Lancet*, *379*(9832), 2198–2205. doi:10.1016/S0140-6736(12)60766-1 PMID:22682466

Jones, M. J., & Solomon, J. F. (2013). Problematising accounting for diversity. *Accounting, Auditing & Accountability Journal*, *26*(5), 668–687. doi:10.1108/AAAJ-03-2013-1255

Lopez, A., Mathers, C., Ezzati, M., Jamison, D., & Muray, C. (2006). *Global burden of disease and risk factors*. Washington, DC: World Bank/Oxford University Press. doi:10.1596/978-0-8213-6262-4

Madison, A. (2001). *The world economy: a millennial perspective*. Paris, France: Organisation for Economic Co-operation and Development. doi:10.1787/9789264189980-en

Metcalfe, J. S. (2002). *Evolutionary economics and creative destruction*. London, UK: Routledge. doi:10.4324/9780203018927

Paris Agreement. (2015). The Paris Agreement Summary. Climate Focus. Briefing Notes. Available at https://climatefocus.com/sites/default/files/20151228%20COP%2021%20briefing%20FIN.pdf

Pearce, D., Groom, B., Hepburn, C., & Koundouri, P. (2003). Valuing the future: Recent advances in social discounting. *World Economy*, *4*, 121–141.

Petkov, M., Birry, A., Plesser, S., & Wilkins, M. (2016). Climate change-related legal and regulatory threats should spur financial service providers to action. S&P global rating. 7-8. S&P Global Publications.

Pfeiffer, A., Hepburn, C., Vogt-Schilb, A., & Caldecott, B. (2018). Committee emissions from existing and planned power plants and asset stranding required to meet the Paris Agreement. *Environmental Research Letters*, *13*(5), 054019. doi:10.1088/1748-9326/aabc5f

Pratt, P. S. (2008). *Valuing a business. the analysis and appraisal of closely held companies* (5th ed.). New York, NY: McGraw-Hill.

Rimmel, G., & Jonall, K. (2013). Biodiversity treporting in Sweden: Corporate disclosure and preparers' view. *Accounting, Auditing & Accountability Journal*, *26*(5), 746–778. doi:10.1108/AAAJ-02-2013-1228

ENDNOTES

1. Valuation in the Oil and Gas Industry: Oil Price. Investor Education Series. Report#6: Everything you need to know to put a realistic value on your investment: https://www.finance-monthly.com/2017/01/valuing-oil-gas-assets-the-complexities-and-key-considerations/
2. World Energy Outlook. Available at: www.iea.org.weo2018/

Chapter 10
Valuation of Banking Sector

Ahmad Aref Almazari
King Saud University, Saudi Arabia

ABSTRACT

This chapter examines in particular the valuation of banks which can be classified into five parts. It introduces several valuation approaches to find out whether there is a superior method. This chapter starts with a description of bank regulations and their impact on bank valuations and continues with an overview of valuation approaches. The second part applies the banking sector decision Models. The third section shows banking sector valuation models. The fourth part presents the input factors that are needed to value a company. In the last part, financial statements have been used to analyze the main ratios of the Bank of America, and the calculated values were then compared over time (2014-2018) to assess the explanatory power of the bank.

INTRODUCTION

Banks have regulatory bodies and they are subject to maintain capital adequacy as per the mandate. The regulations of capital adequacy are defined by Basel III norms for the banks. They are capital adequacy ratio, Tier 1 capital, Tier 2 capital, Tier 3 capital and minimum capital adequacy which they have to maintain. When regulatory norms are laid on banks they also have to calculate risk weighted assets. Basel III focused on enhancing the financial system thereby enhancing the quality as well as quantity of regulatory capital in addition to liquidity of banks.

Another important point in what distinguishes a bank from any other business is the way a bank is regulated. The Basel Committee on Banking Supervision is the main regulatory standard setter for banks. The committee defines general guidelines and standards on the supervisory of banks. The central bank governors of the G10 formed it in 1974 after the breakdown of the Bretton Woods system. The main objectives at that time were to set minimum capital requirements to enhance the financial stability of the market. A consultative paper known as Basel 1 or The Accord proposed “a minimum capital ratio of capital to risk-weighted assets of 8% to be implemented by the end of 1992” (“A brief history of the Basel Committee,” 2013).

DOI: 10.4018/978-1-7998-1086-5.ch010

The following Basel 2 and Basel 3 Accords further increased the capital requirements and regulated the ways banks generate income still with the goal to strengthen financial stability. ("Basel Committee on Banking Supervision Charter," 2013).

This chapter examines in particular the valuation of banks which can be classified into five parts. First part introduced the aims and importance of the chapter. Second part focuses on banking sector decision Models literature review. The third part focuses on banking sector valuation models by using different models. The fourth part estimated the input factors needed to value a company or a bank. The fifth part discusses the main financial ratios with the help of financial statements of Bank of America for the years, 2014-2018 as a sample for analysis.

It is quite challenging to assess the value of a bank. Banks differ from other companies in multiple ways, which necessarily leads to different valuation approaches. Additionally, banks are traditionally highly leveraged; Bank of America for example has a debt to equity ratio of 7.87% in 2018 (Bank of America, Financial Statements 2005-2019). Today, many banks generate their revenues not only from lending money and receiving interest, but from many sources like asset management fees and other services. In general, there are three main forms of income for a bank, interest income, fee income and trading and other income (Koller et al., 2010).

It is assumed that the valuation methods in this chapter can be used to find the strength and weaknesses of the financial position of the commercial banks. As well as, it is assumed that it is impossible to implement any method that will measure all financial performance of a bank. There is a nearly unlimited number of relative valuation multiples that are commonly used, but the decision on which to choose is heavily dependent on the industry.

This chapter investigated the valuation methods of banking sector. It also aimed at studying financial statements of banks. A business valuation can be done in two ways. First way is by estimating the cash flows and calculating the intrinsic value. Second way is to compare the market value of its shares when compared to other business of similar type. Valuation process is considered very important because it help the banks analysts to find the strength and weaknesses of the financial position of their business. At the same time, valuation is a challenging task for the financial analyst. It involves study of various parameters of the business. The first important element of valuation is the nature of business. The second element is the regulatory changes to be incorporated by these firms as mandatory which influence the firm's value. The third important element is the accounting rules, and standards which changes according to the regulations creates an impact on the value of the firms.

BANKING SECTOR DECISION MODELS (LITERATURE REVIEW)

This part of the chapter examines some previous studies about the theories and their decision models in valuation of banking sector.

Although the Basel Accord regulation defines the lower limit of the Capital Adequacy Ratio, national banks may determine higher ratios for example for systemic relevant banks. The risk-weighted assets RWAs and the tier one and tier two capital are then used to calculate the capital adequacy ratio (CAR) ("Reserve Bank of New Zealand, 2007").

$$\text{Capital Adequacy Ratio} = \frac{Tier1\ Capital + Tier2\ Capital}{Risk\ Weighted\ Assets}.$$

When doing a valuation for investment purposes, one needs to assume that the market is not strong efficient according to the efficient market hypothesis, otherwise the share price of a stock multiplied by the number of shares outstanding would always be the same as the intrinsic value of a company. Therefore, valuation practitioners assume that the market is at the most, semi-strong efficient but will correct mispricing over time. When doing relative valuation one assumes that the market prices assets correctly on average, but is wrong on individual assets (Damodaran, 2013).

The intrinsic value represents the theoretical worth of an asset. Meaning, "Price is what you pay, value is what you get" (Buffet, 2008). The intrinsic value of an asset represents the accumulated benefits received from that asset. Not every asset has an intrinsic value but every asset has a market price as long as it has a market.

There are multiple approaches to assess the intrinsic value of a company, but in general they share one specific characteristic. "Companies create value for their owners by investing cash now to generate more cash in the future" (Koller, Goedhart, & Wessels, 2010). For most companies it is sufficient to have a positive cash flow or in total a positive return on investment (ROI) Therefore, when talking about banks, only what increases income or decreases risks adds value to them.

Intrinsic valuation tries to assess the value of a company based on the specific characteristics of a company. Bancel and Mittoo conducted a survey on 356 European valuation experts in 2012 to gain insight on how practitioners make use of valuation methods. Their survey shows that nearly 80 percent of the respondents use a discounted cash flow model (2014). The DCF model is a tool for intrinsic valuation and consist of the discounted cash flows that the asset will generate in the future, the estimated growth rate and the risk of the company. Therefore, only cash-flow generating assets can be valued with an intrinsic valuation approach as the following formula shows:

$$Vo = \sum_{t=1}^{\infty} \frac{E(CFt)}{(1+r)t}.$$

where;

V = Is the present value of the asset.
E(CF) = Are the expected cash-flows.
r = Is the discount factor.

The two-stage dividend discount model is used in literature which can be split into two or more stages of dividend growth to estimate the value more realistically. The first growth stage is usually called the high-growth stage and the second is called the stable-growth stage. Hence, one should see the high-growth stage as the expected dividend growth rate in the foreseeable future and the stable-growth stage as the long-term constant perpetual dividend growth rate. Sometimes, it is argued that the stable-growth stage is lower "(...) because of limited growth opportunities (...)" Dermine, (2008). The general formula for a two stage DDM is presented below **(CFA Institute, n.d.)**

$$\text{Present Value of Equity} = \sum_{t=1}^{N} \frac{Do(1+g)t}{(1+r)t} + \frac{PVn}{(1+r)n}$$

Where;

g = Is the short-term growth rate.
t = Is the short-term growth period.
PVn= Is the present value of the company in year N.
N= Is the long-term growth period.
r= Is the cost of capital.

In relative valuation the investor compares the price of one asset, for example the price of a publicly traded company, with the price of an asset that share specific characteristics. The important part is to find an asset or group of assets that are in fact comparable. In summary, applying the multiple approach implies, that the market prices assets on average correctly but the market is weak in pricing individual companies (Damodaran, 2013). There is a nearly unlimited number of relative valuation multiples that are commonly used, but the decision on which to choose is heavily dependent on the industry the target asset is in.

For banks, entity value multiples like the commonly used firm Value/ Sales or Firm Value/ EBITDA cannot be easily adopted to the bank industry. Because, in case of banks, the value or the operating income cannot be simply determined, Damodaran, (2009). However, multiples that can be used for banks are equity valuation multiples like the Price/ Earnings (P/E) multiple or the Price to Book value ratio (P/BV) as recommended by Damodaran (2009).

The formula for the Price Earnings Ratio is:

$$\text{Price Earnings Ratio} = \frac{\text{Price per Share}}{\text{Earning per Share}}$$

Nevertheless, the P/E ratio is commonly used not just to estimate whether a company might be overvalued- or undervalued, but also to compare the ratio over time and to look for discrepancies that may unveil a short-term orientation of the company (Liu, Nissim, & Thomas, 2007). Research shows that the accounting earnings multiples dominate cash flow and dividend multiples, and that the best performance is exhibited by forecast earnings since they project the least dispersion of pricing errors. This result is quite impressive since the earnings forecasts must provide the futuristic view of the profitability in a better way than the historical measures. This result is supported by another research that used multiples to forecast prices of initial public offerings (IPO) and found that forward looking earnings multiples are more accurate than historical ones (Kim & Ritter,1999).

The process to value banks or any other publicly traded company with the price to book value ratio, also known as market-to-book value ratio (MBV), is similar to other relative valuation approaches. However, the price to book value ratio is especially common for the valuation of banks, as the marked-to-market process is more commonly used with financial service companies than with non-financial companies, making the price to book value multiple more meaningful for banks. The multiple approach in general, normally starts with the selection of comparable banks, then the market-to-book value for each of these banks is then determined through division of the current market value of shares with the book value of equity as reported in the balance sheet of the company (Dermine, 2008).

$$\text{Price} - \text{to} - \text{Book Value Ratio} = \frac{\text{Price per Share} \times \text{Shares Outstanding}}{\text{Total Assets} - \text{Total Liabilities}}$$

Although this valuation approach requires, compared for example to the discounted cash flow approach, just two inputs per company i.e. current share price and stated book value of equity, that can be easily observed, there is a catch to it.

BANKING SECTOR VALUATION MODELS

When a number of valuation models are used, it provides less biased value for a company. Various models under use are discussed here.

The Free Cash Flow Equity Model

The free cash flow equity model is nothing but a DCF (Discounted Cash Flow) valuation method which makes use of free cash flow to equity. This remains the overall cash flow made available to the common equity shareholders of the company and this is not the dividends which they get. It corresponds to the calculation of free cash flow equity from the balance sheet changes and it also emphasizes the changes present in the composition of assets and liabilities of the company. When the net income is subtracted with increased equity and when added with other comprehensive income which is necessary for a firm to grow, one can calculate the free cash flow equity (Koller & Goedhart, 2005).

$$\text{FCFE} = \text{NI} - \Delta\text{assets} + \Delta\text{liabilities}$$

This method is otherwise known as free cash flow equity valuation method which is more or less equal to the Dividend Discount model. However, the dividends are replaced by the discounted free cash flows. The model formula is as follows.

Vo

where:

Vo = Value of the company
FCFE = Free cash flows to equity
r = Cost of equity
g = Long-term growth rate

FCFE Formula starting with Net Income

FCFE Formula = Net Income + Depreciation & Amortization + Changes in WC + Capex + Net Borrowings

FCFE Formula Starting from EBIT

FCFE Formula = EBIT – Interest – Taxes + Depreciation & Amortization + Changes in WC + Capex + Net Borrowings

FCFE Formula Starting from FCFF

FCFE Formula = FCFF – [Interest x (1-tax)] + Net Borrowings

The Dividend Discount Model

One can evaluate the model with the help of dividend discount model too. Having a long history of valuing a company or a bank, this model allots price equal to present value of all the future dividends. While the latter is basically dependent on the growth rate of the net profit excluding the retained earnings. Either the investor gets the net profit or it gets reinvested within the firm itself. This in turn benefits the investors finally. This model's share price is primarily based on the assumptions given above due to which this model is good enough to be used. The dividend discount valuation model formula is given below.

$$Vo = \sum_{t=1}^{N} \frac{divt}{(1+r)t} + \frac{divn(1+g)}{(r-g)n}$$

where:

Vo = The present value of the company
divt = Dividend at time t
divn = Expected dividend after the forecast period
r = Discount rate or cost of equity
g = Long-term growth

The Residual Income Valuation Model

The residual income valuation model is developed on the basis of company value which is equal to the capital invested in addition to what is created in addition to the cost of equity. The capital invested for a firm is nothing but its equity at book value. Return on Equity (ROE) remains a good measure to evaluate the value produced for the investors. The value of the firm remains higher when there is a large difference exists between the ROE and the required rate of return, when there are risks involved with the company. Cost of Equity (COE), on the other hand, denotes the risks involved with the company and it projects the cost opportunities available when investing in a share.

Since there is not much weight upon the terminal, the residual income remains the suitable option for dividend and free cash flow models. In RIM model, the firm that do not pay dividends can be valued and there will be negative values for expected free cash flows (Stowe & John D, 2007). The formula for the residual income valuation model is as follows:

$$Vo= Bo + \sum_{t=1}^{N}\frac{RI}{(1+re)t}+\frac{RIn}{(re-g)n}=Bo+\sum_{t=1}^{N}\frac{(ROEt-re)Bt}{(1+re)t}+\frac{(ROEt-re)Bn}{(re-g)n}$$

where:

Vo =The present value of the company.
Bo = Current book value of the equity.
Bt = Book value of equity at time t.
RI = Residual Income.
ROE = Return on equity.
re = Cost of equity.
g = Long-term growth rate.

The Justified P/BV Model

Having Gordon's growth model as a base, this model makes use of long-term sustainable figures such as cost of equity, target P/BV, ROE and growth. This model attempts to calculate P/BC ratio based on which the banks can easily trade as per the long-term values discussed above. This valuation type is too sensitive to handle since it may undergo changes based on underlying assumptions and forecasts. At times, the intuition may also be taken into account rather than the estimation using historical figures. In this scenario, the long-term growth figure is considered as the economic growth and once the forecasted period ends, the ROE is generated based on the predicted figures of the balance sheet and income statement. However, the challenging feature is that when there is a wrong assumption, it may result in a large over or under estimation of the fair value of the bank. This model's formula is as follows (Jean, 2009):

$$P/BV\ (target) = \frac{(ROE-g)Bn}{(COE-g)n}*BVPS*\left[\frac{1}{(1+r)1}*\frac{1}{(1+r)2}*\ldots*\frac{1}{(1+r)2}\right]$$

where:

P/BV = Price to book value.
ROE = Return on equity.
COE = Cost of equity.
g = Long term growth rate.
BVPS = Book value Per Share.

INPUT FACTORS

Estimating Input Factors

Input factors are always needed to value a company. How many input factors one needs is dependent on the valuation model one uses? Generally speaking, one can say that the more input factors the model requires, the more complex it becomes. Complexity in valuation should be avoided as the more complex it becomes, the more mistakes one can make and the explanatory power of that model becomes questionable.

The Capital Asset Pricing Model

To calculate the cost of capital for an intrinsic valuation, the Capital Asset Pricing Model (CAPM) is considered, ignoring that more complex calculations, like the Arbitrage Pricing Model (APM) or Multifactor models exist, because CAPM is the easiest and most often used model. The CAPM formula to calculate the cost of equity is as follows: Eugene F. Fama & Kenneth R. Frenchm (2004).

$$E(R) = rf + \beta\,(Rm - rf)$$

where

E(R) = The expected return.
Rf = The risk-free rate.
Rm = Required return of the market.
β = The unlevered beta.

Beta Factor

The beta factor is an important factor and necessary to calculate the cost of capital with the CAPM model. The beta is the slope of the regression line calculated with this formula:

$$\beta = \frac{\mathrm{cov}(\text{Stock, Market})}{\mathrm{var}(\text{Market})}$$

As can already be seen from the formula, the calculation of the beta requires the stock price and the index values. For stock listed companies these data are easy to obtain from various sources on the Internet. For non-stock listed companies or not yet stock listed companies that simply have no share price history, the formula cannot be calculated. In this case, one can calculate an average beta for a similar group of companies and use this beta as a best estimate of the target company's beta.

When selecting a reasonable index for the beta factor calculation, one has to make sure that not one single company dominates the index as this would result in a beta of close to one, which makes the beta factor in this case meaningless. The domination of one single company in an index is most likely in smaller countries that have just a few large cap companies and many mid and low cap companies like it was the case with Nokia in Finland in the 2000s (Damodaran, 2013).

Bank managers are aware of the fact that a more volatile business model will reduce the intrinsic value and probably try to reduce the volatility where possible. A lower debt-to-equity ratio results in a lower beta factor consequently reflecting a lower systemic risk (Gardner, McGowan Jr., & Moeller, 2010).

On the contrary, a higher debt-to-equity ratio will likely decrease the return on equity of the bank. To counteract this development, bank managers will probably invest in riskier assets that promise a higher return, again increasing the risk of the bank (Neus, 2010). In our case, the Bank of America debt-to-equity ratio was low (see Table.2)

Risk Free Rate

The risk-free rate is just the required rate of return for a theoretically risk-free asset, as risk-free is in practice not possible. Triple A rated government bonds are commonly considered to be risk-free. Government bonds however have different interest rates, depending on the time horizon. A ten-year zero-coupon bond has typically a higher interest rate than a three-month zero-coupon bond of the same country and the choice made by the analyst may have a high impact on the CAPM calculation. Damodaran recommends using the same time horizon for the zero coupon bond as for the forecasted cash flows (Damodaran, 2012).

The Equity Risk Premium (ERP)

The Equity Risk Premium (ERP) is the required return necessary to cover the additional risk for an asset that is not risk free. The calculation of the ERP can be done by either looking in the past or trying to estimate the future ERP, both approaches have their downsides and are just best estimates. The decision about which ERP to take for an asset is very subjective and differs from one investor to another. There are many surveys that ask investors for their personal equity premium and some surveys are repeatedly undertaken over several years. One survey conducted by Fernandez showing different equity risk premiums for 51 countries (Fernandez & Carabias, 2006), or the survey of Bancel and Mittoo just asking for a general market risk premium, show that for well developed countries like European countries, the range is between 5.5% for Germany and 7.3% for Greece on average. Furthermore, both surveys show that these risk premiums change over time (Bancel & Mittoo, 2014). Additionally, Bancel and Mittoo showed that "valuation experts use both historical and expected market risk premiums (58% versus 42%)" for a discounted cash flow analysis (2014). The second possible approach, next to the survey approach, is to look at what the market earned historically in contrast to the risk free rate. The third approach is "to back out an equity risk premium from market prices today" (Damodaran, 2014a).

In addition to a country risk premium that includes the political risk in a country, one could add as many risk premiums as one could think of. This could for example be a risk premium for firm size or maturity of a company (Damodaran, 2013).

Estimating Growth

Estimating growth is one of the most important input factors and one of the most difficult to estimate. In finance however many academics developed tools to come up at least with an approach. Banks, and other organizations, which regularly publish their findings were not able to forecast the future growth in gross domestic product accurately and even worse, seemed to be, on average, too overoptimistic (Kelm, 2014).

For banks forecasting the future is even more critical. In 2008 the French bank Societé General announced that the junior trader Jérôme Kerviel, made a loss of 4.9 billion euros within one year ("French Bank Says Rogue Trader Lost $7 Billion - NYTimes.com, 2008"). Although this could be a one-time event that will not happen in the future again, it is not. Before and after this events similar ones had happened before and afterwards, all over the world. Additionally, in the last decade banks had to set aside huge amounts of provisions for legal disputes and fines. However, according to Aswath Damodaran the expected growth rate is calculated as the return on equity multiplied with the retention ratio estimating growth, using EPS (2012). For that, one needs to calculate the return on equity (ROE) as well as the retention ratio

$$\text{Return on Equity}= \frac{\text{Net Income actual year}}{\text{Book Value of Equity previous year}}$$

$$\text{Retention Ratio}= 1- \frac{\text{Dividends}}{\text{Net Income}}$$

The expected growth rate is then calculated, based on the existing fundamentals by multiplying the return on equity with the retention ratio.

Expected Growth Rate Existing Fundamentals = ROE * Retention Ratio

These formulas are easy to apply but have the disadvantage that they just take into account the performance of the previous year, which will result into a too optimistic valuation if the last year was extraordinarily good or into a too pessimistic valuation if the last year was especially bad. For banks, the net income and the dividends necessary for the calculation of the expected growth rate varies strongly from year to year.

Normalizing Fundamentals

Normalizing is an essential part in valuing a company, which eases out extraordinary successful years as well as special events that led to low or negative income. Instead of the net income of the actual year Damodaran uses the four-year average of net income throughout to normalize fundamentals, following Damodaran's approach (2013).

$$\text{Normalized Return on Equity}= \frac{\text{Average Net Income 2003-2007}}{\text{Book Value of Equity 2006}}$$

$$\text{Retention Ratio}= 1- \frac{\text{Dividends2007}}{\text{Average Net Income2003} - 2007}$$

The idea behind is to take care of extraordinary events, which will most likely not happen again in the near future. As a result, the evaluator needs to estimate the severity of economic effects, the length of the effect and whether these effects are globally or regionally limited. In the case that the event is regionally, one would need to assess the severity according to whether the bank generates revenues in that specific region and if so, what portion of revenues in relation to total revenues is generated in that region.

FINANCIAL ANALYSIS

The following important references were used to add value on the present study:

Moyer, McGuigan& Rao (2018). Lawrence J. Gitman r & Chad J. Zutter (2014)
https://www.myaccountingcourse.com/accounting-dictionary/f

LIQUIDITY RATIOS

The concept of 'Liquidity Ratio' is used for the analysis of an organization's ability to pay its current or long-term liabilities when they become due or current respectively. In other terms, these ratios are used to display an organization's cash levels and their capability to convert assets into cash for the payment of liabilities and other considerable current obligations.

The use of liquidity measures the amount of cash contained in a business and how it will be easy for an organization or a company to gain cash or conversion of assets into viable cash. Many companies find aspects such as inventory, accounts receivable, and trading securities which are easy to be exchanged as cash within short period. Hence, all assets are considered for the calculation of liquidity for a company. Some of the most commonly used liquidity ratios are as follows:

The Current Ratio

Current ratio is utilized as a measure of the ability of a bank to pay off its liabilities that are short terms with its current assets through the calculation of liquidity and efficiency ratio. It is an important liquidity measure since short-term liabilities are deemed to become due within the next fiscal year. Cash, marketable securities, and cash equivalents tend to be converted with ease in a very short span of time which means that banks that have huge amounts of current assets could be used to pay off current liabilities when they are due without the need to sell long-term assets. A current ratio that is higher is most favorable than the current ratio that is lower since it displays the fact that banks could make current debt payments more easily. The calculation of current ratio is given as:

Current Ratio = Current Asses/Current Liabilities

According to Bank of America balance sheet the current assets $1673852 and the current liabilities are $1821951 for the year 2018. Bank of America current ratio would be calculated like this:

Current Ratio for the Bank of America (2018) = $1673852 / $1821951 = 0.92 Times

As displayed above, the Bank of America is found to have few current assets which could be used to pay-off its current liability over the years. This fact displays the highly leveraged and risky scenario faced by the bank. Banks tend to prefer at least a current ratio of 1 or 2 so that the current liabilities can be encompassed by the current assets (Refer Table 1).

Debt to Capital Ratio

The debt to capital ratio is deemed as a liquidity ratio used for the calculation of a bank or a company's use of financial leverage through the comparison of its total obligations and total capital. In other terms, such a metric is used to measure the proportion of a company's debt to finance its operations than the use of its own capital.

Such a ratio could be used as a risk measurement metric that allows the calculation of a bank's ability to handle revenue down turns since it highlights the relationship between debt and financing of equity. With the increase in the ratio, there is an increase in the risk to shareholder and lenders; however, this is not always the case since a high ratio is not always a bad thing to happen. For example, the financial institutions often tend to have high debt levels since these functions are intensive of capital. This measure also translates into a higher debt to capital ratio however this does not mean its insolvency as well. The calculation of debt to capital ratio is as follows:

Debt to Capital Ratio = Total Debt / Total Debt + Shareholders Equity
Debt to Capital Ratio for the Bank of America (2018) = 2089182 / 2089182 + 265325 = 88.73%

The debt to capital ratio for the Bank of America is high over the years, but there is a well handling of downturn in revenues.

LEVERAGE OR SOLVENCY RATIOS

Solvency ratio, otherwise known as leverage ratio is used as a metric to measure the ability of a bank to sustain the operations more indefinitely through the comparison of the levels of debt with assets, equity, and earnings. In other terms, the solvency ratio tends to identify the concerns within a bank and the ability of a firm to pay its bill in longer span of time. In general, the concepts of solvency ratios and liquidity ratios are often confused with one other. Though they both are used for the measurement of a bank's ability to pay off its obligations, the solvency ratios are used to focus on the sustainability of

Table 1. The bank of America liquidity ratios (2014-2018)

Ratios	Formula	2018	2017	2016	2015	2014
Current Ratio	Current Asses/Current Liabilities	0.92 Times	0.91 Times	0.90 Times	0.92 Times	0.94 Times
Debt to Capital Ratio	Total Debt / Total Debt + Shareholders Equity	88.73%	88.29%	87.83%	88.05%	88.43%

a firm on a long term instead of its current liabilities. The ratios are used as the ways to measure pay off long term obligations to bondholder, creditors, and banks. Better solvency ratios tend to indicate the financial soundness or creditworthiness of a bank in long term. Some of the most commonly used solvency ratios are as follows:

The Debt to Equity Ratio

The debt to equity ratio is deemed to compare the total debt with that of total equity of a bank. Being a liquidity ratio, it displays the percentage of financing of a bank that comes from investors and creditors. If the debt to equity ratio is high, it indicates the increased creditor financing than investor financing (meaning increased usage of bank loans than shareholder funding). This ratio is calculated using the formula:

Debit to Equity Ratio = Total Liabilities/Total Equity
Debit to Equity Ratio for the Bank of America (2018) = 2089182/ 265325 = 7.87 times

A debt to equity ratio that is valued at 1 denoting that both the creditors and investors got same amount of shares in business assets. When the debt to equity ratio is low, it means the financial stability of a business is high. Banks with high values of debt to equity are judged to contain high risks for the investors and creditors than banks that possess low ratio. This ratio is deemed to be high in the Bank of America.

The Equity Ratio

The equity ratio is a metric used for the measurement of assets which are financed by the investment of the owners through the comparison of the total bank's equity and total assets. This is an investment leverage or otherwise termed as solvency ratio.

The equity ratio tends to highlight sustainable and solvent business concepts which are two financially important concepts. The first concept displays the leveragability of a bank and how the same is with debt. The second concept conversely show the total assets owned by the bank outright by investors. In general terms, the increased value of equity ratios is favorable for banks. It is deemed that equity financing is cheap than debt financing since the interest expenses are associated with debt financing. Organizations with high ratios of equity should have less debt service and financing costs than banks with low ratios. Equity ratio is calculated using the formula:

Equity Ratio= Total Equity/ Total Assets
Equity Ratio for the Bank of America (2018) =265325/2354507 = 11.27%

From the above calculation, it is deemed that the ratio of Bank of America during the year 2018 is found to be pretty low which means the investors tend to fund more assets with debt. It was found that around 11 per cent of the assets of the bank are owned by shareholders and not its creditors which is the same case for the rest years. Based on the industry, we can decide whether the ratio is healthy or not.

Debt Ratio

Debt ratio is deemed to be a solvency ratio and acts as a metric to measure the total liabilities of a bank as a total asset percentage. In other words, the debt ratio is used to display the ability of a company to pay off its liabilities with its own assets. This means the debt ratio is used as a measure on how many assets that could be used to sell to pay off liabilities. A low ratio is deemed to be more favorable to pay liabilities than high ratios. A low debt ratio displays the increased stability of business with increased longevity since low ratio banks have low debt on the overall range. Each industry tends to have its own debt benchmarks. As stated previously, banks tend to have their own debt considerations. The formula to calculate it is given below:

Debt ratio= Total Liabilities/Total Assets
Debt ratio for the Bank of America (2018) = 2089182 /2354507 = 88.73%

However, the debt ratio for the Bank of America (2018) was very highly leveraged and riskier over the years.

The Equity Multiplier

Being a financial leverage ratio, the equity multiplier generally assess the assets of a bank which are bankrolled by its shareholders. This is usually done by a comparison to total assets with that of the equities of the shareholder. Otherwise, it can also be said that the equity multiplier exhibits the percentage of assets bankrolled or owned by the shareholders. When there is higher ratio, it can be understood that more assets are funded through debt than through equity. During the instance, when the assets of a bank are predominantly funded by debt, the bank is considered to be riskier for investors and creditors since it is highly leveraged.

The Equity Multiplier = Total Assets / Total Stockholder's Equity.
The equity multiplier for the Bank of America (2018) = 2354507/265325 = 8.87%

It can be observed that 8.87% is the ratio for Bank of America which denotes the fact that the bank debts levels are predominantly higher. In this DuPont analysis, the researcher also utilized the multiplier ratio in order to propagate the impact of leverage upon a bank's return on equity. As per DuPont analysis, when the multiplier ratios are higher, it may report higher returns on equity.

The Times Interest Earned Ratio

Interest coverage ratio or the times interest earned ratio is nothing but a coverage ratio which calculates the balanced amount of income which could be made use of, to overcome the future interest expenses.

The times interest ratio is sometimes considered as a solvency ratio since it analysis the capability of a bank to do interest and debt service payments. Due to the scenario that these interest payments are paid on a long-term basis, usually these are considered as ongoing and fixed expense. Alike the most cases of fixed expenses, when the banks are unable to payback, it goes bankrupt and ceased. So, this ratio is

Table 2. The bank of America leverage ratios (2014-2018)

Ratios	Formula	2018	2017	2016	2015	2014
Debt to Equity Ratio	Total liabilities /Total Equity	7.87%	7.54%	7.22%	7.37%	7.64%
Equity Ratio	Total Equity/ Total Assets	11.27%	11.71%	12.17%	11.95%	11.57%
Debt to Assets ratio	Total Debts /Total Assets	88.7%	88.3%	87.8%	88.1%	88.4%
The equity multiplier or Financial Leverage	The Equity Multiplier = Total Assets / Total Stockholder's Equity.	8.87 Times	8.54 Times	8.22% Times	8.37% Times	8.64% Times
The Times Interest Earned Ratio	Earnings Before Interest and Taxes (EBIT)/ Interest Expenses	0.61 Times	0.50 Times	0.43 Times	0.37 Times	0.10 Times

also viewed as a solved ratio. This ratio denotes the number of times, a bank is able to pay the interest before it subtracts the tax income. So it is obvious that when the ratio is large, then it becomes highly favorable compared to small ratios. The formula to calculate the times interest earned ratio is as follows.

The Times Interest Earned Ratio= Earnings Before Interest and Taxes (EBIT)/ Interest Expenses
The Times Interest Earned Ratio for the Bank of America (2018) = $34584/56663 = 0.61 times

It can be observed that the times interest earned ratio is low in case of Bank of America. In such scenario, the creditors go for a bank that has high 'times interest ratio' since it is evident that the bank is able to pay back the interest payments on due date.

EFFICIENCY OR ACTIVITY RATIOS

Efficiency ratios which are otherwise called as activity ratios evaluate the performance of banks or companies with regards to the utilization of assets in generating income. Efficiency ratios are usually considered when the banks collect money from customers i.e., revenue making. These ratios enable the bank management, investors and creditors to understand the operations and profitability factor of the bank. The profitability ratios and efficiency ratios are proportionate to each other. When the banks are efficient enough in handling their resources for revenue generation, they become profitable. The most common efficiency ratios are discussed below.

The Asset Turnover Ratio

One of the efficiency ratio i.e., asset turnover ratio, analyses the capability of a bank in generating revenues from its assets through a comparison of net revenues and average total assets. Otherwise, this ratio declares a company's efficiency in leveraging its assets for revenue making.

Average total assets are generally determined through the addition of beginning and ending values of total asset balances and dividing the resultant value by two. So, when there is higher ratio, it becomes highly favorable. When there is higher turnover ratio present for the bank, it can be understood that it leverages its assets efficiently. Based on the industry standards, the asset turnover ratio is decided using the following formula alike other ratios.

Asset Turnover Ratio= Net Revenues/ Average Total Assets
The asset turnover ratio for the Bank of America (2018) = 110584/ 2317871 = 0.047

It can be observed that the Bank of America (2018)'s ratio is 0.037 which is the least for rest of years. This denotes that the Bank of America generated only 037 cents for every dollar of its assets in the year 2018.

Return on Revenue

Operating profit margin or otherwise the Return on Revenue (ROR) is an important financial ratio which determines the efficiency of a bank when it comes to generating profits out of its revenue. Otherwise, it can also be stated that the performance of a bank is determined by assessing the percentage of total bank revenues which has been converted into bank profits. ROR (Return on Revenues) is generally considered as an indicator of both efficiency and profitability ratios.

This efficiency ratio is predominantly taken into account by the investors and creditors since it projects the percentage of money made by the bank, using its revenues, during a certain period. This calculation can be utilized to do compare a bank's performance for a fixed period or compare two different sized bank's performance during a certain period of time.

Return on Revenues = Operating Profit / Net Revenues
Return on revenues ratio for the Bank of America (2018) = 34584 / 110584 = 31.27%

As we can see, the Bank of America (2018) converts 31.27 percent of it is revenues into profits, this ratio was less in the previous years. When a bank wish to enhance its net operating income, it is suggested to either emphasize on reduction on its expenses or increase in its revenues.

Fixed Asset Turnover

Fixed asset turnover ratio is one of the efficiency ratios which analyzes the ROI (Return On Investment) of a bank's investment upon a property, plant and/or equipment through a comparison of net revenues with that of the fixed assets. Both creditors as well as the investors make use of this ratio to get insights about the bank in terms of their utilization of equipment in generating revenues. This is an important concept for the investors since they always look for approximate ROI prior to investment. When there is a higher turnover ratio, it denotes that the smaller assets are efficiently made use of, by the bank to generate large amount of revenues. The formula to calculate this ratio is as follows.

Fixed Asset Turnover = Net Revenues / Fixed Assets
Fixed Asset Turnover ratio for the Bank of America (2018) = 110584/9906 = 11.16 Times.

As you can see, the Bank of America (2018) generates more eleven times revenues than the net book value of it is assets. The bank should compare this metric with other banks similar in its industry. It remains critical to compare and contrast the ratios with other banks' ratios in the industry.

The Goodwill to Assets Ratio

Being a financial ratio, the goodwill to assets ratio performs a comparison of intangible assets, for instance, unique position in the industry, brand name or customer list, with that of the total assets held by the bank. This comparison is done in order to understand whether the goodwill is recorded properly.

Goodwill and reputation goes in parallel and goodwill acts as a huge asset in business terms for both a company as well as a bank. The accounting term goodwill paves an easy path for the companies to convert its reputation as monetary benefits. In spite of the fact that it is important and it contributes significant value, the goodwill must be compared with other assets at the time of evaluating a bank's value.

Goodwill to Total Assets Ratio = Goodwill / Total Assets
Goodwill to total assets ratio for the Bank of America (2018) =68951 / 2354507 = 2.93%

When there is an increasing goodwill-to-assets ratio, it denotes that the goodwill acquired is outperforming other asset values. The acquisition of Nokia by Microsoft remains a good example for this scenario. After one year of acquisition, Microsoft wrote off over four billion USD of goodwill, just because the company understood that Nokia was overpaid for which it is not worthy. In line with this, the goodwill ratio for the Bank of America was almost in the same range.

PROFITABILTY RATIOS

Gross Margin Ratio

Being a profitability ratio, the gross margin ratio makes a comparison of the business' gross margin with net revenues. The business' gross margin is determined by subtracting the cost of goods sold from net revenues. The net revenue is the value achieved when the gross revenues are subtracted by returns or refunds. It is obvious that only when there is higher ratio, it remains favorable. When there is higher ratio, it denotes that the bank sells their services at higher profit percentage. When higher gross margin ratios are achieved by the company, it has a lot of money in excess to spend for its operating expenses, for instance, rent, utilities, salaries etc.,

Gross Margin Ratio = Gross Margin/ Net Revenues
Gross margin ratio for the Bank of America (2018) = 91247 / 110584 = 82.51%

Table 3. The bank of America efficiency or activity ratios (2014-2018)

Ratios	Formula	2018	2017	2016	2015	2014
Asset Turnover Ratio	Net Revenues/ Average Total Assets	0.037	0.037	0.037	0.037	0.04
Return on Revenues	Operating Profit / Net Revenues	31.27%	29.14%	26.71%	23.73%	8.22%
Fixed Asset Turnover	Net Revenues / Fixed Assets	11.16 Times	10.84 Times	10.25 Times	9.86 Times	9.64 Times
Goodwill to Assets	Goodwill / Total Assets	2.93%	3.02%	3.28%	3.57%	3.70%

It can be observed that 82.51 percent is, the Bank of America's gross margin ratio which is the highest in the rest of years and among other players in the banking industry itself. In other words, it can be said that the bank has 82.51 percent sales revenue to take care of its operating costs even after it paid its inventory costs.

The Profit Margin Ratio

Being a profitability ratio, the profit margin ratio assess the amount of net income earned for every dollar sales generated through a comparison of net income and the bank's net revenues. Otherwise, it can be noted that the profit margin ratio gives the percentage of revenues available, once the business had paid all its expenses. This ratio is generally used by the creditors and investors to assess the effectiveness of a bank in converting its revenues into net income.

Profit Margin Ratio= Net Income/Net Revenues
The profit margin ratio for the Bank of America (2018) = 26696 / 110584 = 24.14%

As you can see, the Bank of America (2018) converted 24.14 percent of their revenues into profits and was able to convert more of these revenues into profits. But in the previous years they made less revenue, because their expenses were high.

The Return on Assets Ratio (ROA)

Being a profitability ratio, the Return on Total Assets or the Return On Assets (ROA) ratio determines the net income generated by the total number of assets in a certain period through comparison of net income with that of the average total assets. Otherwise, the Return on Assets ratio or ROA determines the efficiency of a bank in asset management for profit generation during a specific time period. This ratio is generally taken into account by both management as well as the investors to assess the bank's performance in converting its investments in assets into profits.

Return On Assets Ratio= Net Income/ Average Total Assets
The return on assets ratio for the Bank of America (2018) = 28147 / 2317871 = 1.20

It is obvious that only when there is a higher ROA present, the investors will be interested since the ROA value denotes the bank's efficiency in asset management thus producing excellent increased net income. ROA is mostly used in the comparison of banks within the same industry since different industries consider assets differently. The Bank of America had a low ROA over a period of time. For example, the software companies make use of computers and servers while it is large and expensive equipment in case of construction companies.

Return On Capital Employed (ROCE)

Being a profitability ratio, ROCE (Return on Capital Employed) determines the efficiency of a bank in generating profits from its capital employed, through a comparison of net operating profit and capital employed. Otherwise, the investors get insights about the dollars of profits generated by return on every dollar capital employed. This ratio is done on the basis of two critical calculations such as capital employed and operating profit. The net operating profit is usually termed as EBIT (Earnings Before Interest and Taxes) whereas the capital employed is mostly referred as a company's total assets excluding its all current liabilities. It is obvious that only a high ratio is preferred by the investors since it denotes the high amount of dollars profit generated for every dollar of capital employed. Investors keep an eye on the ratio to understand the efficiency of a bank in utilizing the capital employed in addition to its long-term financing strategies.

Return on Capital Employed Formula =Net Operating Profit/ Total Assets – Current Liabilities
Return on capital employed ratio for the Bank of America (2018) = 34584 / 2354507 – 1821951 = 6.5%

It can be understood that the Bank of America (2018) had a 6.5 percent return which was less when compared to previous years. Otherwise, it can be said that the banks with large cash reserves usually skew this ratio since the cash is generally included in the employed capital computation in spite of the fact that it is not technically employed yet.

The Return on Equity Ratio (ROE)

Being a profitability ratio, ROE (Return on Equity) determines the capability of a bank in terms of profit generation based on the investments of its shareholders. Otherwise, it can be said as the amount of profit generated for every dollar of common stockholder's equity. This remains a critical factor for the potential investors since they need to get an overview of the bank's efficiency in using its money to generate net income. Further, ROE is a good indicator to assess whether the management is effective or not when it comes to utilization of equity financing to fund the operations and grow the company.

The Return On Equity Ratio= Net Income/ Shareholder's Equity.
The Return On Equity Ratio for the Bank of America (2018) = 28147/242999 = 11.6%

It is obvious that the higher ROE ratios are better compared to lower ratios though one need to consider other bank's ratios in the industry. As there are various levels of investors and income present in every industry, ROE cannot be taken as a factor to execute a comparison among the banks outside their industries in an effective manner.

Return On Invested Capital (ROIC)

Being a financial ratio, ROIC (Return on Invested Capital) determines the strategy of a bank in investing the shareholders' money to make profit out of it. Otherwise, it can be said that the ROIC determines the performance of a bank management by assessing its utilization of shareholders' and bondholder's money in order to generate additional revenues. ROIC is also used as a measure by the investors to make a comparison among the banks across industries, so as to arrive at the conclusion on which bank or management team outperforms in terms of generating revenues from the owner's investments. With high ROIC ratio, the management can be termed as better performing in terms of bank operations and investing the money of shareholders and bondholders.

The return on invested capital formula =Net Income – Dividends/ Total Capital Invested
Return on Invested Capital for the Bank of America (2018) = 28147/508324 = 5.7%

It can be understood that the ratio for the Bank of America in (2018) is .057 which was low in the previous years. This denotes that the bank generates 057 cents as income, for every dollar invested in it. Based on the industry, this could be taken as a low return. It must be remembered always that this ratio is the best when comparing the bank's performance for multiple years.

DuPont Analysis

Being a financial ratio, the DuPont analysis, otherwise termed as DuPont model works on the basis of ROE (Return On Equity) ratio which is utilized to assess the ability of a bank in terms of increasing its ROE. Otherwise, it can be said that this model breaks down the ROE ratio to elaborate the way which banks can follow to increase its return for investors. The model suggests a bank to increase its ROE, on the basis of these three performance measures, through the maintenance of high profit margin, effective leveraging of assets and increasing the asset turnover. In 1920s, this analysis was developed by Dupont Corporation, which was named after it. The basic formula is as follows.

In Dupont analysis, there are three main components of ROE ratio are present.
DuPont Analysis = Profit Margin ×Total Asset Turnover × Financial Leverage
Profit Margin = Net Income/ Net Revenues
Total Asset Turnover = Net Revenues / Average Total Assets
Financial Leverage =Total Assets / Total Equity
The DuPont ratio for the Bank of America in (2018) = 0.2414×0.037×8.87= 7.92%

Over the years, it can be observed that the Bank of America have completely different operations. This model enables the investors compare similar kind of banks like these with similar ratios. Then the investors are free to apply the perceived risks with the business model of each bank.

Table 4. The bank of America profitability ratios (2014-2018)

Ratios	Formula	2018	2017	2016	2015	2014
Gross Margin Ratio	Gross Margin/ Net Revenues	82.5%	87.1%	89.4%	88.7%	88.7%
Net Profit Margin Ratio	Net Income/Net Revenues	24.14%	16.57%	17.23%	15.43%	4.62%
Return on Assets Ratio	Net Income/ Average Total Assets	1.20	0.80	0.81	0.74	0.26
Return on Capital Employed	Net Operating Profit/ Total Assets – Current Liabilities	6.5	5.5	5.0	4.2	1.5
Return on Equity	Net Income/ shareholder's equity	11.6%	7.4%	7.4%	6.8%	2.5%
Return on Investment	Net Income – Dividends/ Total Capital Invested	5.7%	3.7%	3.7%	3.2%	1.1%
DuPont Analysis	Profit Margin ×Total Asset Turnover × Financial Leverage	7.9%	5.23%	5.24%	4.78%	1.60%

MARKET RATIOS

Earnings Per Share (EPS)

Being a market prospect ratio, Earnings Per Share (EPS) otherwise called as net income per share, determines the amount of net income generated for every share of stock outstanding. Otherwise, it can be described as the amount of money received for every share of stock when all the profits were distributed to outstanding shares by year end. The preferred dividends should get rid of net income when calculating earnings per share. This might be attributed to the fact that the EPS calculates the income available to common stockholders alone. Preferred dividends are confined only for the preferred shareholders and common shareholders cannot access it. It is always better to have higher earnings per share than lower ratio since the higher ratio denotes a bank to be profitable whereas the company got more profits to share among its shareholders.

Earnings per share= net income - preferred dividends / weighted average common shares outstanding
Earnings per share or basic earnings per for the Bank of America (2018)= 26696/ 10097= $2.64

It can be observed that the EPS of Bank of America for the year 2018 is $2.64 whereas it was low in previous years. This denotes that each share would get a total of 2.64 dollars if the quality distributed every dollar of income to its shareholders.

Book Value Per Share (BVPS)

Book Value Per Share (BVPS) is nothing but a ratio that is utilized to execute a comparison between the common shareholder's equity to the number of shares outstanding. When a firm dissolves, the amount received by all the shareholders is nothing but BVPS. This is widely utilized in relative valuation and generally to compare the market value of one share of a bank. When the BVPS of a bank is higher than its market value per share, then the stock is undervalued, denoting that it executes trade for a lesser price than what is decided by the market.

BVPS = (common shareholder's equity – preferred stock) / number of shares outstanding = ($277536–$0) / 10097 = $27.4

Since the market price of this stock is $27.4, it remains good valued and can be applied for the rest of the years.

The Price to Book Ratio

Being a financial valuation tool, the Price to Book ratio (P/B or market to book ratio) is utilized to assess whether the stock of a bank is overvalued or undervalued through comparing the price of all outstanding shares with the bank's net assets. Otherwise, it can be said as a determination of difference that exist between the book value and the total share price of the bank.

Usually, the investors make use of both formats discussed above in order to critically assess whether a bank is overpriced or underpriced. For instance, when the P/B ratio is more than 1, it denotes that the investors wish to pay excess to the bank than its actual worth of net assets. On the other hand, when the market book ratio is less than 1, it can be understood that the bank's stock price is sold lesser than its actual worth of net assets.

Price to Book Ratio = market price per share / book value per share
Price to Book Ratio for the Bank of America (2018) = $2.64/27.4 = 0.096

It can be observed that the market price of the Bank of America was less than 1 over the years denoting the fact that it could be considered undervalued since the investors wish to pay less for the assets than they are worth though they have a good reason for this.

CONCLUSION

Valuation models add confidence to an investment, there are certain limitations attached to that. The more complex a valuation model becomes and the more time one spends with carefully estimating the intrinsic value of bank, the more confident one becomes about the intrinsic value of a bank. The different valuation methods have shown, that no one model is superior over another. For some banks, some valuation methods seem to have a higher explanatory power than for others. However, this chapter introduced the most appropriate approaches for valuation of banks. It discussed some previous studies included theories and decision models, valuation models, input factors and financial analysis of banking sector.

The most comprehensive method in this chapter is described in section 5. It is assumed that the valuation methods can be used to find the strength and weaknesses of the financial position of the commercial banks. Although, it was not easy to find some data, but it is very accurate and the only model that takes the most regulatory capital into account.

Furthermore, it is assumed that it is impossible to implement any method that will measure all financial performance of a bank. In fact, all models that are presented in this chapter require some assumptions about the future, which makes intrinsic values very subjective and can just be best estimates. There is a nearly unlimited number of relative valuation multiples that are commonly used, but the decision on which to choose is heavily dependent on the industry, as a matter of fact valuation takes different tracks from one industry to other. However, in the end the analyst decides which method he or she wants to use. This study can be used as an overview and guideline to select the proper valuation method.

Table 5. The bank of America Efficiency or Activity Ratios (2014-2018)

Ratios	Formula	2018	2017	2016	2015	2014
Earnings per share	net income - preferred dividends / weighted average common shares outstanding	$2.64	$1.63	$1.57	$1.38	$0.43
Book Value per Share (BVPS)	(common shareholder's equity – preferred stock) / number of shares outstanding	$27.4	$26	$26.5	$24.7	$23.2
Price to Book Ratio	market price per share / book value per share	0.096	0.063	0.059	0.056	0.019

REFERENCES

Bancel, F., & Mittoo, U. R. (2014). *The gap between theory and practice of firm valuation: Survey of European valuation experts*. SSRN Electronic Journal. doi: 10.2139srn.242038

Bank for International Settlement. (2013). A brief history of the basel committee. Retrieved from http://www.bis.org/bcbs/history.pdf

Bank of America Financial Statements. (2014-2018). Retrieved from https://www.macrotrends.net/stocks/charts/BAC/bank-of-america/balance-sheet and https://www.macrotrends.net/stocks/charts/BAC/bank-of-america/income-statement

Damodaran, A. (2009). Valuing financial service firms– The big picture, (April), pp. 1–34. Retrieved from people.stern.nyu.edu/adamodar/pdfiles/papers/finfirm09.pdf

Damodaran, A. (2012). *Valuation - tools and techniques for determining the value of any asset* (3rd ed., p. 155). Hoboken, NJ: John Wiley & Sons.

Damodaran, A. (2013). Session 1: An introduction to valuation some initial thoughts. Retrieved from https://itunes.apple.com/us/course/id780803998

Damodaran, A. (2014a). *Equity risk premiums (ERP): determinants, estimation and implications*. (2014 ed.). SSRN Electronic Journal. doi: 10.2139srn.240919

Dermine, J. (2008). Bank valuation: With an application to the implicit duration of nonmaturing deposits. Retrieved from http://ssrn.com/abstract=1314884

Eugene, F. & Kenneth, R. (2004). The capital asset pricing model: Theory and evidence. *Journal of Economic Perspectives, 18*(3), 25–46 (4.2). Retrieved from www-personal.umich.edu/~kathrynd/JEP.FamaandFrench.pdf

Fernandez, P., & Carabias, J. M. (2006). *Union Fenosa 1991-2005*. SSRN Electronic Journal. doi:10.2139srn.914160

Gardner, J., McGowan, C., Jr. & Moeller, S. E. (2010). Using Microsoft Corporation to demonstrate the optimal capital structure trade-off theory. *Journal of Economics and Finance Education, 9*(2), 29–37. Retrieved from https://www.economics-finance.org/jefe/fin/Gardner.Finance.Vol.9(2).pdf

John, D. S. (2007). *Equity asset valuation* (2nd ed., p. 252). Retrieved from https://theequityanalyst.files.wordpress.com/2015/08/equity-asset-valuation.pdf

Kelm, M. (2014). Geldanlage: Die Nutzlosigkeit von Kapitalmarktprognosen. Retrieved from http://www.wallstreet-online.de/nachricht/6703396-geldanlagenutzlosigkeit-kapitalmarktprognosen

Kim, M., & Ritter, J. R. (1999). Valuing IPOs. *Journal of Financial Economics, 53*(3), 409–437. doi:10.1016/S0304-405X(99)00027-6

Koller, T., Goedhart, M., & Wessels, D. (2010). *Valuation: Measuring and managing the value of companies* (5th ed.). John Wiley & Sons. Retrieved from elibrary.bsu.az/books_200/N_1.pdf

Lawrence, J., Gitman, R., & Chad, J. Z. (2014). *Principles of managerial finance, student value edition* (14th ed.). Pearson.

Liu, J., Nissim, D., & Thomas, J. (2007). Is cash flow king in valuations? *Financial Analysts Journal, 63*(2), 1–13. https://pdfs.semanticscholar.org/7331/01e3253efca1173adf6c76715fdd45aeef38.pdf. doi:10.2469/faj.v63.n2.4522

Moyer, McGuiga, & Rao (2018). Contemporary financial management, 14th Edition, Cengage Learning.

Reserve Bank of New Zealand. (2007). Capital adequacy ratios for banks - simplified explanation and example of calculation. Retrieved from http://pages.stern.nyu.edu/~igiddy/articles/capital_adequacy_calculation.pdf

Zikoh, J. (2009). Strategic valuation of Danske Bank Group. Copenhagen Business School, Master thesis (3.4). Retrieved from https://www.myaccountingcourse.com/accounting-dictionary/f

KEY TERMS AND DEFINITIONS

Capital Adequacy: Is the ratio of the Bank's capital to its risk. It is a term that shows the relationship between the Bank's sources of capital and the risks surrounding the Bank's assets and any other operations.

Discounted Cash Flow: Is a valuation technique used to estimate the attractiveness of an investment opportunity.

Financial Analysis: Financial analysis is a process aimed at assessing ways of investing and employing money in companies. It is a study of the financial information of a particular enterprise or project in order to understand cash flows, profits, and expenditures.

Intrinsic Value: The intrinsic value is the actual value of the business or an asset based on a basic perception of its true value including all aspects of the business in terms of both tangible and intangible factors.

Liquidity Ratios: Liquidity is defined as the ability of the Company to obtain cash and liquidity ratios measure the ability to repay obligations when they fall due.

Profitability Ratios: Is a measure of the financial metrics used to assess a company's ability to make profits that are comparable to its expenses and related costs over a given time period.

Residual Income: Is the amount of income the individual has after paying all personal debts and expenses such as mortgages that have been repaid.

Return on Assets (ROA): Is a measure of the profitability of a company relative to its total assets. The return on assets gives an idea of the management's efficiency in using its assets for profit.

Return on Equity (ROE): Is the net income attributable to the equity ratio. The ROE estimates the profitability of the business by showing the amount of profits the company generates with the money invested by the shareholders.

The Capital Asset Pricing Model: (CAPM), identifies stock risk by knowing the sensitivity of the return of the security and comparing it to the change in market returns.

APPENDIX

Table 6. Bank of America Income Statement 2014-2018

Annual Data in Millions of US $ except per share data	2018	2017	2016	2015	2014
Revenue	**110584$**	**100264$**	**93662$**	**93514$**	**96829$**
Cost of Goods Sold	19337	12912	9961	10549	10935
Gross Profit	**91247**	**87352**	**83701**	**82965**	**85894**
Research and Development Expenses	-	-	-	-	-
SG&A Expenses	56663	58139	58680	60778	76995
Other Operating Income or Expenses	-	-	-	-	-
Operating Expenses	76000	71051	68641	71327	88866
Operating Income	**34584**	**29213**	**25021**	**22187**	**7963**
Total Non-Operating Income	-	-	-	-	-
Pre-Tax Income	**34584**	**29213**	**25021**	**22187**	**7963**
Income Taxes	6437	10981	7199	6277	2443
Income After Taxes	**28147**	**18232**	**17822**	**15910**	**5520**
Other Income	-	-	-	-	-
Income from Continuous Operations	**28147**	**18232**	**17822**	**15910**	**5520**
Income from Discontinued Operation	-	-	-	-	-
Net Income	**26696**	**16618**	**16140**	**14427**	**4476**
EBITDA	-	-	-	-	-
EBIT	-	-	-	-	-
Basic Shares Outstanding	10097	10196	10284	10462	10528
Shares Outstanding	10237	10778	11047	11236	10585
Basic EPS	**$2.64**	**$1.63**	**$1.57**	**$1.38**	**$0.43**
EPS – Earning Per Share	**$2.61**	**$1.56**	**$1.49**	**$1.31**	**$0.42**

Source:https://www.macrotrends.net/stocks/charts/BAC/bank-of-america/income-statement

Table 7. Bank of America Balance Sheet 2014-2018

Annual Data in Millions of US $ except per share data	2018	2017	2016	2015	2014
Cash On Hand	660377 $	590692$	536032$	536106$	529707$
Notes and Loans Receivables	1013475	999409	963271	950514	941653
Inventory	-	-	-	-	-
Other Current Assets	-	-	-	-	-
Total Current Assets	1673852	1590101	1499303	1486620	1471360
Property, Plant, and Equipment	9906	9247	9139	9485	10049
Long- Term Investment	441753	440130	430731	406888	380461
Goodwill and Intangible Assets	68951	68951	71716	76616	77919
Other Long-Term Assets	160045	172805	177178	164678	164745
Total Long-Term Assets	680655	691133	688764	657667	633174
Total Assets	**2354507**	**2281234**	**2188067**	**2144287**	**2104534**
Total Current Liabilities	1821951	1752386	1665569	1612897	1571015
Long-Term Debt	229340	227402	216823	236764	243139
Other Non-Current Liabilities	37891	34300	39480	38450	46909
Total Long-Term Liabilities	267231	261702	256303	275214	290048
Total Liabilities	**2089182**	**2014088**	**1921872**	**1888111**	**1861063**
Common Stock Net	118896	138089	147038	151042	153458
Retained Earnings	136314	113816	101225	88219	75024
Comprehensive Income	-12211	-7082	-7288	-5358	-4320
Other Shareholders Equity	-	-	-	-	-
Shareholders' Equity	**265325**	**267146**	**266195**	**256176**	**243471**
Total Liabilities and Shareholders' Equity	**2354507**	**2281234**	**2188067**	**2144287**	**2104534**

Source: https://www.macrotrends.net/stocks/charts/BAC/bank-of-america/balance-sheet

Chapter 11
Capital and Liquidity Regulations, Resilience, and Bank Value

Md. Atiqur Rahman Khan
https://orcid.org/0000-0002-5815-2045
Faculty of Business Studies, University of Rajshahi, Bangladesh

ABSTRACT

In the business arena, particularly in the field of corporate finance, the scope of valuation is highly significant. There are several value drivers for a firm. However, due to its nature of business, a bank's valuation is affected by several unique drivers including earnings diversification, risk capabilities, assets mix, and a lot of intangible factors. Since banking is a highly regulated sector, this chapter is designed to address the missing links between Basel capital and liquidity regulations, banking system resilience, and bank valuation.

INTRODUCTION

Valuation is a process to determine the value, in particular, the current economic value of a business by evaluating it's all aspects. The process might include an analysis of the company's management, ownership nature, capital structure, the expected market value of assets, risks, and most importantly future earnings prospects. There might be several reasons behind a firm's valuation, namely, acquisitions and mergers, portfolio management, legal and taxation purpose. However, categorization of assets (tangible and intangible) is the biggest challenge for the managers today which have a significant impact on the firm value. A significant portion of earnings are induced from intangible assets in particular for the financial institutions.

In the business arena particularly in the field of corporate finance, the scope of valuation is highly important. Valuation has much significance in different areas of finance including a firm's financing, investment, and dividend decisions. Within the objective of firm value maximization, the shareholders'

DOI: 10.4018/978-1-7998-1086-5.ch011

wealth maximization principle is incorporated. Further, among all the measures of a listed firm, the stock price is the most observable indicator that can be applied to assess the firm performance. In an efficient market, stock prices of a particular firm immediately reflect all newly disclosed information. Usually, managers' decisions and actions are continuously compared with stock prices performance. A stock price upsurge is often credited to the value creation performance of the management (Kumar, 2016). The intrinsic or true value of stock contains all aspects (tangible and intangible factors) of a company, and these factors affect the perceived as well as the market price of a share.

There is also a crucial role of valuation in financing decisions for investment purposes. IPOs pricing is mainly based on the valuation process. Further, to set a long-term investment strategy, the value of a firm based on fundamental analysis help to understand whether it is overvalued or undervalued. Thus, the role of valuation in portfolio management possesses much importance, as it is an essential part of the fundamental analysis where the firm value is linked to its cash flow features in terms of timing, riskiness, and growth.

Valuation methods can generally be categorized into asset-, earnings-, and market-based valuation. However, in the last few decades, market-based valuation, which is also known as the shareholder value approach, has turned out to be the leading approach for business-performance measurement worldwide (Kumar, 2016). In addition, shareholders' value maximization is the crucial objective for managerial decisions making process in different business sectors, including banks (Stephanie, 2006; Kumar, 2016). Considering the trust-based business nature, shareholder value creation has become the key goal of leading banks.

Scholars have identified several value drivers of banking institutions. Further to be noted, since the banking industry is highly regulated one, although few studies attempted to identify the effect of changing regulations on the stability and resilience of the banking system; no study is focused on whether the added regulations and increased resilience could increase the value of the banking firms as well as the shareholders' wealth. However, there is a vital gap in existing literature whether the changing regulations could bring any value addition to the banks.

To identify the missing links between the new regulations, resilience and the value of the banking institutions, the remaining discussions are divided into additional 4 sections. While Section 2 presents how to value a bank, and the value drivers identified so far. Based on Basel initiatives, the regulations and resilience of the banking system are portrayed in Section 3. Section 4 addresses the effect of regulations on banks' value. Lastly, Section 5 presents the concluding remarks.

VALUING A BANK

When valuing a bank, three matters are important. First, which valuation methods are appropriate for banks? Second, are any customization required for the standard methods for valuation; and third, on the basis of value drivers, how the customization be done? As outlined earlier, the shareholder value approach i.e. equity-based approach is better for baking institutions. However, the focus should be spotted on the value drivers. The key aspect of decision making in investment and asset management relies on a thoughtful study of the valuation as well as the sources of value. In addition to the fundamental factors, like, earnings, cash flows, revenue; business nature and risk-oriented factors are needed to be considered in the valuation.

Value drivers are required to be directly connected to the creation of shareholder value and to be measured by both operational and financial KPIs which must consider operating performance and long-term growth. In addition, since the sustainability and environmental issues are the main concern for scholars and policymakers in the present situation, the externalities should also be assessed in fixing the KPIs. The specific value drivers associated with bank valuation are stated below:

Common Value Drivers

Sales, costs, and investments are the three common financial drivers of value creation. In terms of relative measurement, sales growth, growth in earnings, growth in free cash flow, and return on investment are more vital financial drivers (Miller et al., 2004). Empirical studies (Damodaran, 2002; Kazlauskiene & Christauskas, 2008; Jennergren, 2013) find a number of significant value drivers – profit margin, earnings per share (EPS), corporate tax rate, cost of capital, working capital, asset turnover, and return on equity. It is often argued that in value creation EPS plays the most significant role. However, the two widely recognized accounting performance measures – EPS and sales growth are neither persistent nor predictive; and thus have the inadequate scope in forecasting shareholder returns (Mauboussin, 2012). In addition, EPS and earnings or sales growth are not capable to consider the cost of investment. Important to note that, value creation occurs if the management can generate value beyond the resource costs, comprising the cost of capital.

Strategic and Operational Value Drivers

In line with Stephanie (2006) and Kumar (2016), four strategic and operational drivers can be identified and those may influence the major financial indicators related to cost, income, and risk structure of a bank. Firstly, the 'business mix' plays a crucial role behind the value creation, as banks provide diversified services to their customers. As the proxy for business mix, 'income diversification' can be used. Intensive banking products (A higher degree diversification) is associated with the fee-based business model. On the other hand, low diversification denotes the outmoded interest income based (loan focused) model. Secondly, the 'branch structure' and its parameter (customers/branch) would significantly affect the income and cost structure and thus the value of a bank. In a competitive environment, the third driver, 'cost efficiency' plays a vital role. This could be measured by the operational cost per employee. Lastly, greater 'risk-bearing capacity' is considered as a unique feature of the best performing banks. The loan loss provision (LLP) to interest income ratio delivers an essential indication about the risk-bearing capabilities of a bank.

Intangible Value Drivers

The complex interaction of assets mix (tangible and intangible) which is known as the 'economic DNA' may value or devalue a bank. Over time, the importance of intangible assets has been increasing in banks, and gradually these assets have been recognized as the vital drivers of KPIs and in creating value. This matter is much vital for banking institutions as they usually possess and operate various categories of commercial intangible assets which construct the majority part of their asset portfolios.

Major intangible KPIs include product quality, skilled workforce, technology, know-hows, customer satisfaction, customer loyalty, number of new customers, patents, trademarks, copyrights, brand name, reputation, workplace safety, employee satisfaction, and customer's inclination to product promotion (Hall, 1992; Pike et al., 2005; Kumar, 2016). These KPIs ensure competitive advantage and accordingly higher value for modern companies. Among the recognizable intangible KPIs, brand value is the most significant. A strong brand can easily catch the customer confidence about the product and service quality and convey a sense of mission inside the company.

In banking institutions, few unique intangible factors are identifiable, which have a significant impact on valuation. As pointed out by Reilly (2010), these factors include operating systems and procedures; relations with main depositors; relationship with mortgagors, credit card holders, and other borrowers, regulatory approvals, service marks and service names, and trained and assembled workforce.

Loan Growth and Bank Value

Loan growth is expected to have a procyclical nature. Usually, during the economic recovery and expansionary phases, demand for bank loans increases significantly (Keeton, 1999); business growth improves borrowers loan repayment capacity and net worth (Bernanke, Gertler, & Gilchrist, 1996); in effect, enhanced loan performance and profitability of banks boost their value. Thus, loan growth usually has a significant positive impact on bank value.

However, this relationship may vary along with the size and earnings nature of banks. Compared to large banks, at small and medium banks, faster loan growth induces higher valuations (Niu, 2016). Further, large banks usually possess a lower ratio of loans to total earning assets, and also a greater level of nonperforming loans ratio. Zemel (2015) has documented that for high earning banks, loan growth plays a positive role in bank value in terms of stock price while the relationship is proved to be negative for low earning banks.

Geographic Diversification and Bank Value

Geographic diversification can increase the bank value as the greater geographic diversification would improve internal capital markets and diversify funding sourcing (Cetorelli and Goldberg, 2012), lessen the degree to idiosyncratic local shocks (Goetz et al., 2016). Further, greater geographic diversification can bring many variations in value estimation for banks in emerging countries, compared to banks in developed countries. A higher level of inter-regional diversification may affect negatively on the valuation of while a higher level intra-regional diversification can induce to value enhancement of banks in the emerging country (Yildirim and Efthyvoulou, 2018).

REGULATIONS AND RESILIENCE OF THE BANKING SYSTEM

In the process of valuing banks, the scholars and researchers have identified a number of drivers as outlined in Section 2. However, operational complexities, as well as risk dimensions of banks, have been increasing over time. Further, economic imbalances would certainly increase the vulnerabilities of the financial system (Khan and Sadique, 2019). Targeting to enhance the resilience of banks from being protected against those risks, regulators and policymakers have introduced a number of new measures. Although the empirical studies are very limited, it is anticipated that the recent regulatory measures can improve the resilience and thus contribute towards the value creation of banks.

Basel Capital and Liquidity Regulatory Measures

Banking instability induced from financial crises would be extremely costly for bringing severe systematic imbalances (Khan et al. 2019). Targeting to strengthen the international banking system after the global financial crisis in last decade, there is a wide unanimity among the scholars, economists, and regulators on the necessity to take on uniform regulations (Cappiello et al. 2010; Abdel-Baki 2012). It is argued that the strength and resilience of the global financial system are essential to be increased by introducing tighter capital and liquidity requirements to tolerate the major future crises (Basel Committee on Banking Supervision, BCBS, 2016; IIF, 2011). As a consequence, a new regulation (Basel III) has been developed, while Basel IV is at the doorstep. Before,

Basel III, the improved version of Basel II, has emerged in 2010. However, since 2013, the implementation process of the Basel III standards has been initiated by the banks (Gatzert & Wesker, 2011). The inspiration behind the introduction of Basel III was to enhance the stability of the global banking system by increasing the resistance of banks to protect them from future financial and economic crises. The major two features of Basel III related to capital and liquidity requirements are summarized below:

Capital Requirement

Banks require to maintain 'Common Equity Tier 1 (CET 1)' (paid-up capital and retained earnings) 4.5% (raised from 2% as prescribed in Basel II). Further, since 2015, the 'mandatory Tier 1 capital' has to be increased from 4% to 6% (BCBS, 2011).

An additional capital known as 'capital conservation buffer (CCB)' of 2.5% is introduced to strengthen the banking system's resilience to face financial crises in the future. This buffer will raise the CET 1 obligation from 4.5% to 7%. This phase has commenced from the start of 2016.

Leverage Ratio

In off-balance sheet exposures and in securitization transactions, extremely high levels of leverage were piled-up by banks which were a prime root of the last global financial crisis. Thus, to restrict excessive leverage in the banking sector, BCBS has initiated a leverage ratio, which is calculated as:

$$Leverage\ Ratio = \frac{Tier1\ Capital}{Total\ Assets} \geq 3\% \qquad (1)$$

The total assets are required to be calculated by adding 10% of off-balance sheet exposures with the on-balance sheet assets without any adjustment for risk level. In this way, a non-risk-based leverage ratio supplements the capital requirement (Metha, 2012). It is to be believed that this ratio can surely protect banks against the "model risk and measurement error"[1] (BCBS, 2011). The implementation of this ratio is started in 2017.

Liquidity Coverage Ratio (LCR) and Net Stable Funding Ratio (NSFR)

BCBS has also initiated two new liquidity requirements – the liquidity coverage ratio (LCR) and the net stable funding ratio (NSFR) (BCBS, 2013). The LCR obliges banks to maintain adequate liquidity in terms of 'unencumbered high-quality assets' in a one-month horizon to persist against a critical liquidity crisis (BCBS, 2015). Since 2015, the implementation of the LCR has been initiated. The LCR is to be measured by using the following equation:

$$LCR = \frac{Stock\ of\ HQLA}{Total\ net\ cash\ out\ flows\ over\ the\ next\ 30\ calendar\ days} \geq 100\% \tag{2}$$

The stock of high-quality liquid assets (HQLA) includes 'level 1 assets' plus 'level 2 assets' as defined by BCBS (2013). The 'level 1 assets' comprises "cash; central bank reserves; marketable securities representing claims on or guarantees by sovereigns, central banks, IMF, non-central bank public sector entities, etc.; and debt securities issued by sovereigns or central banks. The 'level 2 assets' includes marketable securities subject to 20% risk-weights, and AA- and above rated corporate bonds."

The second liquidity measure, net stable funding ratio (NSFR) requires banks to increase the long-term funding sources and limit the dependence on short-term funding; accordingly, the resilience of banks would be enhanced (BCBS, 2015). The NSFR is measured as per the following equation:

$$NSFR = \frac{Available\ amount\ of\ stable\ funding}{Required\ amount\ of\ Stable\ funding} \geq 100\% \tag{3}$$

The NSFR is calculated over a one-year horizon. As pointed out by King (2013), NSFR is initiated to lessen the funding risk which could be induced from the assets-liabilities mismatches. Thus, banks are expected to have a huge liquidity level to protect them in a severe liquidity crisis situation in the economy.

Impact of Basel III Regulation on the Stability and Resilience of Banks

The Basel III regulation, in terms of added capital and liquidity measures, has been proved to be effective in increasing the resilience of the banks. The new regulations have increased the resilience of the banks by capturing all the related risks including credit, liquidity, operational, market, strategic, residual, concentration, environmental, and securitization risks. The additional capital requirement increases the shock absorption capacity of banks, and the LCR and NSFR would reduce the liquidity crisis during the systematic disasters, and in effect, in the long run, macroeconomic benefits would be carried.

Empirical studies support these claims. Hossain et al. (2018) have documented that higher capital requirements enhance the overall stability in the financial system by limiting banks' intentions to take extreme risks, and at the same time, by enhancing their loss-absorbing capability. Similarly, Laeven & Levine (2009), and Abdel-Baki (2012) have also revealed that higher capital levels ensure the stability and solvency of banks. The resilience of well-capitalized or solvent banks is high enough to handle possible losses in economy-wide crises period (Berger & Bouwman, 2013; Tsai and Chen 2015).

Further, in spite of maintaining the required capital level as per Basel II, a number of banks faced huge troubles in managing liquidity level properly in a crisis period (BCBS, 2014). In a liquidity distress situation, accompanying with economy-wide financial crises, banking panic is a common phenomenon (Ivashina & Scharfstein, 2010), which ultimately affects the resilience of banks severely. In this context, Angora & Roulet (2011) have evidenced that NSFR can significantly improve the resilience of the banking system. Similarly, Chalermchatvichien et al. (2014) reveal higher NSFR significantly reduces the distress of banks thus increase the resilience. Hossain et al. (2018) have also argued that the NSFR and LCR enhance the resilience of banks.

However, the scholars and regulators concern that the regulation would adversely affect the banking system and also macroeconomy as well. The added capital and liquidity measures may uplift the funding cost and thus the lending rate of banks, which might make loans costlier (Aiyar et al. 2014), which would possibly reduce the loan volume and obstruct the economic activity in the short- as well as in the medium-term (Locarno, 2011). In effect, the economic output (GDP) is likely to go down (Noss & Toffano, 2016).

On the contrary, although the added regulatory requirement would increase the funding costs, concurrently the increased stability in the financial system would reduce the possibility of financial and economic crisis. Accordingly, the economy could save output loss by avoiding such crisis. In different studies, Yan et al., (2012), Parcon-Santos & Bernabe (2012), Bernabe & Jaffar (2013) have found Basel III would result added cost and output loss, but the final impact would be a net gain in GDP.

BASEL REGULATIONS AND BANK VALUE

From the previous discussion, it can be argued that added regulations would certainly improve the stability and resilience of individual banks and the whole banking systems. In addition, such regulation can restrain loan growth which would decrease the credit risk in a way of reducing non-performing loans, and accordingly helps to maintain financial system stability (Chavan & Gambacorta, 2018).

The increased stability of banks would rise their assets' performance by reducing non-performing loans. The operational efficiency would also be increased, as the banks are more resilient to shocks induced from all sorts of risks containing credit, liquidity, and market risks. In addition, to meet up the regulatory cost, instead of increasing lending price, banks in competitive markets would definitely try to control the operational and administrative costs, and accordingly, this process would also increase the operational efficiency. This two-way enhancement of operational efficiency would definitely contribute to increase the earnings, reputation, and in effect the value of the banks.

It is also to be noted that the net GDP gain (due to added regulations) would boost economic activities, which subsequently would increase the loan volume and earnings of the banks, and accordingly increase the banks' value.

CONCLUSION

On the basis of the previous discussions, it can be summarized that the new capital and liquidity requirements of Basel III would certainly increase the resilience and stability in the banking, financial, and as a whole in the economic systems. Existing empirical research support this argument. It is also convincible that the added stability and resilience may increase the operational efficiency and performance and as a result, the value of the banks would be increased. However, there is a scope for empirical research in future to support this argument.

REFERENCES

Abdel-Baki, M. A. (2012). The impact of Basel III on emerging economies. *Global Economy Journal*, 12(2).

Aiyar, S., Calomiris, C. W., & Wieladek, T. (2014). Does macro-prudential regulation leak? Evidence from a UK policy experiment. *Journal of Money, Credit and Banking*, *46*(s1), 181–214. doi:10.1111/jmcb.12086

Angora, A. & Roulet, C. (2011). Liquidity assessment and the use of liquidity ratio as defined in the Basel III accords to identify bank distress. Working paper, Université de Limoges, France. Retrieved from http://iriaf.univpoitiers.fr/colloque2011/article/v1s2a2.pdf

Basel Committee on Banking Supervision (BCBS). (2011). Basel III: A global regulatory framework for more resilient banks and banking systems. Revised, June. BIS, Basel. Available at https://www.bis.org/publ/bcbs189.htm

Basel Committee on Banking Supervision (BCBS). (2013). Basel III: The liquidity coverage ratio and liquidity risk monitoring tools. BIS, Basel. Available at https://www.bis. org/publ/bcbs238.htm

Basel Committee on Banking Supervision (BCBS). (2014). Impact and implementation challenges of the Basel framework for emerging market, developing and small economies. BCBS Working Paper No. 27, Bank for International Settlement, Basel. Retrieved from http://www.bis.org/bcbs/publ/wp27.pdf

Basel Committee on Banking Supervision (BCBS). (2015). Net stable funding ratio disclosure standards. BIS, Basel. Available at https://www.bis.org/bcbs/publ /d324.htm

Basel Committee on Banking Supervision (BCBS). (2016). Basel Committee on Banking Supervision Charter. Bank for International Settlement, Basel. Retrieved from http://www.bis.org/bcbs/charter.htm

Berger, A. N., & Bouwman, C. H. (2013). How does capital affect bank performance during financial crises? *Journal of Financial Economics*, *109*(1), 146–176. doi:10.1016/j.jfineco.2013.02.008

Bernabe, E. M., Jr. & Jaffar, J. (2013). Gauging the macroeconomic impact of Basel III on Malaysia. Staff paper no. 87. Research and Training Centre, SEACEN.

Bernanke, B., Gertler, M., & Gilchrist, S. (1996). The financial accelerator and the flight to quality. *The Review of Economics and Statistics*, *78*(1), 1–15. doi:10.2307/2109844

Cappiello, L., Kadareja, A., Kok, C., & Protopapa, M. (2010). *Do bank loans and credit standards have an effect on output? A panel approach for the euro area. ECB Working Paper No. 1150.* Frankfurt, Germany: European Central Bank. Retrieved from https://www.ecb.europa.eu/pub/pdf/scpwps/ecbwp1150.pdf

Cetorelli, N., & Goldberg, L. S. (2012). Liquidity management of U.S. global banks: Internal capital markets in the great recession. *Journal of International Economics*, *88*(2), 299–311. doi:10.1016/j.jinteco.2012.05.001

Chalermchatvichien, P., Jumreornvong, S., & Jiraporn, P. (2014). Basel III, capital stability, risk-taking, ownership: Evidence from Asia. *Journal of Multinational Financial Management*, *28*, 28–46. doi:10.1016/j.mulfin.2014.09.001

Chavan, P., & Gambacorta, L. (2018). Bank lending and loan quality: An emerging economy perspective. *Empirical Economics*, 1–29. doi: 10.100700181-018-1436-5

Damodaran, A. (2002). *Investment valuation: Tools and techniques for determining the value of any asset* (2nd ed.). New York, NY: John Wiley & Sons.

Gatzert, N. & Wesker, H. (2011). A comparative assessment of Basel II/III and solvency II. Friedrich-Alexander-University of Erlangen-Nuremberg, Nuremberg, Germany.

Goetz, M. R., Laeven, L., & Levine, R. (2016). Does the geographic expansion of banks reduce risk? *Journal of Financial Economics*, *120*(2), 346–362. doi:10.1016/j.jfineco.2016.01.020

Hall, R. (1992). The strategic analysis of intangible resources. *Strategic Management Journal*, *13*(2), 135–144. doi:10.1002mj.4250130205

Hossain, M. Z., Khan, M. A. R., & Sadique, M. S. (2018). Basel III and perceived resilience of banks in the BRICS economies. *Applied Economics*, *50*(19), 2133–2146. doi:10.1080/00036846.2017.1391999

Institute of International Finance (IIF). (2011). The cumulative impact on the global economy of proposed changes in the banking regulatory framework. IIF Net Cumulative Impact Study, IIF, Washington, D.C. Retrieved from https://www.iif.com/system/files/nciseptember2011.pdf

Ivashina, V., & Scharfstein, D. (2010). Bank lending during the financial crisis of 2008. *Journal of Financial Economics*, *97*(3), 319–338. doi:10.1016/j.jfineco.2009.12.001

Jennergren, L. P. (2013). Technical note: Value driver formulas for continuing value in firm valuation by discounted cash flow model. *The Engineering Economist*, *58*(1), 59–70. doi:10.1080/0013791X.2012.729876

Kazlauskiene, V., & Christauskas, C. (2008). Business valuation model based on the analysis of business value drivers. *Econ. Eng. Decis.*, *57*(2), 23–31.

Keeton, W.R. (1999). Does faster loan growth lead to higher loan losses? *Federal Reserve Bank of Kansas City Economic Review*, Second Quarter, 57-75.

Khan, M. A. R., & Sadique, M. S. (2019). A forward looking small semi-structural macroeconomic model for Bangladesh. *Journal of Developing Areas*, *53*(2), 43–61. doi:10.1353/jda.2019.0020

Khan, M. A. R., Sadique, M. S., & Wadud, I. K. M. (2019). How vulnerable are commercial banks to macroeconomic shocks? The case of Bangladesh. *Current Analysis on Economics & Finance*, *1*, 2019.

King, M. R. (2013). The Basel III net stable funding ratio and bank net interest margin. *Journal of Banking & Finance*, *37*(11), 4144–4156. doi:10.1016/j.jbankfin.2013.07.017

Kumar, R. (2016). *Valuation -theories and concepts*. Academic Press.

Laeven, L., & Levine, R. (2009). Bank governance, regulation and risk taking. *Journal of Financial Economics*, *93*(2), 259–275. doi:10.1016/j.jfineco.2008.09.003

Locarno, A. (2011). The macroeconomic impact of Basel III on the Italian economy. Questioni di Economia e Finanza, Occasional papers. Retrieved from http://ssrn.com/abstract=1849870

Mauboussin, M. J. (2012). The true measure of success. *Harvard Business Review*, 46–56.

Metha, M. (2012). Demystifying Basel III for Indian banks. International Conference on Technology and Business Management, Delhi University, India.

Miller, T. W., Mathisen, R. E., & McAllister, J. P. (2004). Estimates of the sensitivities of the value of the firm to profitability, growth and capital intensity. *J. Account. Finance Res.*-Winter II. 20-33.

Niu, J. (2016). Loan growth and bank valuations. *The Quarterly Review of Economics and Finance*, *61*, 185–191. doi:10.1016/j.qref.2016.02.001

Noss, J., & Toffano, P. (2016). Estimating the impact of changes in aggregate bank capital requirements on lending and growth during an upswing. *Journal of Banking & Finance*, *62*, 15–27. doi:10.1016/j.jbankfin.2015.09.020

Parcon-Santos, H. C. & Bernabe, E. M., Jr. (2012). The macrocosmic effects of Basel III implementation in the Philippines: A preliminary assessment. BSP Working Paper, the Philippines.

Pike, S., Roos, G., & Marr, B. (2005). Strategic management of intangible assets and value drivers in R&D organizations. *R & D Management*, *35*(2), 111–124. doi:10.1111/j.1467-9310.2005.00377.x

Reilly, R. F. (2010). Intangible asset identification and valuation in the bank and thrift industries. *Intangible Asset Valuation Insights*. Winter.

Stephanie, G. (2006). *Bank and shareholder value - an overview of bank valuation and empirical evidence on shareholder value for banks*. Wiesbaden, Germany: Deutscher Universitats-Verlag.

Tsai, J.-Y., & Chen, S. (2015). How does equity capital cost affect bank performance during a financial crisis? *Applied Economics*, *47*(42), 4459–4474. doi:10.1080/00036846.2015.1030569

Yan, M., Hall, M. J. B., & Turner, P. (2012). *A cost and benefit analysis of Basel III: Some evidence from the UK*. Leicestershire, UK: School of Business and Economics, Loughborough University.

Yildirim, C., & Efthyvoulou, G. (2018). Bank value and geographic diversification: Regional vs global. *Journal of Financial Stability*, *36*, 225–245. doi:10.1016/j.jfs.2018.04.003

Zemel, M. (2015). The information content of loan growth in banks. Working Paper. Available at http://ssrn.com/abstract=255711

ENDNOTE

1 Model risk and measurement error arises when a financial model is used to measure a bank's risks but the model fails to capture the risks involved or may have errors in measuring it. The stability or resilience of banks would be reduced due to severe model risks associated with low-risk loans Kiema and Jokivuolle (2014).

Chapter 12
"Designing Optimal Valuation Model of Bank Stocks": Empirical Evidence for Iran Banking Systems

Saeed Soltani
University of Bordeaux, France

ABSTRACT

The growth and diversification of investment and management property have development requirements, so achieving first place economically requires transfer of share of ownership from government to private sector. One of the major requirements of these operations is pricing of shares through stock exchange. The accurate and transparent assessment in assignment of stock value has great importance. So, it has been tried to design optimal model and then determine the bank stock value in public offerings. In this regard, the review of conventional models of stock valuation has been analyzed and the effect of functional variables and balance sheet on the value of bank stocks is investigated. In the statistical stage, the relevant tests have been accepted for 16 banks in Tehran Stock Exchange and Iranian OTC market on a three-year timeframe. The results of research lead to design and specify the optimal model for evaluating of Bank stock.

INTRODUCTION

The ownership structure of banks and their fundamental role in the national economy is a key factor in economic and financial development process. In Iran, some of the institutions as well as public organizations governmental and nongovernmental have a considerable stock of these banks and institutions, non-bank credit that may be based on Article 105 and 106 of Article 44 of the constitution are compelled to transfer the bulk of these stocks. Studies of Pricing Initial Public Offerings are reported the existence of two features: First of all stocks in initial public offering are usually under intrinsic value of pricing: Second, mentioned stock has poor performance of the stock in the long term than other companies .One of the most common methods of privatization agencies is their ceding of shares through the provision of the Stock Exchange.

DOI: 10.4018/978-1-7998-1086-5.ch012

Intrinsic value analysis and comparison with the market price of the share is very important for analysts. The main purpose of this comparison is to recognize whether now the target stock is cheap (below the real price) or expensive (over the real price), if a share is cheap, the market has not been found the impact of fundamental factors that is determined a higher price than the market price for shares.

Analysis of intrinsic value is accompanied with limits ranging from a variety of risks in the pricing of stock. The intrinsic value of the companies' shares depends on how the continued growth, but the future is always faced with uncertainty and cannot be predicted desirable. Due to the ambiguity of the question arises: Is it possible to determine the optimal model for the valuation of bank stocks?

In this article two topics are examined: 1. Determine effective variables and their relation to the valuation of bank stocks 2: optimization model valuation of bank stocks in initial public offering by relying variables inherent values are calculated using different valuation models and accounting variables. There are currently 20 private banks and non-bank credit institution in exchange and OTC listed and some are awaiting the arrival mentioned markets. Assignment of this category shares only in 2013 has been allocated more than 300 trillion riyals and more than %20 of the market value of the Iranian capital. The results help to investors to know affecting factors the determination of prices of bank shares in the initial public offering.

Figure 1. Segmentation of a variety of valuation methods

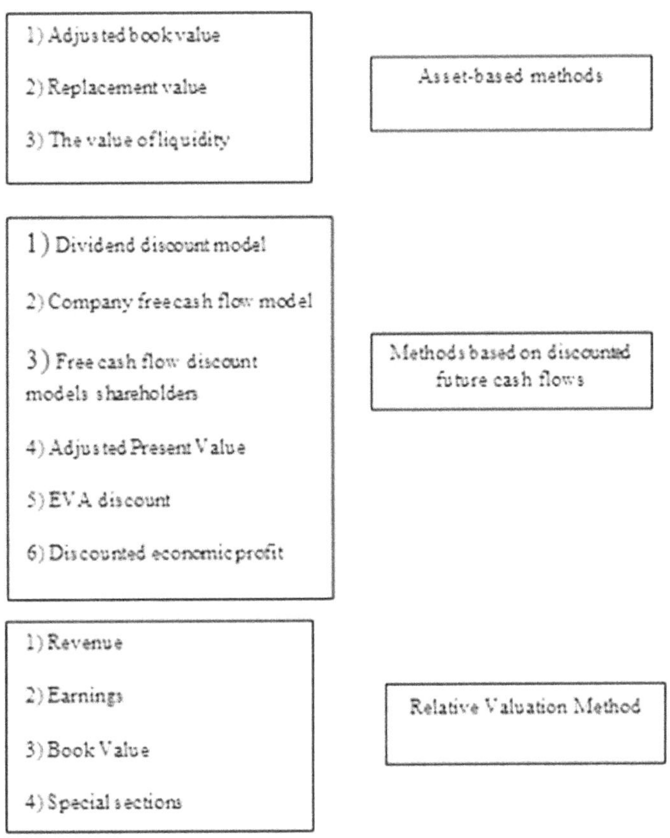

Generally, the company's value is being used in a simple and basic relationship resulting from the balance sheet.

Corporate Value = the value of equity + value of corporate debt

Some alternative valuation methods, their focus is on the left side of this equality, while others consider the company as a whole, it means they have considering the right side of equation. Sometimes they are used in combination. Generally, Company valuation different models can be divided into several following general topics:

1. Asset Based Valuation Model
2. Discounted Cash flow Valuation Model
3. Dividend discount Models(DDM)
4. Discounted Free Cash flow Valuation Model
5. Relative Valuation Model

In case Capital Market has the necessary efficiency, basically, there is no need to analyze the securities; because their prices reflect the intrinsic value of them, and investors can easily take their investment decisions, but In case it is questioned, securities analysis and portfolio selection should be through proper investment, the expected returns achieved (Fama,1998).

In the dividend discount model is the value of a stock is the present value of dividends expected to contribute. Assuming that the share transaction has an unlimited life, the value of the contribution will be as follows.

$$V=\sum_{t=1}^{t=\infty}\frac{\mathbf{DPS}_t}{(1+\mathbf{K}_e)} \tag{1}$$

DPS = Expected dividend per share in the time t
Ke =the expected rate of Shareholders

In the case of the privatization is expected to have stable dividend growth, in this case, we will use the Gordon growth formula.

$$V=\frac{\mathbf{DPS1}}{(\mathbf{Ke}-\mathbf{g})}. \tag{2}$$

G = the expected constant growth rate

In general, for the valuation of a stock dividend discount model is required to expense stock rate, the expected dividend payments and expected rate of growth is estimated profit per share over the coming years.

The cost of stock for a monetary or financial institution is covered that risk which also cannot be removed by diversification. The risk is estimated of using beta (In the capital asset pricing model) or buildings (multi-factor models or APM). Expected dividends for each share in a future period could be considered through multiplication of expected earnings per share in that period and the period of expected benefit payments. Rate of dividend to a bank is dividends from profits, as is true for any other institutions. Traditionally, dividend rate of monetary and Financial Intermediation is more than other business units operating in the market. Monetary and financial intermediation will be a much higher interest rate than any other institutions that there are two main reasons: 1. Banks and insurance companies according to the accounting definition require much less capital expenditure than any other institution, 2. Banks and insurance companies has been known as safe payers of high dividends, and over time, have attracted investors who are friendly dividend policy appropriate, and the reason for the change in the dividend policies is difficult.

If dividends are exclusively based on the profitability, the expected growth rate that will determine the company's value, the expected growth rate is in profitability.

Return on Equity × undivided interest rate = the expected growth rate in earnings per share (3)

If we expect that the rate of return on equity is changed over time, the expected growth rate of earnings per share can be calculated as follows.

$(ROE_t) / ROE_t + (\text{Payment benefit ratio -1}) = -ROE_{t+1} + (ROE_{t+1})$ (4)

The Expected Growth Rate in Earnings Per Share

In both formulas, the expected growth rate is a function of undivided interest rate, which indicates the amount of reinvestment and return on equity, return on such investments shows that quality.

The second method of valuation of monetary and financial intermediation is using the excess return model. In such a model, the value of a firm can be calculated as total investment in the company and the present value of excess returns that the company is expected to achieve in the future. The value of equity in an institution can be taken into account as the sum of equity invested in the company and the expected excess return on equity of these investments and future investments.

The present value of the expected excess return on equity of investments + invested equity = equity value (5)

To measure the equity that is recently in invested company, it is usually used book value of equity at the Institute. Book value of equity shares can be affected by share repurchases or atypically (Superior) and random (one time).

In relative valuation model, factors such as the ratio of the value of enterprise value ratios EBITDA and EBIT value cannot simply be accepted as the value of the monetary and financial intermediation. Three ratios of equity that have been used extensively in this area include: ratios of price to earnings, price-to-book and price to sales.

Earnings per share ÷ Market price per share = Ratio Price to the profitability (P / E) (6)

(Book value per share) ÷ (Price per share) = the ratio of price to book value (P / BV) (7)

Growth rate expected variables of the profitability per share are Dividend ratio, determines the relative cost of equity and Return on Equity. Of these fourth variables, Return on Equity has the greatest impact on the ratio of price to book value of equity for monetary and financial intermediation should be stronger than other institutions because equity book value closer to the market value of equity investment in existing assets.

LITERATURE REVIEWS

Asadi and et al (2016) studied the relationship between accounting information, financial condition and stock price in the range of 2005 to 2014. The study population was companies listed on the Tehran Stock Exchange. They found that earnings per share and book value of equity per share are significant correlation with stock prices. In addition, economic conditions with the impact on earnings persistence are changed coefficient of its effect on the stock price.

Damodaran (2002) considers the valuation of financial service firms with the special role of debt in their functioning (similar to opinions of Copeland; Adams, Rudolf). What is special about Damodoran's opinion is that he sees debt for financial service companies as a raw material and not as a source of capital. "Debt is something to be molded into other financial products that can be sold at a higher price and yield a profit. Consequently, capital at financial service firms is more narrowly defined as including only equity capital. This definition is reinforced by the regulatory authorities."

Damodaran also stated two practical problems in valuating banks. The first is that the estimation of cash flows could not be performed without estimating reinvestments; the second is that estimating expected future growth becomes more difficult if the reinvestment rate cannot be measured. Hence, it makes more sense to value equity directly at banks, rather than the entire firm.

Some authors delegated (2014) which have performed to comparative review of supply below the share price in initial public offering of state-owned companies and non-vested stock through the Tehran Stock Exchange as well as identify the affecting factors in a study titled "A comparative analysis of the factors influencing in initial public offering priced below the intrinsic value of state-owned companies and non-governmental". Research findings show that all supply companies in Tehran Stock Exchange, governmental and non-governmental presented below intrinsic value; however no significant difference between the pricing under the government and there is no intrinsic value stocks. As well as only factor in pricing below the intrinsic value of non-public companies is number of employees, and the only factor in pricing below the intrinsic value of state-owned companies is Percent of shares in the initial public offering.

Adams and Rudolf (2010) distinguish the characteristics of banking business into four categories, motivating a distinct valuation approach. First, banking is a heavily regulated industry. Second, banks operate on both sides of their balance sheets, actively seeking profits not only in lending but also in raising capital. Third, banks are exposed to credit default risk, but they also actively seek risk as a part of their business model. Last but not least, the profit and the value of a bank are much more dependent on interest rate risk than other industries.

Some authors (2014) studied affecting factors capital adequacy ratio as the most important driver of the profitability. The time period of the study is 2007 to 2011 years and the research community and private banks. Results showed that these variables liquidity, return on assets, a positive and significant relationship between the size of banks, the share of total assets, facilities, storage facilities and losses on financial leverage have significant and negative correlation With the capital adequacy ratio.

Copeland et al (2000) also paid attention to the fact that bank liabilities consist of customer deposits and borrowings on funds market, which apparently perform the same function, but with a different margin. As a result, the spread between the interest received on loans and the cost of capital is so low that small errors in estimating the cost of capital can result in huge swings in the value of the banks.

Some authors studied the impact of credit risk on banks' the profitability in the range of 2004 to 2010. Non-Current loans to total loans ratio of bad loans to total loan reserves and profitability of the two ratios Return on assets and return on equity were used to measure credit risk. The research sample was consisted of fifteen banks and credit institutions under the supervision of the Central Bank of the Islamic Republic of Iran during the period 2004 to 2010. The results showed that there is significant negative relationship between credit risk and profitability of banks. In other words, with the increase in credit risk, banks have increased the cost, thus reducing their profitability.

Other authors studied affecting factors of the profitability of banks in the period 2002 to 2010 in public and private banks, results of their study show costs play an important role in the profitability of banks, and there is significant negative relationship between the cost and profitability. In addition, important factor in profitability are efficiency ratio variables (earnings per share), the ratio of deposits to assets, the ratio of loans to deposits ratio of profitable assets, the ratio of liquid assets to deposits and bank capital.

Chang et al (2010) have examined pricing of IPOs in Korea during the years 2000 to 2002. The results of their study showed pricing less than 19.7 percent event rate in the securities market of Korea.

Some reports (2010) have compared the low level of pricing in the stock market compared with other Bangladesh countries. Based on their study, the low level of pricing in the stock market Bangladesh 71/480 percent with a standard deviation 24/1217 that this figure compared to studies in other countries was a significant figure. Based on the regression analysis, age and size of the company are positive and negative types of transaction volume with pricing levels were less than the relationship. They did not achieve in connection with the initial public offering and priced less significance than real time.

In general terms, there are four approaches to valuation with numerous sub-approaches within each. The first, asset-based valuation is built around valuing the existing assets of a firm, with accounting estimates of value or book value often used as a starting point. The second, market valuation, estimates the value of an asset by looking at the pricing of 'comparable' assets relative to a common variable like earnings, cash flows, book value or sales. The third, income approach, relates the value of an asset to the present value of expected future cash flows on that asset. The fourth approach, contingent claim valuation, uses option pricing models to measure the value of assets that share option characteristics. Each approach is applicable for bank valuation with several conditions.

Asset-Based Approach

The asset-based valuation of a bank requires valuing the loan portfolio of the bank and subtracting the outstanding debt to estimate the value of equity. It is frequently used to establish the liquidation value of a bank for possible legal proceedings. However, the value-based approach is difficult to apply when the bank enters multiple businesses or regions.

Figure 2. Conceptual Model of Research

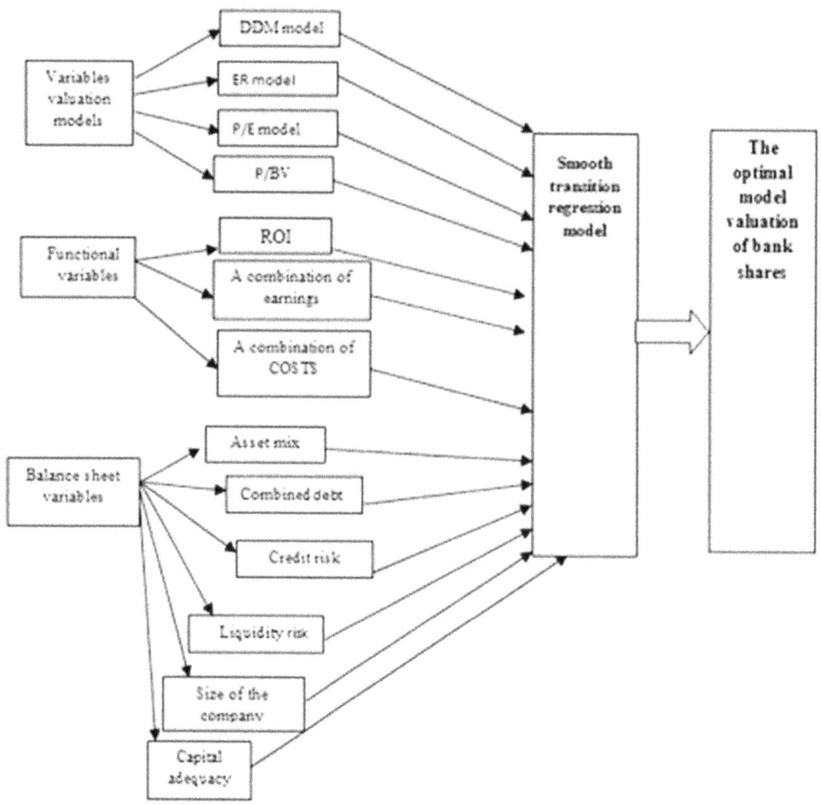

The necessity of the asset-based approach in bank valuation also lies in the testing of the bank's actual book value until the valuation moment, and, consequently, it is a meaningful instrument at the negotiation.

Market Approach

The market approach is probably the simplest way to value a bank. Analysts' conclusions based on this approach could be easily found in business reports on a regular basis, where reasonably comparable guideline companies are defined primarily by expert opinions and multiples' comparisons. The most sufficient multiples for bank valuation are the price-earnings ratio (P/E) and the price-to-book value ratio (P/BV). P/E ratio, as a function of three variables – the expected growth rates in earnings, the payout ratio, and the cost of equity, depicts some specific characteristics for bank valuation revealed previously.

The choice of comparable banks will include banks with similar historical growth rates and risk profiles. The differences between the subject of valuation and the comparable banks should be thoughtfully incorporated into the valuation analysis by several adjustments.

Damodaran (2002) calls attention to the choice of a relevant comparable. Modern banking is a business mix of retail banking, private banking, corporate and investment Banking and trading activities. Also, to find a comparable bank with the same proportions in the banking business model from the outside is relatively hard. As for the P/E ratio specifically, it is liable to a high volatility due to the bank policy to report a profit while creating provisions for credit losses.

Income Approach

The income approach focuses on the conversion of expected future economic benefits into their present value. The discounted cash flow valuation gets the most play in academic research and comes with the best theoretical credentials. It is relevant to concentrate on cash flow and dividends as cash flow proxies for bank valuation.

The common free cash flow on equity method is highly valid for bank valuation, also because it reflects the fact that banks can create value from the liability side of the balance sheet. Figure 1 reveals the logic of the FCFE calculation.

The alternative representation of FCFE is the summation of dividends paid, potential dividends, and equity repurchases and issues.

The dividend discount model (DDM) is another theoretical extension of the neo- classical discounted cash flow models, which applies to banks since they are publicly traded companies. The general form of the model is presented by the formula:

T Value per share of equity = ∑ DPSt tt 1 (1ki)

where

DPSt – expected dividend per share in period t;
ki – cost of equity.

The discussion on inputs and special cases (such as stable growth) could be found in Damodaran (2002). To value a stock, using the dividend discount model, the estimates of the cost of equity, the expected payouts ratios, and the expected growth rate in earnings per share over times are needed. The expected dividend per share in a future period can be written as a product of the expected earnings per share in that period and the expected payout ratio. It allows us to focus on the expected growth in earn-

Table. 1 Free cash flow to equity (bank shareholders)

Balance sheet		**Income statement**
Liabilities	**Assets**	
Growth of shareholders' funds (equity)	New loans	+ Net interest income
- Provisions and unearned income	+/- Securities held (increase/decrease)	+ Net fees and commissions
+/- Deposits (increase/decrease)	+/- Accounts receivable	+/- Securities trading (gains/loses)
+/- Liabilities from dealing activities	+/- Fixed assets (increase/decrease)	+/- Loan loss provision
+/- External debt (increase/decrease)	+/- Net intangible assets	+ Net non-interest income
+/- Accounts payable (increase/decrease)	+/- Cash reserve (increase/decrease)	- Taxes
= Changes in liabilities	= Changes in assets	= Net income
Change in Assets – Change in Liabilities = Growth (change) of capital + Net income = FCFE		

Source: Adapted from Copeland et al. (2000), Antill, Lee & Beninga (2008)

ings (more accessible and reasonable data) and change the payout ratio over time (to reflect changes in growth and investment opportunities). However, the calculation of the discount factor for the model leads to some complications and shortcomings.

The major discussion on the income approach concerns the possibilities of estimating the cost of equity. The cost of equity for a bank has to reflect the portion of the risk in the equity that cannot be diversified away by marginal investment in the stock. Several methods are available to calculate the expected return on equity or discount rate for banks:

- Gordon Growth Model
- An average profitability
- The cost of foreign funds
- Capital Asset Pricing Model (and its extensions)

The influence of risk on the cost of capital is the main concern for researchers. Traditionally, risk is estimated by beta (in CAPM) or betas (in a multifactor or arbitrage pricing model). The estimation of beta-coefficient is usually conducted by regressing the securities' excess return on the market excess return. Some researchers, such as Fama and French (1996), argued against the ability of CAPM to predict returns; nevertheless, the beta-coefficient is widely used to estimate the excess return and the cost of equity.

Damodaran (2002) usually argues the use of regression betas because of the noise in the estimates (standard errors) and the possibility that the firm has changed over the period of the regression. As for usage of regression betas for the valuation of banks, his empirical research suggests that such beta estimates are valid for large and stable financial institutions and if regulatory restrictions have remained unchanged over the period and are not expected to change in the future. He also suggests using the average levered beta for comparable firms as the bottom-up beta for the firm being analyzed.

The income-based approach is a well-recognized and frequently used valuation methodology, which has received wide application in practice, mostly because the bank's value is determined by its future performance, which is of significant concern for shareholders and other suppliers of capital. However, studying the literature and analyzing the empirical findings leads to the conclusion that the value obtained by this approach may be rather subjective, since it is based to a great extent on the appraiser's consideration about the bank's future return and the associated risks. Small modifications of the input variables affect the final value significantly. Moreover, the income approach does not entirely consider the specific characteristics of banking mentioned previously.

Contingent Claim Valuation

Up to this point we have discussed the classical approaches to valuation. In recent years, option pricing models (binominal, Black-Scholes-Merton, etc.), based on more advanced mathematical appliance, have been introduced. We suppose that they might be used for bank valuation as well. The Black-Scholes-Merton model is a function of six input factors: the current price of the underlying stock (S), the dividend yield of the underlying stock (R), the option RtStrike price (X), the risk-free rate over the life of the option contract (e f), the timeRemaining until option expiration (t), and the price volatility of the underlying stock (σ). In terms of the six inputs, the formula for the pricing of a call option on a single share of common stock is

P S * N (d1)Xe f* N (d 2),

where N (d1) and N (d2) – the conditional density functions of the normal distribution $_{\text{with}}$ sigma representing stock price volatility, this is calculated

f 2d1, 2ln(S / X) (R / 2)t .t

The Black-Scholes model is appropriate for valuation of companies, which assets and liabilities measures are comparable by significance. Undoubtedly, the model is feasible for usage in bank valuation, since operations on both assets and liabilities are significant for the banking business structure. The model might be adopted for bank valuation by the following procedures:

1. The risk-free rate is accepted at the same level as in the income approach.
2. The price volatility is calculated from the annual bank statistics. The usage of relatively stable market indexes is also appropriate.
3. Instead of Macalay duration, we suggest to use the weighted average debt turnover s debt duration.
4. S and X variables are determined by the asset-based approach. [7, p.6-7]

Results of empirical studies on the option pricing model applied to bank valuation (such as Giammarino, Schwartz, Zeichner, 1989) imply that the valuation technique should not replace conventional methods of monitoring financial institutions (as a regulation procedure), and do not depict the regulation impact on the performance of banks.

Nevertheless, the special characteristics of banking might be adequately considered in the valuation of banks. Absent attributes should be respected in valuation by the inclusion of additional variables in the model. Adams and Rudolf (2010) proposed a valuation model for banks derived from Merton's (1973) structural model of a firm, Black-Scholes pricing model and concept of matched maturity marginal value of funds (MMMVF). Applying the MMMVF transfer pricing framework and dividend discount model, the proposed model divides the bank's economic value into three separate values: the value of deposit business, the value of loan business and the value of asset- liability management.

To acquire each value the special valuation procedures are performed separately. However, the model has a few shortcomings: (1) it is abstracted from taxes, reserve requirements, minimum capital requirements and other regulatory factors, and (2) it does not include non-cash items in valuation (depreciation, amortization, etc.).

The revealed advantages and disadvantages of each valuation approach with regard to banks are summarized in Figure 2. It is worth mentioning, that each approach is suitable in a specific range of situations. For example, an application of income and contingent claim approaches is limited for banks functioning in emerging markets, due to the lack of information for calculations of the discount factor and the market return.

Table .2 Advantages and disadvantages of the valuation approaches

Valuation Approach	Advantages	Disadvantages
Asset-based approach	- Simple for understanding and practical usage - Does not require guesswork and assumptions	- The most simplified valuation model - Requires access to all of the bank's internal data - Does not consider the long-term development perspectives
Market approach	- Uses actual data - Simple application (derives estimates of value from relatively simple financial ratios) - Does not rely on explicit forecasts - Considers market reaction on bank performance - Reflects the M&A practice	- Most of the important assumptions are hidden (bank's expected growth in earnings, risk and margins) - No good guideline companies exist (therefore, expertise and additional adjustments are required) - Laborious and time-consuming (an immense amount of data has to be processed) - Based on the present situation, resulting in losing long-term trends
Income approach	- Flexible for changes - Considers future expectations - Considers market performance (through excess return on market)	Controversial results (requires projections of future economic benefits) - Requires estimates of appropriate discount rates (also subject to controversy) - Partially based on probabilities and expertise - Problems with application in the emerging markets (due to the lack of market information) - The valuation results can be easily manipulated
Contingent claim valuation	- Captures the specific characteristics of banking better than any other approach	- Regulatory factors are not included - Possible problems with application (requires the building of a mathematical model)

Source: Author's table

METHOD

This article is based on the assessment a review of previous studies, the variables affecting the pricing of bank stocks in initial public offering of common valuation models to identify and be used to calculate the intrinsic value of stock, and then is designed that prices of bank shares are specified in the initial public offering on the stock exchange and Iranian OTC Tehran. This article is an applied target. In terms of implementation process is quantitative, in terms of logic implementation is posteriori, in terms of performance time is Length – retrospective, and the method of data collection is analytical laboratory solidarity. Variable share price in the initial public offering is the dependent variable, and variables inherent value calculated using valuation models are dividend discount model. Model excess return, relative valuation model - price to earnings ratio, relative valuation model - the ratio of price to book value and accounting variables (performance and balance sheet) are independent variables.

To calculate the intrinsic value, the following equation is used:

$$P_0 = \frac{DPS_1}{\left(1+K_e\right)^1} + \frac{DPS_2}{\left(1+K_e\right)^2} + \frac{\left({}^{P1}\!/_{E1} * EPS_2\right)}{\left(1+K_e\right)^2} \quad (8)$$

The variables used in this equation are as follows:

DPS_1: Dividend per share in the year
DPS_2: Dividend per share, in the year after the release
EPS_2: Earnings per share in the year after the release
K_e: Expected rate of return of equity that the rate of return on government bonds plus 5% risk premium in the year can be achieved.
P1/ E1= the division of the final price per share (P1) has been achieved on the earnings per share (E1) at the end of the year.

To calculate the intrinsic value of the excess return model is calculated as follows:

$$P_0 = \frac{ER_1}{(1+K_e)^t} + \frac{ER_2}{(1+K_e)^{t+1}} + BV_{-1} \tag{9}$$

The intrinsic value is calculated using the relative valuation model - the ratio of price to earnings (PE) is as follows:

$P = \text{Mean } (P/E)^{*}E_1$

$\text{Mean } (P/E) = \text{mean } (P_0/E_{-1};\ P0/E_1;\ P1/E_1;\ P2/E_2)$

$E_{1=}$ Earnings per share in the year
$E_{-1\,=}$ Earnings per share in the year prior to release
$E_{2\,=}$ Earnings per share in the next year
$P_{0\,=}$ Share price in the initial public offering
$P_{1=}$ the final price per share at the end of the year
$P_{2=}$ The final price per share at the end of the year after the release of intrinsic value is calculated using relative valuation model - the ratio of price to book value (PBV) is as follows:

$P = \text{Mean } (P/BV)^{*}BV_1$

$\text{Mean } (P/BV) = \text{mean } (P_0/BV_{-1};\ P0/BV_1;\ P1/BV_1;\ P2/BV_2)$

$BV_{1\,=}$ the book value in the year
$BV_{-1=}$ Book value per share in the year prior to release
$_{=}$ Book value per share after the release $_2$BV

The study population is all banks listed on the Tehran Stock Exchange and Iranian OTC. The research sample is selected, both the following criteria:

1. In the period 2002 to 2013 are listed in the Tehran Stock Exchange or Iranian OTC.
2. one year before and one year after its release financial statements have been audited.
3. The period of one year after the release date is not a trading halt, and its shares are traded on the exchange or OTC.

Accordingly, 16 banks were selected as statistical sample. Theoretical Foundations of the study are collected Persian and English books and professional journals and data needed to test the hypothesis with respect to the financial statements, explanatory notes, acceptance and inclusion prospectus, the Securities and Exchange databases and enterprise Stock Exchange (www.codal.Ir, www.rdis.ir and www.tsetmc.com) and new financial software brings.

In this paper to analyze the data, is used paired test and regression model to design model Ghyrkhty-Smooth Transition Regression (STR) which is a kind of nonlinear models. These models are quite flexible, and are able to show different forms of non-linear behavior. Smooth transition regression models are divided in terms of its transition two Logistic Smooth Transition Regression (LSTR) and Exponential Smooth Transition Regression (ESTR). More details on these methods are provided. The collected data is prepared through Excel data file format, and is performed statistical analysis by using software Excel 2010, version 8 E views.

RESEARCH FINDINGS AND RESULTS

Inferential statistical analysis of the research for the intrinsic value is calculated by using of dividend discount valuation model (DDM) and is compared it with the price of shares in the initial public offering for banks as Tables 3 is a sample:

The company has not had dividend profit. :*

Table 3. intrinsic value per share is calculated based on DDM (sums in Rials)

No.	Bank	Release date	P0	The intrinsic value of according to the DDM model
1	Eghtesad Novin	February 4, 2004	3,752	1,034
2	Parsian	December 1, 2003	6,600	934
3	Sarmayeh	June 1, 2011	2,240	-*
4	Tejarat	May 18, 2009	1,201	269
5	Mellat	February 18, 2009	1,050	378
6	Saderat	June 9, 2009	1,001	155
7	Pasargad	August 16, 2011	2,190	498
8	Ansar	August 28, 2011	2,752	259
9	Gardeshgari	July 27, 2011	1,262	160
10	Dey	July 12, 2011	1,499	342
11	Iran ZAMIN	September 27, 2011	1,294	-*
12	Kar Afarin	February 28, 2004	6,938	1,427
13	Hekmat Iranian	January 30, 2012	1,340	39
14	Post Bank	November 2, 2010	2,301	9
15	Middle- East	December 27, 2010	1,239	239
16	Sina	September 25, 2007	1213	392

Inferential statistical related to intrinsic values calculated for sample banks by using the discounted dividend valuation model is as Table 4. The average value calculated for each share of banks in the sample, 383 riyals, the highest calculated value of £ 1,427 belonging to the Bank and the lowest value in numerical terms, the banks have been Iranian capital. Skewness of the normal values calculated density is on average somewhat more than usual.

The intrinsic value is calculated by using valuation model excess return (ER) and is compared it with the price of shares in the initial public offering for stock banks as Table 5 is a sample:

Analytical statistics intrinsic values calculated is based on excess returns for banks in the sample as Table 6. The average value calculated for each share of banks in the sample, £ 1,658, the highest calculated value of £ 3,519 belonging to Ansar Bank and the lowest value in numerical terms, the equivalent of £ 914 has been owned by the Bank Hekmat Iranian. Skewness of the normal values calculated density is on average somewhat more than usual.

The intrinsic value is calculated using relative valuation model - the ratio of price to earnings (PE) and comparison with the share price at the initial public offering sample banks is as Table 7.

Statistics analytical values per share are calculated using the P / E is shown in Table 8.

Table 4. Inferential statistical were calculated intrinsic values based on DDM

Average	383	Median	**264**
Standard deviation	411	Variance	168;898
Skewness	105	Elongation	107
Maximum	1,427	Minimum	0

Table 5. Calculated value based on the excess return (IRR figures)

No.	Bank	Release date	P0	The intrinsic value of according to the ER model
1	Eghtesad Novin	February 4, 2004	3,752	1,919
2	Parsian	December 1, 2003	6,600	2,803
3	Sarmayeh	June 1, 2011	2,240	1,205
4	Tejarat	May 18, 2009	1,201	1,854
5	Mellat	February 18, 2009	1,050	1,371
6	Saderat	June 9, 2009	1,001	1,734
7	Pasargad	August 16, 2011	2,190	1,666
8	Ansar	August 28, 2011	2,752	3,519
9	Gardeshgari	July 27, 2011	1,262	1,294
10	Dey	July 12, 2011	1,499	1,209
11	Iran ZAMIN	September 27, 2011	1,294	1,116
12	Kar Afarin	February 28, 2004	6,938	2,388
13	Hekmat Iranian	January 30, 2012	1,340	914
14	Post Bank	November 2, 2010	2,301	1,173
15	Middle East	December 27, 2010	1,239	951
16	Sina	September 25, 2007	1,213	1,421

Table 6. Statistics calculated intrinsic value analysis based on ER

Average	1,659	Median	**1,396**
Standard deviation	715	Variance	511,923
Skewness	105	Elongation	109
Maximum	3;519	Minimum	914

Table 7. intrinsic value is calculated by using of the PE (sums in Rials)

No.	Bank	Release date	P0	The intrinsic value of according to the P/E model
1	Eghtesad Novin	February 4, 2004	3,752	4,820
2	Parsian	December 1, 2003	6,600	5,377
3	Sarmayeh	June 1, 2011	2,240	1,218
4	Tejarat	May 18, 2009	1,201	1,488
5	Mellat	February 18, 2009	1,050	1,160
6	Saderat	June 9, 2009	1,001	940
7	Pasargad	August 16, 2011	2,190	2,025
8	Ansar	August 28, 2011	2,752	2,468
9	Gardeshgari	July 27, 2011	1,262	1,452
10	Dey	July 12, 2011	1,499	1,640
11	Iran land	September 27, 2011	1,294	1,960
12	Kar Afarin	February 28, 2004	6,938	10,823
13	Hekmat Iranian	January 30, 2012	1,340	1,508
14	Post Bank	November 2, 2010	2,301	5,915
15	Middle East	December 27, 2010	1,239	1,199
16	Sina	September 25, 2007	1,213	1,022

Table 8. Analytical statistics intrinsic values calculated based on P / E

Average	2,487	Median	**1,498**
Standard deviation	723	Variance	7,311;246
Skewness	207	Elongation	706
Maximum	10,822	Minimum	940

Average value per share calculated for the sample banks, 2.487 Rails, the highest calculated value of R10. 822 Rials belonging to the Bank and the lowest value in numerical terms, the equivalent of £ 940 is belonged Iranian Bank Saderat. Skewness of the normal density calculated values around the mean is too conventional.

The intrinsic value is calculated by using relative valuation model - the ratio of price to book value (PBV) and is compared it with the initial public offering for shares in the bank share price sample is based on the table 9.

Statistics analysis of the intrinsic value per share is calculated by using model PBV is shown in Table 10.

Table 9. calculated intrinsic value by using P / BV (Figures in Rials)

No.	Bank	Release date	P0	The intrinsic value of according to the P/BV model
1	Eghtesad Novin	February 4, 2004	3,752	5,310
2	Parsian	December 1, 2003	6,600	11,910
3	Sarmayeh	June 1, 2011	2,240	1,940
4	Tejarat	May 18, 2009	1,201	1,418
5	Mellat	February 18, 2009	1,050	1,145
6	Saderat	June 9, 2009	1,001	1,256
7	Pasargad	August 16, 2011	2,190	2,047
8	Ansar	August 28, 2011	2,752	3,613
9	Gardeshgari	July 27, 2011	1,262	1,309
10	Di	July 12, 2011	1,499	1,834
11	Iran land	September 27, 2011	1,294	1,905
12	Kar Afarin	February 28, 2004	6,938	8,538
13	Iranian Hekmat	January 30, 2012	1,340	1,223
14	Post Bank	November 2, 2010	2,301	3,342
15	Middle East	December 27, 2010	1,239	1,458
16	Sina	September 25, 2007	1,213	1,079

Table 10. Descriptive statistics of calculated intrinsic values based on the model

Average	3,083	Median	1,870
Standard deviation	768	Variance	9,428, 877
Skewness	201	Elongation	402
Maximum	11,910	Minimum	1,079

DISCUSSION

Average of calculated value per share for the sample banks is 3 R 082 Rials, the calculated highest value equivalent 11 R 910 rials is belonged to Parsian Bank, and the lowest value in numerical terms, the equivalent of 1 R 079 Rials is belonged to Sina Bank. Sample skewness somewhat normal and density values are calculated on the average somewhat too conventional.

The results of the solidarity analysis show that PE and PBV variables with a Pearson correlation coefficient of 0.86 and 0.96 respectively, significance at the one percent level and Spearman correlation coefficient of 0.88 and 0.9, statistical significant at one percent, compared to other variables have more correlation with variable-price initial public offering. In addition, calculated intrinsic values based on the excess return and relative value - the ratio of price to earnings and price to book value of more solidarity with each other and can be placed in a category. However intrinsic values of the discounted dividend valuation model show low correlation with other variables. However correlation of this variable is more varied with the results of the excess return compared to the other two models (relative value - the ratio of price to earnings and price to book value).

According to Pearson and Spearman correlation coefficient between functional variables (earnings per share (EPS), Dividends per share (DPS), Price to earnings ratio (PER), Revenue granted facilities (LI), Income from savings and investments (II), Mutual income (MI), Non-Mutual income (NMI), Interest paid to depositors (SP), Bad debt expense (DC) and total costs (TC), variables of earnings per share, dividends of per share, income from deposits and investments, and ratio of price to earnings based on both Pearson and Spearman correlation coefficient have a significant correlation with variable share price in the initial public offering. In addition, variable earnings per share with the Dividends per share and revenue of depositors and investments, variable ratio of price to earnings with the revenue of depositors and investors of variables, mutual and non-mutual incomes, paid interest to depositors and the total costs, variable income from deposit and loan with a variable income investors and mutual incomes, paid interest to depositors, variable of mutual incomes have a significant relationship with total costs, and variable costs for bad debts have a significant relationship with the total costs.

Pearson and Spearman correlation coefficients between the variables balance sheet (bad debt provision (Zmm), Fixed assets (FA), Total assets (TA), Investments (Inv), Deposit with Bank (DB), Deposit loan (QD), Short-term deposits (SD), Long-term deposits (LD), The proportion of profitable assets (DS), Rate exchange agreements (OM2), The ratio of bad debt provision facilities (ZMT), Loans to deposits ratio (TS),The percentage of short-term resource mobilization (TMK), The percentage of long-term resource mobilization (TMB) and the percentage of loan resource mobilization (TMQ) of variables total assets, investment, Short-term and long-term deposits, Profitable assets, ratio of exchange contracts and the percentage of long-term resource mobilization have a significant correlation with the variable share price in the initial public offering. Pearson and Spearman correlation coefficients analysis show that variables of bad debt provision, fixed assets, total assets, investments, short-term deposits and long-term and profitable assets have a significant relation with more variables compared to other variables. In other words, these variables with more variables overlap and can transfer more data.

The results of comparison of several community indicated that at least average results of a valuation model with the average price of shares in the initial public offering sample banks are not equal. In order to determine models which have a significant correlation with the share price in the initial public offering samples of their research, of the two samples paired test was used. In order to test assumptions, are as follows:

H_1: $\mu_{ER} \neq \mu_{IPO}$
H_2: $\mu_{DDM} \neq \mu_{IPO}$
H_3: $\mu_{P/E} \neq \mu_{IPO}$
H_4: $\mu_{P/BV} \neq \mu_{IPO}$

The results of the test above assumptions are explained in Table 12.

Table 11. test results of comparison average intrinsic value and share price in the initial public offering

Amount of statistic F	405
Amount of F statistic at the border ناحیه بحرانی	2049
The significant level (Amount of sig)	0.003

Table 12. Average values inherent paired test results according to various valuation models and the price of shares in the initial public offering

Comparative couples	Amount of t-statistic	The significant level (Amount of sig)
The mean value calculated excess return model and the average share price in the initial public offering	-1.9	0.08
The mean value calculated dividend discount model and the average share price in the initial public offering	-5.1	0.00
The mean value calculated PE model and the average share price in the initial public offering	1.3	0.22
The mean value is calculated PBV model and the average share price in the initial public offering	2.1	0.05

The results showed that with a confidence level %95, average results of evaluation of PE, ER and PBV are equal with the average price of shares in the initial public offering sample banks, and only by the DDM valuation results with the initial public offering share price are not the same research sample banks. And about this model (DDM), calculated values by the model are less than the price of recovered bank stocks their shares in initial offerings.

The results of testing are corresponded this hypothesis with the results of the research of Frankel Lee (1998) that they showed better performance for the relative valuation models and excess return.

Considering that all variables are significantly different from zero at five per cent error, reflect the influence of variables, valuation, performance and balance sheet in the model. The following diagnostic test results have been reported. Obtained results of the diagnostic test are indicated the absence of auto-correlation in residuals model problem. As it can be seen, the results are satisfactory to all stipulations.

The analysis shows while the growth rate of earnings per share is low, two variables of dividends per share and doubtful debt provision are more in evaluating investors. By increasing the growth rate of earnings per share, while the previous two variables in the valuation investors are still concerned, and the two variables earnings per share and compared with the facility to deposit also has given more attention. In addition, the use of relative valuation models to determine the price of a diet high growth in earnings per share is more important. In the fourth part, selected variable transition is earnings per share. And according to the ISTAR model to estimate the initial offering price coefficient was chosen in the stock market. It can be concluded that IPO4 respect to different levels of earnings per share shows a nonlinear behavior.

These results are corresponded with the results of the results Asadi and et al research (2016) and the other researchers mentioned that were known variables earnings per share, dividend per share Total costs and bad debt provision as affecting variables in the assessment of banks, and relative valuation methods were introduced as more efficient methods.

Speed transition between the two regimens growth of production, due to the estimated transition parameter (EPS_{it}) is equal to 10. The above equations indicate when EPS growth is upper and lower, the severity of influencing variables on the share price at the initial public offering of stock is different. The figure below shows how to handle the transition function at different levels of EPS. In other words, when the EPS growth rate comes to about 10 percent, the behavior of the transition function will be changed. Considering that LSTR model is estimated with the $K=1(LSTR_1)$ has the capability of modeling of symmetric variables. s_t is introduced changes to the measurement of phase or period. LSTR1 model can be

Table 13. Estimation of non-linear models with the different specifications of final research model

Variable	Coefficient	The significance level
	Linear section	
Width of origin	239.55	0.003
PE	6.27	0.000
TC	2.55-	0.031
EPS	1.42	0.031
TR	1.06	0.042
CAR	2.78	0.010
FA	1.56	0.006
FD	0.51	0.016
	Non-linear section	
Width of origin	789.4	0.007
PE	1.61	0.048
TC	2.10-	0.052
EPS	1.56	0.021
TR	1.48	0.050
CAR	8.12	0.042
FA	3.20	0.070
FD	0.52	0.075
Gamma Coefficient	8.13	
Coefficient C	0.119	
	Good statistic of model fitting	
The coefficient of determination: 0.95	Akaike statistics: 1.302	Schwartz statistics: 1.397

used to describe the process by which the characteristics of the dynamics are different from one regime to another regime (ie the processes that behave differently from periods of recession boom periods), and the transition is from one regime to another regime done just smooth, reliable and convenient model. On the other hand, $LSTR_2(K=2)$ is appropriate that the dynamic adjustment process in the high and low values s_t similar behavioral and only in the median values show different behavior.

CONCLUSION

The conclusion of the test of secondary research questions, as follows:

At the confidence level %95 regarding significant relationship between the relative valuation models (PE & P / BV) and price of shares in the initial public offering banks examined in the study and at confidence level of %90 a significant relationship between the excess return (ER) and the price of shares in the initial public offering were confirmed. Results of the survey the second hypothesis was stating of the lack of a significant relationship between the DDM and the share price in the initial public offering studied banks.

The results of testing are corresponded this hypothesis with the results of the research of Dastgir and colleagues (2010), Bidgoli and colleagues (2009), Havas Beigi (1998) and Frankel Lee (1998) that they showed better performance for the relative valuation models and excess return.

Based on the results of the study, variable coefficient intrinsic value by using the price to earnings (PE) ratio of price to book value per share model (P / BV) in the level of 5 percent was significantly different from zero. On this basis calculated intrinsic values by using this model provide more power in explaining the initial public offering prices. The results have been suggested the positive impact of the average P / E, and PBV model on the value of each share.

These results are corresponded with the results of Asadi and et al research (2016), Sepehrdoust and Aeini (2014), Shahchera and Jouzani (2013) that stated profit variables of per share are the book value are important variables in the valuation and research results Haibati (2011), Bidgoli et al. (2009) and Pak Din and colleagues (2009) as they think fit the ratio of price to earnings and its resulting model for valuation.

The results also showed that earnings per share variables are effective on the relationship between the other variables with share price in the initial public offering of bank shares, and the price of shares in the initial public offering of the different levels of earnings per share shows a nonlinear behavior. Considering that prices of bank shares is influenced by productivity and profitability, selection earnings per share as a variable in terms of economic is fair and reasonable selection. In the estimated model, earnings per share (EPS), total costs (TC) and total incomes (TR) have a determining role in the price of shares in a public offering.

These results are corresponded with the results of Asadi and et al research (2016), Sepehrdoust and Aeini (2014), Shahchera and Jouzani (2013) that they know earnings per share as an important factor in determining the value of the company and with the researches of Haibati (2011), Bidgoli et al. (2009) and Pak Din and colleagues (2009) that price earnings were introduced an affecting factor in the assessment. This is while Shahchera and Jouzani (2013) in their study pointed out the importance of cost in evaluating banks.

Based on the results of the study, we can conclude that has been shown symmetric behavior shares in the public offering varying degrees of bank deposits. The results of the done reviews have been suggested the positive impact of bad debt provision, the total fixed assets, the ratio of loans to deposits, capital adequacy ratio and total deposits On the bank's shares in the IPO banks. The results are corresponded with the results of Shauvalpour and Ashari (2014) and Shahchera and Jouzani (2013) that were introduced important factors in assessing banks the proportion of loans to deposits, bad debt provision, the volume of assets and capital adequacy.

The final model determines the price of shares in the IPO banks in this study are as follows:

$$\begin{aligned} IPO4_{it} &= 239.5 + 6,27*PE_{it} - 2.55*TC_{it} + 1.42*EPS_{it} + 1.06*TR_{it} + 2.78*CAR_{it} + 1.56*FA_{it} \\ &+0.51*TS_{it} + \left(789.4 + 1.61*PE_{it} - 2.10*TC_{it} + 0.324*EPS_{it} + 1.48*TR_{it} + 8.12*CAR_{it}\right. \\ &\left.+3.20*FA_{it} + 0.52*TS_{it}\right)\left(1 + \exp\left\{8.13\left(EPS_{t} - 0.119\right)\right\}\right)^{-1} \end{aligned}$$

The results show that there is a linear relationship in the conditions of low growth of earnings per share and a non-linear relationship between high growth in earnings per share between the bank and the share price in the IPO price to earnings per share, the total cost, total revenues, capital adequacy ratio, the ratio of loans to deposits. These results are corresponded with the results of the results Asadi and Ismaili Fard research (2016), Sepehrdoust and Aeini (2014), Shahchera and Jouzani (2013) Shavvalpour and Ashari (2014), Haibati (2011) and Pak Din and colleagues (2009) that were known variables earnings per share, dividend per share Total costs and bad debt provision as affecting variables in the assessment of banks, and relative valuation methods were introduced as more efficient methods.

ACKNOWLEDGMENT

Dr. Soltani would like to thank Isa Rezaee for their contributions to this chapter.

REFERENCES

Adams, M. & Rudolf, M. (2010). A new approach to the valuation of banks [online]. Cited 2011-05-06.

Amiri, P. M. & Morteza, A. R. (2009). Prioritize financial factors affecting the price index in the Tehran Stock Exchange using TOPSIS, financial research: No. 26, pp. 61-76.

Antill, *N. & Lee, K. (2008). Company valuation under IFRS.* UK: Harriman House.

Asadi, G. & Ashkani, B. (2016). Investigating the impact of auditor change on stock price. *Audit Knowledge Journal,* 66, pp. 41-60.

Bangladesh Country Review. (2010). Stock market. Bangladesh Country Review, 80-81.

BENNINGA. (2008). *S. Financial Modeling* (3rd ed.). London, UK: The MIT Press.

Boabang, F. (2003). The IPOs of Canadian firms via installment receipts: the opening performance and implications for the short-run efficiency of the Canadian market. *Canadian Journal of Administrative Sciences*/Revue Canadienne des Sciences de l'Administration; 20, 3, pp. 224–233, September 2003.

Bundoo, S. K. (2007). An analysis of IPOS underpricing in Mauritius. *African Journal of Accounting, Economics, Finance and Banking Research, 1*(1), 1–12.

Chang, S. C., Chung, T. Y., & Lin, W. C. (2010). Underwriter reputation, earnings management and the long-run performance of initial public offerings. *Accounting and Finance, 50*(1), 53–78. doi:10.1111/j.1467-629X.2009.00329.x

Chen, K. Y., Lin, K. L., & Zhou, J. (2005). Audit quality and earnings management for Taiwan IPO firms. *Managerial Auditing Journal, 20*(1), 86–104. doi:10.1108/02686900510570722

Chi, J. & Padgett, C. (2002). The performance and long-run characteristics of the Chinese IPO market, U of Reading, ISMA Centre Discussion Paper No. 2002-09.

Copeland. T., Koller, T., & Murrin, J. (2000). Valuation. Measuring and managing the value of companies (3rd ed.). New York, NY: John Wiley & Sons.

Damodaran, A. (2002). *Investment valuation: Tools and techniques for determining the value of any asset.* New York, NY: John Wiley & Sons.

Fama, E. (1998). Market efficiency long run returns and behavioral finance. *Journal of Financial Economics,* 49.

Frankel, R., & Lee, C. M. C. (1998). Accounting valuation, market expectation, and cross-sectional stock returns. *Journal of Accounting and Economics*, *25*(3), 283–319. doi:10.1016/S0165-4101(98)00026-3

Giammarino, R., Schwartz, E., & Zechner, J. (1989). Market valuation of bank assets and deposit insurance in Canada. Canadian Journal of Economics, 22(1), pp. 109–127.

Sepehrdoust, H. & Taibe, A. (2014). Affecting factors in the Iranian bank the capital adequacy ratio during the years 2007- 2011, the Financial Accounting Research: Successive Number 18, Pages 35-50.

Kazerouni, A. R. & Afshari, M. (2006). Article 44 of the constitution and the challenges facing the Iranian private banking. Journal of Political - Economic twenty years, Number 5-6 (s 222), Bahman and Esfand 2014.

Shahchera, M. & Jouzani, N. (2013). The impact on the profitability of state-owned banks and private investors towards Iranian, Monetary and Banking Studies, 12, pp. 20-43.

Mehrani, S. & Nounahalnahr, A. A. (n.d.). Assessment response of less than expected investors in the Tehran Stock Exchange. *Reviews Accounting and Auditing,* 54.

Merton, R. C. (1973). Theory of rational option pricing. *The Bell Journal of Economics and Management Science*, *4*(1), 141–183. doi:10.2307/3003143

Shauvalpour, S. & al-Ash'ari, E. (2014). The effect of the credit risk on the profitability of banks in Iran, Financial Research: Number 2, pp. 229-246.

Chapter 13
Challenges of Stock Prediction

Walid A. Mohammed
https://orcid.org/0000-0003-3756-1138
The University of Salford, UK

ABSTRACT

The challenge of the stock price forecast is the most crucial component for companies and equity traders to predict future revenues. A successful and accurate prediction to the future stock prices ultimately results in profit maximisation. This chapter proposes the use of autoregressive integrated moving average (ARIMA) and the artificial neural networks (ANNs) models to predict the future prices of the stock. Using Walmart's stock index, the results show that both ARIMA and the ANNs models provide accurate forecasting performance. However, for short-term forecasting, the performance of ANNs outperformed ARIMA models.

INTRODUCTION

Stock price forecast is the most crucial component for investors and companies to predict future revenues and any possible negative earnings. The essence of the stock market investments involves high risk and high profits; thus, it is a source of attraction to many businesses, investors and economists. Traditionally, the firm's growth valuation depends on forecasting earnings and cash flows using an appropriate discount rate for cash flows to arrive at the value of the firm. However, this traditional forecasting earning is merely possible if a firm has either positive earnings, comparable firms or a long history of performance. We attempt to overcome this problem and provide appropriate solutions and tools for financial managers and investors to assist in making successful business decisions. In particular, we apply several quantitative techniques with a set of examples which help to forecast and predict the future prices of the stock. It also allows investors and businesses to make informed decisions about whether to buy or sell the stock of interest.

Additionally, the stock market data is prone to non-economic factors such as natural disasters and political decisions; thus, it is naturally noisy and unpredictable. The unpredictability of the stock data is also due to the incomplete information from the past behaviour of the stock market to enable capturing the dependency between future and previous prices (Tay and Cao 2001). The incomplete information

DOI: 10.4018/978-1-7998-1086-5.ch013

concerning the stock market data is often regarded as noisy characteristics, making it a challenge to predict the future price of a stock. Due to the rapid increase in trade and investment, the need for the appropriate tools and methods to mitigate risks and maximise gains equally increased.

To address this issue, we explore several (linear and nonlinear) time series models in the literature with accurate forecasting performances. In the recent competitive forecasting-literature, the aim is to construct models which can predict the future stock prices with greater accuracy. Nonetheless, the literature in exponential smoothing methods still inconclusive, Gardner (2006) developed the work of Brown (1959); and Holt (2004a) from theoretical and practical perspectives. Theoretically, and based on a new class of the state-space models, Gardner introduced a complete statistical rationale for exponential smoothing method. Practically, he developed a robust method for smoothing damped multiplicative trends.[1] ARCH and GARCH models are also essential tools for the analysis of time-series data; however, according to Engle (2001), they are especially useful for the analysis and forecasting volatility. Several other prediction models also made available in the literature, for example, Support Vector Machine models (Sai et al., 2007; Karathanasopoulos et al., 2016); structural time series models and the Kalman filter, (Harvey, 1990). Besides, using Sunspot data, Babu and Reddy (2014) proposed a hybrid ARIMA-ANN model based on a moving-average filter. Their results show that for both one-step and multistep ahead forecast, the proposed hybrid model has higher prediction accuracy.

For more than half a century, linear autoregressive integrated moving average (ARIMA), and the nonlinear artificial neural networks (ANNs) models have dominated time series forecasting area. In this chapter, we investigate with a set of examples, the forecasting performance of the autoregressive integrated moving average (ARIMA) and the artificial neural networks (ANNs) models in predicting the future prices of the stock market. Several distinguishing features of both ARIMA and the ANNs models make them vital tools for valuable forecasting tasks.

The ARIMA model; known as Box-Jenkins methodology, is widely used in the literature as an efficient and accurate tool for forecasting time series data. It can only perform well using a stationary time series data; for other case scenarios, the data should be made stationary (by, differencing) to meet the requirements for accurate forecasting results. Thus, the time series prediction using ARIMA model assumes the case under study generated from linear processes; because it relies on the previous values of the series and the past error-terms for forecasting, (Khashei and Bijari 2010; Wang et al. 2012; Adebiyi and Adewumi 2014).

Artificial neural networks (ANNs) are also one of the most accurate and extensively applied forecasting models in various real-life applications including social, economics, stock problems, engineering and foreign exchange (Khashei and Bijari, 2010). It is because; ANNs are data-driven and self -adaptive methods which can be used as universal function approximators. As nonlinear models, the ANNs received overwhelming attention in recent literature for time series forecasting, in particular, the prediction of the stock market prices.

This chapter contributes to the contemporaneous challenges of the stock price prediction. The aim is to capture challenging and frequently changing prices more quickly and minimise risks to stock market investors and financial decision-makers. Our study contrasts different time series forecasting tools such as ARIMA and ANNs models to accurately predict the future prices of a stock; using Walmart' stock data as an example. Based on daily adjusted closing prices of Walmart's stock index, our predictive results presented here contributes significantly to the higher level of building profitable strategies. Besides, to enhance our contribution reliability, we employ some important technical indicators such as simple moving average (SMA) and moving average convergence/divergence (MACD) as auxiliary forecasting tools.

Our approach is entirely helpful in providing greater accuracy of the stock market's price forecast. The prediction techniques we present here are up-to-date and can be very useful to identify the potential opportunities of buying and selling the stock of interest. The rest of the chapter organised as follows: Section 2 discusses the most relevant literature. Section 3 provides the method and input data, and section 4 discusses the empirical results. Section 5 concludes.

RELATED LITERATURE

The related literature on this topic is overwhelmingly rich mainly, in the area of forecasting, where both ARIMA and the ANNs models extensively studied. As time-series forecasting models, the essential functioning of ARIMA and the ANNs is deep-rooted in interpreting the future information based on observation carried forward from the past, i.e. the previous observations tell us something about the future. That being said, the classical forecasting approach for both ARIMA and ANNs based on regression analysis where the specification of a linear parametric relationship between two variables is essential. The field of linear prediction is dated back to the pioneering work of Kolmogorov (1941) and Wiener (1941), where they set the foundation to solve the *signal extraction* problem. Adelman and Adelman (1959) later emphasised that forecasting models generated from a signal extraction context.

Given the foundation of the linear process, Box and Jenkins (1970) provided a solution to the non-stationarity (by, differencing the data) and suggested that ARIMA models can provide accurate forecasting results. Thus, as forecasting tools, both models ARIMA and the ANNs, acquired the attention in the recent literature mainly, in the field of stock price prediction where the search for accurate results is profound. Tansel et al. (1999) contrast the performance of ANNs with other generic algorithms (Gas) for time series data modelling. They advocate that the linear optimisation techniques performed better than neural networks. To predict the stock's movement direction, Hansen et al. (1999) used both ARIMA and ANNs; their results show that the latter provided more accurate results.

Using Korean stock data index, Lee et al. (2007) compared the forecasting performance of both ARIMA and the ANNs; the ARIMA model generates more accurate forecasting results compared to ANNs. Forecasting the Indian stock index, Merh et al. (2010) tested the performance of hybrid ARIMA and the ANNs. They suggested that in most prediction cases, ARIMA model provided better results than ANNs. In recent literature, hybrid forecasting techniques also applied to time series forecasting, including ANNs and ARIMA models which yield more accurate predicting results (Pai and Lin, 2005; Zhou and Hu, 2008; Khashei and Bijari 2010).

For various real-life applications, Sterba and Hilovska (2010) indicate that both ARIMA and ANNs can provide accurate forecasting results. They used both models to linear and nonlinear applications; their findings show that for linear time series, ARIMA models provide accurate results, whereas, for a nonlinear time series forecasting, the ANNs yields better performance. Wijaya et al. (2010) also contrast the performance of ANNs with ARIMA models on forecasting the Indonesian stock exchange. The authors argued that ANNs generate better forecasting results than ARIMA model. Kara et al. (2011) predicted the direction of the Istanbul stock exchange, using ANNs and SVM. Their findings show that both models are useful; however, the predicting performance of ANNs is more accurate compared to SVM. Nayak et al. (2015) proposed a hybrid SVM with K-nearest Neighbour approach to predict the Indian stock market's profit and loss. Their recommended model scores relatively good results. Dash and Dash (2016) integrated a decision support system with ANNs using efficient computational function and technical analysis rules. The authors concluded that the proposed model engenders the profitable trade's decision points effectively. The literature reviewed here clearly shows for time series forecasting, both ARIMA and ANNs models can provide accurate forecasting results.

After a brief review of the literature, in this chapter, we apply both time series forecasting tools, ARIMA and the ANNs to predict the future prices of Walmart's stock. The aim is to provide more insight to the already existing literature, the forecasting abilities of ARIMA and the ANNs in predicting the future stock's prices. Besides, the chapter will also compare the forecasting performance of both models.

METHOD AND INPUT DATA

Method

To predict Walmart's stock price, in this chapter, we apply autoregressive integrated moving average (ARIMA), the artificial neural networks (ANNs) models and some technical analysis indicators. The technical indicators we apply in this chapter are simple moving average (SMA) and the moving average convergence divergence (MACD). Our study based on historical daily stock prices of Walmart Inc. MATLAB version 2018b is used for implementations.

ARIMA (p, d, q)

In ARIMA models, which also called Box and Jenkins (1970) methodology, the non-stationarity of the data transformed into stationary by adding-up finite differencing to the data points. Using lag polynomial, ARIMA (p, d, q) can be expressed as below:

This can be written as:where p is the integer of autoregressive term, d is the non-seasonal differences integer and q is the forecast error term.

The ANNs Approach

The multi-layer perception (MLPs) ANNs with a single hidden layer is the most broadly applied for its high degree of accuracy in forecasting and prediction, (Zhang G. P. 2003; Chen et al. 2003; Zhang and Min Qi 2005; Zhang et al. 2008). The multi-layer characteristics consist of hidden, input and output connected by acyclic links. A functional relationship between the layers (input and output) can be expressed as follow:

$$X_t = \Psi_0 + \sum_{j=1}^{q} \Psi_j . \Phi\left(\Psi_{0j} + \sum_{i=1}^{p} \Psi_{ij} . X_{t-1} \right) + \varepsilon_t \quad (1)$$

where Ψ_j and Ψ_{ij} are the connection weights (parameters), p & q are the integers of input and output nodes, respectively, and ε_t is the random shock. The most nonlinear activation function used in the model is logistic sigmoid function $g(x) = \frac{1}{1+e^{-x}}$ where, other activation functions (Gaussian, Linear, and Hyperbolic Tangent) can also be applied with diverse modelling applications, Kamruzzaman (2006). The ANNs feed-forward single hidden-layer performs the functional mapping from historical observations of the time series to the future values, Zhang et al. (1998).

Technical Analysis Indicators

Technical indicators are extensively applied in the literature to smooth the data points such as moving averages, volatility indicators, market trend indicators and momentum indicators (Murphy 2009; Fayek et al. 2013; Nayak et al. 2015). In this chapter, we use two important technical indicators, the simple moving average (SMA), and moving average convergence divergence (MACD).

(a) Simple Moving Average (SMA)

According to Nayak et al. (2015b, p. 672), the SMA shown in Figure. 8 smooths the data through the process of replacement, i.e., by replacing each element with the average of neighbouring elements defined within the window which can be expressed mathematically as:

$$\Omega\Lambda_i = \frac{1}{2N+1}\left(\Omega\Lambda(i+N)+\Omega\Lambda(i+N-1)+\ldots+\Omega\Lambda(i-N)\right) \tag{2}$$

where $\frac{1}{2N+1}$ is the span, the smoothed value for the *ith* data point is $\Omega\Lambda_i$ and N is the number of neighbouring data points of either side of $\Omega\Lambda_i$ value. This chapter defines $\Omega\Lambda_i$ as daily adjusted closing prices.

(b) Moving Average Convergence Divergence (MACD)

We use the MACD indicator to assess the price movement of Walmart stock and highlight the potential profit-making opportunities. Calculations of the MACD involve the use of exponential moving average EMA, which can be mathematically expressed as follows:

$$EMA_p = \left(X_p\left(\frac{\Phi}{1+n}\right)\right)+EMA_q\left(1-\left(\frac{\Phi}{1+n}\right)\right) \tag{3}$$

where n is the number of days, Φ represents the smoothing multiplier, p is today's value, and q is the previous day value. Different periods (number of days) can be used to calculate the MACD. In this chapter, we apply a 26-period exponential moving average (EMA) from a 12-period EMA; the formula for calculating the MACD is as follows:

$$MACD = 12PeriodEMA - 26PeriodEMA \tag{4}$$

The above calculations generate the MACD line along with a nine-day EMA of MACD often called the signal-line. Figure. 9 demonstrates the MACD results for Walmart Inc.

Input Data

The data applied in this chapter is a historical daily stock price, which consists of open, low, high, close, adjusted close and volume. Daily stock prices data are extensively applied in academic studies (Kim 2003; Brownlees and Gallo, 2006; Ariyo et al. 2014; Henrique et al. 2018). The daily prices data selected are for the period of five years with 1356 observations, obtained from Yahoo Finance for availability. The adjusted closing prices indices were chosen for MACD indicator for modelling and predicting the potential opportunities of buying and selling the stock of interest, in our study is Walmart Stock. That is because the adjusted closing prices represent the daily behavioural activities of the index.

EMPIRICAL RESULTS

ARIMA (p, d, q) Model for Walmart Stock Price Index

The empirical estimation and results we generate in this chapter are based on daily historical data for Walmart stock prices, covering the period from January 02, 2014, to May 22, 2019. Figure 1 displays the original patterns of the data series. Before applying the ARIMA model, first, we transform the data into stationary by removing the linear trend from the data, using MATLAB function (*detrend*). This process enables us to focus our analysis on the fluctuations in the data about the trend.

Figurer 1. Walmart Stock Prices Index

Figurer 2. Graphical representation for Walmart stock price in 2018

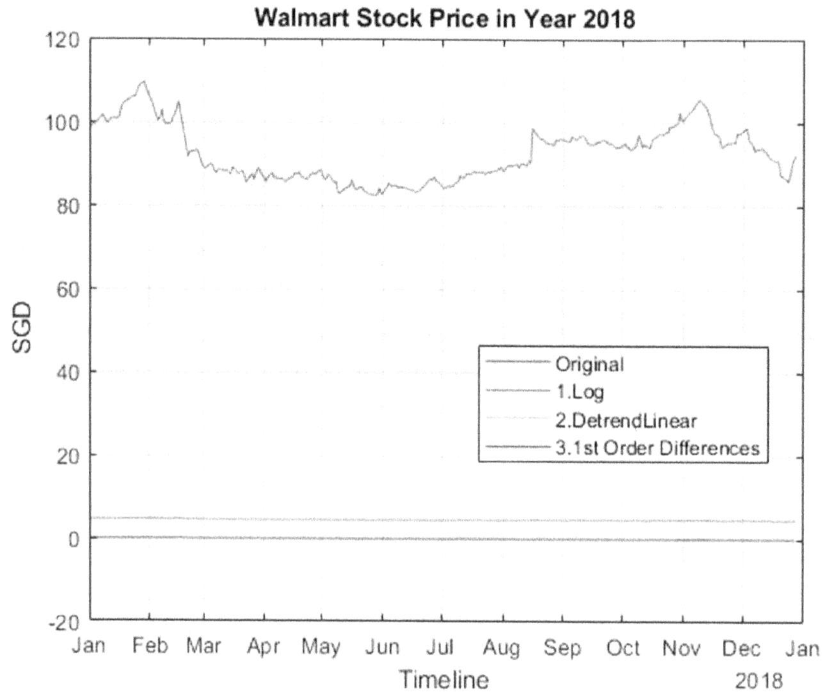

However, Figure 2 below, visualises the stock prices data for the year 2018, as expected, the detrended data has a mean almost close to zero, which helps to reduce the overall variations from the data.

To develop the best ARIMA model for Walmart's daily stock prices, we follow an extensive set of criteria for modelling and forecasting purposes as follows:

1. Since the data under investigation is a time-series data, we further examine whether the data series is stationarity or nonstationary, using autocorrelation and partial autocorrelation functions (ACF & PACF) developed by Box et al. (2015). These statistical tests enable us to identify series with serial correlations, examine the effectiveness of moving average (MA) model, and to identify the significant auto-regressive (AR) lags for model identification. Figureure 3 and 4 for (ACF) and (PACF) respectively depict the analysis results. The result outcomes suggest that the first order differencing is enough to transform the data into stationary to satisfy the ARIMA model requirements, which has a constant conditional mean and variance.
2. The ACF and PACF results also indicate that at 0 lag spikes, the autocorrelation is relatively high, and dies at a first-order lag.

That means, after differencing the data, we should use MA (0) and AR (0) for the best model development. Moreover, the cyclical trend indicates the stationarity of the data.

3. Considering relatively small Bayesian and Akaike Information Criterions (BIC & AIC), and relatively small standard error of the regression (SER).

Figure 3. Graphical representation for (ACF)

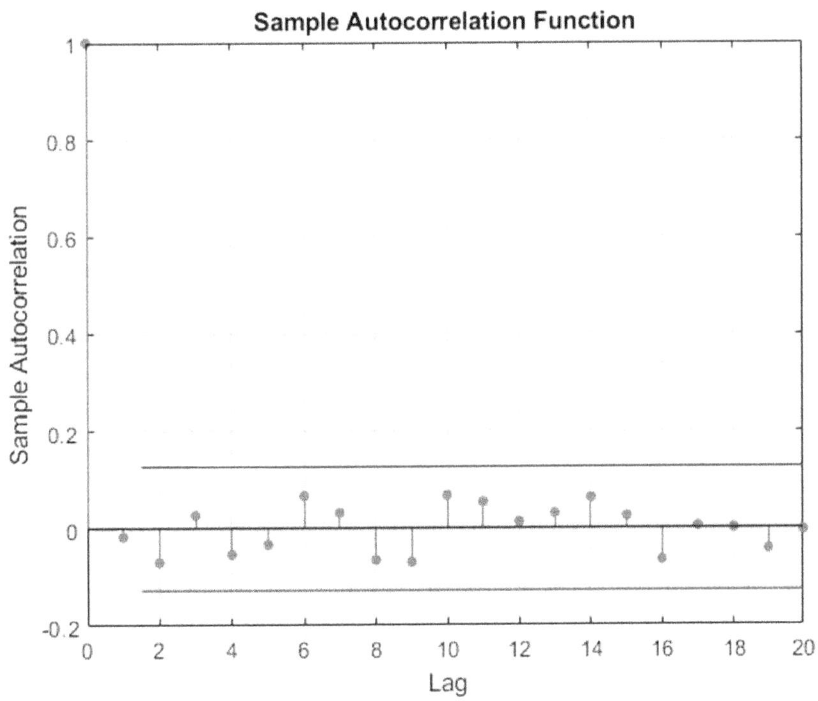

Figure 4. Graphical representation for (PACF)

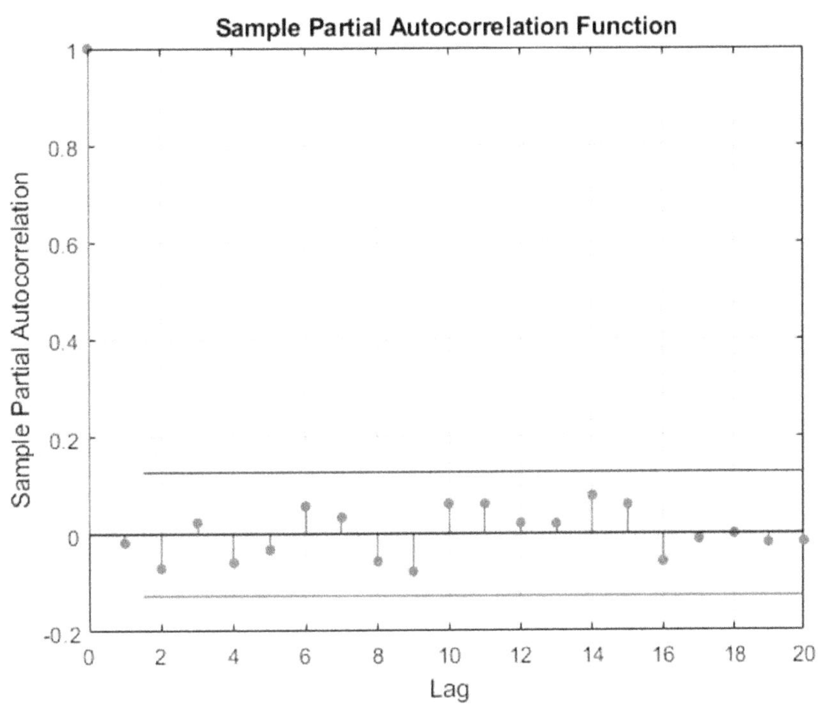

The exploratory data analyses we present above suggest that ARIMA (0, 1, 0) is the best model to provide an accurate prediction of Walmart stock prices for the year 2018. Table 1 shows several diagnostic statistical results of the analyses and Figure 5 depicts ARIMA (0, 1, 0).

The result in Figure 5 reflects the graphical performance of ARIMA (0, 1, 0) in predicting Walmart stock prices, which is impressive as expected. It also indicates that the predictive capabilities of ARIMA (0, 1, 0), can yield a more accurate forecasting result. To enhance the reliability and accuracy of our findings presented in Figure 5, it is always good to compare the fitness of different ARIMA models. To evaluate the performance of ARIMA (0, 1, 0) results shown in Figure 5, we apply ARIMA (1, 2, 1) as an auxiliary tool. Figure 6 gives a clear graphical representation of the predicting outcome.

Looking at the results presented in both Figure 5 and 6, the comparison of ARIMA models (0, 1, 0) and (1, 2, 1) performances in predicting the stock prices for the year 2018 is almost identical. The results are compelling evidence that both ARIMA models (0, 1, 0 and 1, 2, 1) under investigation can provide higher forecasting performances. However, to investigate this argument further, we combine both ARIMA models to test their capabilities of forecasting Walmart stock prices for the years 2018 and 2019. By combining ARIMA models, the aim is to improve forecasting performance and obtain accurate and reliable results. The test will also show an impressive result, i.e. which ARIMA model has a higher forecasting performance. To assess the forecasting performance of proposed models, we use 1H of the year 2018; that is six months of Walmart's Adjusted Close. That is because the Adjusted Closing prices represent more accurate reflections of Walmart's stock value. For back-testing, the first month of the year 2018, is used as an out-of-sample data. Figure 7 depicts the forecasting results for ARIMA models (0, 1, 0) and (1, 2, 1).

Table 1. ARIMA (0, 1, 0) MODEL (GAUSSIAN DISTRIBUTION)

	Value	Standard Error	T-Statistic	P-Value
Constant	0.025534	0.092859	0.27497	0.78334
Variance	2.0523	0.062978	32.587	6.1715e-233
Table comparison = 9×3 table				
Var 1	**Var 2**	**Var 3**		
Arima (0,1,0)	893.21	900.25		
Arima (1,1,1)	892.23	899.28		
Arima (1,1,2)	891.58	898.62		
Arima (1,2,1)	899.45	906.49		
Arima (1,2,2)	892.67	899.71		
Arima (2,1,1)	891.59	898.63		
Arima (2,1,2)	891.55	898.59		
Arima (2,2,1)	897.59	904.63		
Arima (2,2,2)	892.67	899.71		
Log Likelihood	**=-444.6044**			
AIC	**=893.2089**			
BIC	**=900.2518**			
R. Squared	**=0.960**			

Figure 5. ARIMA (0, 1, 0) of Walmart stock for the year (2018)

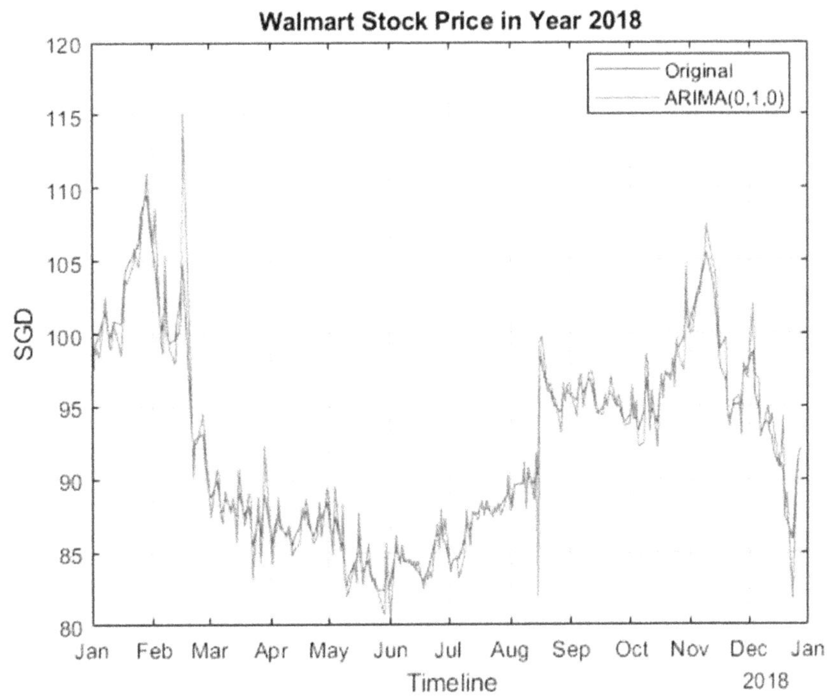

Figure 6. ARIMA (1, 2, 1) of Walmart stock for the year (2018)

Figure 7. ARIMA random walk model (0, 1, 0) and ARIMA (1, 2, 1) forecast performance

The results in Figure 7 show that both ARIMA models are very useful tools for forecasting time series data. However, in the above example, and based on the criteria listed in the previous section, we observe that ARIMA (1, 2, 1) yields more accurate forecasting results than a random walk, ARIMA (0, 1, 0). In addition to the findings presented above, we also apply trend analysis to smooth Walmart's stock prices, using technical indicators such as simple moving average (SMA) and moving average convergence/divergence (MACD). The MACD indicates whether to buy or sell the stock, Figure 8 and 9 visualise the results of SMA and MACD, respectively.

We observe from Figure 9 that the MACD line crosses the signal line at various locations indicating possible trade opportunities.

The ANN Model for Walmart Stock

The creation of the ANNs model for Walmart stock, based on Adebiyi et al. (2014) involves two essential steps. First, we build the network topology which consists of the number of hidden layers, the number if selected hidden neurons and the number of input neurons (10), and the number of output neurons (one, in this study). Second, network training which involves selecting the network type and algorithm (in our research, Feed-forward backpropagation algorithm) training function (TRAINGDM), training and target data input, selecting functions; learning (LEARNGDM), performance (MSE) and transfer (TANSIG) function.

Figure 8. SMA for Walmart stock prices

Figure 9. MACD for Walmart stock prices

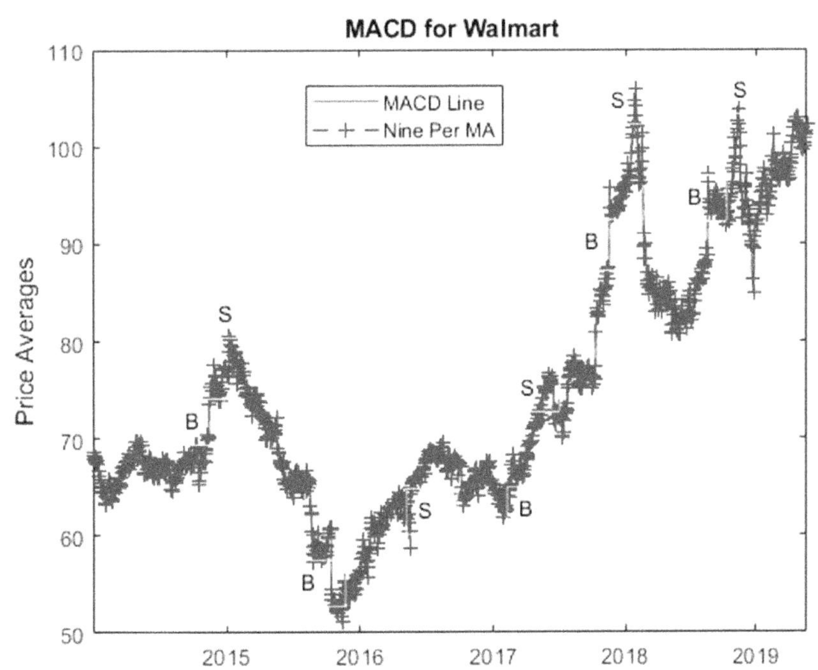

To build a robust ANN model for Walmart stock, we use short-term historical data from February 2, 2019, to April 30, 2019, including a day of the week as input. The first 60 days it used as training data and the last 30 days used to test the model's prediction performance.

Figure 10 graphically reflects the performance of different network training sessions for various network structure models. The best performance of the network structure models is the one that returns the smallest Mean Square Error (MSE) as it gives accurate prediction outcomes.

To identify the best model, carefully, we select training and testing data, and the model was trained with 20 epochs. In addition, we also note the mean square error (MSE) generated from each training sessions of various network structure. Figure 11 depicts the predicted data obtained by the backpropagation neural network (BPNN) for Walmart stock, including testing, validation, training and total data.

The ANN Model Results

After several network training using ANNs, the network structure with the smallest mean square error (MSE) at epoch 14, which depicted in Figure 10 is the best network structure to provide high forecasting performance. Table 2 presents the results generated from the testing period and Figure 12 reflects the correlation accuracy.

Figure 10. Graphical result of the best in network training of ANN for Walmart stock

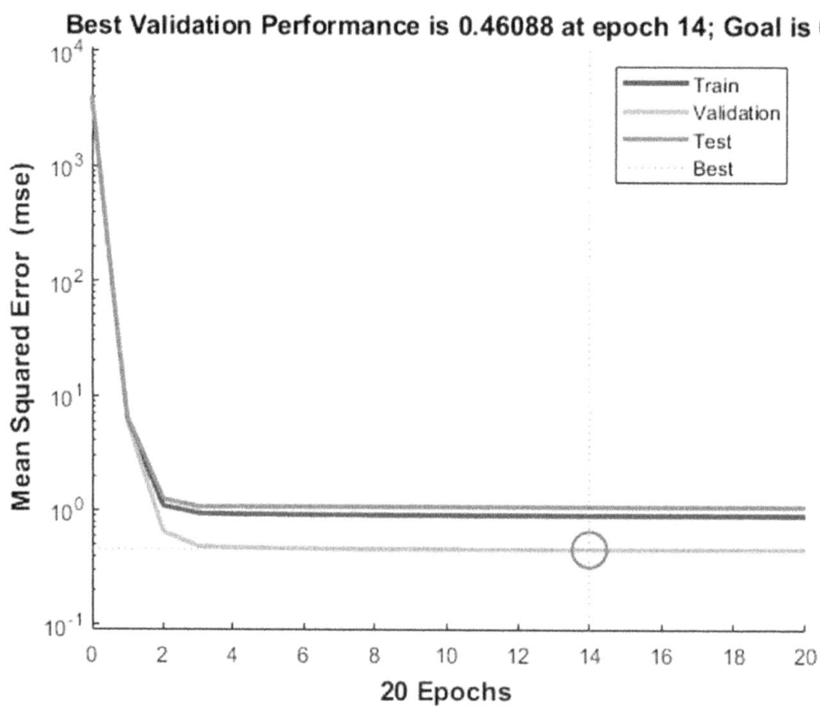

Figure 11. Walmart Stock predicted data for testing, training, validation and the total data generated by BPNN.

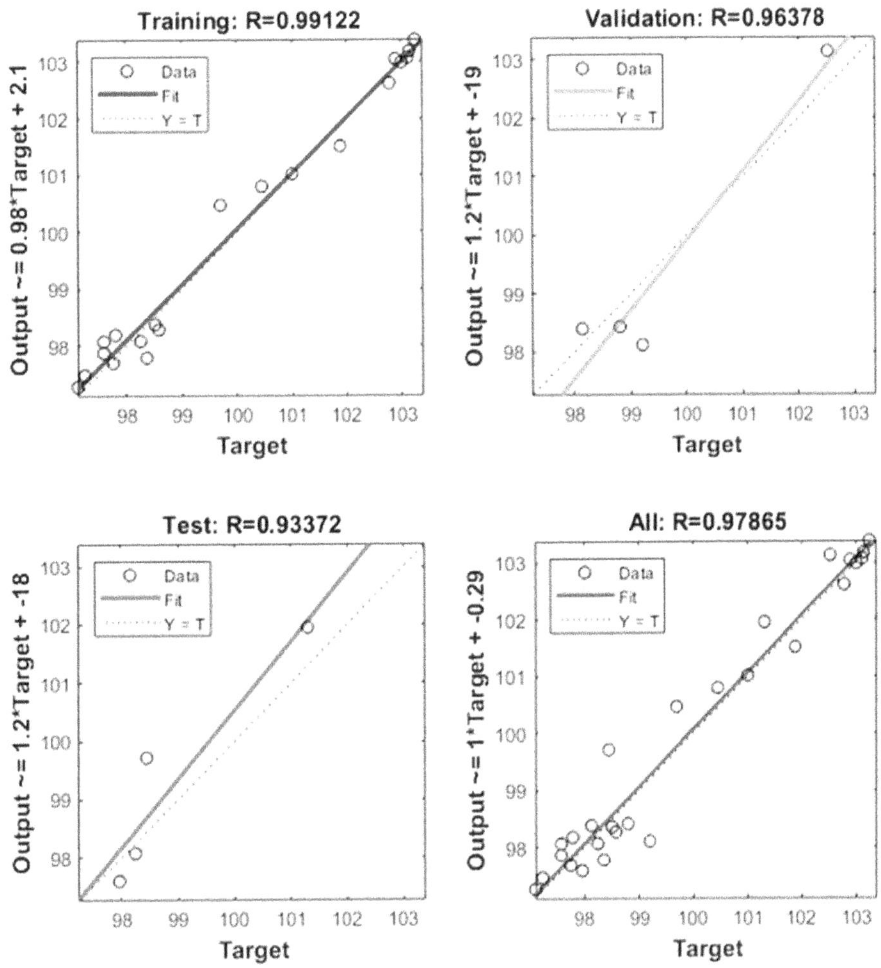

CONCLUSION

The empirical results presented in this chapter suggest that both ARIMA and the ANNs models provide accurate forecasting performances, judging from the forecast error for both models. This argument based on the quantitative methods applied above using Walmart's daily stock prices data as an illustrative example. The results have shown no significant differences between the two models in terms of their predicting abilities. This finding is in line with the work by Sterba & Hilovska (2010) and Adebiyi et al. (2014). However, it can be argued that for a short-term forecasting period, the performance of ANNs is better than ARIMA models. That is due to the nature of the stock prices, which are incredibly dependent on newly revealed information; therefore, they are naturally unpredictable for long-term.

Table 2. ANN results for Walmart stock index.

Sample Period	Actual Values	Predicted Values	Forecast Error
01/04/2019	97.03	96.82	0.00493
02/04/2019	96.43	95.94	0.00508
03/04/2019	96.68	96.19	0.00506
04/04/2019	97.59	96.11	0.01516
05/04/2019	98.31	97.93	0.00386
08/04/2019	98.71	98.23	0.00486
09/04/2019	98.17	98.11	0.00061
10/04/2019	99.07	98.76	0.00312
11/04/2019	100.27	99.08	0.00468
12/04/2019	101.02	100.56	0.00455
15/04/2019	101.89	101.43	0.00451
16/04/2019	102.39	102.07	0.00312
17/04/2019	102.61	102.17	0.00428
18/04/2019	102.63	102.18	0.00438
22/04/2019	101.83	100.37	0.01433
23/04/2019	102.53	102.07	0.00448
24/04/2019	102.98	102.11	0.00844
25/04/2019	102.97	101.52	0.01408
26/04/2019	100.99	99.53	0.01445
29/04/2019	101.02	100.56	0.00455
30/04/2019	102.03	101.84	0.00447

Figure 12. Graphical representation of ANN model to the actual stock prices against forecasted values for Walmart stock index.

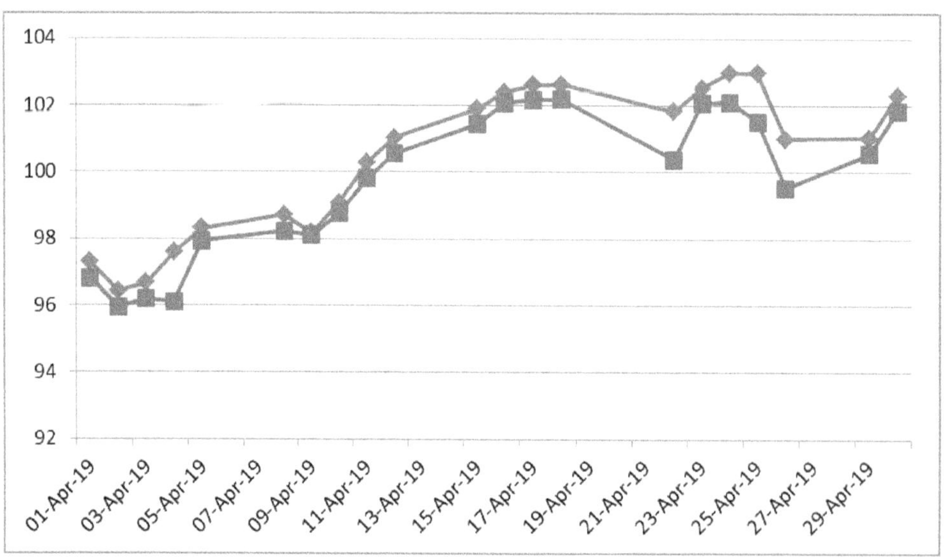

Our study presents an extensive empirical analysis and results to meet the contemporaneous challenges of the stock price prediction. Based on daily stock data, we examined the performance of ARIMA and the ANNs models to test their abilities in predicting the future prices of the stock in this case, Walmart stock. The results show that the forecasting performance of both ARIMA and the ANNs models are equally significant and can achieve excellent results to solve real-life stock price prediction. However, in this study, we observe that ARIMA (1, 2, 1) model yields more accurate forecasting results than random walk, ARIMA (0, 1, 0) model. As times series forecasting models such as ARIMA and ANNs acquire the central attention of the investment decision-makers; nevertheless, for long-term prediction, their performance is not always satisfactory.

Additionally, because the stock price data is inherently unstable, however, some empirical evidence in the literature (Jain and Kumar 2007; Khashei and Bijari 2010; Sterba and Hilovska 2010) argue, using the hybrid-method reduces model uncertainty in time series forecasting. Thus, given the findings presented in this chapter and the vast empirical evidence in the literature, the future forecasting techniques using hybrid-method can yield more accurate results than traditional artificial neural networks.

REFERENCES

Adebiyi, A. A., Adewumi, A. O., & Ayo, C. K. (2014). Comparison of ARIMA and artificial neural networks models for stock price prediction. *Journal of Applied Mathematics*, 2014.

Adelman, I., & Adelman, F. L. (1959). The dynamic properties of the Klein-Goldberger model. *Econometrica*, *27*(4), 596–625. doi:10.2307/1909353

Ariyo, A. A., Adewumi, A. O., & Ayo, C. K. (2014, March). Stock price prediction using the ARIMA model. In *2014 UKSim-AMSS 16th International Conference on Computer Modelling and Simulation* (pp. 106-112). IEEE. 10.1109/UKSim.2014.67

Babu, C. N., & Reddy, B. E. (2014). A moving-average filter-based hybrid ARIMA–ANN model for forecasting time series data. *Applied Soft Computing*, *23*, 27–38. doi:10.1016/j.asoc.2014.05.028

Brown, R. G. (1959). *Statistical forecasting for inventory control*. McGraw/Hill.

Brownlees, C. T., & Gallo, G. M. (2006). Financial econometric analysis at ultra-high frequency: Data handling concerns. *Computational Statistics & Data Analysis*, *51*(4), 2232–2245. doi:10.1016/j.csda.2006.09.030

Chen, A. S., Leung, M. T., & Daouk, H. (2003). Application of neural networks to an emerging financial market: Forecasting and trading the Taiwan Stock Index. *Computers & Operations Research*, *30*(6), 901–923. doi:10.1016/S0305-0548(02)00037-0

Dash, R., & Dash, P. K. (2016). A hybrid stock trading framework integrating technical analysis with machine learning techniques. *The Journal of Finance and Data Science*, *2*(1), 42–57. doi:10.1016/j.jfds.2016.03.002

Engle, R. (2001). GARCH 101: The use of ARCH/GARCH models in applied econometrics. *The Journal of Economic Perspectives, 15*(4), 157–168. doi:10.1257/jep.15.4.157

Fayek, M. B., El-Boghdadi, H. M., & Omran, S. M. (2013). Multi-objective optimization of technical stock market indicators using gas. *International Journal of Computers and Applications, 68*(20).

Gardner, E. S. Jr. (2006). Exponential smoothing: The state of the art—Part II. *International Journal of Forecasting, 22*(4), 637–666. doi:10.1016/j.ijforecast.2006.03.005

Hansen, J. V., McDonald, J. B., & Nelson, R. D. (1999). Time series prediction with genetic-algorithm designed neural networks: an empirical comparison with modern statistical models. *Computational Intelligence, 15*(3), 171–184. doi:10.1111/0824-7935.00090

Harvey, A. C. (1990). *Forecasting, structural time series models and the Kalman filter.* Cambridge University Press. doi:10.1017/CBO9781107049994

Henrique, B. M., Sobreiro, V. A., & Kimura, H. (2018). Stock price prediction using support vector regression on daily and up to the minute prices. *The Journal of Finance And Data Science, 4*(3), 183-201.

Hipel, K. W., & McLeod, A. I. (1994). *Time series modelling of water resources and environmental systems* (Vol. 45). Elsevier. doi:10.1016/S0167-5648(08)70655-5

Jain, A., & Kumar, A. M. (2007). Hybrid neural network models for hydrologic time series forecasting. *Applied Soft Computing, 7*(2), 585–592. doi:10.1016/j.asoc.2006.03.002

Kamruzzaman, J. (Ed.). (2006). Artificial neural networks in finance and manufacturing. Hershey, PA: IGI Global. doi:10.4018/978-1-59140-670-9

Kara, Y., Boyacioglu, M. A., & Baykan, Ö. K. (2011). Predicting direction of stock price index movement using artificial neural networks and support vector machines: The sample of the Istanbul Stock Exchange. *Expert Systems with Applications, 38*(5), 5311–5319. doi:10.1016/j.eswa.2010.10.027

Karathanasopoulos, A., Theofilatos, K. A., Sermpinis, G., Dunis, C., Mitra, S., & Stasinakis, C. (2016). Stock market prediction using evolutionary support vector machines: An application to the ASE20 index. *European Journal of Finance, 22*(12), 1145–1163. doi:10.1080/1351847X.2015.1040167

Khashei, M., & Bijari, M. (2010). An artificial neural network (p, d, q) model for timeseries forecasting. *Expert Systems with Applications, 37*(1), 479–489. doi:10.1016/j.eswa.2009.05.044

Kim, K. H. (2003). Dollar exchange rate and stock price: Evidence from multivariate cointegration and error correction model. *Review of Financial Economics, 12*(3), 301–313. doi:10.1016/S1058-3300(03)00026-0

Kim, K. J. (2003). Financial time series forecasting using support vector machines. *Neurocomputing, 55*(1-2), 307–319. doi:10.1016/S0925-2312(03)00372-2

Kolmogoroff, A. (1941). Interpolation und extrapolation von stationaren zufalligen folgen. *Izvestiya Rossiiskoi Akademii Nauk. Seriya Matematicheskaya, 5*(1), 3–14.

Lee, C. K., Sehwan, Y., & Jongdae, J. (2007). Neural network model versus SARIMA model in forecasting Korean stock price index (KOSPI). *Issues in Information Systems*, *8*(2), 372–378.

Merh, N., Saxena, V. P., & Pardasani, K. R. (2010). A comparison between hybrid approaches of ANN and ARIMA for Indian stock trend forecasting. *Business Intelligence Journal*, *3*(2), 23–43.

Murphy, J. J. (2009). *The visual investor: how to spot market trends* (Vol. 443). John Wiley & Sons.

Nayak, R. K., Mishra, D., & Rath, A. K. (2015). A naïve SVM-KNN based stock market trend reversal analysis for Indian benchmark indices. *Applied Soft Computing*, *35*, 670–680. doi:10.1016/j.asoc.2015.06.040

Ord, K. (2004). Charles Holt's report on exponentially weighted moving averages: An introduction and appreciation. *International Journal of Forecasting*, *20*(1), 1–3. doi:10.1016/j.ijforecast.2003.09.016

Pai, P. F., & Lin, C. S. (2005). A hybrid ARIMA and support vector machines model in stock price forecasting. *Omega*, *33*(6), 497–505. doi:10.1016/j.omega.2004.07.024

Sai, Y., Yuan, Z., & Gao, K. (2007, November). Mining stock market tendency by RS-based support vector machines. In *2007 IEEE International Conference on Granular Computing (GRC 2007)* (pp. 659-659). IEEE. 10.1109/GrC.2007.104

Sterba, J., & Hilovska, K. (2010). The implementation of hybrid ARIMA neural network prediction model for aggregate water consumption prediction. *Aplimat—. Journal of Applied Mathematics*, *3*(3), 123–131.

Tay, F. E. & Cao, L. (2001). Application of support vector machines in financial time series forecasting. *Omega, 29*(4), 309-317.

Taylor, J. W. (2003). Exponential smoothing with a damped multiplicative trend. *International Journal of Forecasting*, *19*(4), 715–725. doi:10.1016/S0169-2070(03)00003-7

Wang, J. J., Wang, J. Z., Zhang, Z. G., & Guo, S. P. (2012). Stock index forecasting based on a hybrid model. *Omega*, *40*(6), 758–766. doi:10.1016/j.omega.2011.07.008

Wiener, N. (1942). The extrapolation, interpolation and smoothing of stationary time series with engineering applications: DIC Contract 6037, a research pursued on behalf of the National Defense Research Council (Section D2) at the Massachusetts Institute of Technology. Massachusetts Institute of Technology.

Wijaya, Y. B., Kom, S., & Napitupulu, T. A. (2010, December). Stock price prediction: Comparison of Arima and artificial neural network methods-an Indonesia stock's case. In *2010 Second International Conference on Advances in Computing, Control, and Telecommunication Technologies* (pp. 176-179). IEEE. 10.1109/ACT.2010.45

Zhang, G. P. (2003). Time series forecasting using a hybrid ARIMA and neural network model. *Neurocomputing*, *50*, 159–175. doi:10.1016/S0925-2312(01)00702-0

Zhang, G. P., & Qi, M. (2005). Neural network forecasting for seasonal and trend time series. *European Journal of Operational Research*, *160*(2), 501–514. doi:10.1016/j.ejor.2003.08.037

Zhou, Z. J., & Hu, C. H. (2008). An effective hybrid approach based on grey and ARMA for forecasting gyro drift. *Chaos, Solitons, and Fractals*, *35*(3), 525–529. doi:10.1016/j.chaos.2006.05.039

ENDNOTE

1 According to Taylor (2003), multiplicative exponential smoothing involves modelling the local slope by smoothing the successive ratios of the local level which leads to a forecast function that is product of level and growth rate.

Chapter 14
The Valuation of a Firm With Alternative Projects

Cem Berk
Kirklareli University, Turkey

Mustafa Dilmen
Infratech Industrial Heating Systems, Turkey

ABSTRACT

The value of a firm is equal to the value of all projects in its assets. Investment decision is taken based on expected costs, knowledge of techniques, and risk perception; all of which are parameters of firm valuation. The research in this chapter is based on a real company in the household appliance industry. The company has a factory storage in Istanbul, Turkey. Two alterative heating projects (infrared and natural gas) are developed for the storage space according to project characteristics and heating requirements. The initial investments and operating costs are determined by market prices. According to the results, electric infrared heating is most of the time more favorable when the ceiling is high. An investment decision specifically for the factory storage is made. A discussion section on results is also available. Heating and cooling is a strategic industry for European Commission. The research can guide academicians and practitioners in this field.

INTRODUCTION

Laro and Pratt (2011) point out that the first step in determining the value of a firm is to define the concept of value. Although the most relied definition is fair value, there are others such as investment value, intrinsic value, and transaction value. Fair value is defined as the current value in a market where both buyer and seller are willing and knowledgeable and they are not in a rush to buy and sell. Investment value is the value specific for an investor. Especially for firms, the value of a firm may be different for different investors due to synergy considerations. Intrinsic value is the theoretical value that is independent from market conditions and is likely to be computed by an analyst. Transaction value requires a history of previous sales where the firm or benchmark firms are sold either completely or partially.

DOI: 10.4018/978-1-7998-1086-5.ch014

According to Matschke et al. (2010) valuation is the process of determining a value for a specific valuation object for someone who is interested in the value of valuation object which is most of the time monetary. For the purposes of this book, valuation refers to firm (also called as business, or company). The valuation may be for the whole firm or for the part of it such as a facility, project or division, and shares of the company.

Mercer and Harms (2008) argue that the value of a firm can be best determined by the current value of all cash flows to the firm which are forecasted with the assumption that the firm has infinite life and discounted to today where project risks are considered.

As explained by Feldman(2005), several issues arise while valuing a private firm. Some of these include deciding which valuation technique is adequate, determining the amount of discount buyers may demand in the market, valuing affiliates, tax considerations and method to determine cost of capital.

According to Damodaran (2001) there are three approaches to valuation. The first one is discounted cash flow which is previously mentioned. The second one is relative valuation which requires the use of one / combination of multiples and benchmark firms. And the third one is contingent claim valuation where option pricing model is used.

The value of a firm is equal to the net present value of the all of the projects which it has in its assets. Kodukula and Papudesu (2006) think that project valuation is a critical process where a dollar value is determined for a project. They think that a proper project valuation require to subtract life time project costs from project revenues. The important factors for project valuation are to determine the initial and operating phase cash flows for the entire project life, discount rate, and availability of management decisions. These decisions ("real options") include deferring, abandoning, expanding, and contracting the project.

Investment decision is one of the core concepts of corporate finance. Virlics (2013) thinks that investment decision is taken based on expected costs, knowledge of techniques, and risk perception all of which are parameters of firm valuation. Investment is an allocation of resources. And since the resources are scarce, it is crucial to allocate the funds to correct project/ projects to avoid bankruptcy.

Lukashevich et al. (2018) see investment decisions as often being a selection of alternatives under constraints. In firm valuation, we have budgetary constraints among alternative projects. It may not possible to operate with multiple projects in parallel. Moreover, in some projects, accepting a project might mean rejecting the alternative because the alternative is no longer necessary to apply or there are technical constraints such as lack of space, license, equipment and staff. These projects are mutually exclusive. Therefore, the most attractive project needs to be chosen. The alternative investment projects may be selected based on a combination of capital budgeting techniques such as net present value, profitability index, internal rate of return, return on investment and payback period.

The motivation of this paper is to propose a framework for firm valuation in heating and cooling industry. Heating and cooling is a strategic industry for European Union. It consumes roughly half of the energy in EU. European commission targets demand reduction, use of renewable energy, and reduction in waste heat. This is also critical for energy supply security. There is clearly a need to renew the current systems with new energy efficient ones. In addition 75% of the resources come from fossil fuels and it is clear that decarbonization process would help meet climate change objectives. Therefore, this research can guide these new projects to be properly appraised. (European Commission, 2016)

In this study, two different heating projects are designed for the factory storage of a real-life company. The projects are alternatives and mutually exclusive. One of the projects include natural gas radiant tubular type heating while in the other electric infrared heaters are used. For the specific properties of the storage, the appropriate heaters are chosen for the projects and placing of the units is planned. The initial investments are determined for the alternatives by using the best offers in the market for several investment items. Then the operating costs which are natural gas, electricity, and maintenance costs are determined for both projects based on heating requirements and the properties of the heaters selected. Finally, alternative projects are compared based on net present values of the projects and investment decision is made.

The rest of the chapter is organized as follows. Section 2 demonstrates some of the important works available in the literature. In section 3, presentation of the research scope and net present value method are given. In Section 4, research results and investment decision is provided. Section 5 includes some discussion on research results and further decision-making criteria. Finally, in section 6, concluding remarks are given.

Background

Buying a heating equipment is an investment even if it is used at home. Capital budgeting techniques might therefore be used for the decision to buy the equipment. Mutually exclusive projects as applied in this research can also be valued with net present value. (NPV)

Wurtzebach and Waller (1983) work on energy efficient home components that generate energy cost savings. For the purchase to be financially feasible, during the life span of the equipment the present value of cost savings generated by the purchase should exceed the monetary value of the purchase. This is also known as a positive net present value project. (NPV) Mutually exclusive projects such as choosing from several efficient water heaters can also be valued with the same technique. On the other hand, according to the principle of value additivity, the value of a home which includes a positive NPV energy efficient component increases by the amount of NPV.

In the literature, there are different approaches to valuation in energy industry. Accounting information is used in firm valuation. Net book value is an accounting measure to compute the value of assets after depletion, depreciation, amortization and impairment.

According to Harris and Ohlson (1987), there may be different methods used while capitalizing exploration costs of oil and gas companies. These are full costing method and successful efforts method. However in oil and gas industry, there are uncertainties that arise due to the fact that future cash flows are not known as success of the exploration is yet to be determined. This is a well-known challenge in firm valuation in energy industry.

According to Thompson et al. (2004), there are many factors to be considered when making valuation in the energy industry. Some of these include optimization of the energy system to generate maximum net expected cash flows, energy price changes, and environmental factors.

They developed models for valuation of hydroelectric and thermal power plants. The models include optimization of the systems, such as capacity and equipment to be selected. Energy price is known to be mean reverting and might have price peaks. There are many environmental concerns including the minimum and maximum amount of water to be used.

Key performance indicators (KPI) are also used in firm valuation. It is an accounting based value showing the performance of the firm. There is no universally accepted KPI however, some are used more frequently in certain industries.

Osmundsen et al. (2006) used a KPI – RoACE for valuing international oil and gas companies. RoACE is the net revenue adjusted for minority shares and net financial items after tax as a percentage of average capital employed. Capital employed is the sum of funds collected from shareholders and net interest-bearing debt. They find that changes in valuations are explained by the changes in the price of oil, oil and gas production and reserve replacement.

The weighted average cost of capital (WACC) is known as the weighted average cost of all funds used to finance a firm's assets. These funds include shareholders' equity and liabilities. Generally, firms target projects with a return on investment (ROI) value higher than WACC. For valuation practice, due to this expectation of return, expected cash flows are often discounted by WACC.

Pierru and Babusiaux (2008) study the valuation of an international firm where different tax schemes are available for different projects. It's known that interest is tax deductible in most countries and this creates a "tax shield" effect which increases firm value. The cost of debt is therefore reduced by the amount of tax rate as a common practice in calculation of WACC. However, when there are multiple tax schemes an international company might optimize its debts according to these rates. They therefore argue that for an international company such as an oil company with multiple fields can use ATWACC (after tax weighted average cost of capital) as an improved version of WACC for valuation purposes.

The cash flow assumptions used in firm valuation are often not precise. If risk and uncertainty exist there are additional techniques that can be applied. These include sensitivity analysis, simulation, decision tree, and real options.

Ucal and Kahraman (2009) think that energy investments have special properties such as long duration, capital intensive nature, and risk and uncertainty. They conclude that fuzzy real options may be used to minimize these effects.

Real options are often used in valuation. There are some works in the field of heating valuation which use this technique. They try to model the system like financial derivatives. Because management decisions are much like options contracts. The rest of the work is then to solve the math by using options valuations techniques.

Kienzle and Anderson (2010) proposed a model with Monte Carlo simulations technique and real options method to value energy hubs. Because depending on the volatility of the market prices of energy inputs, the operation of energy hubs can be adapted. An energy hub is a system where there are multiple inputs such as electricity and natural gas and multiple outputs such as electricity, heating and cooling.

Tobin's q is a market based firm valuation technique. It is calculated by dividing market value of the firm to the replacement value of the assets. The ratio is especially high when the company has high amount of intangible assets.

Gilje and Taillard (2017) study Tobin's q as an indicator of firm value. They specifically work on the relationship between hedging and firm value. Hedging can be achieved by obtaining financial derivatives. Basis risk can exist in this process which is the difference between the price of underlying asset and the actual asset. They find that as a result of basis risks, firms tend to sell assets, reduce investments, and lower financial leverage.

MAIN FOCUS OF THE CHAPTER

Presentation of the Scope of the Research

This study is based on X household appliance company which was established in 2001 in Istanbul, Turkey. The company is one of the leading brands in Turkey. For confidential reasons the company will be mentioned as X company in the rest of this research.

X Company has a daily production capacity of 25.000 units and a total facility space of 55.000 m^2 around the World. The company has 350 staff members.

The heating Project will take place in a prefabricated area of 1.300 m^2. The place has a width of 23, 33 m, length of 55, 79 m and height of 9 m. The place is previously inadequately heated by local electric heaters.

The building is prefabricated, the ceiling is high, the area to be heated is large and the doors are open due to loading and unloading which lead to losses of heat. The investment decision is to choose from industrial infrared electric and natural gas heaters.

The heating project will take place in the factory storage the properties of which is previously mentioned. There are 40 staff members working in the building. The building is facing the south. The sketch of the project area where the local heating investment will take place is given in Figure 1.

In this study two different projects are developed for the heating of this building. The alternative projects are natural gas heating and electric heating. For each of the projects, the amount and type of the heaters are determined. The initial investment and operating costs are obtained by the best offers of the suppliers in the market. These costs are then discounted with net present value method. Investment decision is made based on these results.

Net Present Value Method

As mentioned in the background section of this paper, there are several methods used in valuing energy firms. These include capital budgeting techniques such as internal rate of return, payback period and profitability index.

The firm analyzed in this chapter has two mutually exclusive projects. An important consideration is which method to choose in valuing the firm. The decision is straightforward in this case since net present value method is known to be superior when mutually exclusive projects exist.

Net present value – NPV (also called discounted cash flow – DCF) is the most common technique used in firm valuation. Most of the time NPV is required before contingent valuation. Therefore, understanding fundamentals of the technique is crucial in applying different techniques of valuation.

Figure 1. Sketch of the factory storage

The formula for NPV used in firm valuation is given below. As indicated by Damadoran (2011), the value of firm is calculated by the present value of cash flows generated by the firm. A company has three types of cash flows which are operating, investment, and financing. For firm valuation purposes, only cash flows related to operating and investment and taxes are used in this phase. The discount factor is WACC – weighted average cost of capital. N indicates number of years in which cash flows are generated.

$$Value\ of\ Firm = \sum_{t=1}^{t=N} \frac{CF\ to\ firm\ t}{(1+WACC)^t}$$

In order to effectively describe how net present value is calculated the famous machine question of Fisher (1907) can be asked in a different way. Because this illustration of Fischer for machine valuation, is today common practice for firm valuation. This technique is also used as the method of this study.

An investor wants to yield 5% interest from an investment of 10 machines each of which generates \$ 100 income annually. The cost of renewal for all machines per year is the cost of one machine which is \$ 772. What should be the price investor needs to pay for buying the machines? The answer turns out to be \$ 4.556. Because net income divided by interest gives the investment required. (\$ 100 * 10- \$ 772) / 5% = \$ 4.556

The mathematical proof is available in the reference for readers who are interested. But what is more interesting for valuation purposes is why this result happens to be \$ 4.556.

One of the machines is new and will generate the return for the next 10 years. The next machine has a life of 9 years. Decreasing in the same trend, the duration of the last machine is one year. So the answer to the question of the amount of the investment required should be exactly equal to the income generated by this machines which is calculated by the net present value under the 5% target return.

The net present value is the present value of return generated and notated by "a" discounted by interest rate "i "for next year, that is a / (1 +i). Note that 1 is used in the formula to indicate that interest is invested together with principle to generate return during the life of investment. The next year the present value of return a would be a / (1 +i) 2. And in the final year the present value of the income is a / (1 +i) m where m is the investment duration. Note that the denominator is increasing over time to reflect time value of money.

The value of the machine in our example may be computed with the following Net Present Value (NPV) formula. v_1 in the formula is the NPV for the machine.

$$V_1 = \frac{a}{(1+i)^1} + \frac{a}{(1+i)^2} + \ldots + \frac{a}{(1+i)^{m-1}} + \frac{a}{(1+i)^m}$$

The income generated in this example is constant, allowing a special technique called annuity. However, the income might be different for different years as in this research. The same formulation will be valid except the annuity notated by "a" will be different each year. That would be a more generalized case of this specific example.

Returning to the example, the income of the first machine is computed with the following formula.

$$V_1 = \frac{100}{(1+0,05)^1} + \frac{100}{(1+0,05)^2} + \ldots + \frac{100}{(1+0,05)^9} + \frac{100}{(1+0,05)^{10}}$$

This can be computed to obtain \$ 772. One needs to compute all 10 terms to obtain the result. Note that for the second machine there will be 9 terms that is the project life of the project. (m=9) The last term which is 100 / (1+0,05) 10 would disappear. For the third machine m=8 and it would decrease so on.

Once again since this is a special case, for the ease of calculation annuity formula, table, spreadsheet or calculator can also be used. And the summation of the net present income of all machines gives the required investment of \$ 4.556. (\$772 + \$711 + \$646 + \$578 + \$508 + \$433 + \$355 +272 + \$186 +\$95)

SOLUTIONS AND RECOMMENDATIONS

Valuation of the Natural Gas Heating

The quantity and type of heaters are determined by m^2 area to be heated in natural gas radiant heating systems. For the factory storage of the X Company, 55kW – BH55 ST type heater is chosen. This is a tubular type radiant heater appropriate for 1.300 m^2 space.

Each heater has a capacity of 300 m^2 area heating. Therefore 5 BH55 ST natural gas radiant heaters are required. They consume 5, 73 Nm^3/h of natural gas and 500 W electricity per hour. The length of the heater is 19 m. The placing of the heaters in the project area is designed and shown in plan view in Figure 2.

The amount of investment required for the natural gas heating units and installation is given in Table 1. The investment amount is determined by the best offers of the major companies in the market. Accordingly, the natural gas heating project requires an initial investment of € 10.380.

The current natural gas price is TL 0, 09088778 (Turkish Lira) /kWh. 1 m3 is roughly equal to 10 kW. As mentioned above each BH 55 ST natural gas tubular radiant heater consumes 5.73 m^3/h of natural gas. Therefore for 5 units, an hourly natural gas operating cost of TL 28,65 is required. The devices operate 10 hours actively during the day considering heating requirements. This is a daily natural gas consumption of TL 286, 67. For 6 months heating, and 20 working days per month, the annual natural gas operating cost is TL 34.400 or € 7.013.

Each heating unit consumes 500 Watt / hour electricity. Since there are 5 devices, an hourly electricity consumption of 2,5 kW is required. For 10 hours heating requirement / day and 6 months heating an annual electricity consumption of 3.000 kW/ year is required. The electricity price is TL 0,2532/ kWh. Therefore, an annual electricity consumption of TL 759,6 or € 154,87 is required.

Figure 2. Industrial Radiant Natural Gas Heater Placing

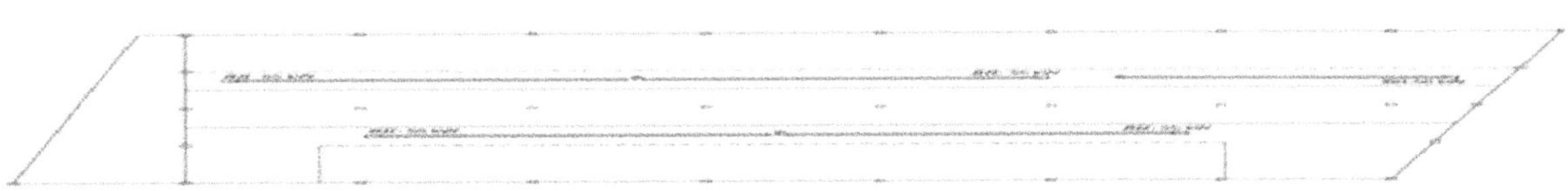

Table 1. Calculation of Investment Required

1.	Initial Investment (EURO)	Unit Price	Amount	Total Price
1.1.	Heating Device	1.400,00	5	7.000,00
1.2.	Control Panel	250,00	1	250,00
1.3.	Flue Exit Set	110,00	3	330,00
1.4.	Installation	500,00	1	500,00
1.5.	Electrical Installation	300,00	1	300,00
1.6.	Connection Hose	30,00	5	150,00
1.7.	Project Fees	1.850,00	1	1.850,00
Total Investment (EURO)				10.380,00

Each device requires an annual maintenance of TL 300. Therefore for 5 heaters, an annual maintenance cost of TL 1.500 or € 305, 82 is required.

The discount rate can be computed as the summation of risk-free rate and risk premium. Eurobond periodic interest with a duration of 7 years for the Republic of Turkey is 3, 25%. A risk premium of 1% is applied for the project. The discount rate is therefore computed as 4, 25%.

As shown in Table 2, annual operating cost is obtained as the summation of natural gas, electric consumption and maintenance costs. Annual operating cost for the first operating year is 7.013,39 + 154, 87 + 305, 81 = € 7.474,08. The operating cost for the following years is computed with an assumption of 1% annual inflation rate. The net present value of operating costs is € 45.728,44. The total lifetime cost of the natural gas heating project including the initial investment is € 56.108,44.

$$NPV = \frac{7.474,08}{(1+k_i)^1} + \frac{7.548,82}{(1+k_i)^2} + \frac{7.624,31}{(1+k_i)^3} + \frac{7.700,55}{(1+k_i)^4} + \frac{7.777,55}{(1+k_i)^5} + \frac{7.855,33}{(1+k_i)^6} + \frac{7.933,88}{(1+k_i)^7}$$

$$NPV = \frac{7.474,08}{(1+0,0425)^1} + \frac{7.548,82}{(1+0,0425)^2} + \frac{7.624,31}{(1+0,0425)^3} + \frac{7.700,55}{(1+0,0425)^4} + \frac{7.777,55}{(1+0,0425)^5} + \frac{7.855,33}{(1+0,0425)^6} + \frac{7.933,88}{(1+0,0425)^7}$$

NPV = € 45.728,44 + € 10.380,00 = € 56.108,44.

Valuation of the Electric Heating

In electric infrared electric heating, the type and amount of heaters are determined by the m^2 area of the space to be heated. The space where heating system will be applied is 1.300 m2. When technical properties of the electric infrared heaters are considered IR-CH90 9 kW heater model is chosen as the heater of the project.

Table 2. Cash Flow for Natural Gas Heating Project

	t=0	Year 1	Year 2	Year 3	Year 4	Year 5	Year 6	Year 7
1. Initial Investment (EUR)	10.380,00							
2. Operating Cost (EUR)		7.474,08	7.548,82	7.624,31	7.700,55	7.777,55	7.855,33	7.933,88
2.1. Natural Gas Consumption		7.013,39	7.083,53	7.154,36	7.225,91	7.298,17	7.371,15	7.444,86
2.2. Electricity Consumption		154,87	156,41	157,98	159,56	161,15	162,77	164,39
2.3. Maintenance Cost		305,8166	308,87	311,96	315,08	318,23	321,42	324,63

Figure 3. Industrial Electric Heater Placing

Each heater has a 90 m^2 area heating capacity. Therefore 13 IR-CH90 are planned to be placed in the factory storage as in Figure 3. Each heater consumes 9 kW/h electric energy per hour.

The initial investment includes several equipment and installation. The prices of these are determined by choosing the best offers in the market. The amount of initial investment required is € 5.250. The calculation of the investment is presented in Table 3.

The major operating cost of the industrial electric heater is the cost of electric energy. Each device consumes 9kW/h electric energy per hour. The total electric energy consumption for the 13 devices in an hour is therefore 117 kW/h. For 10 hours of heating in a day, daily electric energy consumption is 1.170 kW/day. As mentioned in the valuation of the natural gas heating, electric price is 0, 2532/ kW/h.

Daily energy consumption is therefore TL 296, 24. For 20 working days / month and 6 months working, the operating cost of electricity is TL 5.924,88 / month, and TL 35.549,28 / year or € 7.247,71.

Another operating cost for electric heating is maintenance. Each IR-CH90 industrial infrared electric heater has TL 80 cost of maintenance / year. This is an annual cost of TL 1.040 for 13 heaters or € 212, 03.

Annual total operating cost is computed as the summation of electric cost and maintenance cost. So the operating cost for the first operating year is 7.247,71 + 212, 03 = € 7.459,74. Cash flow for the electric heating project is given in Table 4. The operating cost for the following years are computed under the

Table 3. Calculation of the Investment Required

1.	Initial Investment (EURO)	Unit Price	Amount	Total Price
1.1.	Industrial Type Electric Heater- 9 kW- CH-IR 90	250,00	13	3.250,00
1.2.	Electrical Installation	1.000,00	1	1.000,00
1.3.	Control Panel	500,00	1	500,00
1.4.	Installation	500,00	1	500,00
Total Cost (EURO)				5.250,00

Table 4. Cash Flow for the Electric Heating Project

	t=0	Year 1	Year 2	Year 3	Year 4	Year 5	Year 6	Year 7
1. Initial Investment (EUR)	5.250,00							
2. Operating Cost (EUR)		7.459,74	7.534,34	7.609,68	7.685,78	7.762,64	7.840,26	7.918,66
2.1. Electricity Consumption		7.247,71	7.320,18	7.393,39	7.467,32	7.541,99	7.617,41	7.693,59
2.2. Maintenance Cost		212,0329	214,15	216,29	218,46	220,64	222,85	225,08

assumption of 1% annual inflation rate. Net present value of the operating costs when discounted with 4, 25% as in the valuation of the natural gas heating section of this study is € 45.670,72. The total lifetime cost for the electric infrared heating system including the initial investment is therefore € 50.890,72.

$$\text{NPV} = \frac{7.459,74}{(1+k_i)^1} + \frac{7.534,34}{(1+k_i)^2} + \frac{7.609,68}{(1+k_i)^3} + \frac{7.685,78}{(1+k_i)^4} + \frac{7.762,64}{(1+k_i)^5} + \frac{7.840,26}{(1+k_i)^6} + \frac{7.918,66}{(1+k_i)^7}$$

$$\text{NPV} = \frac{7.459}{(1+0,0425)^1} + \frac{7.534}{(1+0,0425)^2} + \frac{7.609}{(1+0,0425)^3} + \frac{7.685}{(1+0,0425)^4} + \frac{7.762}{(1+0,0425)^5} + \frac{7.840}{(1+0,0425)^6} + \frac{7.918}{(1+0,0425)^7};$$

NPV = € 45.640,72 + € 5.250 =€ 50.890,72.

Investment Decision

Two projects are developed for the heating of the factory storage of the X Company. The projects are mutually exclusive. In other words, only one of them can be applied. Therefore, the project with better capital budgeting results should be preferred. The capital budgeting technique used in this study is net present value.

The projects have two main components. These are initial investment and operating costs. The operating costs are close to each other; net present value of € 45.728,44 for the natural gas heating project and € 45.640,72 for the electric heating project. It should also be noted that roughly 94% of the natural gas heating operating costs is natural gas cost which is a fossil fuel. Whereas for the electric heating project roughly 98% of the operating costs are electric energy costs which may be generated by renewable energy sources.

Although out of scope of this study, these types of voluntary emission reductions may result in direct and indirect cash returns to the firm which reduces the carbon emissions often through governmental incentives, market-based solutions and public relations efforts. This might sometimes be a factor in investment decision.

For the initial investment, there is a dramatic difference. Investment is € 10.380 for natural gas heating project and €5.250 for the electric heating project. Therefore, total net present values of investment required are € 56.108,44 for natural gas heating project and € 50.890,72 for electric project. This is a potential € 5.217,72 of cost saving and more 10% of difference in NPV of these projects. Therefore, electric infrared heating system should be preferred over the alternative project of natural gas radiant tubular heating. More considerations are given in the following section.

DISCUSSION

Methodological Discussion

The method used in this chapter is Net Present Value. The method is the most reliable when comparing mutually exclusive projects as in this chapter. However, one should be aware that in different valuations where there are not mutually exclusive projects other methods could be more reliable.

According to Milis et al. (2009), payback period measures the time required for the cash flows to cover initial costs of the investment. According to the authors this is the least reliable technique. Because this would lead to the selection of projects with fast payback while disregarding those with long project duration. Considering most energy investments have long project duration, this method may not be very effective for the industry.

Internal rate of return is the discount rate computed when cash inflows are to equal cash outflows. This is an improvement because this is a dynamic method where time value of money is considered and is suitable with long project durations. However, there are still some weaknesses. The result of the method is a percentage which makes it difficult to compare projects with different size and time pattern. Most importantly, when mutually exclusive projects exist, due to the inability to determine discount rate project risks cannot accurately be reflected in valuation.

Finally, it should be noted that net present value is accurate if assumptions are correctly determined. The assumptions are cash flow to the firm, discount rate and appraisal period. Note that in this study cash flows are determined by using real market prices and using escalations when needed, discount rate computation is given and appraisal period is based on economic life of the equipment.

Project Discussion

There are three electric lamps all of which has 3kW power within each 9kW industrial electric infrared heater. This embodies a cost saving potential due to the ability to operate each of them separately. These lamps also have different wave lengths which results in different surface heat and reaction times. The use of short wavelength halogen infrared lamps may result in energy efficiency.

Contrary to central heating, combi type singular natural gas heating, electric infrared heating systems are effective in local heating. The heaters might be turned off in the places that aren't used or that heating is not required.

Infrared heaters can be activated in the region to be heated, and they have the potential to heat the specific region locally within 3-5 minutes where the light is effective. In addition, the electric heaters are easily installed, and upon demand can be deinstalled and reinstalled to where they are needed. For this no project drawings, costs and official permits are required.

Power control is not fully applicable in natural gas radiant heating systems where the ceiling is high. Long wave heating property of the systems requires time to reach the target heating level. Energy consumption in this period should also be considered.

As seen in the results of our study, natural gas heating systems generally have higher initial investment and installation costs than electric heating systems. The deinstallation and reinstallation of natural gas radiant systems is more difficult and takes time when compared to electric infrared heating systems. Yet, this requires project drawings and official permits.

In addition, some natural gas radiant heating systems with no fluke gives the excess gas to the place to be heated which is harmful for human health and environment.

Despite these factors natural gas radiant heating systems have energy cost advantage in buildings with low ceiling and good insulation when compared to electric infrared heating systems.

The decision for heating systems have many choosing criteria such as geographical conditions, ceiling height, building insulation, roof insulation, number of doors and windows, and whether there is air flow inside.

Additional criteria might include the properties of the place to be heated, the requirements of the users, installation and operating costs, energy costs, sustainability and availability of energy, whether it is environmentally friendly, not harmful for human health and safety, easily applicable to the place to be heated, appropriate for decorative concerns, guarantee period, availability of maintenance service, cost and quality of spare parts.

FUTURE RESEARCH DIRECTIONS

Determining the assumptions correctly is key for an accurate valuation model. However, this is not always easy in a dynamic industry. As Vorsatz et al. (2015) point out, there are incentives in the heating and cooling industry which promote efficiency gains. In addition, firms tend to decrease their energy costs by renewing their heating and cooling projects. However, in some workplaces, the temperature is not comfortable. Therefore, despite improvements in unit energy costs, total energy costs may not decrease for these cases.

In addition, heating and cooling energy consumption may not remain constant which is a consideration in valuing these projects. The increases in GDP tend to increase energy consumption. However, efficiency gains and tendency to work in smaller areas should be considered in future research.

The viability of models in this field can be maintained by a careful consideration of the factors above. The valuation in this chapter considers both current and future expected energy consumption. The equipment and installation costs are determined by the best offers in the market. Researchers are encouraged to check the prices by the time of their research. The actual natural gas and electricity prices and future changes also need to be forecasted. There may be also possible changes in the required heating and cooling levels through the life of the project. The Eurobond price is also obtained as an indicator for cost of capital. This market price should also be obtained for future research.

For further research, valuation for externalities can be included. It is a known fact that the carbon emissions generated by the industry constitutes a burden for the environment. These effects can be quantified and analyzed in valuation. On the other hand, there are also some cases where companies generate extra income by the emission reductions which might be considered in future research.

CONCLUSION

As explained by Pinto et al. (2010) valuation process include analyzing the firm, financial statements, and other disclosures, creating a pro forma budget, choosing the valuation model, preparing the valuation and decision making.

Koller et al. (2010) explain drivers of value. In firm valuation, value is created when discounted cash flows (DCF) increase. Therefore, the value is created when there is a positive difference between the discounted value of cash invested and cost of investment. In other words, value is created by a sustainable increase in ROIC – return on invested capital and revenue.

As Graham (2016) suggests investors need to be aware of risks. If a bond issuing company have debts of $ 10 billion and they have $ 30 billion, there is a margin of safety of $20 billion before the bondholders would suffer a loss. Similarly, we know in firm valuation that there is a probability that expected cash flows might not be realized. Therefore as a safety margin, a risk premium is included within the discount rate in valuation.

The literature review shows that in the field of energy and particularly in heating valuation, one needs to consider optimization of the system before the actual valuation. Therefore in this research, the place to be heated is modelled with two alternative projects. These projects are developed with real life products and costs which are best applicable to the project. A quick generalization of the research results in this respect is that when the ceiling is high, electric infrared systems are preferred over natural gas heating. Conversely, when ceiling is low natural gas may be preferred.

Many inputs of the valuation can be categorized in two major groups. These are initial investment and operational costs. For most of the cases, initial investment for electric infrared systems are lower than that of the natural gas heating projects. However, the operating costs vary based on the project characteristics.

Two alternative projects are designed and valued in this study. The total costs of natural gas project (€ 56.108) is higher than that of electric heating project. (€ 50.891) The investment decision is electric project for this case which also brings renewable energy production potential as an additional environmental gain.

A procedure for design of the project based on area and heating and cooling requirements is given. The computation of various initial and operating costs is discussed. There is a need to use actual prices by using market offers for equipment and installation and energy costs. The market rate of Eurobond is also obtained for the research. The possible changes in these variables should also be considered for valuation.

Heating and cooling industry is one of the strategic areas chosen by European Commission to battle against climate change. Due to the incentives in this field, many projects are expected to be developed. This research might help academicians and practitioners in this field on how to properly develop and value companies in the industry.

REFERENCES

Damodaran, A. (2001). *Investment valuation*. Wiley.

European Commission. (2016). Overview of support activities and projects of the European Union on energy efficiency and renewable energy in the heating & cooling sector, *Horizon 2020, Framework Programme 7 and Intelligent Energy Europe programmes of the European Union,* 2.

Feldman, S. J. (2005). *Principles of private firm valuation.* Wiley.

Fisher, I. (1907). *The rate of interest: its nature, determination and relation to economic phenomena.* MacMillan Company.

Gilje, E. P., & Taillard, J. P. (2017). Does hedging affect firm value? evidence from a natural experiment. *Review of Financial Studies, 30*(12), 4122. doi:10.1093/rfs/hhx069

Graham, B. (2016). *The intelligent investor.* Harper Business Essentials.

Harris, T. S., & Ohlson, J. A. (1987). Accounting disclosures and the market's valuation of oil and gas properties. *The Accounting Review, 62*(4), 654.

Kienzle, F., & Andersson, G. (2010). Location-dependent valuation of energy hubs with storage in multi-carrier energy systems, *IEEE, Conference Paper,* 6.

Kodukula, P. & Chandra, P. (2006). *Project valuation using real options: a practitioner's guide.* J. Ross.

Koller, T., Goedhart, M., & Wessels, D. (2010). *Valuation: measuring and managing the value of companies.* McKinsey Company.

Laro, D., & Pratt, S. P. (2011). *Business valuation and federal taxes: procedure, law and perspective.* Wiley.

Lukashevich, N., Svirina, A., & Granin, D. (2018). Multilevel prognosis of logistics chains in case of uncertainty: information and statistical technologies implementation. *Journal of Open Innovation: Technology, Market, and Complexity, 4*(2), 4.

Matschke, M. J., Brosel, G., & Matschke, X. (2010). Fundamentals of functional business valuation. *Journal of Business Valuation and Economic Loss Analysis, 5*(1), 3.

Mercer, Z. C., & Harms, T. W. (2008). *Business valuation: an integrated theory.* Wiley.

Milis, K., Snoeck, M., & Haesen, R. (2009). *Evaluation of the applicability of investment appraisal techniques for assessing the business value of IS services.* Katholieke Universiteit Leuven. doi:10.2139srn.1517656

Osmundsen, P., Asche, F., Misund, B., & Mohn, K. (2006). Valuation of international oil companies. *Energy Journal,* 53.

Pierru, A. & Babusiaux, D. (2008). Valuation of investment projects by an international oil company: a new proof of a straightforward rigorous method, *OPEC Energy Review,* 197.

Thompson, M., Davison, M., & Rasmussen, H. (2004). Valuation and optimal operation of electric power plants in competitive markets. *Operations Research, 52*(4), 561. doi:10.1287/opre.1040.0117

Ucal, I., & Kahraman, C. (2009). Fuzzy real options valuation for oil investments. *Baltic Journal of Sustainability, 15*(4), 653.

Virlics, A. (2013). Investment decision making and risk. *Procedia Economics and Finance*, *6*, 170. doi:10.1016/S2212-5671(13)00129-9

Vorsatz, D. U., Cabeza, L. F., Serrano, S., Barreneche, C., & Petrichenko, K. (2015). Heating and cooling energy trends and drivers in buildings. *Renewable & Sustainable Energy Reviews*, *41*, 97.

Wurtzebach, C. H., & Waller, N. G. (1983). The feasibility, underwriting, and valuation of residential energy components. *The Appraisal Journal*, 68.

Chapter 15
Valuation of Logistics Hubs:
A Case Study From Turkey

Musa Gün
https://orcid.org/0000-0002-5020-9342
Recep Tayyip Erdogan University, Turkey

ABSTRACT

Logistics structures playing significant roles in the economic development of countries are irreversible investments. The exact valuation of them could be difficult due to various uncertainties and problems. This chapter illustrates a methodological way to be able to make an investment decision about the creation of a logistics hub in Of-Iyidere region. Under given assumptions, the study findings indicate that (1) the investment has a positive net present value under three different cost of capital rates, which are 7.5%, 10%, and 15%; (2) the internal rate of return is 18.5%; (3) the payback period is 7 years 8 months; and (4) the discounted payback periods are calculated as 10 years 1 month, 11 years 3 months, and 14 years 11 months according to the aforementioned cost of capital rates. Moreover, the chapter discusses basic project valuation challenges and presents solutions to improve the practice of logistics hub appraisal. So, the paper exhibits an essential guidance and policy support tool to highlight the potential of logistics hub infrastructures in Turkey.

INTRODUCTION AND BACKGROUND

According to the data of Clarksons Research, which is the world's leading provider of integrated shipping services, on average 80 percent of the world trade is realized by maritime transport (Clarksons Research, 2019). There are several participants in the sector and the flow of funds constitutes an essential share for the world trade. In the sector where the risks are high, making the right investments at the right time is the most important key to success in the market. From this perspective, among the developing countries, Turkey connects the centers of production and consumption since it takes place in the most geographically and economically convenient location where it is close to many countries and borders. To be able to benefit from this important advantage, there is a need for logistics hub center where many

DOI: 10.4018/978-1-7998-1086-5.ch015

integrated logistics activities such as transportation, distribution, storage, handling, export, import, and transit trade could be carried out easily. Similar to the world trade transport data, approximately 85 percent of Turkey's foreign trade is transported by sea (Turkish Chamber of Shipping, 2018). The great proportion of maritime transport in trade has constituted a source of motivation for this study. The high share of maritime transport within the trade volume as well as the specific risks of the sector show that the logistics hubs and ports where sea transportation is carried out should be subject to special consideration and valuation.

Palšaitis and Bazaras (2004) and Europlatforms (2004) define the logistics centers as the hub of a specific region where all logistics activities related to transport and distribution both for national and international transit are carried out on a commercial basis by various operators. These activities may include many integrated services such as storage, handling, consolidation, decomposition, customs clearance, export, import and transit operations, infrastructure services, insurance and banking, consultancy, and production. Starting from the local scale, the logistics center can be a regional, international and global center of attraction as far as its technical and legal infrastructures and geographical locations permit this. Turkey could be considered as a regional transportation project area in this context. However, global developments and inter-country economic cooperation have made countries face serious competition in world markets. In this fierce competition environment, both the countries and the enterprises need to make new capital investments in order to be successful and to survive. Therefore, especially in developing countries such as Turkey, capital investments will be a natural extension of these developments in the future.

The most important step in the development of trade relations between the European Union (EU) Countries and Central Asia and the Caucasus is the transportation corridor. In 1993, EU Commission - via the Brussels Declaration- has started to implement the Transport Corridor Europe-Caucasus-Asia (TRACECA) project, *an international transport program involving the European Union and 14 member States of the Eastern European, Caucasian and Central Asian region*, in order to strengthen the trade and transportation of Azerbaijan, Armenia, Georgia, Kazakhstan, Kyrgyzstan, Tajikistan, Turkmenistan and Uzbekistan to integrate them with the international economy. On 8 September 1998, the project started with the approval by the State Parliament of total 12 countries including Turkey, Ukraine, Moldova, Romania, and Bulgaria. The accomplishment of this project aiming at the development of trade and transportation systems in order to improve the cooperation between countries depends primarily on the realization of international issues such as international road, air transportation, railway and sea transportation systems, traffic prominence, environmental sensitivity, transportation security, and competitiveness in the transfer of goods.

The western part of Turkey, which is located at the center position of this transportation corridor, has the required size and the capacity in terms of maritime transport. However, both the Ministry of Transport and Infrastructure data and the analyses carried out within the scope of TRACECA project reveal the need for an alternative port and logistics center to the ports of Batum and Sochi in the eastern part of this transportation corridor. With the completion of the Baku-Tbilisi-Kars railway, Ovit connection tunnel and Rize-Erzurum road by the end of 2016, both the east-west and north-south axes will provide a national and international transport corridor. The Of-Iyidere watershed, located on the TRACECA transit route, will be the opening point of the region with the Batumi-Samsun railway project. In 2013, in this respect, the Turkish Ministry of Environment and Urbanization has declared Of-Iyidere region, which is located on the border of Rize and Trabzon, as a special project area for the establishment of a logistics center area including a port logistics hub. Undoubtedly, these expectations and developments increased the importance of capital investments. The use of the right methods and criteria in the valuation of capital investments will be an important factor in the realization of the objectives of the economy and enterprises. The increasing importance of capital investments has become a specific area of academic discipline. In other words, the project valuation has begun to be dealt with especially in academic programs as a subject of specialization in recent years.

Logistics transport structures are key components of the national asset portfolio. The role of ports has taken several different forms and development paths. Transport structures are irreversible investments and require long-time commitment maintenance and operation. In most of the cases, the decision to invest in transport structure is not simple, mainly, because of the complications in the planning process, the high amount of capital needed to invest, and a large number of stakeholders involving in the decision-making process. The decision-making process is more complicated in large transport structure projects, where the project sustainability is strongly related to financial viability as well as economic development prospects in medium and long terms. Therefore, these projects should be dealt with in detail and be carefully analyzed. Within this context, this study aims to examine and implement the valuation techniques on the basis of the Of-Iyidere logistics hub project. A model has been developed to calculate the value of the investment by using the discounted cash flow approach which is is a widely used valuation method based on future expectations. In this regard, another goal of the study is to present a projection to the market actors and the decision-makers, as well as to contribute to the literature by providing a broad perspective to academicians and researchers. In addition, the paper discusses some specific challenges as an issue in many studies like Pawlik et al. (2011), Beresford et al. (2012), Bergqvist et al. (2016), and Dimitriou (2018) confronted with the valuation of logistics hubs and ports. According to a systematic approach, the analysis framework where the valuation issues are tackled and the key messages to the decision-makers are addressed in this study. The study does not just present a pure valuation but also it provides a systematic approach to policymakers, academics, and other researchers about a specific subject such as logistics hub. The lack of the systematic approach hinders the processes of logistics hub implementation. The contribution of the paper, therefore, is essential not only for academia but also for the business world. Furthermore, the topic examined exhibits an essential guidance and policy support tool to highlight the logistics hub infrastructures potential and demonstrates a vision on the future development of logistics in Turkey.

The structure of this chapter is organized as follows. After, the introductory and background section, the paper provides a broad discussion of the topic incorporating difficulties and remedies under the heading of the challenges and solutions in the valuation of logistics projects. The next section presents the methodological framework. Then, the author performs the valuation of the sample project in detail covering load estimation, initial investment cost, operating expenses and income, and application of the valuation methods on the predicted cash flows. And lastly, the study ends with the findings and recommendations for future research directions.

CHALLENGES AND SOLUTIONS IN VALUATION OF LOGISTICS PROJECTS

The transportation sector not only makes significant contributions to the economic growth, but also requires building operational productivity, efficient infrastructure, and services (Dimitriou et al., 2015; Macharis and Bernardini, 2015; Dimitriou, 2018). It seems impossible for public or private organizations or entrepreneurs to invest especially in the capital-intensive projects without making a feasibility study in an environment under tight budget constraints where resources are scarce. Making investment decisions in transportation projects such as logistics hub is often not a simple and easy process. The challenges in the planning phase, the determination of the logistics area, the course of actions to be carried out before the detection of the amount of capital to be invested, and a large number of stakeholders involved in this process are the factors that make the valuation process and investment decision difficult. The decision-making process becomes complicated by the size of the transportation project (Beresford et al., 2012). The sustainability, implementation, and financially feasibility of the project depends on the prospects and developments in the medium and long terms. In this regard, this paper tries to present a methodological approach to be able to make strategic decisions including investment decision about the creation of a logistics hub in Of-Iyidere region.

Valuation of large transportation structures, such as logistics hubs, includes the rationale for the construction of the project, strategic issues, cost-benefit analysis, risks and uncertainties, financial sustainability, and economic impact of the project (Crescenzi and Rodríguez, 2012). Therefore, investors and other stakeholders focus on these different constituents in the decision-making process in order to be able to invest in a transport project (Bergqvist et al., 2016). Dimitriou and Sartzetaki (2016) analytically conceptualize this process by illustrating the dynamic behaviors, uncertainties, and interdependencies of these constituents as shown in Figure 1 below.

Considering concrete steps across the investment decision-making process of a project can be an influential approach to make it more resilient and more profitable for all stakeholders. The decision-making process for investing in large transportation projects is conceived as a multi-parameter analysis

Figure 1. Phases in the decision-making process
Source: Dimitriou and Sartzetaki, 2016

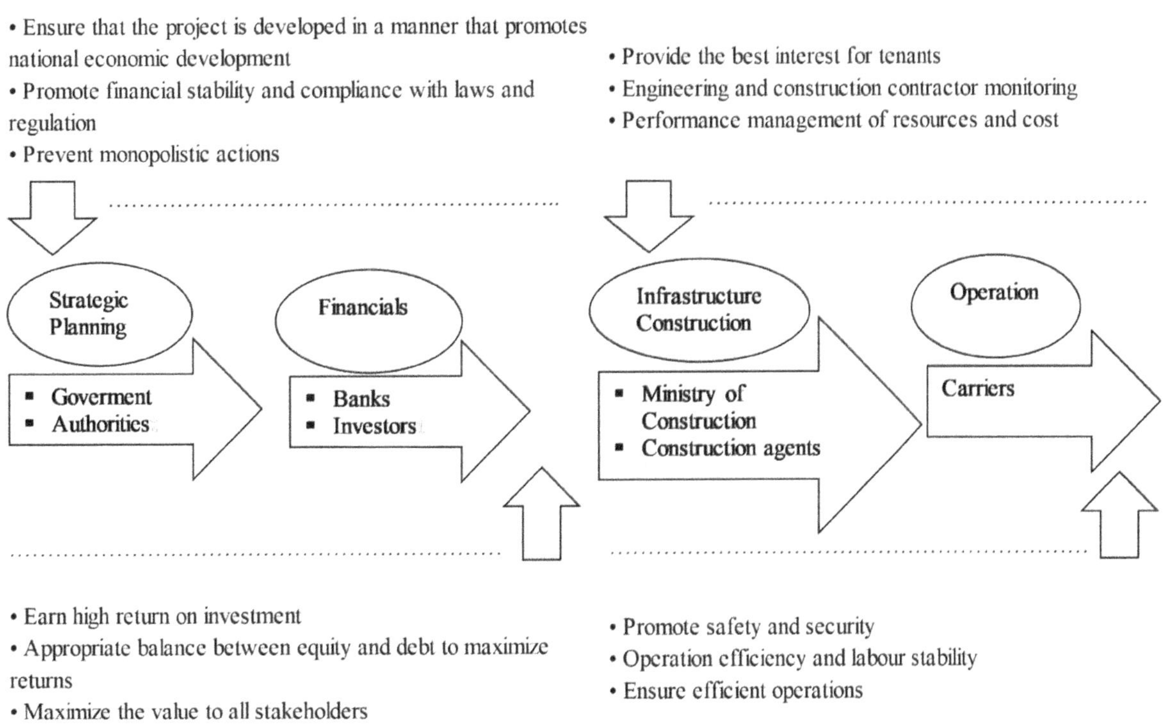

with the undermentioned subtitles. Within the scope of project valuation, it is of course not possible to be able to produce solutions to all the challenges that are put forward in the case of a logistics hub in this limited preparatory work. Nevertheless, possible solutions have been tried to offer in light of the suggestions provided by both the academic literature and business applications.

Strategic Planning

Strategic planning comprises project development with precise forecasts and assumptions on the essential variables including demand, prices, earnings, capital and other expenditures, and external factors for the project feasibility. According to Dimitriou and Sartzetaki (2016), basically, governments and project appraisers are responsible parties for the consideration of strategic planning. In addition, the responsible parties should also maintain alternative plans for possible volatility and adverse scenarios. On the other hand, planning and management of possible joint risks stem from early-stage decisions regarding project structures and design could be expressed as other challenges that should be struggled against. In this stage, all prospective risks that could be faced by contractors and investors should be born in mind.

Employing a risk-based viewpoint probably offers a systematic framework which helps the decision-making process to be easier. Particularly, planning stages of large transport construction projects such as logistics hub centers are the processes that need serious efforts to identify, qualify and measure the risks which may be encountered both during the completion and subsequent economic life of the projects. Government authorities and project specialists should take care not to ignore any adverse circumstances and scenarios that could seriously damage the success of the projects. The aim of a project valuation that will cover all possible risks is to create processes for investors and other decision-makers to be able to choose the most appropriate investment option. In such a way, the most favorable investment decision should include the choices that provide the desired profit for investors and contribute to regional and national economic development. On the whole, the cash flows obtained in this preliminary study and various cost of capital rates reflect all possible assumptions, the work of the technical expert team in the field, various scenario analyzes, load estimations, and projections for the future. Briefly, the cash flows and discount rates are the results of all activities subject to the strategic plan. The findings of the study in this direction provide practical guidance to the decision-makers and investors.

Strategic planning should also take the location selection into account for the establishment of logistics hubs. Location determination is the selection of the most suitable area for the investment to be made. When it is considered the various studies such as Lee et al., 2009; Li et al., 2011; Feng et al., 2013; Ünal and Derindere Köseoğlu, 2014 on the logistics hub, it can be summarized that the decision of location selection is a long-term strategic planning process which includes the size, geographical location, number of the logistics facilities, and also which requires macro and micro perspectives. In the macro analysis, the geographic location of the logistics hub is examined. The number, size, and location of the required facilities are determined with the participation of senior managers by taking into account the customer service level and logistical costs. In the macro analysis, the location is selected by considering the positioning according to market, product or both market and product. On the other hand, qualitative and quantitative factors such as transportation cost, proximity to customers, suppliers or customs, land and construction costs, zoning status, expropriation risk, proximity to the current and future main transportation roads, land topography and ground characteristics, infrastructure facilities, ease of access of personnel, traffic density, climate (altitude, dominant wind facing the road), expansion possibility, taxes and incentives, and environmental impacts are taken into consideration in the microanalysis. All these technical and engineering works within the framework of microanalysis were carried out by the technical expert team of the project. The types of investments and the determination of the investment amount in the following parts of the study are generated through the findings obtained by the technical endeavors. Normally, logistics hubs should be located along the transport corridors as stated in the studies of Hanaoka and Regmi (2011) and Monios and Lambert (2013). Apparently, a similar approach is taken in order to choose the location of this new logistics hub. Thus, Of-Iyidere region which is located on the TRACECA transit route is determined as the project area for the creation of this logistics hub. Moreover, we apply the public involvement to be able to tackle the problem of location selection. As aforementioned, the decision of the Turkish Ministry of Environment and Urbanization on this issue has guided us in the determination of location.

Financial Analysis

Investors seek profitable projects to invest their money. While determining the profitable projects, they apply various valuation techniques such as Net Present Value (NPV), Payback Period (PB), Discounted Payback Period (DPB) and Internal Rate of Return (IRR) as many capital budgeting decisions are taken by utilizing these methods (Drury, 2005; Bhandari, 2009; Dymowa, 2011; De Souza, 2012; Pyles, 2014).

The payback period approach is the easiest to calculate and widely preferred method in practice to determine the time horizon when an investment project necessitates paying for itself, whereas it ignores the time value of money. On the other hand, the discounted payback period method, which is more popular in business practice, incorporates the time value of money. In this regard, the discounted payback period method has both the ability of reflection the investment's useful life and it considers the risks of the project as proposed by Mao (1970) and Bhandari (2009). Meanwhile, the internal rate of return technique is another method which prices the risks of the investments (Boussabaine, 2013). Apart from these techniques, the net present value method offers a standardized approach and superior project valuation criteria (Keown et al., 2013; Vitollo and Cipparone, 2014). However, it doesn't reflect the project's period since it is based on an assumption that the project has a certain period of life. This pitfall could be overcome by DPB approach. Therefore, the literature proposes not to use any investment valuation techniques alone. Thus, in order to be able to tackle the problem of using which valuation methods for this logistics hub project we follow the studies in the literature and apply some of the aforementioned methods as used in similar studies such as Ankobiah (2001), Baird and Valentine (2006), Meidute (2007), Bhandari (2009), and Hanaoka and Regmi (2011).

The main purpose of financial analysis is to use the project cash flow forecasts in order to be able to measure the suitable net return indicators. Project specialists compare cash inflows and cash outflows within the scope of financial analysis in order to decide whether the projects are profitable or not. Cash inflows and outflows are:

- any kind of achievable gain arising from sales of products or services
- cash inflows from the financial resources including tax and other types of government incentives
- initial investment expenditures
- operation and management expenditures
- reimbursement of credit and interest payments, if any
- tax payments and other disbursements such as dividend payments

Estimating the initial investment expenditures and the economic life of the project, in other words, the time horizon for the project are the first steps in the financial analysis stage. The time horizon refers to the years in which the cash flows are forecasted. The time horizon for the port projects is determined as 25 years in similar studies such as Dimitriou (2018). Therefore, we apply the academic literature to determine the time horizon for the valuation of the Of-Iyidere logistics hub project. The following step is the estimation of operating and management costs as well as all prospective revenues. Operational costs such as salary payments, management expenses, and other expenses are foreseen for the acquisition of goods and services. These are the expenditures consumed within each accounting period. A project can be sustained financially if the cash inflows continue in the future. The most important problem here is the timing of cash payments and revenues. Project experts should be able to demonstrate that cash inflows and cash outflows overlap throughout the project lifecycle. The financial success of the project could be ensured by the positive cumulative cash flows to be generated over the project time horizon. The final stage of the financial analysis comprises the assessment of project financial performance. This step is the process of evaluating the return on capital of the project beneficiaries who could be public or private entrepreneurs.

Economic Impact Analysis

In project valuations, it should not only be considered whether the project is financially feasible for the investors but also the contribution of the project to the economic prosperity of the neighborhood and nation should be appraised. When a logistics hub project is built within a specified region, a number of economic consequences will certainly occur within that region and also within that country. Consideration of these consequences includes their identification, measurement, and also judgment as to their social contribution. In this respect, economic impact analysis is a way for assessing the effects of a project or investment on the economy of a particular region or country (Davis, 1990). It is a major analysis method for decision-making and provides a measure of strategic goal achievement that complements the cost-benefit analysis and financial feasibility.

However, just basing on a financial cost-benefit analysis may ignore the perspective of society as a whole. In other words, the market price of a product is not a sufficient indicator of its true value for the specified region, nation, or whole society since the external effects play a significant role for the contribution of the investment project. Therefore, the economic impact analysis should include additional indirect influences and revenue-generating of other contributions (Engel et al., 2010; Pawlik et al., 2011). It should be noted that considering these types of secondary effects is important for economic analysis and could be a significant impact on the appraisal of the project. In order to be able to appraise these externalities, the external factors should be identified, quantified and assigned with a monetary value to them. Here the aim is to achieve a balance between the financial sustainability and economic contribution of the investment.

To summarize briefly, economic impact analysis addresses the contribution of existing industries, facilities and activity centers. It also emphasizes the effects on the offering better-paying jobs in the industries which are providing greater stability and future income growth opportunities. The results of the economic impact analysis could be indicators of strategic economic improvement consequences and side effects. Furthermore, the features of economic impact analysis method could serve the outputs in a straightforward way that matter to stakeholders including policymakers and investors. The economic impact analysis, which is a substantial challenge in project valuation, requires a separate study on its own. Thereby, the economic impact analysis could not be included in the scope of this study and it is proposed as a further research topic. Nevertheless, the job opportunities for the project itself could be considered as an economic impact (Schade, 2006).

Financing the Projects

The achievement of a financially feasible and viable transportation structure project depends on clear identification of both long term economic benefits and its impact on the overall business. The financing market of transportation structure projects has gone through a process of significant evolution starting from the years mid of the 2000s. Various improvements such as changes in economic conditions and strict financial regulations have caused a reallocation of financial flows from the traditional banking sector to a more contemporary institutional investment sector. So, the different types of financing strategies have been developed together with the transformation in the financial market. There are many ways to finance transportation structures like logistics hubs. Basically, the public sector could take part in such big projects and also a number of hybrid forms could be a concern. The alternative funding schemes could be public funding, funding from the investment bank and financial institutions, public-private partnership, or solely private investment.

In the private investment model, the required financing is provided by a private investor or a group of investors. Private companies, enterprises or individuals could be private investors who finance the project. Private investors may use their own money or borrow from the national or international financial markets. Together with the private sector, the public can participate in this financing and form a public-private partnership. A public-private partnership is a cooperative arrangement between one or more public and private sectors. The past few decades have seen a clear trend towards public across the world making greater application of public-private coordination. Especially the 2008 financial crisis has introduced high interest in the financial market and thus in the cost of capital of investments. Financing constraints on public resources due to the crisis highlights the significance of new structure investments and increased interest in financing mechanism like private sector as an alternative additional source of funding in order to meet the funding gap and to be able to boost regional and national economic growth.

On the other hand, solely public funding - as its name signifies - incorporates government budget money invested in the project. The budgetary fund's participants could be local governments, subdivisions of ministries, public organizations, or other institutions. The assets of investments are owned by the State and the State manages and operates the project. Funds for the project could also be achieved by investment banks and financial institutions. Domestic bank financing could be stringent with financial restrictions due to the narrow, concentrated and illiquid characteristics of the national banking sector. The tightening of banking could also impede international financing of transportation projects. Once the projects are proved to be viable, large international banks could be another scenario for finance. This plot study presents the feasibility of the project. However, the financing model of the project is a matter to be determined by the public authority due to various restrictions on the amendments. Though, the findings of hub investments projects in many countries show that the financial burden could be overcome through public-private partnerships (Ng and Gujar, 2009; Bergqvist et al., 2010; Antai and Olson, 2013; Monios, 2011; Monios and Wilmsmeier, 2012; Pekin and Macharis, 2013; Roso, 2013).

METHODOLOGICAL FRAMEWORK

Scope and Aim of the Study

The scope of this study covers the financial valuation of a logistics hub planned to be established in Of-Iyidere region of Turkey. Within this context, the study aims to test the financial viability of the project by using the undermentioned project valuation methods. The paper also shows the ways of obtaining crucial required data needed for appraising the investment.

Apart from applying various methods such as net present value and internal rate of return in project valuation studies, it is important to accurately estimate the cash inflows and outflows of the project and to determine the opportunity cost that constitutes the risk of the project. After obtaining the cash flows and discount rate, various valuation methodologies are applied to determine whether the project is feasible or not. Figure 2 below provides the basic inputs required for investment valuation.

The requirements for project or investment valuation can be grouped under three headings. The first is the possible cash flows related to the project including initial investment amount, cash inflows, and cash outflows. The second is the period in which the cash flows will occur. The time period can be expressed as the economic life of the project. Thirdly, the cost of capital constitutes the risk of the project. This shows the rate of return expected by the project participants who are the debt owners or equity owners. It is also called the opportunity cost. Once all these inputs have been obtained, it could be decided whether the investment project is financially feasible or not by using various project valuation methods such as net present value and internal rate of return. This study is conducted in this direction with the purpose of making recommendations to improve the practice of valuation of the logistics hub.

Figure 2. Core inputs needed for valuation

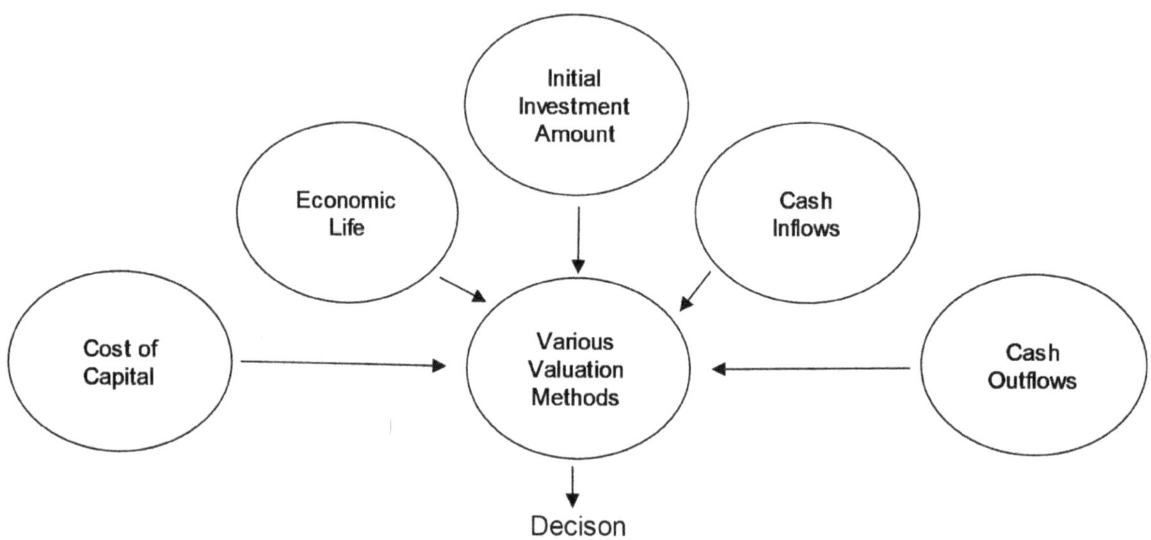

The Methodology of the Study

The basic problems that face projects specialists in investment valuation are the measurement of value and profit. There are different ways to do such measurement but there is a need for a theoretically sound basis, useful and verifiable information, practical approach, defined time frame, and professional expertise. The logistics hub authorities, government, and private investors have different interest in the valuation of the project and could prefer various valuation methods. To measure the value of a project, there is a need to add together all future net benefits or expected cash flows and discount or adjust such future flows to cater for inflation (Nobes, 1997). There are four main methodologies paid attention in any valuation. These are earnings-based valuation methods, asset-based methods, market-based methods, and industry-specific methods (Gordon, 1962).

Among the various methods which are applied for valuation of logistics hubs, the most commonly used is the discounted cash flow practices in earnings-based valuation methods (Ankobiah, 2001; Baird and Valentine, 2006; Meidute, 2007). The discounted cash flow method is based on the assumptions that the value of a project to the investors is the present value of the expected future net cash inflows to be derived from the investment. When the method is applied to the logistics hub, in this case, the value of the project, is calculated by discounting the operating cash flows before interest and after-tax, adding the value of surplus assets, and deducting interest-bearing debts (Cass, 1998).

After determining the expected cash flows, various techniques, which can be used for examining projects and preparing feasibility reports, can be listed as follows: payback method, the average rate of return, internal rate of return, net present value, and profitability index. In this study, net present value, payback, discounted payback, and internal rate of return methods are utilized. The amount of investment required to be made has been determined by engineering and other technical studies. In order to determine the cash inflows, the cargo estimations and the number and types of incoming ships to the port have been tried to be predicted. Income and expense estimations are based on unit service revenue and expenditures data obtained from various stakeholders in the sector. After that, expected future cash flows are discounted at the various cost of capital rates.

In other respects, the type of currency to work with and the weighted average cost of capital rate are among the problems considering when using the discounted cash flow method. Due to currency differentials especially as a result of inflation and also most of the input costs are in terms of foreign currency, cash flows are projected using the American dollar (USD) and discount rates are calculated on a consistent basis. The weighted average cost of capital is calculated through an assessment of the rates of return demanded by the funding providers (debt and equity owners). Other constraints that need to be solved when applying discounted cash flows for a logistics hub comprehending a port could be specified as:

- forecasting traffic intensity and income projections depending on the expected future demand, competition, and the nature of the sector
- appraising expected future operating expenses based on labor capacity, cargo capacity, and operating competence
- analyzing capital expenditures to be affected by the potential of alternative financing methods such as leasing arrangements, conditions of existing facilities, and unexpected changes
- disposition of one-off payments and receipts covering inherited liabilities and predictions on scrap or residual values (Cass, 1998).

PILOT APPLICATION: THE CASE OF A LOGISTIC HUB PROJECT IN TURKEY

General Information about the Project

Within the scope of the TRACECA project, countries have planned and implemented investments which aim at strengthening their logistics infrastructure. Among these investments, Baku-Tbilisi-Kars railway, Ovit connection tunnel and Rize-Erzurum road, which were completed by the end of 2016, will provide an east-west corridor in terms of international transportation and a north-south corridor in terms of national transportation. With the Batumi-Samsun railway project that is planned to be constructed, Of-Iyidere basin which is the point of region opening to the sea will possess a port logistics hub feature in terms of transportation.

The Eastern Black Sea Region is strategically important with its position on the Caucasus Corridor opening to Europe and Central Asia. The completion of the Ovit tunnel will provide an advantage in North-South freight movement and especially in Iranian transit freight. In line with these developments, the Ministry of Environment and Urbanization has approved the Iyidere region as a "Special Project Area" for the creation of a logistics hub.

Within the scope of the project, technical and other engineering affairs related to the land ownership and exploitation of the region, the topography and geotechnical situation of the region, transportation facilities, and economic structure are supported by Recep Tayyip Erdogan University Scientific Research Project Office (Project ID / No: 177 / 2013101.10.2). The data related to the project valuation are obtained from the outputs of these technical and engineering affairs that are implemented by the various experts in their fields. Therefore, the reliability of the data used in this study is quite high.

The cash flows, which form the basis of the valuation issue, are obtained as a result of the works made within the framework of the aforementioned project. In this study, it is estimated that this logistics hub will have a port with a capacity of 34.4 million tons. It is assumed that the hub will work with 75% capacity and it is estimated that approximately 14.5 million tons (1.1 million TEU) of this load will be a container, 3.5 million tons will be general and bulk cargo, and 7.8 million tons will be liquid cargo. Ship types and numbers proportional to the estimated loads have also been analyzed in various scenarios. In the first years, it is predicted that small ships would come more due to the low volume of cargo, and in the following years, the probability of incoming ships to the port would increase in proportion to the size and cargo volume of the ships.

Estimation of Load Potential

In 2010, Republic of Turkey Ministry of Transport and Infrastructure prepared the "Transportation Coastal Structures Master Plan" covering the maritime sector for the next twenty years. According to the cargo and capacity estimations of this plan for the Black Sea region, the container, general and bulk cargo, liquid cargo, and Ro-Ro foreign trade are foreseen as 2,475,410 TEU, 65,729,245 tons, 5,381,525 tons and 274,929 numbers respectively in 2030. Considering the load capacities of the existing ports, a surplus of 34,475,241 tons are anticipated for 2030. The estimated surplus value indicates that additional investment is needed for the Black Sea Region in the coming years. In this respect, capacity estimations are made by using scenario analysis for Of-Iyidere port and logistics hub. It is assumed that 75% of the total surplus of 34,475,241 tons expected to occur in 2030 will be handled in this port and hub. The distribution of this total load as a container, general and bulk cargo and liquid cargo is given in Table 1.

This distribution and estimation have been done by considering historical load data for the region, past economic growth, predicted economic growth in the future, economic and commercial relations with neighboring countries within the framework of regional developments, superior features from neighboring ports, transportation connections to the inner regions of the project area, especially the local economic growth in the Southeastern Anatolia Project (GAP) region, and foreign trade volumes. In addition, the potential cargo types and quantities in neighboring countries have been taken into account. Taking into consideration all of these, handling amounts and capacity usage rates to be expected to realize in the 1st, 5th, 10th, and 15th years are shown in Table 1.

While making predictions, various scenario analyses have been created and grouped under three headings as "pessimistic situation", "average situation", and "optimistic situation". Afterward, a single load estimation is obtained by taking the weighted averages of these different scenarios created. Therefore, the cash flows presented in Table 6 are calculated based on this single load estimation. As a result of the statistical estimates showing the normal distribution characteristics in the scenarios created, it is expected that the cargo amounts will increase by 6% for the pessimistic situation, 12.5% for the average situation and 14.2% for the optimistic situation annually.

More than half of the total handling at the Black Sea ports consists of general and bulk cargo such as coal, ore, iron, and steel (Directorate General of Merchant Marine, 2018). When the foreign trade volume of the targets countries with Turkey is analyzed, it is understood that Turkey has a developed foreign trade relationship based on a wide variety of products with Iran, Azerbaijan, Georgia, and the Turkic Republics (Turkish Statistical Institute, 2018). Of-Iyidere port and logistics hub has strategic position especially for the export of cereals in Kazakhstan, cotton and liquid cargo in Turkmenistan, and chemical products and precious metals in Iran. For example, after the grain harvest in Kazakhstan, exports of this product have problems due to seasonal conditions. Kazakhstan has to use Russian ports for export and has difficulties in exporting because of the closed ports due to winter conditions. However, this problem will be eliminated by Of-Iyidere port and logistics area. For container traffic, Of-Iyidere port and logistics area, which may be the closest port to these countries, will have an important position in the east-west axis of world trade.

Expected Ship Types

The ships expected to arrive at the logistics hub and their characteristics are presented in Table 2 in line with the technical features of the port obtained by engineering works and the freight demand forecasts.

Due to the low volume of cargo in the first few years, it is expected that small ships will arrive more frequently. It is assumed that the probability of ships approaching the port in the coming years will increase in proportion to the size and volume of the ships. In the estimation of the financial analysis, it is

Table 1. Cargo and Capacity Estimation (Ton)

Years	Container	General and Bulk Cargo	Liquid Cargo	Total	Capacity Usage Rate	Total Capacity
1	2,655,705	628,138	1,389,937	4,673,780	14%	34,475,241
5	3,723,468	881,243	1,972,932	6,577,643	19%	
10	6,710,727	1,589,258	3,594,711	11,894,695	35%	
15	14,561,348	3,449,958	7,845,125	25,856,430	75%	

Table 2. Expected Ships

Ship Types	Average Draft (m)	Cargo Carrying Capacity
Container Ships		
Panamax	13	3.000-5.100 TEU
Feedermax	12	2.000- 3.000 TEU
Feeder	10	1.000- 2.000 TEU
Small Feeder	9	0-1.000 TEU
General and Bulk Cargo Ships		
Handy Max	12	> 20.000-60.000 Mt
Koster	7	< 20.000 Mt
Liquid Cargo Ships		
Seawaymax	12	10.000 - 60.000 DWT
Koster	9	0 – 10.000 DWT

* Mt:Metric Tons, 1 Metric Ton= 1,000 Kilogram; Dwt: Deadweight tonnage, 1 Deadweight tonnage= 1,016 Kilogram
1 TEU (Twenty-Foot Equivalent Unit) refers to a standard 20′ (20-foot) shipping container and it has approximately 34 cubic meter capacity.

assumed that the carrying capacities of Panamax type ships, Feedermax type ships, Feeder type ships, and Small Feeder type ships incoming to the container terminal will be 4,000 TEU, 2,500 TEU, 1,300-1,600 TEU, and 1,000 TEU respectively. Calculations are made assuming that the carrying capacities of Handymax type ships incoming to the general and bulk cargo terminal will be 45,000 tons and the Koster type ships will be 10,000 tons. And lastly, it is assumed that Seawaymax type ships incoming to the liquid cargo terminal will have a carrying capacity of 44,291 DWT (approximately 45,000 tons) and the Koster type ships will have 1,476 DWT (approximately 1,500 tons) capacity.

Initial Investment Costs

All calculations related to investment costs, revenue and expenses are made in USD. First of all, the areas to be used for the port, container terminal, general and bulk cargo terminal and liquid cargo terminal are determined. Within the scope of the project, construction of breakwaters, berthing docks, handling vehicles, container terminal stacking areas, container storage buildings, cold storage, maintenance buildings, general and bulk cargo storage areas, truck and vehicle park, and customs and administration buildings are planned.

According to the load potential and capacity estimation, a place of 37 hectares will be sufficient for the project area. The container yard, general cargo area, liquid cargo tanks, bulk cargo (for grain storage) silo area, and custom and administration building area are destined as 320,000 m^2, 10,000 m^2, 15,000 m^2, 5,000 m^2 respectively. The details of the fixed initial investment expenditures are given in Table 3.

The estimated total cost of fixed investment (construction costs, purchase of cranes and other handling equipment) is calculated as the US $ 328,641,175. Crane purchases, equipment and construction costs, which will be widely used in fixed investments for years, have been discounted with the determined cost of capital rate of the project.

Table 3. Fixed Investment Costs

Type of work unit	Quantity	Amount (USD)
Dredging	2,200,000 m^3	11,000,000
Mobilization		500,000
Breakwater	2,544,494 m^3	27,480,535
Accropode	210,860 m^3	42,699,150
Accropode patent right	210,860 m^3	316,290
Breakwater concrete wall	21,472 m^3	2,147,200
Breakwater laboratory experiment		300,000
Container dock	21,000 m^2	42,000,000
Bulk cargo dock	9,000 m^2	18,000,000
Dock riprap	464,000 m^3	3,248,000
Other construction costs		7,950,000
Bulk cargo cranes	4 units	10,000,000
Container cranes	9 units	90,000,000
Forklift, weighbridge, other equipment, and vehicles		70,000,000
New crossroads construction	1 unit	3,000,000
Total		**328,641,175**

Operating Expenses

Operating expenses are divided into two parts as personnel and general administrative expenditures. Expenses are calculated annually, estimated at 15 years and kept constant after that. The number of technical and administrative personnel is planned to be around 100 for the first year. The number of employees is expected to reach approximately 400 people at the end of 15 years together with the increasing business volume. General administrative expenses consist of fuel, energy, water, communication, maintenance, overhead and unexpected expenditures. The expenses of the 1st year, 5th year, 10th year and 15th year regarding the estimations are presented in the following Table 4.

It is assumed that the annual general administrative expenses will be constant as of the 15th year. Such assumptions are frequently used in the calculation of cash flows of long-term projects.

Table 4. Operating Expenses by Years (US $)

Years	Personnel Expenses	General Administrative Expenses	Total Operating Expenses
1	1,563,000	1,221,600	2,784,600
5	2,412,921	1,484,862	3,897,783
10	4,943,886	1,895,103	6,838,988
15	10,669,715	2,418,684	13,088,400

Operating Income

Operating incomes are calculated by considering the load potential from Eastern Anatolia, Southeastern Anatolia, Iran, Iraq, Azerbaijan, and Turkic Republics. The revenues of the logistics center are expected to be generated by:

- Services provided to the ship (pilotage, towing, moorage, berthing, anchoring, waste reception)
- Services provided to the freight (shipping, unloading, shifting, limbo, container reinforcement, security service)
- Terminal revenues (loading and unloading of trailers, custom inspection, bulk goods inspection, container washing, container consolidation, bulk solid packaging, cold air container in-warehouse monitoring, cold air container testing, assembly, and disassembly)
- Storage service revenues
- Other service revenues

Data on revenue items are obtained from the Turkish Chamber of Shipping, Regional Harbor Offices, agencies, and freight companies. The calculations are done by using average fare per item according to the ship capacity. According to this data, for example, the average daily service charge is the US $ 8,178 for the ships of 29,000-30,000 gross tonnage. While determining the service revenues, the number of incoming ships is found according to the probability of ships arriving in years. Then, the average service charge and the number of ships are multiplied and the service charge is calculated. In the analysis, the charges for the 1,000-50,000 gross tonnage ships vary between 742 and 13,263 US Dollars. By using these values, the service items given to the ships in Table 5 are reached.

The services provided to the freight are categorized under three parts as general and bulk cargo, container, and liquid cargo. The average loading and unloading unit service cost for the container, general and bulk cargo, and liquid cargo are estimated at the US $ 130, US $ 4.5 and the US $ 2.25, respectively. These prices are multiplied by the estimated load of potential amounts over the years. Then other service charges (shifting, limbo, etc.) added to these and the related values in Table 5 below are obtained. Operating income is kept constant after the 15th year, as the assumption is made in the estimation of operating expenses. As a result of all these assumptions, the expected operating income including services provided to the ship, services provided to the freight, terminal service income, storage service income and other service income calculated over the years are presented in Table 5.

Table 5. Expected operating income by years (USD)

Income sources	1st Year	5th Year	10th Year	15th Year
Revenues from services provided to the ship	3,598,622	5,312,326	10,150,883	23,279,791
Revenues from services provided to the freight	32,972,832	46,282,302	83,498,407	181,279,577
Terminal service income	4,416,722	6,215,873	11,240,487	24,434,327
Storage service revenues	2,145,411	3,017,014	5,452,094	11,847,374
Other service revenues	4,416,722	6,215,873	11,240,487	24,434,327
Total	47,550,309	67,043,388	121,582,357	265,275,396

The calculation method of income can be summarized as follows:

- Load and capacity estimations which take place under the heading of load potential on the terminal basis are used.
- Operating income is classified as revenues from services provided to the ship, revenues from services provided to the freight, terminal service income, storage service income and other service income.
- In the calculation of the revenues from services given to the ship, the number of future ships is calculated for each terminal by taking into consideration the probability of ships arriving, the expected amount of cargo, and the capacities of the ships.
- The revenues from the services given to the freight are calculated by multiplying the estimated load amounts expected for each terminal and the service charges.
- The length of stay in the port is estimated according to the capacities of the ships and the terminal service income is calculated by multiplying the number of ships and the length of stay with the average service charges.
- Storage and other service revenues are also estimated based on the load potential capacities. The average fees calculated for these services are multiplied by the estimated load potential.

Determination of Time Horizon and Discount Rate of the Project

Other important inputs needed to evaluate projects or investments are discount rate and valuation period as shown in Figure 2. The discount rate is the average rate of return expected by the project financiers. This ratio constitutes the weighted average cost of capital (WACC) of that business. The weighted average cost of capital expresses its blended cost of capital across all sources, basically including equity and debt. The cost of each type of capital is weighted by its percentage of total capital and they are added together. As it is well known (Miller and Modigliani, 1958), it could be formulated as below:

$$\text{WACC} = \text{cost of equity} \times \%\ \text{equity} + \text{cost of debt} \times \%\ \text{debt} \times (1 - \text{tax rate}) \quad (1)$$

The cost of capital can be calculated by adding the cost of debt to the cost of equity which is determined by modern methods such as the capital asset pricing model. The main idea the capital asset pricing model based on is that the investors demand an additional expected return, called as the risk premium if they are asked to accept additional risk. In this regard, the model gives an accurate estimation of the relationship that should be recognized between the risk of an asset and its expected return. The expected return for the investors indicates the cost of the project. Thus the capital asset pricing model contributes a benchmark rate of return for assessing feasible investments (Treynor, 1962; Sharpe, 1964; Mossin 1966; Lintner, 1969; Black et al., 1972). However, conventional techniques such as the Gordon model may also be preferred (Gordon, 1962). In addition, factors such as market interest rate, inflation rate, sector risk, and country risk are among the main variables determining the cost of capital. On the other hand, when investors invest in more risky projects rather than simply a risk-free return instrument such as a bond, they will naturally expect a higher return relative to the risk they endure. In this context, when the investors assess this investment which will be made in Turkey, the cost of capital will be proportional to the cost of credit received from a national or international market and foreign currency deposit rates or Eurobonds returns. USD denominated deposit returns vary between 2% and 3% and Eurobond returns vary between 5% and 7% on average according to various maturities as June of 2019 (Central Bank of Turkish Republic, 2019). Moreover, loan interest rates, which represent borrowing costs, are around 18% - 20% for USD currency in the national market (Central Bank of Turkish Republic, 2019). In the international market, this ratio is more affordable. For example, the cost of USD syndicated loan obtained by Akbank in international markets in March 2019 is Libor + 2.5% (Akbank, 2019).

There will be no difference between the pre-tax and post-tax value of the cost of debt due to various tax exemptions and incentives provided by the government in the region, in other words, the tax shield of the debt will be eliminated. In addition, if the credit default swap spread (CDS) which shows the credit risk is added to the cost of capital as a risk factor, the new average cost of capital can be expressed as follows:

$$WACC_{(new)} = Libor + Spread + CDS \quad (2)$$

While 5-year CDS rate of Turkey was around 300 pips in March 2019, it has passed 500 pips in May 2019. As of the end of June 2019, it is below 400 (Worldgovernmentbonds.com, 2019). An average of 450 pips CDS rate represents an additional cost of 4.5%. The 12-month USD Libor varies between 2.5% and 3.0% in 2019 (Global-rates.com, 2019). In this case, considering the average values in 2019, the cost of capital will be around 10%. Particularly due to the high volatility in developing markets and rapid change in market conditions, it is not possible to determine the exact rate of the cost of capital. Additionally, the valuation turns to a complex problem in most project finance investments since the project leverage changes over time. Thus, the use of a single discount rate is inappropriate. The way to tackle this problem of changing leverage is to use multiple discount rate (Esty, 1999; Mandron, 2000). Therefore, while performing this sample project valuation, the calculations are made by using three different costs of capital rates which are 7.5%, 10%, and 15%.

The value of logistics hub consisting of port, land, infrastructure, superstructure, and equipment depends on the alternative use for these assets, the maintenance schedule and the economic life. Valuation of port equipment is generally done taking into consideration the useful economic life and depreciation worth of the items. Some valuation practices are specifically required by regulation standards. In this example, the average useful life of the facilities and equipment in the logistics hub is 25 years. Therefore, the time horizon for the sample project is based on a 25-year period. Moreover, Dimitriou (2018) suggests the time horizon for the port projects as 25 years.

Valuation of the Investment

In the valuation of the investment, Net Present Value (NPV), Internal Rate of Return (IRR), Payback Period (PB), and Discounted Payback Period (DPB) methods are used to determine the financial feasibility of the project. The NPV analysis is the calculation method in order to find the value of cash flows over the economic life of a project or investment. The cash inflows and outflows are discounted to the present with a weighted average cost of capital. In other words, NPV is the difference between the present value of cash inflows and the present value of cash outflows. For a project to be acceptable according to this method, the NPV must be equal to or greater than zero. On the other hand, IRR is the discount rate that makes the project's net present value equal to zero. This rate represents the return on investment in case the costs of the project are met and it is an important indicator that can be used to express the profitability of the investment. On the other hand, PB method indicates how long it takes for a project to recoup its investment. The method allows investors to be able to make a comparison among

Table 6. Cash flows of the project

Years	Initial Investment Amount	Available Cash	Depreciation and Amortization	Net Cash Flow
-	- 328,641,175			- 328,641,175
1		17,142,223	13,145,647	30,287,870
5		30,927,144	13,145,647	44,072,791
10		69,625,468	13,145,647	82,771,115
15		172,708,188	13,145,647	185,853,835
25		172,708,188	13,145,647	185,853,835

alternative investment opportunities. So, they could decide on a project that reimburses their investment in the shortest period. Starting from the first year, the expected cash flows are collected cumulatively over the years and the year in which the total value reaches the positive is determined as the payback time. The decision rule in this method is to minimize the time taken for the return of investment. Meanwhile, DPB differs from the PB by aspects of taking uncertainties and risks into account. That is to say, it incorporates the time value of money.

The literature has shown that the economic appraisals of the logistics hubs including the establishment of a seaport project more often perceive NPV as a method superior to other decision-making criteria (Magni, 2009; Panova and Hilmola, 2015). On the other hand, Bowen (1984) and Bhandari (2009) propose the discounted payback period technique, which is widespread in business practice, for the investment selection and risk measure especially when uncertainty is involved in the decision-making process. To re-express, the valuation methods have different characteristics and troubles as stated in the *Financial Analysis* section. Therefore, it is not right to use any method alone. The cash flows constituting the valuation of the project by years are given in Table 6.

The initial investment amount is calculated (*by taking the average of the various cost of capital rates*) as the present value of the expenses to be made during the project life cycle. It is assumed that the capacity utilization rate will reach 75% in the 15th year and will remain constant after that. Therefore, cash flows are kept constant after 15th years.

As a result of the investment valuation, the net present value is calculated separately with a discount rate of 7.5%, 10% and 15% over a 25 year period. The net present value of the project is calculated as 688,822,320 USD, 422,460,582 USD, and 116,934,421 USD respectively according to three possible financing costs. For the acceptance of the project, it is sufficient that the net present value is greater than or equal to zero. The project internal rate of return is calculated as 18.5% and the payback period is calculated as 7 years 8 months. When the risks, which are represented by the discount rates, in other words, the costs of capital (7,5%, 10%, and 15%), are taken into consideration, the discounted payback periods are calculated as 10 years 1 month, 11 years 3 months, and 14 years 11 months.

Although the risk of the project varies according to parameters such as the expectation of the investor, the minimum value of the expected profitability rate is considered as the cost of capital. When making an investment decision, the IRR is compared with the profitability ratio expected by the investors. As a result of the comparison, the acceptance or rejection of the project is decided. If the project's internal rate of return is higher than the expected profitability rate of the project, the project is accepted and if not, the project is rejected. The discount rate used in the calculation of the net present value, in other words, the cost of capital also refers to the expected rate of return of the project beneficiaries. The calculated 18.5% IRR is higher than all three possible financing costs and it meets the return expectations of the fund providers. Therefore, the project is acceptable.

CONCLUSION AND AVENUES FOR FUTURE RESEARCH

Logistics hub or center is described as an area in which all activities such as storage houses, centers for storing bulk cargo, parking, custom clearance, export-import transactions, and all other facilities related to the transportation are carried out on a commercial basis by various operators (Palšaitis and Bazaras 2004; Europlatforms, 2004).

On average 80 percent of the world trade is realized by maritime transport (Clarksons Research, 2019). Similarly, among the emerging economies, Turkey has a share of 85% transportation by sea in foreign trade (Turkish Chamber of Shipping, 2018). Turkey, which is located at the center position of TRACECA transport corridor project, connects the centers of production and consumption through taking place in a geographically and economically convenient place where it is close to many countries and borders. To be able to benefit from this important advantage, there is a need for a logistics hub center where the logistics facilities could be carried out easily. The western part of Turkey which is near the crossroads of trade within the scope of the TRACECA project has enough size and the capacity in terms of maritime transport. Furthermore, together with the completion of the Baku-Tbilisi-Kars railway, Ovit connection tunnel, and Rize-Erzurum road by the end of 2016, both the east-west and north-south axes of Turkey will provide a national and international transport corridor. The Of-Iyidere watershed, located on the TRACECA transit route, will be the opening point of the region through the Batumi-Samsun railway project. In this respect, the Turkish Ministry of Environment and Urbanization has declared Of-Iyidere province as a special project area for the creation of a logistics center area including a port logistics hub in 2013.

On the other hand, transport structures such as logistics hubs are irreversible investments and require long-time commitment maintenance and operation. In most of the cases, the decision to invest in transport structure is not simple, mainly, because of the complications in the planning process, the high cost of the investment amount, and the involvement of various stakeholders in the decision-making process. Therefore, these projects should be dealt with in detail and be carefully analyzed.

Additionally, before estimating the value of the project, we tried to address and tackle some basic challenges issues such as Engel et al., 2010; Pawlik et al., (2011); Hanaoka and Regmi (2011); Beresford et al., (2012); Monios and Lambert (2013); Bergqvist et al., (2016); Dimitriou (2018), and researches, that is difficult to list all of them here, referred to the different parts of the study. For example, Kapros et al. (2005) state that the techniques used to appraise logistics hub structures are usually limited to conventional financial or social valuation methods that use descriptive terms and have quantification problems. On the other hand, Tsamboulas and Dimitropoulos (1999) state that there are no standardized methods for the assessment of "node types" infrastructures, such as logistics hub although standards exist in many countries for the valuation of "link types" infrastructures, such as roads and railways. Logistics hub projects have more complex valuation factors and the success of them depends on several variables due to the diversity of roles, features, and stakeholders involved. Similarly, Song (2003) discusses the factors attributed to the success of the logistics hub and offers solutions which are often intangible and less accessible appraisal methods. Some of the problems associated with the valuation practice of logistics hub enclosing a port include the determination of the initial investment costs, estimation of the maintenance expenditures, operating expense and income, calculation of economic life of the hub, estimation of the cost of capital, and agreement on residual or disposal value of the hub. Also, unclear legal and regulatory procedures, inappropriate processes for conversion and repatriation of profits, obstacles in dealing with labor unions, and risk of unexpected changes to agreed terms and conditions could be significant challenges in the valuation phase (Cass, 1998). Moreover, the locational elements of a logistics hub are important to outline (Lee et al., 2009; Li et al., 2011; Feng et al., 2013; Ünal and Derindere Köseoğlu, 2014). The typical logistics hub will be at or near the crossroads of trade connections and have to be well integrated within the facility and its extensive intermodal functionality. In brief, the valuation of a logistics hub could be heavily executed due to various uncertainties and problems but a careful analysis of the situation could provide solutions to the benefit of all parties involved in.

Accordingly, this chapter examines the concept of the logistics hub, basically port logistics, and analyzes its applicability in the province of Of-Iyidere, Turkey. The study has illustrated the project valuation methods to the problem of the investment of a new logistics hub. Different methods are applied for valuation of logistics hub but the most commonly used is discounted cash flow method (Ankobiah, 2001; Baird and Valentine, 2006; Meidute, 2007). Within this context, this study aims to examine and implement the discounted cash flow approach for the valuation of the logistics hub in Of-Iyidere restrict. To do so, first, the load potential is estimated by considering the historical data and future expectations basically based on the foreign trade volume. Then, the initial investment cost is determined through the endeavor of technical and engineering experts in the scope of the project which is stated in the acknowledgment part of this study. After that, operating expenses and revenues are estimated by means of the field study which involves the coordination with the Turkish Chamber of Shipping, Regional Harbor Offices, agencies, and freight companies. According to the cargo and capacity estimations of "Transportation Coastal Structures Master Plan" for the Black Sea region, the container, general and bulk cargo, liquid cargo, and Ro-Ro foreign trade are foreseen as 2,475,410 TEU, 65,729,245 tons, 5,381,525 tons and 274,929 numbers in 2030, respectively. Considering the load capacities of the existing ports, a surplus of 34,475,241 tons are anticipated for 2030. In line with the load potential and capacity estimation, a place of 37 hectares will be sufficient for the project area including the container yard, general cargo area, liquid cargo tanks, bulk cargo, silo area, and custom and administration buildings. The estimated total cost of fixed investment (construction costs, purchase of cranes and other handling equipment) is calculated as the US $ 328,641,175. The life cycle of the project is assumed as 25 years and the cash flows are discounted by the various cost of capital rates due to the high fluctuation in financial markets.

As a result of the investment valuation, the net present value is calculated separately using different discount rates which are 7.5%, 10% and 15% over a 25-year period. The net present value of the project is calculated as 688,822,320 USD, 422,460,582 USD, and 116,934,421 USD respectively according to three possible financing costs. The project internal rate of return is calculated as 18.5% and the payback period is determined as 7 years 8 months. The calculated 18.5% IRR is higher than all three possible financing costs and it meets the return expectations of the fund providers. Therefore, the project is feasible. On the other hand, the discounted payback periods are determined as 10 years 1 month, 11 years 3 months, and 14 years 11 months in accordance with the aforecited cost of capital rates. Unfortunately, the discounted payback periods corresponds to almost half of the project's life cycle.

The valuation methodology and the implementation steps, used in this study could be integrated with a valuation of large-scale project studies such as Mandron (2000), Meidute (2007), Pawlik et al. (2011), and Panova and Hilmola (2015). On the other hand, the elaborated financial valuation including

(a) estimation of initial cost, operating cost, and operating income, (b) basic challenges and solutions, (c) cooperation with technical and engineering experts in their fields to acquire reliable data for the valuation, and (d) providing a guidance for the creation of a new logistics hub by considering a wider point of view through not focusing on just one subject of valuation makes this study distinguished from other similar researches such as Esty (1999), Kapros et al. (2005), Bergqvist et al. (2010), Hanaoka and Regmi (2011), Feng et al. (2013), and Macharis and Bernardini (2015). In this respect, the study presents a projection to the market actors and the decision-makers, as well as it contributes to the literature by providing a broad perspective to the academicians and the researchers. In other words, the study does not just present a pure valuation but also it provides a systematic approach to policymakers, academics, and other researchers on a specific subject such as logistics hub. The lack of the systematic approach hinders the processes of logistics hub implementation. The contribution of the paper, therefore, is essential not only for academia but also for the business world. Furthermore, the topic examined exhibits an essential guidance and policy support tool to highlight the potential of logistics hub infrastructures and demonstrates a vision on the future development of logistics in Turkey.

Nevertheless, the project valuation is a very comprehensive issue, which incorporates the analysis of whether the project is financially feasible for investors or not as well as various economic impacts for the region and country. Therefore, further studies could be carried out on a valuation by taking the indirect economic contributions of the investment into account. Moreover, the risk management processes, which are not discussed in-depth, are essential since risks may cause the deviation of future cash flows from the expected ones, as well as the postponement of the payback periods of the investment. However, especially the risks are treated in a deficient manner in project valuation studies for the large-scale projects although they are high in such mega projects (Bruzelius et al., 2002). In other saying, the management of various risks during the phases of the investment of this logistics hub project still presents a considerable challenge from the practical and theoretical points of view.

ACKNOWLEDGMENT

I would like to thank the Research Project Office of Recep Tayyip Erdogan University that supported this project (Project ID/No: 177/2013101.10.2).

REFERENCES

Akbank. (2019). *Investor relations*. Retrieved from https://www.akbank.com/en-us/investor-relations/Pages/News.aspx

Ankobiah, M. (2001). *Valuation of port assets: impact on the financial performance of port and the national economy*. (Unpublished master dissertation). World Maritime University, Malmo, Sweden.

Antai, I., & Olson, H. (2013). Interaction: A new focus for supply chain vs supply chain competition. *International Journal of Physical Distribution & Logistics Management*, *43*(7), 511–528. doi:10.1108/IJPDLM-06-2012-0195

Baird, A. J., & Valentine, V. F. (2006). Port privatisation in the United Kingdom. *Research in Transportation Economics, 17*, 55–84. doi:10.1016/S0739-8859(06)17003-1

Beresford, A., Pettit, S., Xu, Q., & Williams, S. (2012). A study of dry port development in China. *Maritime Economics & Logistics, 14*(1), 73–98. doi:10.1057/mel.2011.17

Bergqvist, R., Falkemark, G., & Woxenius, J. (2010). Establishing intermodal terminals. *World Review of Intermodal Transportation Research, 3*(3), 285–302. doi:10.1504/WRITR.2010.034667

Bergqvist, R., Wilmsmeier, G., & Cullinane, K. (Eds.). (2016). *Dry ports–a global perspective: challenges and developments in serving hinterlands*. New York, NY: Routledge Publishing.

Bhandari, S. B. (2009). Discounted payback period-some extensions. *Journal of Business and Behavioral Sciences, 21*(1), 28–38.

Black, F., Jensen, M. C., & Scholes, M. (1972). The capital asset pricing model: Some empirical tests. *Studies in the theory of capital markets, 81*(3), 79-121.

Boussabaine, A. (2013). *Risk pricing strategies for public-private partnership projects*. Hoboken, NJ: John Wiley & Sons. doi:10.1002/9781118785812

Bowen, P. A. (1984). A hypothesis: Portfolio theory is elegant but useless. *The Investment Analysts Journal, 13*(24), 17–21. doi:10.1080/10293523.1984.11082227

Bruzelius, N., Flyvbjerg, B., & Rothengatter, W. (2002). Big decisions, big risks. Improving accountability in mega projects. *Transport Policy, 9*(2), 143–154. doi:10.1016/S0967-070X(02)00014-8

Cass, S. (1998). *World port privatisation: finance, funding and ownership: a cargo systems report*. London, UK: IIR Publications.

Central Bank of Turkish Republic. (2019). *Interest Rate Statistics, Statistics Department, Data Management Division*. Retrieved from https://www.tcmb.gov.tr/wps/wcm/connect/EN/TCMB+EN/Main+Menu/Statistics/Interest+Rate+Statistics

Clarksons Research. (2019). *Shipping review and outlook*. Retrieved from https://www.crsl.com/acatalog/shipping-review-and-outlook.html

Crescenzi, R., & Rodríguez-Pose, A. (2012). Infrastructure and regional growth in the European Union. *Papers in Regional Science, 91*(3), 487–513. doi:10.1111/j.1435-5957.2012.00439.x

Davis, H. C. (1990). *Regional economic impact analysis and project evaluation*. Vancouver, Canada: UBC Press.

De Souza, G. F. M. (2012). *Thermal power plant performance analysis*. London, UK: Springer. doi:10.1007/978-1-4471-2309-5

Dimitriou, D. J. (2018). *Economic impact and project financing equilibrium to assess large transport infrastructure projects*. Working papers SIET. Retrieved from http://www.sietitalia.org/wpsiet/WP_SIET_2018_2_Dimitriou.pdf

Dimitriou, D. J., Mourmouris, J. C., & Sartzetaki, M. F. (2015). Economic impact assessment of mega infrastructure pipeline projects. *Applied Economics*, *47*(40), 4310–4322. doi:10.1080/00036846.2015.1026591

Dimitriou, D. J., & Sartzetaki, M. F. (2016). Decision framework for cross-border railway infrastructure projects. *International Journal of Social, Behavioral, Educational, Economic Business and Industrial Engineering*, *10*(11), 3531–3536.

Dimitriou, D. J., & Sartzetaki, M. F. (2016). Sustainable development variables to assess transport infrastructure in remote destinations. *World Academy of Science, Engineering and Technology, International Journal of Civil, Environmental, Structural Construction and Architectural Engineering*, *10*(10), 1343–1350.

Directorate General of Merchant Marine. (2018). *Load Statistics*. Retrieved from https://atlantis.udhb.gov.tr/istatistik/istatistik_yuk.aspx

Drury, C. (2005). *Management accounting for business* (3rd ed.). London, UK: Thomson Learning.

Dymowa, L. (2011). *Soft computing in economics and finance*. Heidelberg, Germany: Springer. doi:10.1007/978-3-642-17719-4

Engel, E. M., Fischer, R. D., & Galetovic, A. (2010). The economics of infrastructure finance: Public-private partnerships versus public provision. *EIB papers*, *15*(1), 40-69.

Esty, B. C. (1999). Improved techniques for valuing large-scale projects. *The Journal of Structured Finance*, *5*(1), 9–25. doi:10.3905/jsf.1999.320177

Europlatforms EEIG. (2004). Logistics centres directions for use. *a report by Europlatforms EEIG*.

Feng, F., Li, F., & Zhang, Q. (2013). Location selection of Chinese modern railway logistics center based on DEA-Bi-level programming model. *Research Journal of Applied Sciences, Engineering and Technology*, *6*(5), 812–818. doi:10.19026/rjaset.6.4125

Global-rates.com. (2019). *US Dollar LIBOR rates*. Retrieved from https://www.global-rates.com/interest-rates/libor/american-dollar/2019.aspx

Gordon, M. J. (1962). *The investment, financing, and valuation of the corporation*. Homewood, IL: RD Irwin.

Hanaoka, S., & Regmi, M. B. (2011). Promoting intermodal freight transport through the development of dry ports in Asia: An environmental perspective. *IATSS Research*, *35*(1), 16–23. doi:10.1016/j.iatssr.2011.06.001

Jorgensen, A. (2007, September). *A perspective on freight transport in South Africa*. Notes presented at a special interest group meeting, Johannesburg, South Africa.

Kapros, S., Panou, K., & Tsamboulas, D. A. (2005). Multicriteria approach to the evaluation of intermodal freight villages. *Transportation Research Record: Journal of the Transportation Research Board*, *1906*(1), 56–63. doi:10.1177/0361198105190600107

Keown, A. J., Martin, J. D., Petty, J. W., & Scott, D. F. (2013). *Foundations of finance: the logic and practice of financial management*. USA: Pearson Education.

Lee, K. L., Huang, W. C., & Teng, J. Y. (2009). Locating the competitive relation of global logistics hub using quantitative SWOT analytical method. *Quality & Quantity*, *43*(1), 87–107. doi:10.100711135-007-9087-1

Li, Y., Liu, X., & Chen, Y. (2011). Selection of logistics center location using Axiomatic Fuzzy Set and TOPSIS methodology in logistics management. *Expert Systems with Applications*, *38*(6), 7901–7908. doi:10.1016/j.eswa.2010.12.161

Lintner, J. (1969). The valuation of risk assets and the selection of risky investments in stock portfolios and capital budgets: A reply. *The Review of Economics and Statistics*, *51*(2), 222–224. doi:10.2307/1926735

Macharis, C., & Bernardini, A. (2015). Reviewing the use of multi-criteria decision analysis for the evaluation of transport projects: Time for a multi-actor approach. *Transport Policy*, *37*, 177–186. doi:10.1016/j.tranpol.2014.11.002

Magni, C. A. (2009). Investment decisions, net present value and bounded rationality. *Quantitative Finance*, *9*(8), 967–979. doi:10.1080/14697680902849338

Mandron, A. (2000). Improved techniques for valuing large-scale projects: A follow-up. *The Journal of Structured Finance*, *6*(1), 33–45. doi:10.3905/jsf.2000.320185

Mao, J. C. (1970). Survey of capital budgeting: Theory and practice. *The Journal of Finance*, *25*(2), 349–360. doi:10.1111/j.1540-6261.1970.tb00513.x

Meidute, I. (2007). Economical evaluation of logistics centres establishment. *Transport*, *22*(2), 111–117. doi:10.3846/16484142.2007.9638108

Miller, M., & Modigliani, F. (1958). The cost of capital. Corporate Finance and the Theory of Investment. *The American Economic Review*, *48*, 261–297.

Monios, J. (2011). The role of inland terminal development in the hinterland access strategies of Spanish ports. *Research in Transportation Economics*, *33*(1), 59–66. doi:10.1016/j.retrec.2011.08.007

Monios, J., & Lambert, B. (2013). The heartland intermodal corridor: Public private partnerships and the transformation of institutional settings. *Journal of Transport Geography*, *27*, 36–45. doi:10.1016/j.jtrangeo.2012.03.015

Monios, J., & Wilmsmeier, G. (2012). Giving a direction to port regionalisation. *Transportation Research Part A, Policy and Practice*, *46*(10), 1551–1561. doi:10.1016/j.tra.2012.07.008

Mossin, J. (1966). Equilibrium in a capital asset market. *Econometrica*, *34*(4), 768–783. doi:10.2307/1910098

Ng, A. Y., & Gujar, G. C. (2009). Government policies, efficiency and competitiveness: The case of dry ports in India. *Transport Policy*, *16*(5), 232–239. doi:10.1016/j.tranpol.2009.08.001

Nobes, C. (1997). *Introduction to financial accounting* (4th ed.). London, UK: International Thomson Business Press.

Palšaitis, R., & Bazaras, D. (2004). Analysis of the prospectives of intermodal transport and logistics centres in Lithuania. *Transport, 19*(3), 119–123. doi:10.3846/16484142.2004.9637963

Panova, Y., & Hilmola, O. P. (2015). Justification and evaluation of dry port investments in Russia. *Research in Transportation Economics, 51*, 61–70. doi:10.1016/j.retrec.2015.07.008

Pawlik, T., Stemmler, L., Baird, A. J., & Helch, M. (2011). The value of container terminal investment to ocean carrier strategy. *Maritime Economics & Logistics, 13*(3), 319–341. doi:10.1057/mel.2011.8

Pekin, E., & Macharis, C. (2013). A GIS-based analysis of the potential for freight villages in Turkey. *World Review of Intermodal Transportation Research, 4*(2-3), 157–174. doi:10.1504/WRITR.2013.058980

Pyles, M. K. (2014). *Applied corporate finance questions, problems and making decisions in the real world.* New York, NY: Springer.

Roso, V. (2013). Sustainable intermodal transport via dry ports–importance of directional development. *World Review of Intermodal Transportation Research, 4*(2-3), 140–156. doi:10.1504/WRITR.2013.058976

Schade, W. (2006). Assessing economic impacts of large-scale transport infrastructure projects: case of Lyon–Turin corridor. *Transportation Research Record: Journal of the Transportation Research Board, 1960*(1), 142–151. doi:10.1177/0361198106196000118

Sharpe, W. F. (1964). Capital asset prices: A theory of market equilibrium under conditions of risk. *The Journal of Finance, 19*(3), 425–442.

Song, K. (2003). The Korean hub strategy. (Unpublished master's dissertation). *Massachusetts Institute of Technology,* Cambridge.

Treynor, J. L. (1962). Jack Treynor's toward a theory of market value of risky assets. Available at https://ssrn.com/abstract=628187

Turkish Chamber of Shipping. (2018). *Maritime Sector Report.* Retrieved from https://www.denizticaretodasi.org.tr/Media/SharedDocuments/sektorraporu/2017_sektor_en.pdf

Turkish Statistical Institute. (2018). *Foreign Trade Statistics.* Retrieved from http://www.tuik.gov.tr/UstMenu.do?metod=temelist

Ünal, G., & Derindere Köscoğlu, S. (2014). Revealing the freight market risk in Istfix shipping area. *International Journal of Shipping and Transport Logistics, 6*(6), 593–610. doi:10.1504/IJSTL.2014.064904

Vitolo, G., & Cipparrone, F. (2014). Strategic implications of different criteria for project portfolio selection. In *Global Conference on Business & Finance Proceedings*, 9, 1, pp. 427-434. Institute for Business & Finance Research.

Worldgovernmentbonds.com. (2019). *Turkey 5 Years CDS.* Retrieved from http://www.worldgovernmentbonds.com/cds-historical-data/turkey/5-years/

ADDITIONAL READING

Bichou, K. (2014). *Port operations, planning and logistics*. London: Informa Law from Routledge. doi:10.4324/9781315850443

Bolumole, Y. A., Closs, D. J., & Rodammer, F. A. (2015). The economic development role of regional logistics hubs: A cross-country study of interorganizational governance models. *Journal of Business Logistics*, *36*(2), 182–198. doi:10.1111/jbl.12088

Hesse, M. (2004). Logistics and freight transport policy in urban areas: A case study of Berlin-Brandenburg/Germany. *European Planning Studies*, *12*(7), 1035–1053. doi:10.1080/0965431042000267894

Higgins, C. D., & Ferguson, M. R. (2011). *An exploration of the freight village concept and its applicability to Ontario*. McMaster Institute for Transportation and Logistics.

Jaržemskis, A. (2007). Research on public logistics centre as tool for cooperation. *Transport*, *22*(1), 50–54. doi:10.3846/16484142.2007.9638096

Krishnan, R., Desai, A., Ngoc, H. V. T., Tarannum, N., & Phan, T. (2012). A Case Study of Singapore as a Logistics Cluster. In M. Garg & S. Gupta (Eds.), *Cases on Supply Chain and Distribution Management: Issues and Principles* (pp. 1–35). IGI Global. doi:10.4018/978-1-4666-0065-2.ch001

Roso, V. (2007). Evaluation of the dry port concept from an environmental perspective: A note. *Transportation Research Part D, Transport and Environment*, *12*(7), 523–527. doi:10.1016/j.trd.2007.07.001

Singh, A., Chhetri, P., & Padhaye, R. (2016). Understanding the port-centric logistics clusters: concepts, characteristics, and measurements. In A. N. Dwivedi (Ed.), *Innovative Solutions for Implementing Global Supply Chains in Emerging Markets* (pp. 257–272). IGI Global. doi:10.4018/978-1-4666-9795-9.ch017

Taniguchi, E., & Van Der Heijden, R. E. (2000). An evaluation methodology for city logistics. *Transport Reviews*, *20*(1), 65–90. doi:10.1080/014416400295347

Yang, Y. C., & Chen, S. L. (2016). Determinants of global logistics hub ports: Comparison of the port development policies of Taiwan, Korea, and Japan. *Transport Policy*, *45*, 179–189. doi:10.1016/j.tranpol.2015.10.005

KEY TERMS AND DEFINITIONS

Cost of Capital: All kinds of resources used by the businesses have a cost. The cost of capital or the cost of funding is the weighted average cost of any kind of financial resources used or intended to be used. The importance of the calculation of the cost of capital could be listed as follows: (a) The cost of capital is used as the discount rate in the valuation of investment projects, (b) The capital structure and the cost of capital affect the success and the profitability of the businesses, (c) It is necessary to know the cost of capital for decisions such as leasing, long-term financing, and working capital policy. Moreover, the components of the cost of capital are the equity, preferred shares, undistributed profits and debts including long term liabilities and short term loans such as bank loans, financial bills, and vendor credits. While estimating the cost of capital, the cost of each resource constituting the capital structure of the business is calculated separately, then the average cost of capital is calculated by considering the weight of these resources in the capital structure. Furthermore, it is assumed that operating risk, profit distribution policy and capital structure will not change when calculating the cost of capital.

Credit Default Swap Spread: The credit default swap (CDS) is a type of credit derivative product. Credit derivatives provide transferring credit risk, which is the possibility that one of the contract parties will not able to fulfill his obligations, from one contractor to another one. Accordingly, credit derivatives are the tools that help banks, financial institutions and investors manage this risk. For example, if a debtor cannot pay the debts, losses will occur on the investments and these losses can be compensated by credit derivatives. Banks and investors prefer credit derivatives over insurance contracts because of their low transaction costs, quick payments and more liquidity. Within this context, CDS could be considered as an insurance transaction that is made to guarantee the receivable of the creditor. The cost of this insurance is the spread determined by the CDS rates. In other words, the price of a credit default swap is referred to as its spread. The spread is expressed by the basis points. For instance, a company CDS has a spread of 300 basis point indicates 3% which means that to insure $100 of this company's debt, an investor has to pay $3 per year. The higher the risk of debt, the higher the CDS point is. The increase in CDS rates indicates that the risk of the debt or the economy has increased. Thus, beyond the insurance function against the default risk, CDS provides insight into the countries' risks. Especially foreign investors primarily analyze the CDS of the country while they are making an investment in that country.

Logistics Center: The logistics center is a hub of a specific region where all logistics activities related to transport and distribution both for national and international transit are carried out on a commercial basis by various operators. These activities include many integrated services such as storage, handling, consolidation, decomposition, customs clearance, export, import and transit operations, infrastructure services, insurance and banking, consultancy, and production. In order to be able to carry out these mentioned operations, a logistics center should be equipped with all facilities. The terms logistics center, logistics hub, and logistics freight are generally used interchangeably.

Project Valuation: Project valuation refers to the analysis of the investment projects in order to determine the benefits and costs of the investments. With regard to this, the analysis aims to decide which projects to choose and to determine whether an investment project will be implemented or not. That is to say, the project valuation is a detailed study that includes investigating and evaluating whether any investment is practically applicable. The study mainly covers research and evaluations on market, technical and financial issues. Moreover, in general terms project valuation is a comprehensive process that detects the price of anything. This process could contain the worth determination of various assets from stocks, options, and mutual funds to patents, trademarks, and properties. Before launching any investment the entrepreneurs assess and analyze different factors such as project environment, cash flows, profitability, risks, technical solutions, regional and social effects, and other necessary information according to the scope of the project in order to be able to determine the worth of it.

Southeastern Anatolia Project: The Southeastern Anatolia Project (GAP) is an integrated program covering the development and services of urban and rural infrastructure, transportation, industry, education, health, and other sectors, as well as dams, hydroelectric power plants, and irrigation facilities in the Euphrates- Tigris Basin and upper Mesopotamia plains. In this respect, the program is one of the biggest projects in the history of the Turkish Republic. The project area covers 9 cities which are Adıyaman, Batman, Diyarbakır, Gaziantep, Kilis, Mardin, Siirt, Şanlıurfa, and Şırnak. These provinces make up approximately 11% of Turkey in both geographical and population terms. The project aims to increase the income level and strengthen the living standards of the local population by using the region's resources, increasing productivity, providing employment opportunities, and what is more, the project intends to decrease the economic disparities between the region and other parts of the country. Thus, it contributes to national economic development and social stability.

TEU: It is a type of measurement standing for Twenty-Foot Equivalent Unit which is used to measure a ship's cargo-carrying capacity. The dimensions of one TEU are equal to that of a standard 20′ (20-foot) shipping container and it has a volume of approximately 34 cubic meters. In other words, the term TEU expresses the capacity of a container ship in a uniform manner, the number of containers that the ship can load is converted into a number of containers of the smallest size, i.e. those that are twenty feet in length.

TRACECA: It is the abbreviation of Transport Corridor Europe-Caucasus-Asia. This transport corridor project is an inter-state program that aims at improving international transport and political-economic progress in the European Union, the Black Sea, Caucasus, and Central Asia. Moreover, specifically, the program intends to strengthen the trade and transportation of Azerbaijan, Armenia, Georgia, Kazakhstan, Kyrgyzstan, Tajikistan, Turkmenistan and Uzbekistan to integrate them with the international economy.

Compilation of References

Abdel-Baki, M. A. (2012). The impact of Basel III on emerging economies. *Global Economy Journal*, 12(2).

Abell, J., & Krueger, T. (1989). Macroeconomic influences on beta. *Journal of Economics and Business*, *41*(2), 185–193. doi:10.1016/0148-6195(89)90016-7

Achleitner, A. K., & Nathusius, E. (2003). Syndizierung von Venture-Capital-Deals. *Entrepreneur des Jahres–NEWS*, *2*, 8.

Adams, M. & Rudolf, M. (2010). A new approach to the valuation of banks [online]. Cited 2011-05-06.

Adams, C. A., & Whelan, G. (2009). Conceptualising future change in corporate sustainability reporting. *Accounting, Auditing & Accountability Journal*, *22*(1), 118–143. doi:10.1108/09513570910923033

Adebiyi, A. A., Adewumi, A. O., & Ayo, C. K. (2014). Comparison of ARIMA and artificial neural networks models for stock price prediction. *Journal of Applied Mathematics*, 2014.

Adelman, I., & Adelman, F. L. (1959). The dynamic properties of the Klein-Goldberger model. *Econometrica*, *27*(4), 596–625. doi:10.2307/1909353

Adler, M., & Dumas, B. (1983). International portfolio choice and corporation finance: A synthesis. *The Journal of Finance*, *38*(3), 925–984. doi:10.1111/j.1540-6261.1983.tb02511.x

Aiyar, S., Calomiris, C. W., & Wieladek, T. (2014). Does macro-prudential regulation leak? Evidence from a UK policy experiment. *Journal of Money, Credit and Banking*, *46*(s1), 181–214. doi:10.1111/jmcb.12086

Akbank. (2019). *Investor relations*. Retrieved from https://www.akbank.com/en-us/investor-relations/Pages/News.aspx

Aktaş, R.; Başçı S., Değere Dayalı Yönetim ve Firma Değerinin Tespiti, chapter 11, Sakarya Üniversitesi Sürekli Eğitim Uygulama ve Araştırma Merkezi.

Alibhai, S., & … . (2018). *Interpretation and Application of IFRS Standards*. UK: John Wiley.

Amiri, P. M. & Morteza, A. R. (2009). Prioritize financial factors affecting the price index in the Tehran Stock Exchange using TOPSIS, financial research: No. 26, pp. 61-76.

Angora, A. & Roulet, C. (2011). Liquidity assessment and the use of liquidity ratio as defined in the Basel III accords to identify bank distress. Working paper, Université de Limoges, France. Retrieved from http://iriaf.univpoitiers.fr/colloque2011/article/v1s2a2.pdf

Ankobiah, M. (2001). *Valuation of port assets: impact on the financial performance of port and the national economy*. (Unpublished master dissertation). World Maritime University, Malmo, Sweden.

Ansar, A., Caldecott, B., & Tilbury, J. (2013). *Stranded assets and the fossil fuel divestment campaign: what does divestment mean for the valuation of fossil fuel assets? Stranded assets programme. Smith School of Enterprise and Environment.* University of Oxford.

Antai, I., & Olson, H. (2013). Interaction: A new focus for supply chain vs supply chain competition. *International Journal of Physical Distribution & Logistics Management*, *43*(7), 511–528. doi:10.1108/IJPDLM-06-2012-0195

Antill, *N. & Lee, K. (2008). Company valuation under IFRS.* UK: Harriman House.

Antoniou, A., Guney, Y., & Paudyal, K. (2008). The determinants of capital structure: capital market-oriented versus bank-oriented institutions. *Journal of Financial and Quantitative Analysis*, *43*(1), 59–92. doi:10.1017/S0022109000002751

Ariyo, A. A., Adewumi, A. O., & Ayo, C. K. (2014, March). Stock price prediction using the ARIMA model. In *2014 UKSim-AMSS 16th International Conference on Computer Modelling and Simulation* (pp. 106-112). IEEE. 10.1109/UKSim.2014.67

Ark, A. H. (2002). Risk Sermayesi: Tarihsel Gelişimi ve Türkiye Ekonomisinin Yeniden Yapılandırılmasında Potansiyel Rolü ve Önemi. *Activefinans, 82vd.*

Asadi, G. & Ashkani, B. (2016). Investigating the impact of auditor change on stock price. *Audit Knowledge Journal,* 66, pp. 41-60.

Aswath, D. (2010). *Estimating risk parameters.* Stern School of Business.

Atkins, J., & Maroun, W. (2018). Integrated extinction accounting and accountability: Building an ark. *Accounting, Auditing & Accountability Journal*, *31*(3), 750–786. doi:10.1108/AAAJ-06-2017-2957

Babu, C. N., & Reddy, B. E. (2014). A moving-average filter-based hybrid ARIMA–ANN model for forecasting time series data. *Applied Soft Computing*, *23*, 27–38. doi:10.1016/j.asoc.2014.05.028

Baird, A. J., & Valentine, V. F. (2006). Port privatisation in the United Kingdom. *Research in Transportation Economics*, *17*, 55–84. doi:10.1016/S0739-8859(06)17003-1

Bancel, F., & Mittoo, U. R. (2004). Cross-country determinants of capital structure choice: a survey of European firms. *Financial Management*, 103–132.

Bancel, F., & Mittoo, U. R. (2014). *The gap between theory and practice of firm valuation: Survey of European valuation experts*. SSRN Electronic Journal. doi:10.2139srn.242038

Bangladesh Country Review. (2010). Stock market. Bangladesh Country Review, 80-81.

Bank for International Settlement. (2013). A brief history of the basel committee. Retrieved from http://www.bis.org/bcbs/history.pdf

Bank of America Financial Statements. (2014-2018). Retrieved from https://www.macrotrends.net/stocks/charts/BAC/bank-of-america/balance-sheet and https://www.macrotrends.net/stocks/charts/BAC/bank-of-america/income-statement

Banz, R. W. (1981). The relationship between return and market value of common stocks. *Journal of Financial Economics*, *9*(1), 3–18. doi:10.1016/0304-405X(81)90018-0

Barnes, S. A. (n.d.). *The Uber dilemma: Valuing startup and early stage companies with negative earnings.* Retrieved from https://files.constantcontact.com/85e69272601/1234ed1a-3764-40fc-9ff5-fbdce61aa83b.pdf

Barnett, V., & Lewis, T. (1994). *Outliers in statistical data.* Chichester, UK: Wiley.

Basel Committee on Banking Supervision (BCBS). (2011). Basel III: A global regulatory framework for more resilient banks and banking systems. Revised, June. BIS, Basel. Available at https://www.bis.org/publ/bcbs189.htm

Basel Committee on Banking Supervision (BCBS). (2013). Basel III: The liquidity coverage ratio and liquidity risk monitoring tools. BIS, Basel. Available at https://www.bis. org/publ/bcbs238.htm

Basel Committee on Banking Supervision (BCBS). (2014). Impact and implementation challenges of the Basel framework for emerging market, developing and small economies. BCBS Working Paper No. 27, Bank for International Settlement, Basel. Retrieved from http://www.bis.org/bcbs/publ/wp27.pdf

Basel Committee on Banking Supervision (BCBS). (2015). Net stable funding ratio disclosure standards. BIS, Basel. Available at https://www.bis.org/bcbs/publ /d324.htm

Basel Committee on Banking Supervision (BCBS). (2016). Basel Committee on Banking Supervision Charter. Bank for International Settlement, Basel. Retrieved from http://www.bis.org/bcbs/charter.htm

Basu, S. (1977). Investment performance of common stocks in relation to their price-earnings ratios: A test of the efficient market hypothesis. *The Journal of Finance*, *12*(3), 129–156.

Beck, U. (1992). Risk society: towards a new modernity, London, UK.

Beck, U. (1997). Sub-politics: Ecology and the disintegration of institutional power. *Organization & Environment*, *10*(1), 52–65. doi:10.1177/0921810697101008

Belkaoui, A. R. (2000). Accounting theory: Thomson Learning, London, UK, 4th ed.

BENNINGA. (2008). *S. Financial Modeling* (3rd ed.). London, UK: The MIT Press.

Beresford, A., Pettit, S., Xu, Q., & Williams, S. (2012). A study of dry port development in China. *Maritime Economics & Logistics*, *14*(1), 73–98. doi:10.1057/mel.2011.17

Berger, A. N., & Bouwman, C. H. (2013). How does capital affect bank performance during financial crises? *Journal of Financial Economics*, *109*(1), 146–176. doi:10.1016/j.jfineco.2013.02.008

Bergqvist, R., Falkemark, G., & Woxenius, J. (2010). Establishing intermodal terminals. *World Review of Intermodal Transportation Research*, *3*(3), 285–302. doi:10.1504/WRITR.2010.034667

Bergqvist, R., Wilmsmeier, G., & Cullinane, K. (Eds.). (2016). *Dry ports–a global perspective: challenges and developments in serving hinterlands*. New York, NY: Routledge Publishing.

Bernabe, E. M., Jr. & Jaffar, J. (2013). Gauging the macroeconomic impact of Basel III on Malaysia. Staff paper no. 87. Research and Training Centre, SEACEN.

Bernanke, B., Gertler, M., & Gilchrist, S. (1996). The financial accelerator and the flight to quality. *The Review of Economics and Statistics*, *78*(1), 1–15. doi:10.2307/2109844

Bernstein, P. L. (1996). *Against the gods. the remarkable story of risk*. Chichester, UK: John Wiley.

Bezant, M. & Rogers, D. (2016). *Asset – based valuation floor or flawed valuation?* An FTI Consulting White Paper, Dec. 2016. Retrieved from www.fticonsulting.com

Bhandari, L. (1988). Debt/equity ratio and expected common stock returns: empirical evidence. *The Journal of Finance*, *43*(2), 507–528. doi:10.1111/j.1540-6261.1988.tb03952.x

Bhandari, S. B. (2009). Discounted payback period-some extensions. *Journal of Business and Behavioral Sciences*, *21*(1), 28–38.

Black, A. & Wright, P. (2001). *In search of shareholder value: Managing the drivers of performance,* 2nd ed., Financial Times Prentice Hall.

Black, F., Jensen, M. C., & Scholes, M. (1972). The capital asset pricing model: Some empirical tests. *Studies in the theory of capital markets, 81*(3), 79-121.

Blank, S., & Dorf, B. (2014). *Startup: manual do empreendedor.* Alta Books Editora.

Boabang, F. (2003). The IPOs of Canadian firms via installment receipts: the opening performance and implications for the short-run efficiency of the Canadian market. *Canadian Journal of Administrative Sciences*/Revue Canadienne des Sciences de l'Administration; 20, 3, pp. 224–233, September 2003.

Borch, K. (1969). A note on uncertainty and indifference curves. *The Review of Economic Studies, 36*(1), 1–4. doi:10.2307/2296336

Bornholt, G. (2013). The failure of the capital asset pricing model (CAPM): An update and discussion. *Abacus, 49*(S1), 36–43. doi:10.1111/j.1467-6281.2012.00382.x

Borsa İstanbul. (2016). *Startup Valuation.* https://bfb.az/wp-content/uploads/2016/10/Startup-Valuation.pdf

Boussabaine, A. (2013). *Risk pricing strategies for public-private partnership projects.* Hoboken, NJ: John Wiley & Sons. doi:10.1002/9781118785812

Bowen, P. A. (1984). A hypothesis: Portfolio theory is elegant but useless. *The Investment Analysts Journal, 13*(24), 17–21. doi:10.1080/10293523.1984.11082227

Bowman, R. (1979). The theoretical relationship between systematic risk and financial (accounting) variables. *The Journal of Finance, 34*(3), 617–630. doi:10.1111/j.1540-6261.1979.tb02129.x

Bradley, M., Jarrell, G. A., & Kim, E. H. (1984). On the existence of an optimal capital structure: Theory and evidence. *The Journal of Finance, 39*(3), 857–878. doi:10.1111/j.1540-6261.1984.tb03680.x

Brigham, E. F., & Daves, P. R. (2014). *Intermediate financial management.* Cengage Learning.

Brouwer, W. B., Niessen, L. W., Postma, M. J., & Rutten, F. F. (2005). Need for differential discounting of costs and health effects in cost effectiveness analyses. *BMJ (Clinical Research Ed.), 331*(7514), 446–448. doi:10.1136/bmj.331.7514.446 PMID:16110075

Brown, L. D., Huefner, R. J., & Sanders, J. R. (1995). A test of the reliability of current cost disclosures, accounting theory: A contemporary review. Orlando, FL: Harcourt Brace.

Brownlees, C. T., & Gallo, G. M. (2006). Financial econometric analysis at ultra-high frequency: Data handling concerns. *Computational Statistics & Data Analysis, 51*(4), 2232–2245. doi:10.1016/j.csda.2006.09.030

Brown, P., & Walter, T. (2013). The CAPM: Theoretical validity, empirical intractability and practical applications. *Abacus, 49*(S1), 44–50. doi:10.1111/j.1467-6281.2012.00383.x

Brown, R. G. (1959). *Statistical forecasting for inventory control.* McGraw/Hill.

Brush, C. G., Carter, N. M., Gatewood, E. J., Greene, P. G., & Hart, M. M. (2006). The use of bootstrapping by women entrepreneurs in positioning for growth. *Venture Capital, 8*(1), 15–31. doi:10.1080/13691060500433975

Bruzelius, N., Flyvbjerg, B., & Rothengatter, W. (2002). Big decisions, big risks. Improving accountability in mega projects. *Transport Policy, 9*(2), 143–154. doi:10.1016/S0967-070X(02)00014-8

Bundoo, S. K. (2007). An analysis of IPOS underpricing in Mauritius. *African Journal of Accounting, Economics, Finance and Banking Research*, *1*(1), 1–12.

Bunea-Bontas, C. A. (2013). *Valuation techniques used in fair value* (pp. 97–104)., Retrieved from www.strategicmanagerial.ro/pdf

Caldecott, B. (2018). *Stranded assets and the environment. risk, resilience and opportunity. routledge explorations in environmental studies*. Routledge. doi:10.4324/9781315651606

Cappiello, L., Kadareja, A., Kok, C., & Protopapa, M. (2010). *Do bank loans and credit standards have an effect on output? A panel approach for the euro area. ECB Working Paper No. 1150*. Frankfurt, Germany: European Central Bank. Retrieved from https://www.ecb.europa.eu/pub/pdf/scpwps/ecbwp1150.pdf

Cass, S. (1998). *World port privatisation: finance, funding and ownership: a cargo systems report*. London, UK: IIR Publications.

Central Bank of Turkish Republic. (2019). *Interest Rate Statistics, Statistics Department, Data Management Division*. Retrieved from https://www.tcmb.gov.tr/wps/wcm/connect/EN/TCMB+EN/Main+Menu/Statistics/Interest+Rate+Statistics

Cetorelli, N., & Goldberg, L. S. (2012). Liquidity management of U.S. global banks: Internal capital markets in the great recession. *Journal of International Economics*, *88*(2), 299–311. doi:10.1016/j.jinteco.2012.05.001

CFA Institute. (2019). *Free Cash Flow Valuation*. Retrieved from https://www.cfainstitute.org/membership/professional-development/refresher-readings/2019/free-cash-flow-valuation

Chalermchatvichien, P., Jumreornvong, S., & Jiraporn, P. (2014). Basel III, capital stability, risk-taking, ownership: Evidence from Asia. *Journal of Multinational Financial Management*, *28*, 28–46. doi:10.1016/j.mulfin.2014.09.001

Chambers, N. (2009). *Firma Değerlemesi*. İstanbul, Turkey: Beta Basım Yayın.

Chandra, P. (2011). *Corporate valuation and value creation* (1st ed.). Delhi, India: Tata McGraw-Hill Education.

Chang, S. C., Chung, T. Y., & Lin, W. C. (2010). Underwriter reputation, earnings management and the long-run performance of initial public offerings. *Accounting and Finance*, *50*(1), 53–78. doi:10.1111/j.1467-629X.2009.00329.x

Chan, L. C., Yasushi, H., & Josef, L. (1991). Fundamentals and stock returns in Japan. *The Journal of Finance*, *46*(5), 1739–1789. doi:10.1111/j.1540-6261.1991.tb04642.x

Chavan, P., & Gambacorta, L. (2018). Bank lending and loan quality: An emerging economy perspective. *Empirical Economics*, 1–29. doi:10.100700181-018-1436-5

Chen, A. S., Leung, M. T., & Daouk, H. (2003). Application of neural networks to an emerging financial market: Forecasting and trading the Taiwan Stock Index. *Computers & Operations Research*, *30*(6), 901–923. doi:10.1016/S0305-0548(02)00037-0

Cheng, S. R., & Shiu, C. Y. (2007). Investor protection and capital structure: international evidence. *Journal of Multinational Financial Management*, *17*(1), 30–44. doi:10.1016/j.mulfin.2006.03.002

Chen, K. Y., Lin, K. L., & Zhou, J. (2005). Audit quality and earnings management for Taiwan IPO firms. *Managerial Auditing Journal*, *20*(1), 86–104. doi:10.1108/02686900510570722

Chi, J. & Padgett, C. (2002). The performance and long-run characteristics of the Chinese IPO market, U of Reading, ISMA Centre Discussion Paper No. 2002-09.

Cho, D. (1988). The impact of risk management decisions on firms value: gordon's growth model approach. *The Journal of Risk and Insurance*, *55*(1), 118–131. doi:10.2307/253284

Cingöz, A. (2014). İndirgenmiş Nakit Akımlari Yöntemine Göre Firma Değerleme ve Enerji Sektöründe Bir Uygulama, Selçuk University, Doctoral Study, Konya, İstanbul.

CISL. (2014). *The value of responsible investment. The moral, financial and economic case for action*. University of Cambridge.

Clarksons Research. (2019). *Shipping review and outlook*. Retrieved from https://www.crsl.com/acatalog/shipping-review-and-outlook.html

Çoban, M. & Saban, M. (2006). Türkiye'de risk sermayesi uygulaması ve sorunları. *Muhasebe ve Finansman Dergisi*, (31), 131-140.

Cohen, K. J., Hawawini, G. A., Maier, S. F., Schwartz, R. A., & Whitcomb, D. K. (1983a). Estimating and Adjusting for the Intervalling-Effect Bias in Beta. *Management Science*, *29*(1), 135–148. doi:10.1287/mnsc.29.1.135

Cohen, K. J., Hawawini, G. A., Maier, S. F., Schwartz, R. A., & Whitcomb, D. K. (1983b). Friction in the trading process and the estimation of systematic risk. *Journal of Financial Economics*, *12*(2), 263–278. doi:10.1016/0304-405X(83)90038-7

Copeland. T., Koller, T., & Murrin, J. (2000). Valuation. Measuring and managing the value of companies (3rd ed.). New York, NY: John Wiley & Sons.

Copeland, T., Koller, T., & Murrin, J. (1996). *Valuation: Managing and measuring the value of companies*. New York, NY: John Wiley & Sons.

Crescenzi, R., & Rodríguez-Pose, A. (2012). Infrastructure and regional growth in the European Union. *Papers in Regional Science*, *91*(3), 487–513. doi:10.1111/j.1435-5957.2012.00439.x

Damodaran, A. (1999). The dark side of valuation: firms with no earnings, no history and no comparables.

Damodaran, A. (2008). What is the riskfree rate? A search for the basic building block. Stern School of Business, New York University, December.

Damodaran, A. (2009). Valuing financial service firms– The big picture, (April), pp. 1–34. Retrieved from people.stern.nyu.edu/adamodar/pdfiles/papers/finfirm09.pdf

Damodaran, A. (2009). *Valuing young, startup and growth companies: estimation issues and valuation challenges*. Available at SSRN 1418687.

Damodaran, A. (2009). Valuing young, start-up and growth companies: estimation issues and valuation challenges. Stern School of Business, New York University, May.

Damodaran, A. (2012) Valuing firms with negative or abnormal earnings. 3rd Edition. Investment valuation: Tools and techniques for determining the value of any asset. In A. Damodaran (Ed.), Investment valuation: tools and techniques for determining the value of any asset, University Edition. iBooks.

Damodaran, A. (2013). Session 1: An introduction to valuation some initial thoughts. Retrieved from https://itunes.apple.com/us/course/id780803998

Damodaran, A. (2018). Equity risk premiums (ERP): Determinants, estimation and implications. Stern School of Business, New York University, March.

Damodaran, A. (2019). Damodaran online. Available at http://pages.stern.nyu.edu/~adamodar/

Damodaran, A. (2001). *Investment valuation*. Wiley.

Damodaran, A. (2002). *Investment valuation: Tools and techniques for determining the value of any asset*. New York, NY: John Wiley & Sons.

Damodaran, A. (2005). *Valuation approaches and metrics: a survey of the theory and evidence*. New York, NY: Stern School of Business.

Damodaran, A. (2012). *Valuation - tools and techniques for determining the value of any asset* (3rd ed., p. 155). Hoboken, NJ: John Wiley & Sons.

Damodaran, A. (2014a). *Equity risk premiums (ERP): determinants, estimation and implications.* (2014 ed.). SSRN Electronic Journal. doi:10.2139srn.240919

Damodaran, A. (n.d.). Growth rates and terminal value. *DCF Valuation.*

Dasgupta, P. (2001). *Human well-being and the natural environment.* New York, NY: Oxford University Press. doi:10.1093/0199247889.001.0001

Dash, R., & Dash, P. K. (2016). A hybrid stock trading framework integrating technical analysis with machine learning techniques. *The Journal of Finance and Data Science*, *2*(1), 42–57. doi:10.1016/j.jfds.2016.03.002

David, S. (2018, Dec. 5). 7 business valuation methods all entrepreneurs should know [Web log post]. Retrieved from https://www.fundera.com/blog/business-valuation-methods

Davis, G. F., & Cobb, J. A. (2010). Resource dependence theory: Past and future. *Research in the Sociology of Organizations*, *28*(1), 21–42. doi:10.1108/S0733-558X(2010)0000028006

Davis, H. C. (1990). *Regional economic impact analysis and project evaluation*. Vancouver, Canada: UBC Press.

De Jong, A., Kabir, R., & Nguyen, T. T. (2008). Capital structure around the world: the roles of firm-and country-specific determinants. *Journal of Banking & Finance*, *32*(9), 1954–1969. doi:10.1016/j.jbankfin.2007.12.034

De Oliveira, F. B., & Zotes, L. P. (2018). Valuation methodologies for business startups: A bibliographical study and survey. *Brazilian Journal of Operations & Production Management*, *15*(1), 96–111. doi:10.14488/BJOPM.2018.v15.n1.a9

De Souza, G. F. M. (2012). *Thermal power plant performance analysis.* London, UK: Springer. doi:10.1007/978-1-4471-2309-5

De Winter, J. C., & Dodou, D. (2010). Five-point Likert items: T test versus Mann-Whitney-Wilcoxon. *Practical Assessment, Research & Evaluation*, *15*(11), 1–12.

DeAngelo, H., & Masulis, R. W. (1980). Optimal capital structure under corporate and personal taxation. *Journal of Financial Economics*, *8*(1), 3–29. doi:10.1016/0304-405X(80)90019-7

Demirguc-Kunt, A., & Maksimović, V. (1994). *Capital structures in developing countries: evidence from ten country cases* (Vol. 1320). World Bank Publications.

Demuth, A. (n.d.). *Income approach and the discounted cash flow methodology.* Retrieved from https://globalarbitrationreview.com/chapter/1151372/income-approach-and-the-discounted-cash-flow-methodology

Dermine, J. (2008). Bank valuation: With an application to the implicit duration of nonmaturing deposits. Retrieved from http://ssrn.com/abstract=1314884

Diaconu, P. & Coman, N. (2006). *Accounting research from the globalization perspective.* Available at https://ssrn.com

Dimitriou, D. J. (2018). *Economic impact and project financing equilibrium to assess large transport infrastructure projects*. Working papers SIET. Retrieved from http://www.sietitalia.org/wpsiet/WP_SIET_2018_2_Dimitriou.pdf

Dimitriou, D. J., Mourmouris, J. C., & Sartzetaki, M. F. (2015). Economic impact assessment of mega infrastructure pipeline projects. *Applied Economics*, *47*(40), 4310–4322. doi:10.1080/00036846.2015.1026591

Dimitriou, D. J., & Sartzetaki, M. F. (2016). Decision framework for cross-border railway infrastructure projects. *International Journal of Social, Behavioral, Educational, Economic Business and Industrial Engineering*, *10*(11), 3531–3536.

Dimitriou, D. J., & Sartzetaki, M. F. (2016). Sustainable development variables to assess transport infrastructure in remote destinations. *World Academy of Science, Engineering and Technology, International Journal of Civil, Environmental, Structural Construction and Architectural Engineering*, *10*(10), 1343–1350.

Dimson, E. (1979). Risk measurement when shares are subject to infrequent trading. *Journal of Financial Economics*, *7*(2), 197–226. doi:10.1016/0304-405X(79)90013-8

Directorate General of Merchant Marine. (2018). *Load Statistics*. Retrieved from https://atlantis.udhb.gov.tr/istatistik/istatistik_yuk.aspx

Donaldson, G. (1961). *Corporate debt capacity: a study of corporate debt policy and the determination of corporate debt capacity*. Boston, MA: Division of Research, Harvard University.

Douma, S. W., & Schreuder, H. (2008). *Economic approaches to organizations*. Pearson Education.

Drobetz, W., & Wanzenried, G. (2006). What determines the speed of adjustment to the target capital structure? *Applied Financial Economics*, *16*(13), 941–958. doi:10.1080/09603100500426358

Drury, C. (2005). *Management accounting for business* (3rd ed.). London, UK: Thomson Learning.

Dymowa, L. (2011). *Soft computing in economics and finance*. Heidelberg, Germany: Springer. doi:10.1007/978-3-642-17719-4

eFinancial Models. (2016). *Discounted cash flow model*. Retrieved from https://www.efinancialmodels.com/2016/12/28/dcf-model-calculating-discounted-cash-flows/

Ehrhardt, M. C., & Brigham, E. F. (2016). *Corporate finance: A focused approach*. Cengage Learning.

Ekberg, M. (2007). The parameters of the risk society: a review and exploration. *Current Sociology*, *55*(3), 343–366. doi:10.1177/0011392107076080

Elkington, J. (1997). Cannibals with forks: The triple bottom line of 21st century business. Capstone.

Elmas, B., Yılmaz, H., & Yalçın, S. (2017). Firma Değerlemesinde İndirgenmiş Nakit Akımları Yönteminin Kullanımı: Bıst Bilişim Endeksinde Yer Alan Firmalar Üzerinde Bir Uygulama. *Atatürk Üniversitesi İktisadi ve İdari Bilimler Dergisi*, *31*(5), 1221–1238.

Elsas, R., & Florysiak, D. (2015). Dynamic capital structure adjustment and the impact of fractional dependent variables. *Journal of Financial and Quantitative Analysis*, *50*(5), 1105–1133. doi:10.1017/S0022109015000496

Engel, E. M., Fischer, R. D., & Galetovic, A. (2010). The economics of infrastructure finance: Public-private partnerships versus public provision. *EIB papers*, *15*(1), 40-69.

Engle, R. (2001). GARCH 101: The use of ARCH/GARCH models in applied econometrics. *The Journal of Economic Perspectives*, *15*(4), 157–168. doi:10.1257/jep.15.4.157

Ercan, M. K., Öztürk, M. B., & Demirgüneş, K. (2003). Değere Dayalı Yönetim ve Entelektüel Sermaye, Gazi Kitabevi, 1st ed., Ankara, Turkey.

Ercan, M., Öztürk, M., Küçükkaplan, İ., Başçı, Demirgüneş, K. (2006). Firma Değerlemesi ve Banka Uygulaması. İstanbul, Literatür Yayıncılık.

Ernst & Young. (2013). Appling IFRS in real estate. Retrieved from www.eyjapan.jp

Ertugrul, M. (2008). Değer-Fiyat Ayrımı ve İşletme Değeri: Kuramsal Bir Bakış. *Eskişehir Orhangazi Üniversitesi İİBF Derigisi*, *3*(2), 143–154.

Esty, B. C. (1999). Improved techniques for valuing large-scale projects. *The Journal of Structured Finance*, *5*(1), 9–25. doi:10.3905/jsf.1999.320177

Eugene, F. & Kenneth, R. (2004). The capital asset pricing model: Theory and evidence. *Journal of Economic Perspectives, 18*(3), 25–46 (4.2). Retrieved from www-personal.umich.edu/~kathrynd/JEP.FamaandFrench.pdf

European Commission. (2016). Overview of support activities and projects of the European Union on energy efficiency and renewable energy in the heating & cooling sector, *Horizon 2020, Framework Programme 7 and Intelligent Energy Europe programmes of the European Union,* 2.

Europlatforms EEIG. (2004). Logistics centres directions for use. *a report by Europlatforms EEIG.*

Fabozzi, F., & Francis, J. C. (1978). Beta as a random coefficient. *Journal of Financial and Quantitative Analysis*, *13*(1), 101–115. doi:10.2307/2330525

Faccio, M., & Xu, J. (2015). Taxes and capital structure. *Journal of Financial and Quantitative Analysis*, *50*(3), 277–300. doi:10.1017/S0022109015000174

Faff, R. W., Gray, S., & Tan, K. J. K. (2016). A contemporary view of corporate finance theory, empirical evidence and practice. *Australian Journal of Management*, *41*(4), 662–686. doi:10.1177/0312896216632032

Fama, E. (1998). Market efficiency long run returns and behavioral finance. *Journal of Financial Economics,* 49.

Fama, E. F., & French, K. R. (1988). Dividend yields and expected stock returns. *Journal of Financial Economics*, 22.

Fama, E. F., & French, K. R. (1992). The Cross-Section of Expected Returns. *The Journal of Finance*, 47.

Fama, E. F., & French, K. R. (1992). The cross-section of expected stock returns. *The Journal of Finance*, *47*(2), 427–465. doi:10.1111/j.1540-6261.1992.tb04398.x

Fama, E., & French, K. (2004). The capital asset pricing model: theory and evidence. *The Journal of Economic Perspectives*, *18*(3), 25–46. doi:10.1257/0895330042162430

Fan, J. P., Titman, S., & Twite, G. (2012). An international comparison of capital structure and debt maturity choices. *Journal of Financial and Quantitative Analysis*, *47*(1), 23–56. doi:10.1017/S0022109011000597

Fayek, M. B., El-Boghdadi, H. M., & Omran, S. M. (2013). Multi-objective optimization of technical stock market indicators using gas. *International Journal of Computers and Applications*, *68*(20).

Feldman, S. J. (2005). *Principles of private firm valuation.* Wiley.

Feng, F., Li, F., & Zhang, Q. (2013). Location selection of Chinese modern railway logistics center based on DEA-Bi-level programming model. *Research Journal of Applied Sciences, Engineering and Technology*, *6*(5), 812–818. doi:10.19026/rjaset.6.4125

Fernandez, P. (2013). WACC: definition, misconceptions and errors, IESE Business School, University of Navarra, November.

Fernandez, P., & Carabias, J. M. (2006). *Union Fenosa 1991-2005*. SSRN Electronic Journal. doi:10.2139srn.914160

Financial Accounting Standards Board (FASB) (1999-2000). Statement of Financial Accounting Concepts. John Wiley & Sons Inc.

Financial Accounting Standards Board (FASB). (1999-2000). Statement of financial accounting concepts. Hoboken, NJ: John Wiley & Sons.

Fischer, E. O., Heinkel, R., & Zechner, J. (1989). Dynamic capital structure choice: Theory and tests. *The Journal of Finance*, *44*(1), 19–40. doi:10.1111/j.1540-6261.1989.tb02402.x

Fisher, I. (1907). *The rate of interest: its nature, determination and relation to economic phenomena*. MacMillan Company.

Frankel, R., & Lee, C. M. C. (1998). Accounting valuation, market expectation, and cross-sectional stock returns. *Journal of Accounting and Economics*, *25*(3), 283–319. doi:10.1016/S0165-4101(98)00026-3

Frank, M., & Goyal, V. (2009). Capital structure decisions: which factors are reliably important? *Financial Management*, *38*(1), 1–37. doi:10.1111/j.1755-053X.2009.01026.x

Freear, J., Sohl, J. E., & Wetzel, W. (2002). Angles on angels: Financing technology-based ventures- a historical perspective. *Venture Capital: An International Journal of Entrepreneurial Finance*, *4*(4), 275–287. doi:10.1080/13691060022000024923

French, K. R., Schwert, G. W., & Stambaugh, R. F. (1987). Expected stock returns and volatility. *Journal of Financial Economics*, *19*(1), 3–29. doi:10.1016/0304-405X(87)90026-2

Gardner, J., McGowan, C., Jr. & Moeller, S. E. (2010). Using Microsoft Corporation to demonstrate the optimal capital structure trade-off theory. *Journal of Economics and Finance Education, 9*(2), 29–37. Retrieved from https://www.economics-finance.org/jefe/fin/Gardner.Finance.Vol.9(2).pdf

Gardner, E. S. Jr. (2006). Exponential smoothing: The state of the art—Part II. *International Journal of Forecasting*, *22*(4), 637–666. doi:10.1016/j.ijforecast.2006.03.005

Gartner, W. B. (1985). A conceptual framework for describing the phenomenon of new venture creation. *Academy of Management Review*, *10*(4), 694–706. doi:10.5465/amr.1985.4279094

Gatzert, N. & Wesker, H. (2011). A comparative assessment of Basel II/III and solvency II. Friedrich-Alexander-University of Erlangen-Nuremberg, Nuremberg, Germany.

Giammarino, R., Schwartz, E., & Zechner, J. (1989). Market valuation of bank assets and deposit insurance in Canada. Canadian Journal of Economics, 22(1), pp. 109–127.

Giddens, A. (1990). *The consequences of modernity*. Stanford, CA: Stanford University Press.

Giddens, A. (1991). *Modern and self-identity: self and society in the late modern age*. Cambridge: Blackwell Publishing.

Giddens, A., & Pierson, C. (1998). *Conversations with Anthony Giddens: Making sense of modernity*. Cambridge, UK: Polity Press.

Gilje, E. P., & Taillard, J. P. (2017). Does hedging affect firm value? evidence from a natural experiment. *Review of Financial Studies*, *30*(12), 4122. doi:10.1093/rfs/hhx069

Global-rates.com. (2019). *US Dollar LIBOR rates*. Retrieved from https://www.global-rates.com/interest-rates/libor/american-dollar/2019.aspx

Gniewosz, G. (1990). The share investment decision process and information use: An exploratory case study. *Accounting and Business Research*, *20*(79), 233–230. doi:10.1080/00014788.1990.9728880

Goetz, M. R., Laeven, L., & Levine, R. (2016). Does the geographic expansion of banks reduce risk? *Journal of Financial Economics*, *120*(2), 346–362. doi:10.1016/j.jfineco.2016.01.020

Goken, G., & Teraman, O. (2018). Importance of synergistic value in the context of business combination: A case study from Turkey. *Economics*, *6*(1), 49–60.

González, V., & González, F. (2008). Influence of bank concentration and institutions on capital structure: new international evidence. *Journal of Corporate Finance*, *14*(4), 363–375. doi:10.1016/j.jcorpfin.2008.03.010

Gopalan, R., Nanda, V., & Seru, A. (2007). Affiliated firms and financial support: Evidence from Indian business groups. *Journal of Financial Economics*, *86*(3), 759–795. doi:10.1016/j.jfineco.2006.09.008

Gordon, M. J. (1962). *The investment, financing, and valuation of the corporation*. Homewood, IL: RD Irwin.

Graham, B. (2016). *The intelligent investor*. Harper Business Essentials.

Graham, J. R. (2000). How big are the tax benefits of debt? *The Journal of Finance*, *55*(5), 1901–1941. doi:10.1111/0022-1082.00277

Graham, J. R., & Harvey, C. R. (2001). The theory and practice of corporate finance: Evidence from the field. *Journal of Financial Economics*, *60*(2-3), 187–243. doi:10.1016/S0304-405X(01)00044-7

Graham, J. R., Leary, M. T., & Roberts, M. R. (2015). A century of capital structure: the leveraging of corporate America. *Journal of Financial Economics*, *118*(3), 658–683. doi:10.1016/j.jfineco.2014.08.005

Graham, J., & Leary, M. (2011). A review of empirical capital structure research and directions for the future. *Annual Review of Financial Economics*, *3*(1), 309–345. doi:10.1146/annurev-financial-102710-144821

Gravelle, H., & Smith, D. (2001). Discounting for health effects in cost-benefit and cost-effectiveness analysis. *Health Economics*, *10*(7), 587–599. doi:10.1002/hec.618 PMID:11747043

Gray, R. H., Owen, D. L., & Adams, C. (1996). *Accounting and accountability: changes and challenges in corporate social and environmental reporting*. London, UK: Prentice Hall.

Grinblatt, M., & Titman, S. (1992, December). The persistence of mutual fund performance. *The Journal of Finance*, *47*(5), 1977–1984. doi:10.1111/j.1540-6261.1992.tb04692.x

Hall, R. (1992). The strategic analysis of intangible resources. *Strategic Management Journal*, *13*(2), 135–144. doi:10.1002mj.4250130205

Hampel, F. R. (1974). The influence curve and its role in robust estimation. *Journal of the American Statistical Association*, *69*(346), 383–393. doi:10.1080/01621459.1974.10482962

Hanaoka, S., & Regmi, M. B. (2011). Promoting intermodal freight transport through the development of dry ports in Asia: An environmental perspective. *IATSS Research*, *35*(1), 16–23. doi:10.1016/j.iatssr.2011.06.001

Hansen, J. V., McDonald, J. B., & Nelson, R. D. (1999). Time series prediction with genetic-algorithm designed neural networks: an empirical comparison with modern statistical models. *Computational Intelligence*, *15*(3), 171–184. doi:10.1111/0824-7935.00090

Harris, M., & Raviv, A. (1991). The theory of capital structure. *The Journal of Finance*, *46*(1), 297–355.

Harris, T. S., & Ohlson, J. A. (1987). Accounting disclosures and the market's valuation of oil and gas properties. *The Accounting Review*, *62*(4), 654.

Harry, M. (1952). Portfolio selection. *The Journal of Finance*, *7*(1), 77–91.

Harvey, A. C. (1990). *Forecasting, structural time series models and the Kalman filter*. Cambridge University Press. doi:10.1017/CBO9781107049994

Hatto, P. (2010). Standards and standardization handbook. *European Research Area*. Retrieved from https://www.iec.ch

Hemphill, L., Lim, J. L. C., Adair, A., & McGreal, S. (2014). *The Role of International Valuation Standards in Influencing Valuation Practice in Emerging & Established Markets*. Retrieved from www.rics.or/research

Hendriksen, E., & Michael, B. (1992). *Accounting theory* (1st ed.). Homewood, IL: Richard Irwin.

Henrique, B. M., Sobreiro, V. A., & Kimura, H. (2018). Stock price prediction using support vector regression on daily and up to the minute prices. *The Journal of Finance And Data Science, 4*(3), 183-201.

Hipel, K. W., & McLeod, A. I. (1994). *Time series modelling of water resources and environmental systems* (Vol. 45). Elsevier. doi:10.1016/S0167-5648(08)70655-5

Hitcher, J. R. (2003). *Financial valuation*. Hoboken, NJ: John Wiley & Sons.

Hong Kong Institute of Certified Public Accountants. (2018). *Conceptual Framework for Financial Reporting 2018*. Hong Kong. International Valuation Standards (IVS). Retrieved from www.ivsc.org and http://www.iasplus.com/standard/ias40.htm

Hong Kong Institute of Certified Public Accountants. (2018). Hong Kong: Conceptual Framework for Financial Reporting.

Horngren, T. C., Datar, S. M., & Rajan, M. (2015). Cost accounting A managerial emphasis, 15th ed. (Global Edition), Pearson Education Limited.

Hossain, M. Z., Khan, M. A. R., & Sadique, M. S. (2018). Basel III and perceived resilience of banks in the BRICS economies. *Applied Economics*, *50*(19), 2133–2146. doi:10.1080/00036846.2017.1391999

Hovakimian, A., Hovakimian, G., & Tehranian, H. (2004). Determinants of target capital structure: The case of dual debt and equity issues. *Journal of Financial Economics*, *71*(3), 517–540. doi:10.1016/S0304-405X(03)00181-8

Huber, P. J. (1981). *Robust statistics*. New York, NY: John Wiley. doi:10.1002/0471725250

İçerli, M. Y., & Akkaya, G. C. (2001). KOBİlerin Finansal Problemlerinin Çözümünde Risk Sermayesi Finansman Modeli. *DEÜ-SBE Dergisi*, *3*(3), 61–70.

IISD. (2018). Unburnable carbo: Getting the signals right for investors in low- and lower- middle-income countries. Available at https://www.shareweb.ch/site/Development-Policy/Documents/formAttachments/IISD%20for%20SDC%20on%20Unburnable%20Carbon%20copy-edited%2026%20June%202018.pdf

Ilsjan, V. & Kask, K. (2014) *Practical issues in the valuation of real properties with special references to income approach & financial reporting purpose*. Retrieved from https://www.researchgate.net/publication/29137708

Institute of International Finance (IIF). (2011). The cumulative impact on the global economy of proposed changes in the banking regulatory framework. IIF Net Cumulative Impact Study, IIF, Washington, D.C. Retrieved from https://www.iif.com/system/files/nciseptember2011.pdf

International Financial Reporting Standards (IFRS). (2012). Measuring the Fair Value of Unquoted Equity Instruments (Updated in February 2013). Retrieved from http:www.ifrs.org/use-around-the –world/Education

International Valuation Standards Council (IVSC). (2007). *International Valuation for Financial Reporting Valuation Under International financial reporting Standards*. Retrieved from wwwanzvps.api.org.au

International Valuation Standards Council (IVSC). (2014). Illustrative Examples Chapter 1 – Bases of Value, Exposure – Draft – Jan – 14-0%.pdf.

International Valuation Standards Council (IVSC). (n.d.). International Valuation for Financial Reporting (IVA1). Retrieved from www.anzvps.api.org.au

International Valuation Standards Council (IVSC). (n.d.). International Valuation Standards 1 Market value –Basis of valuation, 4.1.

IPCC (2019). Refinement to the 2006 IPCC Guidelines for National Greenhouse Gas Inventories.

Isoraite, M. (2016). Marketing Mix Theoretical Aspects, *International Journal Research Granthaalayah, 4*(6), 25-37. Retrieved from www.grathaalayah.com

Ivashina, V., & Scharfstein, D. (2010). Bank lending during the financial crisis of 2008. *Journal of Financial Economics, 97*(3), 319–338. doi:10.1016/j.jfineco.2009.12.001

Jain, A., & Kumar, A. M. (2007). Hybrid neural network models for hydrologic time series forecasting. *Applied Soft Computing, 7*(2), 585–592. doi:10.1016/j.asoc.2006.03.002

Jarret, J., Woodcock, J., Griffiths, U. K., Chalabi, Z., Edwards, P., & Roberts, I. (2012). Effect of increasing active travel in urban England and Wales on costs to the national health service. *Lancet, 379*(9832), 2198–2205. doi:10.1016/S0140-6736(12)60766-1 PMID:22682466

Jenkins, D. S. (2003). The transitory nature of negative earnings and the implications for earnings prediction and stock valuation. *Review of Quantitative Finance and Accounting, 21*(4), 379–404. doi:10.1023/B:REQU.0000004784.30694.0c

Jennergren, L. P. (2013). Technical note: Value driver formulas for continuing value in firm valuation by discounted cash flow model. *The Engineering Economist, 58*(1), 59–70. doi:10.1080/0013791X.2012.729876

Jensen, M. (1972). Optimal utilization of market forecasts and the evaluation of investment performance in mathematical methods in investment and finance. In G. P. Szego & K. Shell (Eds.), Mathematical methods in finance. North-Holland, 1972, 311-335.

Jensen, M. (1968). The performance of mutual funds in the period 1945-1964. *The Journal of Finance, 23*(May), 389–416. doi:10.1111/j.1540-6261.1968.tb00815.x

Jensen, M. C. (1986). Agency costs of free cash flow, corporate finance, and takeovers. *The American Economic Review, 76*(2), 323–329.

Jensen, M. C., & Meckling, W. H. (1976). Theory of the firm: Managerial behavior, agency costs and ownership structure. *Journal of Financial Economics, 3*(4), 305–360. doi:10.1016/0304-405X(76)90026-X

Jimari, R., & Kumar, B. (2015). Drivers of firm's value: panel data evidence from Indian manufacturing industry. *Asian Journal of Finance & Accounting, 7*(2).

John, D. S. (2007). *Equity asset valuation* (2nd ed., p. 252). Retrieved from https://theequityanalyst.files.wordpress.com/2015/08/equity-asset-valuation.pdf

Johnstone, D. (2013). The CAPM debate and the logic and philosophy of finance. *Abacus, 49*(S1), 1–6. doi:10.1111/j.1467-6281.2012.00378.x

Jones, M. J., & Solomon, J. F. (2013). Problematising accounting for diversity. *Accounting, Auditing & Accountability Journal, 26*(5), 668–687. doi:10.1108/AAAJ-03-2013-1255

Joos, P., & Plesko, G. A. (2005, July). Valuing loss firms. *The Accounting Review, 80*(3), 847–870. doi:10.2308/accr.2005.80.3.847

Jorgensen, A. (2007, September). *A perspective on freight transport in South Africa*. Notes presented at a special interest group meeting, Johannesburg, South Africa.

Kamps, J., & Pólos, L. (1999). Reducing uncertainty: a formal theory of organizations in action. *American Journal of Sociology, 104*(6), 1776–1812. doi:10.1086/210223

Kamruzzaman, J. (Ed.). (2006). Artificial neural networks in finance and manufacturing. Hershey, PA: IGI Global. doi:10.4018/978-1-59140-670-9

Kam, V. (2000). *Accounting theory. Translation by Al-mosul University published hall* (1st ed.). Mosul Iraq.

Kapros, S., Panou, K., & Tsamboulas, D. A. (2005). Multicriteria approach to the evaluation of intermodal freight villages. *Transportation Research Record: Journal of the Transportation Research Board, 1906*(1), 56–63. doi:10.1177/0361198105190600107

Karathanasopoulos, A., Theofilatos, K. A., Sermpinis, G., Dunis, C., Mitra, S., & Stasinakis, C. (2016). Stock market prediction using evolutionary support vector machines: An application to the ASE20 index. *European Journal of Finance, 22*(12), 1145–1163. doi:10.1080/1351847X.2015.1040167

Kara, Y., Boyacioglu, M. A., & Baykan, Ö. K. (2011). Predicting direction of stock price index movement using artificial neural networks and support vector machines: The sample of the Istanbul Stock Exchange. *Expert Systems with Applications, 38*(5), 5311–5319. doi:10.1016/j.eswa.2010.10.027

Katz, J., & Gartner, W. B. (1988). Properties of emerging organisation. *Academy of Management Review, 13*(3), 429–441. doi:10.5465/amr.1988.4306967

Kazerouni, A. R. & Afshari, M. (2006). Article 44 of the constitution and the challenges facing the Iranian private banking. Journal of Political - Economic twenty years, Number 5-6 (s 222), Bahman and Esfand 2014.

Kazlauskiene, V., & Christauskas, C. (2008). Business valuation model based on the analysis of business value drivers. *Econ. Eng. Decis., 57*(2), 23–31.

Keeton, W.R. (1999). Does faster loan growth lead to higher loan losses? *Federal Reserve Bank of Kansas City Economic Review*, Second Quarter, 57-75.

Kelm, M. (2014). Geldanlage: Die Nutzlosigkeit von Kapitalmarktprognosen. Retrieved from http://www.wallstreet-online.de/nachricht/6703396-geldanlagenutzlosigkeit-kapitalmarktprognosen

Keown, A. J., Martin, J. D., Petty, J. W., & Scott, D. F. (2013). *Foundations of finance: the logic and practice of financial management*. USA: Pearson Education.

Khan, M. A. R., & Sadique, M. S. (2019). A forward looking small semi-structural macroeconomic model for Bangladesh. *Journal of Developing Areas, 53*(2), 43–61. doi:10.1353/jda.2019.0020

Khan, M. A. R., Sadique, M. S., & Wadud, I. K. M. (2019). How vulnerable are commercial banks to macroeconomic shocks? The case of Bangladesh. *Current Analysis on Economics & Finance, 1*, 2019.

Khashei, M., & Bijari, M. (2010). An artificial neural network (p, d, q) model for timeseries forecasting. *Expert Systems with Applications, 37*(1), 479–489. doi:10.1016/j.eswa.2009.05.044

Kienzle, F., & Andersson, G. (2010). Location-dependent valuation of energy hubs with storage in multi-carrier energy systems, *IEEE, Conference Paper*, 6.

Kieschnick, R., & Moussawi, R. (2018). Firm age, corporate governance, and capital structure choices. *Journal of Corporate Finance*, *48*, 597–614. doi:10.1016/j.jcorpfin.2017.12.011

Kim, K. H. (2003). Dollar exchange rate and stock price: Evidence from multivariate cointegration and error correction model. *Review of Financial Economics*, *12*(3), 301–313. doi:10.1016/S1058-3300(03)00026-0

Kim, K. J. (2003). Financial time series forecasting using support vector machines. *Neurocomputing*, *55*(1-2), 307–319. doi:10.1016/S0925-2312(03)00372-2

Kim, M., & Ritter, J. R. (1999). Valuing IPOs. *Journal of Financial Economics*, *53*(3), 409–437. doi:10.1016/S0304-405X(99)00027-6

King, M. R. (2013). The Basel III net stable funding ratio and bank net interest margin. *Journal of Banking & Finance*, *37*(11), 4144–4156. doi:10.1016/j.jbankfin.2013.07.017

Kissin, W. & Zulli, R. (1989). Valuation of a closely held business, *Journal of Accountancy, 16*(6). LGA, CPAs and Business Advisors, 4 Questions to Ask Valuations. Retrieved from https://www.lgallp.com/wp-content/uploads/2018/10/LGA-4-Questions-to-Ask-Valuations.pdf

Klemkosky, R., & Martin, J. (1975). The adjustment of beta forecasts. *The Journal of Finance*, *30*(4), 1123–1128. doi:10.1111/j.1540-6261.1975.tb01027.x

Kodukula, P. & Chandra, P. (2006). *Project valuation using real options: a practitioner's guide*. J. Ross.

Koller, T., Goedhart, M., & Wessels, D. (2010). *Valuation: Measuring and managing the value of companies* (5th ed.). John Wiley & Sons. Retrieved from elibrary.bsu.az/books_200/N_1.pdf

Koller, T., Goedhart, M., & Wessels, D. (2010). *Valuation: measuring and managing the value of companies*. McKinsey Company.

Kolmogoroff, A. (1941). Interpolation und extrapolation von stationaren zufalligen folgen. *Izvestiya Rossiiskoi Akademii Nauk. Seriya Matematicheskaya*, *5*(1), 3–14.

Kotova, M. V. (2013). The theoretical and methodological basis of startups valuation. *Економіка: реалії часу*, 1(11), 107-112.

Kraus, A., & Litzenberger, R. H. (1973). A state-preference model of optimal financial leverage. *The Journal of Finance*, *28*(4), 911–922. doi:10.1111/j.1540-6261.1973.tb01415.x

Kuğu, T. D. (2004). Finansman yöntemi olarak risk sermayesi. *Yönetim ve Ekonomi: Celal Bayar Üniversitesi İktisadi ve İdari Bilimler Fakültesi Dergisi*, *11*(2), 141–152.

Kumar, R. (2016). *Valuation -theories and concepts*. Academic Press.

Laeven, L., & Levine, R. (2009). Bank governance, regulation and risk taking. *Journal of Financial Economics*, *93*(2), 259–275. doi:10.1016/j.jfineco.2008.09.003

Laro, D., & Pratt, S. P. (2011). *Business valuation and federal taxes: procedure, law and perspective*. Wiley.

Lawrence, J., Gitman, R., & Chad, J. Z. (2014). *Principles of managerial finance, student value edition* (14th ed.). Pearson.

Leary, M. T., & Roberts, M. R. (2005). Do firms rebalance their capital structures? *The Journal of Finance*, *60*(6), 2575–2619. doi:10.1111/j.1540-6261.2005.00811.x

Lee, C. K., Sehwan, Y., & Jongdae, J. (2007). Neural network model versus SARIMA model in forecasting Korean stock price index (KOSPI). *Issues in Information Systems*, *8*(2), 372–378.

Lee, K. L., Huang, W. C., & Teng, J. Y. (2009). Locating the competitive relation of global logistics hub using quantitative SWOT analytical method. *Quality & Quantity*, *43*(1), 87–107. doi:10.100711135-007-9087-1

Leys, C., Ley, C., Klein, O., Bernard, P., & Licata, L. (2013). Detecting outliers: Do not use standard deviation around the mean, use absolute deviation around the median. *Journal of Experimental Social Psychology*, *49*(4), 764–766. doi:10.1016/j.jesp.2013.03.013

Lintner, J. (1965). Security prices, risk, and maximal gains from diversification. *The Journal of Finance*, *20*(4), 587–615.

Lintner, J. (1969). The valuation of risk assets and the selection of risky investments in stock portfolios and capital budgets: A reply. *The Review of Economics and Statistics*, *51*(2), 222–224. doi:10.2307/1926735

Liu, J., Nissim, D., & Thomas, J. (2007). Is cash flow king in valuations? *Financial Analysts Journal*, *63*(2), 1–13. https://pdfs.semanticscholar.org/7331/01e3253efca1173adf6c76715fdd45aeef38.pdf. doi:10.2469/faj.v63.n2.4522

Li, Y., Liu, X., & Chen, Y. (2011). Selection of logistics center location using Axiomatic Fuzzy Set and TOPSIS methodology in logistics management. *Expert Systems with Applications*, *38*(6), 7901–7908. doi:10.1016/j.eswa.2010.12.161

Locarno, A. (2011). The macroeconomic impact of Basel III on the Italian economy. Questioni di Economia e Finanza, Occasional papers. Retrieved from http://ssrn.com/abstract=1849870

Lopez, A., Mathers, C., Ezzati, M., Jamison, D., & Muray, C. (2006). *Global burden of disease and risk factors*. Washington, DC: World Bank/Oxford University Press. doi:10.1596/978-0-8213-6262-4

Lukashevich, N., Svirina, A., & Granin, D. (2018). Multilevel prognosis of logistics chains in case of uncertainty: information and statistical technologies implementation. *Journal of Open Innovation: Technology, Market, and Complexity*, *4*(2), 4.

Macharis, C., & Bernardini, A. (2015). Reviewing the use of multi-criteria decision analysis for the evaluation of transport projects: Time for a multi-actor approach. *Transport Policy*, *37*, 177–186. doi:10.1016/j.tranpol.2014.11.002

MacKay, P., & Phillips, G. M. (2005). How does industry affect firm financial structure? *Review of Financial Studies*, *18*(4), 1433–1466. doi:10.1093/rfs/hhi032

Madison, A. (2001). *The world economy: a millennial perspective*. Paris, France: Organisation for Economic Co-operation and Development. doi:10.1787/9789264189980-en

Magni, C. A. (2009). Investment decisions, net present value and bounded rationality. *Quantitative Finance*, *9*(8), 967–979. doi:10.1080/14697680902849338

Manchanda, K. & Muralidharan, P. (2014, January). Crowdfunding: a new paradigm in startup financing. In *Global Conference on Business & Finance Proceedings* (9, 1, 369-374). Institute for Business & Finance Research.

Mandron, A. (2000). Improved techniques for valuing large-scale projects: A follow-up. *The Journal of Structured Finance*, *6*(1), 33–45. doi:10.3905/jsf.2000.320185

Mao, J. C. (1970). Survey of capital budgeting: Theory and practice. *The Journal of Finance*, *25*(2), 349–360. doi:10.1111/j.1540-6261.1970.tb00513.x

Marketwatch. (2019). Corporate tax calculator. Available at https://www.marketwatch.com/graphics/2017/sp-500-company-tax-rates/#/

Markowitz, H. (1959). *Portfolio selection: efficient diversification and investments*. New York, NY: John Wiley & Sons.

Martinsons, M. G. (2002). Electronic commerce in China: Emerging success stories. *Information & Management, 39*(7), 571–579. doi:10.1016/S0378-7206(02)00009-5

Matschke, M. J., Brosel, G., & Matschke, X. (2010). Fundamentals of functional business valuation. *Journal of Business Valuation and Economic Loss Analysis, 5*(1), 3.

Matsumoto, D. A. (2002). Management's incentives to avoid negative earnings surprises. *The Accounting Review, 77*(3), 483–514. doi:10.2308/accr.2002.77.3.483

Mauboussin, M. J. (2012). The true measure of success. *Harvard Business Review*, 46–56.

Mehrani, S. & Nounahalnahr, A. A. (n.d.). Assessment response of less than expected investors in the Tehran Stock Exchange. *Reviews Accounting and Auditing,* 54.

Meidute, I. (2007). Economical evaluation of logistics centres establishment. *Transport, 22*(2), 111–117. doi:10.3846/16484142.2007.9638108

Mercer, Z. C., & Harms, T. W. (2008). *Business valuation: an integrated theory*. Wiley.

Merh, N., Saxena, V. P., & Pardasani, K. R. (2010). A comparison between hybrid approaches of ANN and ARIMA for Indian stock trend forecasting. *Business Intelligence Journal, 3*(2), 23–43.

Merton, R. (1973). An intertemporal capital asset pricing model. *Econometrica, 41*(5), 867–887. doi:10.2307/1913811

Merton, R. C. (1973). Theory of rational option pricing. *The Bell Journal of Economics and Management Science, 4*(1), 141–183. doi:10.2307/3003143

Metcalfe, J. S. (2002). *Evolutionary economics and creative destruction*. London, UK: Routledge. doi:10.4324/9780203018927

Metha, M. (2012). Demystifying Basel III for Indian banks. International Conference on Technology and Business Management, Delhi University, India.

Milis, K., Snoeck, M., & Haesen, R. (2009). *Evaluation of the applicability of investment appraisal techniques for assessing the business value of IS services*. Katholieke Universiteit Leuven. doi:10.2139srn.1517656

Miller, T. W., Mathisen, R. E., & McAllister, J. P. (2004). Estimates of the sensitivities of the value of the firm to profitability, growth and capital intensity. *J. Account. Finance Res.*-Winter II. 20-33.

Miller, D. (1990). Organizational configurations: Cohesion, change, and prediction. *Human Relations, 43*(8), 771–789. doi:10.1177/001872679004300805

Miller, M. H. (1988). The Modigliani-Miller propositions after thirty years. *The Journal of Economic Perspectives, 2*(4), 99–120. doi:10.1257/jep.2.4.99

Miller, M., & Modigliani, F. (1958). The cost of capital. Corporate Finance and the Theory of Investment. *The American Economic Review, 48*, 261–297.

Millington, A. (2000). *An introduction to property valuation* (5th ed.).

Mills, J., Bible, L., & Mason, R. (2002). Defining free cash flow. *The CPA Journal.*

Modigliani, F., & Miller, M. (1958). The cost of capital, corporation finance and the theory of investment. *The American Economic Review, 48*(3), 261–297.

Modigliani, F., & Miller, M. (1963). Corporate income taxes and the cost of capital: A correction. *The American Economic Review, 53*(3), 433–443.

Monios, J. (2011). The role of inland terminal development in the hinterland access strategies of Spanish ports. *Research in Transportation Economics*, *33*(1), 59–66. doi:10.1016/j.retrec.2011.08.007

Monios, J., & Lambert, B. (2013). The heartland intermodal corridor: Public private partnerships and the transformation of institutional settings. *Journal of Transport Geography*, *27*, 36–45. doi:10.1016/j.jtrangeo.2012.03.015

Monios, J., & Wilmsmeier, G. (2012). Giving a direction to port regionalisation. *Transportation Research Part A, Policy and Practice*, *46*(10), 1551–1561. doi:10.1016/j.tra.2012.07.008

Mossin, J. (1966). Equilibrium in a capital asset market. *Econometrica*, *34*(4), 768–783. doi:10.2307/1910098

Motley Fool, Foolish Fundamentals: Free Cash Flow.

Moyer, McGuiga, & Rao (2018). Contemporary financial management, 14th Edition, Cengage Learning.

Murphy, J. J. (2009). *The visual investor: how to spot market trends* (Vol. 443). John Wiley & Sons.

Myers, S. C. (2001). Capital structure. *The Journal of Economic Perspectives*, *15*(2), 81–102. doi:10.1257/jep.15.2.81

Myers, S., & Majluf, N. (1984). Corporate financing and investment decisions when firms have information that investors do not have. *Journal of Financial Economics*, *13*(2), 187–221. doi:10.1016/0304-405X(84)90023-0

Nasser, S. (2016). Valuation for startups—9 methods explained.

National Venture Capital Association–NVCA. (2000). Retrieved from http://www.nvca.org.tr/main/index/html

Nayak, R. K., Mishra, D., & Rath, A. K. (2015). A naïve SVM-KNN based stock market trend reversal analysis for Indian benchmark indices. *Applied Soft Computing*, *35*, 670–680. doi:10.1016/j.asoc.2015.06.040

Ng, A. Y., & Gujar, G. C. (2009). Government policies, efficiency and competitiveness: The case of dry ports in India. *Transport Policy*, *16*(5), 232–239. doi:10.1016/j.tranpol.2009.08.001

Niu, J. (2016). Loan growth and bank valuations. *The Quarterly Review of Economics and Finance*, *61*, 185–191. doi:10.1016/j.qref.2016.02.001

Nobes, C. (1997). *Introduction to financial accounting* (4th ed.). London, UK: International Thomson Business Press.

Nobes, C., & Parker, R. (2008). *Comparative international accounting* (10th ed.). USA: Prentice Hall.

Noss, J., & Toffano, P. (2016). Estimating the impact of changes in aggregate bank capital requirements on lending and growth during an upswing. *Journal of Banking & Finance*, *62*, 15–27. doi:10.1016/j.jbankfin.2015.09.020

Olajide, S. E., Lizam, M., & Olajide, E. B. (2016). Understanding the conceptual definitions of cost, price worth and value, *Journal of Humanities & Social Science, 20*(9), 53-57, Retrieved from www.iosrjournal.org

Ord, K. (2004). Charles Holt's report on exponentially weighted moving averages: An introduction and appreciation. *International Journal of Forecasting*, *20*(1), 1–3. doi:10.1016/j.ijforecast.2003.09.016

Osmundsen, P., Asche, F., Misund, B., & Mohn, K. (2006). Valuation of international oil companies. *Energy Journal*, 53.

Pagourtzi, E., Assimakopoulos, V., Hatzichristos, T., & French, N. (2003). Real estate appraisal: A review of valuation methods. *Journal of Property Investment & Finance*, *21*(4), 383–401.

Pai, P. F., & Lin, C. S. (2005). A hybrid ARIMA and support vector machines model in stock price forecasting. *Omega*, *33*(6), 497–505. doi:10.1016/j.omega.2004.07.024

Pallant, J. (2007). *SPSS survival manual* (3rd ed.). Open University Press.

Palšaitis, R., & Bazaras, D. (2004). Analysis of the prospectives of intermodal transport and logistics centres in Lithuania. *Transport*, *19*(3), 119–123. doi:10.3846/16484142.2004.9637963

Panova, Y., & Hilmola, O. P. (2015). Justification and evaluation of dry port investments in Russia. *Research in Transportation Economics*, *51*, 61–70. doi:10.1016/j.retrec.2015.07.008

Papke, L. E., & Wooldridge, J. M. (1996). Econometric methods for fractional response variables with an application to 401 (k) plan participation rates. *Journal of Applied Econometrics*, *11*(6), 619–632. doi:10.1002/(SICI)1099-1255(199611)11:6<619::AID-JAE418>3.0.CO;2-1

Papke, L. E., & Wooldridge, J. M. (2008). Panel data methods for fractional response variables with an application to test pass rates. *Journal of Econometrics*, *145*(1-2), 121–133. doi:10.1016/j.jeconom.2008.05.009

Parcon-Santos, H. C. & Bernabe, E. M., Jr. (2012). The macrocosmic effects of Basel III implementation in the Philippines: A preliminary assessment. BSP Working Paper, the Philippines.

Paris Agreement. (2015). The Paris Agreement Summary. Climate Focus. Briefing Notes. Available at https://climatefocus.com/sites/default/files/20151228%20COP%2021%20briefing%20FIN.pdf

Parsons, C., & Titman, S. (2007). Empirical capital structure: A review. *Foundations and Trends in Finance*, *3*(1), 1–93. doi:10.1561/0500000018

Pawlik, T., Stemmler, L., Baird, A. J., & Helch, M. (2011). The value of container terminal investment to ocean carrier strategy. *Maritime Economics & Logistics*, *13*(3), 319–341. doi:10.1057/mel.2011.8

Pearce, D., Groom, B., Hepburn, C., & Koundouri, P. (2003). Valuing the future: Recent advances in social discounting. *World Economy*, *4*, 121–141.

Pekin, E., & Macharis, C. (2013). A GIS-based analysis of the potential for freight villages in Turkey. *World Review of Intermodal Transportation Research*, *4*(2-3), 157–174. doi:10.1504/WRITR.2013.058980

Pereiro, L. E. (2002). *Valuation of companies in emerging markets, ABD*. John Wiley & Sons.

Petitt, B. S. & Ferris, K. R. (2013). Valuation for mergers and acquisitions, Pearson Education, 2nd ed.

Petkov, M., Birry, A., Plesser, S., & Wilkins, M. (2016). Climate change-related legal and regulatory threats should spur financial service providers to action. S&P global rating. 7-8. S&P Global Publications.

Pfeiffer, A., Hepburn, C., Vogt-Schilb, A., & Caldecott, B. (2018). Committee emissions from existing and planned power plants and asset stranding required to meet the Paris Agreement. *Environmental Research Letters*, *13*(5), 054019. doi:10.1088/1748-9326/aabc5f

Pierru, A. & Babusiaux, D. (2008). Valuation of investment projects by an international oil company: a new proof of a straightforward rigorous method, *OPEC Energy Review*, 197.

Pike, S., Roos, G., & Marr, B. (2005). Strategic management of intangible assets and value drivers in R&D organizations. *R & D Management*, *35*(2), 111–124. doi:10.1111/j.1467-9310.2005.00377.x

Pratt, P. S. (2008). *Valuing a business. the analysis and appraisal of closely held companies* (5th ed.). New York, NY: McGraw-Hill.

PwCplatform. (2019). *17. Çözüm Ortaklığı Platformu Türkiye Start-up Dünyası, Değerleme Yöntemleri ve Yatırımcı Bakış Açısı*. Retrieved from https://www.pwc.com.tr/tr/Etkinlik/17-platform/sunumlar/turkiye-start-up-dunyasi.pdf

Pyles, M. K. (2014). *Applied corporate finance questions, problems and making decisions in the real world.* New York, NY: Springer.

Rabiu, S., & Ma'aji, M. M. (2016, April). A critical evaluation of measurement & effects of fair value in financial statements. *Innovation Research in Social Science & Strategic Management Techniques, 3*(3), 81–90.

Rajan, R. G. (2012). Presidential address: The corporation in finance. *The Journal of Finance, 67*(4), 1173–1217. doi:10.1111/j.1540-6261.2012.01745.x

Rajan, R. G., & Zingales, L. (1995). What do we know about capital structure? Some evidence from international data. *The Journal of Finance, 50*(5), 1421–1460. doi:10.1111/j.1540-6261.1995.tb05184.x

Ramalho, E. A., Ramalho, J. J., & Coelho, L. M. (2016). Exponential regression of fractional-response fixed-effects models with an application to firm capital structure. *Journal of Econometric Methods, 7*(1). doi:10.1515/jem-2015-0019

Ramalho, J. J., & da Silva, J. V. (2009). A two-part fractional regression model for the financial leverage decisions of micro, small, medium and large firms. *Quantitative Finance, 9*(5), 621–636. doi:10.1080/14697680802448777

Rappaport, A. (1998). *Creating shareholder value: a guide for managers and investors.* New York, NY: Simon and Schuster.

Reilly, R. F. (2010). Intangible asset identification and valuation in the bank and thrift industries. *Intangible Asset Valuation Insights*. Winter.

Reserve Bank of New Zealand. (2007). Capital adequacy ratios for banks - simplified explanation and example of calculation. Retrieved from http://pages.stern.nyu.edu/~igiddy/articles/capital_adequacy_calculation.pdf

Rimmel, G., & Jonall, K. (2013). Biodiversity treporting in Sweden: Corporate disclosure and preparers' view. *Accounting, Auditing & Accountability Journal, 26*(5), 746–778. doi:10.1108/AAAJ-02-2013-1228

Roland, G., & Platt, D. (2011). *Managerial accounting*. USA: Mc Graw-Hill Irwin.

Roll, R. (1977). A critique of the asset pricing theory's tests part 1: on past and potential testability of the theory. *Journal of Financial Economics, 4*(2), 129–176. doi:10.1016/0304-405X(77)90009-5

Roso, V. (2013). Sustainable intermodal transport via dry ports–importance of directional development. *World Review of Intermodal Transportation Research, 4*(2-3), 140–156. doi:10.1504/WRITR.2013.058976

Ross, S. A., Westerfield, R., Jaffe, J. F., & Jordan, B. D. (2013). *Corporate finance* (pp. 353–354). McGraw-Hill/Irwin.

Russell, P. J. (2007). Valuation of imaging centers: alternative methods and detailed description of the discounted cash flow approach. *Journal of the American College of Radiology, 4*(1), 53–64. doi:10.1016/j.jacr.2006.08.019 PMID:17412225

Sai, Y., Yuan, Z., & Gao, K. (2007, November). Mining stock market tendency by RS-based support vector machines. In *2007 IEEE International Conference on Granular Computing (GRC 2007)* (pp. 659-659). IEEE. 10.1109/GrC.2007.104

Salamzadeh, A. & Kawamorita Kesim, H. (2015). Startup companies: life cycle and challenges. In *Proceedings 4th International Conference on Employment, Education and Entrepreneurship (EEE),* Belgrade, Serbia. 10.2139srn.2628861

Salamzadeh, A. (2015). New venture creation: controversial perspectives and theories. *Economic Analysis, 48*(3/4).

Sandra. (2014, Feb. 5). *How to value companies with negative earnings.* Retrieved from http://www.financeninvestments.com/banking/companies-negative-earnings.html

Schade, W. (2006). Assessing economic impacts of large-scale transport infrastructure projects: case of Lyon–Turin corridor. *Transportation Research Record: Journal of the Transportation Research Board, 1960*(1), 142–151. doi:10.1177/0361198106196000118

Scholes, M., & Williams, J. (1977). Estimating betas from nonsynchronous data. *Journal of Financial Economics*, *5*(3), 309–327. doi:10.1016/0304-405X(77)90041-1

Scholz, M., & Reydon, T. A. (2009). Organizational ecology: No Darwinian evolution after all. A rejoinder to Lemos. *Philosophy of the Social Sciences*, *40*(3), 504–512. doi:10.1177/0048393109348866

Schumpeter, J. A. (1934). *The theory of economic development: An inquiry into profits, capital, credit, interest, and the business cycle*. Transaction Publishers.

Sepehrdoust, H. & Taibe, A. (2014). Affecting factors in the Iranian bank the capital adequacy ratio during the years 2007- 2011, the Financial Accounting Research: Successive Number 18, Pages 35-50.

Shahchera, M. & Jouzani, N. (2013). The impact on the profitability of state-owned banks and private investors towards Iranian, Monetary and Banking Studies, 12, pp. 20-43.

Sharpe, W. F. (1964). Capital asset prices: a theory of market equilibrium under conditions of risk. *The Journal of Finance*, *19*(3), 425–442.

Sharpe, W. F. (1964). Capital asset prices: A theory of market equilibrium under conditions of risk. *The Journal of Finance*, *19*(3), 425–442.

Shauvalpour, S. & al-Ash'ari, E. (2014). The effect of the credit risk on the profitability of banks in Iran, Financial Research: Number 2, pp. 229-246.

Skinner, D. J. (1994). Why firms voluntarily disclose bad news. *Journal of Accounting Research*, *32*(1), 38–60. doi:10.2307/2491386

Song, K. (2003). The Korean hub strategy. (Unpublished master's dissertation). *Massachusetts Institute of Technology*, Cambridge.

Spies, F. F. & Wilhelm, D. B. (2005) *A critical analysis of.... when used for financial reporting according to IFRS*. Retrieved from www.prres.net

Statement of Protocols for Co-operation on International Financial Reporting Standards (IFRS) and International Valuation Standards (IVS). (2014). Retrieved from www.ifrs.org

Stephanie, G. (2006). *Bank and shareholder value - an overview of bank valuation and empirical evidence on shareholder value for banks*. Wiesbaden, Germany: Deutscher Universitats-Verlag.

Sterba, J., & Hilovska, K. (2010). The implementation of hybrid ARIMA neural network prediction model for aggregate water consumption prediction. *Aplimat—. Journal of Applied Mathematics*, *3*(3), 123–131.

Strebulaev, I. A. (2007). Do tests of capital structure theory mean what they say? *The Journal of Finance*, *62*(4), 1747–1787. doi:10.1111/j.1540-6261.2007.01256.x

Strebulaev, I. A., & Yang, B. (2013). The mystery of zero-leverage firms. *Journal of Financial Economics*, *109*(1), 1–23. doi:10.1016/j.jfineco.2013.02.001

Sullivan, M. (2007). *Statistics: Informed decisions using data* (2nd ed.). Upper Saddle River, NJ: Pearson Prentice Hall.

Tarter, J. (n.d.). EBITA a useful cash-flow tool, but no substitute for good judgment. Federal Reserve Bank of Cleveland. *Supervision & Regulation Department.*

Tay, F. E. & Cao, L. (2001). Application of support vector machines in financial time series forecasting. *Omega*, *29*(4), 309-317.

Taylor, J. W. (2003). Exponential smoothing with a damped multiplicative trend. *International Journal of Forecasting*, *19*(4), 715–725. doi:10.1016/S0169-2070(03)00003-7

The Institute of Cost and Works Accountants of India. (2010). Business Valuation Management, 12, Sudder Street, Kolkata - 700 016, paper 18.

Theil, H. (1971). *Principles of Econometrics. New York, NY*: John Wiley & Sons.

Thompson, M., Davison, M., & Rasmussen, H. (2004). Valuation and optimal operation of electric power plants in competitive markets. *Operations Research*, *52*(4), 561. doi:10.1287/opre.1040.0117

Titman, S., & Wessels, R. (1988). The determinants of capital structure choice. *The Journal of Finance*, *43*(1), 1–19. doi:10.1111/j.1540-6261.1988.tb02585.x

Tosi, H. L. Jr, & Slocum, J. W. Jr. (1984). Contingency theory: Some suggested directions. *Journal of Management*, *10*(1), 9–26. doi:10.1177/014920638401000103

Treynor, J. L. (1962). Jack Treynor's toward a theory of market value of risky assets. Available at https://ssrn.com/abstract=628187

Triola, M. (2008). *Essentials of statistics* (3rd ed.). Boston, MA: Pearson Addison Wesley.

Tsai, J.-Y., & Chen, S. (2015). How does equity capital cost affect bank performance during a financial crisis? *Applied Economics*, *47*(42), 4459–4474. doi:10.1080/00036846.2015.1030569

Turkish Chamber of Shipping. (2018). *Maritime Sector Report*. Retrieved from https://www.denizticaretodasi.org.tr/Media/SharedDocuments/sektorraporu/2017_sektor_en.pdf

Turkish Statistical Institute. (2018). *Foreign Trade Statistics*. Retrieved from http://www.tuik.gov.tr/UstMenu.do?metod=temelist

Ucal, I., & Kahraman, C. (2009). Fuzzy real options valuation for oil investments. *Baltic Journal of Sustainability*, *15*(4), 653.

Ünal, G., & Derindere Köseoğlu, S. (2014). Revealing the freight market risk in Istfix shipping area. *International Journal of Shipping and Transport Logistics*, *6*(6), 593–610. doi:10.1504/IJSTL.2014.064904

Value-Based Management.net. (n.d.). Earnings before interest, taxes, depreciation and amortization.

Valuing Firms with Negative Earnings. Retrieved from http://pages.stern.nyu.edu/~adamodar/pdfiles/valn2ed/ch22.pdf

Van de Ven, A. H., Hudson, R., & Schroeder, D. M. (1984). Designing new business startups: Entrepreneurial, organizational, and ecological considerations. *Journal of Management*, *10*(1), 87–108. doi:10.1177/014920638401000108

Venanzi, D., & Naccarato, A. (2017). The capital structure choice of European firms: The role of financial system and institutional setting. *International Business Research*, *10*(12), 22–47. doi:10.5539/ibr.v10n12p22

Vesper, K. H. (1990). *New Venture Strategies* (2nd ed.). Englewood Cliffs, NJ: Prentice Hall.

Virlics, A. (2013). Investment decision making and risk. *Procedia Economics and Finance*, *6*, 170. doi:10.1016/S2212-5671(13)00129-9

Vitolo, G., & Cipparrone, F. (2014). Strategic implications of different criteria for project portfolio selection. In *Global Conference on Business & Finance Proceedings*, 9, 1, pp. 427-434. Institute for Business & Finance Research.

Vorsatz, D. U., Cabeza, L. F., Serrano, S., Barreneche, C., & Petrichenko, K. (2015). Heating and cooling energy trends and drivers in buildings. *Renewable & Sustainable Energy Reviews, 41*, 97.

Wang, J. J., Wang, J. Z., Zhang, Z. G., & Guo, S. P. (2012). Stock index forecasting based on a hybrid model. *Omega, 40*(6), 758–766. doi:10.1016/j.omega.2011.07.008

Whittington, G. (2010). Measurement in financial reporting, overview of the central thesis. Journal of Accounting, Finance, and Business Studies, ABACUS, 46(1).

Wiener, N. (1942). The extrapolation, interpolation and smoothing of stationary time series with engineering applications: DIC Contract 6037, a research pursued on behalf of the National Defense Research Council (Section D2) at the Massachusetts Institute of Technology. Massachusetts Institute of Technology.

Wijaya, Y. B., Kom, S., & Napitupulu, T. A. (2010, December). Stock price prediction: Comparison of Arima and artificial neural network methods-an Indonesia stock's case. In *2010 Second International Conference on Advances in Computing, Control, and Telecommunication Technologies* (pp. 176-179). IEEE. 10.1109/ACT.2010.45

Worldgovernmentbonds.com. (2019). *Turkey 5 Years CDS*. Retrieved from http://www.worldgovernmentbonds.com/cds-historical-data/turkey/5-years/

Wurtzebach, C. H., & Waller, N. G. (1983). The feasibility, underwriting, and valuation of residential energy components. *The Appraisal Journal*, 68.

Yan, M., Hall, M. J. B., & Turner, P. (2012). *A cost and benefit analysis of Basel III: Some evidence from the UK*. Leicestershire, UK: School of Business and Economics, Loughborough University.

Yildirim, C., & Efthyvoulou, G. (2018). Bank value and geographic diversification: Regional vs global. *Journal of Financial Stability, 36*, 225–245. doi:10.1016/j.jfs.2018.04.003

Zemel, M. (2015). The information content of loan growth in banks. Working Paper. Available at http://ssrn.com/abstract=255711

Zhang, G. P. (2003). Time series forecasting using a hybrid ARIMA and neural network model. *Neurocomputing, 50*, 159–175. doi:10.1016/S0925-2312(01)00702-0

Zhang, G. P., & Qi, M. (2005). Neural network forecasting for seasonal and trend time series. *European Journal of Operational Research, 160*(2), 501–514. doi:10.1016/j.ejor.2003.08.037

Zhou, Q., Tan, K. J. K., Faff, R., & Zhu, Y. (2016). Deviation from target capital structure cost of equity and speed of adjustment. *Journal of Corporate Finance, 39*, 99–120. doi:10.1016/j.jcorpfin.2016.06.002

Zhou, Z. J., & Hu, C. H. (2008). An effective hybrid approach based on grey and ARMA for forecasting gyro drift. *Chaos, Solitons, and Fractals, 35*(3), 525–529. doi:10.1016/j.chaos.2006.05.039

Zikoh, J. (2009). Strategic valuation of Danske Bank Group. Copenhagen Business School, Master thesis (3.4). Retrieved from https://www.myaccountingcourse.com/accounting-dictionary/f

Zörgiebel, S. (2016). Valuation of IPOs with negative earnings, Goethe University Frankfurt. doi:10.2139srn.2698281

About The Contributors

Sinem D. Köseoğlu was born in Istanbul in 1981, She got Associate Professor of Finance degree in January, 2014 from Inter-University Council in Turkey. She is a graduate of the Business Administration from Istanbul University with a honors degree. Then, Dr. D. Köseoğlu began her master studies in Finance at Istanbul University in 2003 and has held a master degree in finance. While doing her master, She commenced her academic career as a research and teaching assistant of finance for the faculty of Transport and Logistics at Istanbul University in 2004. Dr. D. Köseoğlu began her Ph. D. studies in Finance at the same University in 2006. She has held a Ph.D in Finance with a dissertation of 'Analysis of Risks in International Maritime Transportation Industry and Factors that Affect Cargo Ship Investment Decisions' in 2010. Her Ph.D. dissertation has been published by ERF (Economics Research Foundation) as the best dissertation in 2012. Her article entitled "Market Risk of Index Futures and Stock Indices: Turkey as a Developing Country vs. Developed Countries" has been selected as the best paper by the World Business Institute. Dr. D. Köseoğlu, now freelance consultant, trainer, and researcher.

* * *

Ahmad Aref Almazari is currently a professor of finance and banking in King Saud University-RCC in the department of administrative sciences in Riyadh, Kingdom of Saudi Arabia. I was born in Amman, Jordan in 1967. I obtained my Ph.D. in Business Finance and Economics from Jodhpur University, India in 1995. I published articles in a number of international journals in the field of financial analysis, managerial finance and banking. I am editor in some international journals, and research reviewer and arbitrator for post graduate students, as well as arbitrator for post graduate and under graduate programs and plans. My current research interest includes banks efficiency, liquidity and profitability, working capital management, and financial analysis.

Luis Almanza-Herazo is a full time financial consultant working at Waarde Investment Bank (Barranquilla, Colombia) with 10 years of experience in company and project valuation for diverse industries. His experience as practicioner of finance includes management positions in large and medium Colombian companies. Additionally, he teaches undergraduate courses in Finance. He holds a BSc in International Business Management (Universidad del Norte) and MSc in Finance (Escuela de Administración de Empresas).

Tarana Azimova has graduated her Doctoral Degree Business Administration: Finance from Istanbul University. She is currently an Assistant Professor in Business Administration Department at Nisantasi University, where she delivers various finance and economic related courses. Tarana Azimova has previously worked at Khazar University as an Adjunct Professor, where she delivered various financial courses such as Investments, International Finance and Corporate Finance. Her primary area of interest is Finance and Economics and she is the author of different articles in risk management, innovations in financial markets, and bond markets among others.

Cem Berk is an associate professor of finance in Kirklareli University. He was awarded with the title of associate professorship in 2014. He is a strong education professional with a Doctor of Philosophy (Ph.D.) focused in Accounting and Finance from Marmara University and a Bachelor of Science degree from Bogazici University. His primary research fields are international finance, energy finance and real estate finance.

Rumeysa Bilgin received her PhD in Finance from Istanbul University in 2016. She is currently working as an assistant professor at Istanbul Sabahattin Zaim University. She writes mainly on the capital structure decisions of firms.

Mustafa Dilmen is a doctor of finance in Istanbul Arel University. He is an expert in the heating industry and the owner of Infratech Industrial Heating Systems company. He has a strong background with a Doctor of Philosophy (Ph.D.) focused in Accounting and Finance from Istanbul Arel University, 3 master's degrees; which are financial management from Istanbul University, business administration from Sakarya University and electronic engineering from Sakarya University.

Atif Ghayas is a research scholar in the Department of Business Administration at Frank and Debbie Islam Management complex at Aligarh Muslim University, Aligarh.

Orhan Goker was born in 1947, is now is Adjunct Professor of Finance at Galatasaray University. He is a graduate of the BS in Management from Middle East Technical University. Dr. O. Goker began his MBA studies Syracuse University in 1971. Following his Masters graduation, he began his Ph.D. Study at Istanbul University and received his degree in 1977.

Musa Gün is an Assistant Professor of Finance at Recep Tayyip Erdoğan University. He holds a Ph.D. in Finance from Istanbul University. His areas of research interest include corporate finance, financial economics, international financial markets, capital markets, economics and nonlinear econometric analysis and modeling in finance.

Natalia Hernandez-Vargas is a mathematician with a scientific computing orientation degree from Ruprecht-Karls Universität Heidelberg. Research interests are exploratory multivariate analysis, spatial statistics and Computer-based mathematics education.

Md Atiqur Rahman Khan currently works at the Department of Finance, University of Rajshahi. Earlier he served as an academic at the Department of Finance and Banking in Curtin University Malaysia. He also played an active role as the Associate Dean (R&D) at the Faculty of Business in Curtin University Malaysia. His research interest includes banking system resilience, banking regulations and risk management, macroeconomic dynamics, sustainability and issues in financial systems, and renewable energy. He has experiences in managing research grants, and supervising HDR students.

Benedicto Lukanima is a full-time assistant professor at the Business School of Universidad del Norte, Colombia. He has over 17 years in University teaching, specialising in corporate finance, capital markets, derivatives, and company valuation. He holds a PhD (Finance) from the University of Hull (United Kingdom) and a Master's degree in Internation Banking and Finance from Salford University (United Kingdom). His research interest covers the broad area of investments in capital markets, with specific emphasis in investment return and risk management, corporate decision and value creation, Behavioural aspects in capital markets and portfolio diversification.

Walid Mohammed is a PhD candidate at Salford Business School, University of Salford. His research area is in Economics, with emphasis on financial stability and systemic risk issues. His PhD title, risk in financial markets and financial cycles and he is thesis submission date expected in October 2019. He has worked in different institutions including the NHS, Shell, SMD Exchange, and teaching assistant at the University of Salford.

Luis Sanchez-Barrios is a full time lecturer and researcher at the Business School, Universidad del Norte (Barranquilla, Colombia), since 2003. He teaches graduate and undergraduate courses in Finance and Quantitative Methods. He holds a BSc in Industrial Engineering (Universidad del Norte), an MSc in Industrial Engineering (Universidad de los Andes), an MBA in Financial Management (The University of Hull, England) and a PhD in Management (The University of Edinburgh, Scotland). His PhD thesis was titled: "Alternative profit scorecards for revolving credit". His research interests include: Corporate finance, business finance at the BoP, financial wellbeing, personal finance and profit scoring models.

Faisal Usmani is a Research Scholar in The Department of Business Administration at Frank and Debbie Islam Management complex at Aligarh Muslim University, Aligarh.

Index

T

V

www.ingramcontent.com/pod-product-compliance
Lightning Source LLC
LaVergne TN
LVHW062141300926
849161LV00010B/2592